Constructing and organising crime in Europe

CONSTRUCTING AND ORGANISING CRIME IN EUROPE

PETRUS C. VAN DUYNE
ALEXEY SERDYUK
GEORGIOS A. ANTONOPOULOS
JACKIE H. HARVEY
KLAUS VON LAMPE
(EDS.)

eleven
international publishing

Published, sold and distributed by Eleven International Publishing
Published by Kharkiv National University of Internal Affairs

P.O. Box 85576
2508 CG The Hague
The Netherlands
Tel.: +31 70 33 070 33
Fax: +31 70 33 070 30
e-mail: sales@elevenpub.nl
www.elevenpub.com

Lev Landau avenue 27
Kharkiv, 61080
Ukraine
Tel.: +38 057 7398 181
e-mail: odin.univd@gmail.com
univd.edu.ua

Sold and distributed in USA and Canada

Independent Publishers Group
814 N. Franklin Street
Chicago, IL 60610, USA
Order Placement: +1 800 888 4741
Fax: +1 312 337 5985
orders@ipgbook.com
www.ipgbook.com

Eleven International Publishing is an imprint of Boom uitgevers Den Haag.

Cover image: *Reply of the Zaporozhian Cossacks to Sultan Mehmed IV* by Ilya Repin.

ISBN 978-94-6236-955-9
ISBN 978-94-6274-553-7 (E-book)

Printed in The Netherlands

This volume is based on the peer-reviewed presentations of the authors at the 19th Cross-border Crime Colloquium, hosted by the Kharkiv National University of Internal Affairs, 17-19 June 2018

This project was supported by:
Kharkiv National University of Internal Affairs
Northumbria University
Teesside University
Utrecht University

The Cross-Border Crime Colloquium is an annual event since 1999. It brings together experts on international organized (economic) crime to discuss the latest developments in empirical research, legislation and law enforcement, with a special geographical focus on Western, Central, and Eastern Europe. The Colloquia aim at building bridges in three respects: between Eastern and Western Europe, between scholars and practitioners, and between old and young. The Cross-Border Crime Colloquium has previously been organized in:

2017 Bratislava, Slovak Republic
2016 Newcastle upon Tyne, UK
2015 Prague, Czech Republic
2014 Sarajevo, Bosnia & Herzegovina
2013 Cambridge, UK
2012 Manchester UK
2011 Tilburg, the Netherlands
2009 Gent, Belgium
2008 Belgrade, Serbia
2007 Prague, Czech Republic
2006 Tallin, Estonia
2005 Sarajevo, Bosnia & Herzegovina
2004 Berlin, Germany
2003 Ainring, Germany
2002 Ljubljana, Slovenia
2001 Bratislava, Slovakia
2000 Budapest, Hungary
1999 Prague, Czech Republic

Table of content

Petrus C. van Duyne
The perspective of constructing and organising crime in Europe: an introduction 1

Anna Di Ronco and *Anita Lavorgna*
Constructing migrants as crime and public order problems: comparing local press representations in two Italian cities 19

Trang Nguyen
"Government-sponsored crime": The case of Vietnamese undocumented immigrants in Germany and the UK 49

Jurij Novak
Transnational crime of Chinese origin in the EU: False flags and real concerns 75

Dina Siegel
Human smuggling reconsidered: the case of Lesbos 103

Jonathan Davies
Market dynamics of harm and labour exploitation 123

Anna di Ronco and *Anna Sergi*
From harmless incivilities to not-so serious organised crime activities. The expanded realm of European crime prevention and some suggestions on how to limit it 149

Klaus von Lampe and *Susanne Knickmeier*
How well established is research on organised crime in Germany? 179

Kenneth Murray
Hierarchy, strategic assets and distinctive capabilities in Scottish organised crime 205

Miroslav Scheinost
Changing face of organised crime or old and new usual suspects in the Czech Republic 235

Toine Spapens
Cerca Trova: the Italian mafia on Dutch territory 259

Niels van Wanrooij and *Saraï Sapulete*
Do firearms link organised crime and terrorism in the Netherlands? A Social Network Analysis exploration 289

Anna Markovska, Alexey Serdyuk, Petrus C. van Duyne and *Konstantin Bugaychuk*
Corruption in the daily life of Ukraine 313

Igor Sviatokum, Alexey Serdyuk and *Petrus C. van Duyne*
Police reform in Ukraine. A reconnaissance of perceptions 337

Petrus C. van Duyne and *Brendan Quirke*
Moldova: Small country – big problem! Corruption and a mono-garchy 367

Brigitte Slot and *Linette de Swart*
Assessing the outcomes of anti-money laundering policies. Ambitions and reality 399

Matjaž Jager, *Ciril Keršmanc* and *Katja Šugman Stubbs*
Is corporate social responsibility anything more than a mask for multinational (oil) companies? 417

List of authors

Konstantin Bugaychuk

Research Lab on Crime Enforcement of Kharkiv National University of Internal Affairs, Ukraine

Jonathan Davies

Faculty of Law, Tel Aviv University, Israel

Petrus C. van Duyne

Willem Pompe Institute, Utrecht University, the Netherlands

Matjaž Jager

Institute of Criminology at the Faculty of Law, University of Ljubljana, Slovenia

Ciril Keršmanc

District court in Ljubljana, Slovenia

Susanne Knickmeier

Max Planck Institute for Foreign and International Criminal Law, Freiburg, Germany

Klaus von Lampe

Berlin School of Economics and Law, Berlin, Germany

Anita Lavorgna

University of Southampton, UK

Anna Markovska

School of Humanities and Social Sciences, Anglia Ruskin University, Cambridge, UK

Kenneth Murray

Forensic Accountancy at Police Scotland

Trang Nguyen
Max Weber Kolleg, Erfurt, Germany

Jurij Novak
Institute of Criminology at the Faculty of Law, University of Ljubljana, Slovenia

Brendan Quirke
Manchester University, UK

Anna di Ronco
University of Essex, UK

Saraï Sapulete
Ecorys Netherlands

Miroslav Scheinost
ICSP (Institute of Criminology and Social Prevention) Prague, Czech Republic

Alexey Serdyuk
Research Lab on Crime Enforcement of Kharkiv National University of Internal Affairs, Ukraine

Anna Sergi
University of Essex, UK

Dina Siegel
Willem Pompe Institute, Utrecht University, the Netherlands

Brigitte Slot
Ecorys Netherlands

Toine Spapens
Department of Criminal Law, Tilburg University, The Netherlands

Katja Šugman Stubbs
The Constitutional Court of the Republic of Slovenia

Igor Sviatokum
Research Lab on Crime Enforcement of Kharkiv National University of Internal Affairs, Ukraine

Linette de Swart
Ecorys Netherlands

Niels van Wanrooij
Ecorys Netherlands

The perspective of constructing and organising crime in Europe: an introduction

Petrus C. van Duyne[1]

Introduction

Should the following scenario be considered imaginary? In 2040, the international agreed target of maximum 2^0C climate warming-up was exceeded with one degree. A repeated severe drought made the rivers in Europe unnavigable, causing shortages of raw material supplies. This was followed by severe autumn storms and flooding along the shores of the North Sea causing many casualties and damage to civilians and industry. The public indignation was pronounced: "Why have the authorities done nothing?" Though the causal relation between natural disasters and CO^2 was still not rock-solid proven, this chain of events and public fear of more catastrophes resulted in climate scepticism being met with open hostility. Consequently European policy makers were driven to radical action. CO^2 emission licences were reduced to a minimum and violations brought under a severe a criminal law regime. Unlicensed emitting hot house gases was to be penalised as 'causing severe physical harm', at the same punishment level as qualified assault. That is not all: once this penal clause was accepted, addition criminal legal constructions were applied, such as conspiracy or participation in a criminal organisation, if more than three managers were involved. As the forbidden emission is assumed to make illegal gains which have to be disguised in the books, the offence of money laundering was added to the criminal emission construction. As is normal in legislation, once a new construction is put into the legal system, it soon intertwines with many existing ones, creating a new constructed reality.

---

1 Visiting Professor at Willem Pompe Institute, Utrecht University, The Netherlands.

This can also be considered as a warning: be cautious with fears. Still, such a fear-response criminal law scenario is quite common (Van Duyne, 2004). In fact, it is a cast-iron formula in criminal policy making and law enforcement. Fear implies the perception of a threat that has to be fended off and in our ordered society, governed by the rule of law, a common reaction is to resort to criminal law constructions. Threat, risk, fear, or belief in the 'Terrible Snowman', they can all be driving forces for legislation, apart from material and political interests of the law makers. If a substantial part of the population believes in the threat of the 'Terrible Snowman', it is real enough to feed law making. Naturally, the 'Terrible Snowman' fear is a bizarre rhetoric, but is that more bizarre than the criminalisation of homosexuality or blasphemy? Not long ago in the late 1960s that feeling of fear for homosexuality faded (but never fully) making the relevant criminal law constructions obsolete or empty.[2] Decriminalisation of homosexuality followed in most of the industrialised world – to the joy of the LGBTQ+ communities. But do not dare to be blasphemous and gay (or both) in most of the Muslim countries: that is tempting fate.

Given this importance of emotions in criminal law matters, we can speak of fear management: capturing and maintaining fear, which must be cast in a rational way into a legal mould: legislation and/or budget. Interestingly, once fear is recognised (or fanned) politically, it is unlikely that it will be refuted when no real threat manifests itself. Galeotti (2018) summed up a number of Russian organised crime (OC) threats to the 'West'. But he had to admit that the Russians did not come in the sensational OC outfit or made strategic alliances with the mafias (Rawlinson, 1998). Instead, they came as (criminal) traders which does not stir such high fears. So the fear of "crime from the East" as law enforcement priority, for which in the Netherlands even established a special team (Noord en Oost Nederland), sank into oblivion but the constructions around it lingered on for a while.[3]

---

2 In Europe decriminalisation of homosexuality started in 1791, in France and Andorra. In England and Wales it was decriminalised in 1967, Scotland 1981 and Northern Ireland 1982.
https://en.wikipedia.org/wiki/Sexual_Offences_Act_1967

3 Kernteam Noord en Oost Nederland, Algemene Criminaliteitsbeeldanalyse Oost Europa, 2000-2001.

In the 'fear-of' a specific crime there can also be much ambiguity, which may be reflected in the law enforcement response. For example, the governments and employers in many EU industrial sectors realise that the steady retirement of the older workers must be replaced by migrants to keep production and the economy going. At the same time there is a fear of irregular migration. So, a smart law maker must respond to that dual challenge by moderate law enforcement ("doing something") but not so much that the strawberries remain unharvested or the housing construction is delayed. Threat images may also be exploited to arouse resentments and then display the expected law enforcement firmness: "action is taken". Even if refugees are successfully kept out of countries, such as in Poland and Hungary, the constructions to fend off the threat remain literally in the field.

With so many tasks to stem the tide of a multitude of threats and reduce fears, it is not surprising if governments also drop stitches or show ambiguity or (worse), duplicity, in law enforcement. For example, clamping down on corruption, illegal migration and labour exploitation are emotive election themes (feel good), but a strict policy may affect many vested interests in countries with a tradition of mal-governance or in times of labour shortage. This stapling of legal constructions and ambiguous enforcement leads to legal uncertainty, particularly concerning aliens (Herkes, 2018).

Aliens: problematised, criminalised and exploited

The continuous movement of people is an historic given, whether as *homo sapiens* 'out of Africa' or as Goths during the Germanic migration (Heather, 2009). One tribe landed as Longobards in North Italy, and shaped the region by threatening the Pope Stefanus who in 754 had to call in the Frankish king Pepin the Short to protect him (Norwich, 2013), with fateful, long lasting consequences. Migrating people have rarely been welcomed, unless explicitly invited as 'guest workers'. In that capacity they are not criminal. But nevertheless, "they steal our jobs". Even if they do not steal or are otherwise not more criminal than the rest of the population, they are put into a criminal 'frame', in particular when their numbers are perceived as overwhelming. Then feelings of unsafety start to spread among the people putting the (local) administration under pressure "to do something". Usually this entails tough 'crimmigration' measures to assuage the people.

As *Anna di Ronco* and *Anita Lavorgna* set out in their chapter, such criminal framing is media supported and rather 'politically neutral' in the sense that political left or right do not differ much in their attitude. The authors analysed the media in two North Italian cities, and did not find much differences in the measures passed by both centre-right and centre-left coalitions. While the tune of the authorities' rhetoric differs somewhat (more sensationalist on the side the Lega), they did not differ much in the application of municipalities' criminal and administrative tools. These are intended to sanction an individual's behaviour when it is deemed to affect the quality of life in the city centres. Protection against perceived criminal harm has turned into reducing 'existential uneasiness' caused by aliens 'littering the public space' and affecting the 'decorum'. Was this criminal approach necessary? Instead of constructing this 'decorum loss' in a criminal frame, the authorities could also consider a non-criminal approach: handing out jackets, ties and other 'decorum enhancing' items to the migrants such that they would not be considered as unsightly and 'littering'.

Of course, 'littering the streets' is not a real migrant's choice. In principle they want to make a living. In the end, if not repatriated, most do so legally. Not all irregular migrants succeed in achieving this desired outcome. *Trang Nguyen* describes in her chapter the diversity in vicissitudes of Vietnam migrants arriving in Europe. That occurred in three waves and in which the Vietnamese migrants faced various employment 'choices', though as a rule there was not much to choose. Naturally this depends on the (underground) economic opportunities. In the UK many Vietnamese entered the home-grown cannabis industry ('gardener teams') and in Germany they found an income in the Berlin illegal cigarette market (Nguyen and von Lampe, 2018). Often the previous wave of Vietnamese was already moving towards legal employment and leaving their market place to the newcomers. It testifies to the resilience and dynamism of the Vietnamese enterprising spirit in the underground market. But this is not without hardship and many shattered hopes of earning enough to pay off the smuggling debt and send money home. This financial flow back to Vietnam is also advantageous the Vietnamese government, who willingly and knowingly furthers this migration, particularly from impoverished rural regions. Corruption and deceit are common in this migration business, which blurs the dividing line between state organised migration, and irregular migration with the accompanying smuggling and trafficking.

This ambiguous situation is not unique. In a provocative chapter on transnational crime of Chinese origin in the EU *Jurij Novak* sheds light on the criminal landscape, in which migrants move to and fro, some smuggled, others trafficked, and some migrants operating as seemingly legal entrepreneurs, but fraudulently cutting edges to remain competitive with their local semi-legal branch. His chapter describes the highly confusing situation of the Chinese migrant workers in the Chinese garment industry in the city of Prato, Italy. First, the author does away with a lot of myths around Chinese Triads and Chinese migration of whatever modality. After tidying up these fanciful constructions, the author elaborates the organisation of crime in the textile and garment industry in Prato. Amidst a large Chinese minority of 30.000 to 40.000[4], of which a substantial part remains illegal in the country, Chinese entrepreneurs have established a partly underground garment industry. With an annual estimated profit of 2 billion Euros they serve any chic Italian brand (or forge them). To keep the production costs low and the products competitive, all kinds of law breaking have been observed. By any legal qualification the labourers can be considered as exploited or in a state of modern slavery. Despite that, they have little victimisation awareness, industriously working in long shifts after which they return to their damp and crowded dormitories. Their main concern is to transmit their savings home. Those who pull the strings lead complex production organisations as 'bourgeois' crime entrepreneurs, dwarfing old fashioned organised criminals. For the author these findings lead to the question: shouldn't we investigate the more serious economic forms of organising crime? That is, not focus on the Chinese human smugglers, but on the wealthy underground entrepreneurs, with a respectful face but meanwhile exploiting his fellow countrymen. A rhetoric question.

State supported or enabled human smuggling of Vietnamese, the legal and illegal working relationships in the Prato Chinese textile industry, these findings provide strong indicators to look at migration and the related 'travel service' from another, more anthropological angle as is done by *Dina Siegel* (2010) in her previous work as well as in her chapter devoted the refugee crises on the island of Lesbos, Greece. She juxtaposes the crude

4 All numbers in this volume will be in *normal European* notation: a comma for the decimals and a full stop for the thousands.

rhetoric of policy makers and policy documents to the findings of researchers doing field research at site. At the policy makers' side we find the predictable construction of 'ruthless' networks exploiting the vulnerable position of defenceless refugees. If this rhetoric fails to impress it is reinforced by adding that the smuggling is the work of 'organised crime', always a good adjective to enhance the perception of threat. And indeed, there were organised crime groups operating and there are examples of reckless 'services': unseaworthy ships and unsafe life vests given to refugees on overcrowded boats causing numerous casualties. On the other hand, providing 'cross-border travel services' is a purely consensual business interaction in which the service provider rather heeds the principle: "Don't drown your customers". Obviously, doing so or being 'cruel and rapacious' will not further business. In contrast, the author's fieldwork on Lesbos demonstrated that there were many decent 'travel service providers', though not necessarily good Samaritans: they have a business to run. There is also more surrounding business than the core business of illegal transportation. In fact, many inhabitants profited from the parallel economic opportunities. For example, local transport and catering on the island Lesbos which led to substantial price rises for the arriving migrants. This nuanced, ethnographically supported picture underlines the conclusion of the author that clamping down on smugglers does not solve the problem of the flow of migrants: it is ritual dancing far removed from the daily struggle of people who want to leave harmful misery behind.

Recognising and fending off harm and other mischief

Fleeing misery at home is no guarantee against the fate of landing in other harmful situations in the targeted affluent economies where state and business may enable other forms of exploitation. In cases in which this is unethical there is no crime and one may argue that this goes beyond the narrow borders of criminology. But why? There is no reason to heed these criminal law limitations, according to *Jonathan Davies*, who looks through the 'lens of harm' beyond these narrow borders, namely at what happens on the workplace and in supply chain contexts in terms of harm. This is a valuable extension to a crime-restricted criminology. Indeed, many harmful conditions on the work floor were legal for decades until they were recognised as immoral and, after moral awareness raising actions, considered exploitative and harmful to physical and mental health. In the last resort causing or maintaining such working conditions was criminalised. Nowadays such conditions are approached from the perspective of 'modern slavery'. Developments in labour relationships and working condition should therefore be critically followed also by criminologists: there is an inherent tension between 'sound', meaning cost effective, working processes, and costs saving negligence that may inflict harm to the workers' health and rights. For example, making the corporation leaner and more flexible by dismissing personnel and hiring them back as self-employed enterprises under disadvantageous or harmful conditions: lower pay and no health or labour rights protection. In this way a new proletariat may emerge: 'independent but exploited'. Nevertheless, at the moment not yet categorised as exploitation under a criminal law construction.

Recognising that harm may be inflicted remains inconsequential if not followed by *securitisation*: the cocktail of laws, local administrative and institutional measures to prevent harm and crime. Such a security or crime prevention cocktail tends to expand to all sides as is set out in the chapter by *Anna Di Ronco* and *Anna Sergi* and illustrated with the stiff safety regimes in Italy and the UK. They point at how safety and crime prevention becomes dominant rather through a chain of associations, than through a chain of reasoned arguments. This may work as follows. First, there is nuisance, which is next associated with small crime, which is then connected to serious crime and that again to organised crime, eventually to its 'transnational' manifestation. In fact, 'safety thinking' is shaping a safety construction that knows no boundaries. And what about the principles of proportionality and subsidiarity? These words are repeated at all EU levels time and again, but then become subordinated to safety thinking in which these rational principles hardly play a role. The authors present Italy as a good example where getting a safe and 'clean' public space is a prime priority. Indeed, incivilities, hanging around on squares, making noise or making jibes at passers-by make people feel uncomfortable and unsafe in the public space. Correctly or not, a subsequent associative bridge to crime and irregular migrants is easily made. Basically people with a different appearance are considered 'unwanted' and subjected to administrative punitive measures and bans to make the white middle class feel more comfortable. This security extension is not only an Italian xenophobia driven legal construction. In the UK, by a court order one can be severely restricted in one's freedom of movement or coming together in the public space if one is associated with a 'gang', a vaguely defined criminal law concept that leaves the police with a lot of latitude. In the case of drug involvement one is upgraded to 'organised crime'. From the rule of law and the freedom of movement perspective, the EU should scrutinise these limiting legal constructions. However, that would be at odds with its own created European Crime Prevention Network (EUCPN). Will that institution disseminate best practices and at ther same time point at the mitigating requirement of proportionality? The authors express their doubt: in the politicised simplified construction of prevention and fear of crime there little room for this extra dimension. After all, one does not win elections by invoking proportionality when taking advantage of voters' fears is the winning card.

More than mischief: organised crime and business goes on

What about fear of organised crime? Would that not be an ultimate 'winning card' in elections? Here we have a paradox: indeed, organised crime has for a long time figured on the top of the political priority pyramid (Lampe, 2016). From the late 1980s till the present, the threat image of OC functioned as an associative 'crowbar' argumentation as we saw in the previous chapter: in Italy as well as in the UK 'organised crime' was used to lend the proposed policies more weight: who can oppose a freedom restricting crime prevention policy when the source of harm is allegedly 'organised crime' related. This implies that 'organised crime' remains in the general consciousness as a kind of keynote with a variable volume depending on the 'tune' of other political opportunities. Being a constant tune it is present for adding weight to a theme by adding the bridge-concept 'nexus'. For example the "nexus of . . . organised crime". Success guaranteed. Therefore, the way OC is constructed still deserves our critical attention (von Lampe, 2016).

With such multiple use one expects a lot of research activity and an accompanying availability of research funds. Is that the case? In their chapter on research on organised crime in Germany *Klaus von Lampe* and *Susanne Knickmeier* refute this expectation: compared to the political interest there is generally a shortage of basic empirical research, with the exception of the Netherlands. The authors made a meticulous stock taking and analysis of the OC research landscape in Germany over a period of 2008-2017 for which they collected research projects, dissertation projects and academic publications of German-based researchers on OC issues. This must be seen against the backdrop of the OC situation as presented in numerous police reports and media publications. Contrary to expectation, the type and subjects of research projects did not reflect the public OC image and concerns. In fact, measured by output the picture is fragmented. In general, there is a scarcity of empirical research compared to the large numbers of publicised studies, though in the beginning, around 1990, Germany had taken the lead in Europe. But after 2000, it seems to have lagged behind as is illustrated by the low output from 2008-2014, after which it started to catch up. Nevertheless, there remains a gap between the subjects of public attention in Germany and research interest. For example, the so-called Arabic Clans, outlaw biker groups, and phenomena such as organised residential burglary. It remains to be seen whether recently launched studies into these thematic areas will lead to more than just sporadic research output. One may wonder whether this lack of coherence is due to lack of a proper construction of the OC concept. And if such a construction cannot be drawn up, under the principle of scientific parsimony it should be discarded. That is not done either: the OC flag remains on top, while the underlying reality changes, as the next chapters on Scotland and the Czech Republic demonstrate.

Regarding the construction of OC in Scotland, *Kenneth Murray* raises the question concerning the working in network relations or in a hierarchy. Though in the criminological literature there is a tendency to interpret OC from the perspective of networks, for the Scottish organised crime landscape the author takes a middle position. Taking the wholesale cocaine traffic as the field of description, he constructs a hierarchic *and* a network interaction for the handling of the contraband. Unsurprisingly, the wholesale importation of contraband requires hierarchy: access abroad, oversight and scrutiny for the handling along the intermediate transport steps. These are distinctive capabilities that are inherent to a hierarchic organisation. Once the commodities have landed at retail distribution level, there is more need of flexible handling of the goods within network relations. However, for the reverse flow, the financial handling of the revenues, the *criminal money management*, higher expertise and oversight are required as special operational abilities. For this task a hierarchically enforced financial discipline is an essential asset also if financial tasks are out-coursed. Naturally, there may be network relationships between hierarchic organisations. At the end of the chapter we get a warning that the validity of the OC construction may have only a geographic validity: it may mainly apply to the mid-Scotland central belt between Glasgow and Edinburgh. Up north the illicit market landscape appears to be more open. It is a warning to address the validity question seriously: what seems to be a valid construction can evaporate across territories and times. "Panta rhei", all is changing, as Heracleitos would say.

This is almost literally the title of the chapter by *Miroslav Scheinost*: the changing face of organised crime, as it appears in his description of the past decades in the Czech Republic. The author leads us through the changing landscape of organised crime: from the 'virgin' years of the socialist society, where organised crime was not even thought of, to 'socialist organised crime', to the post-socialist transition epoch, till the present day where 'organised crime' has moved into higher circles. It could be considered the underlining of the statement that 'organised crime always adapts' itself to new circumstances and opportunities. Is that correct? If it is the same criminals who change their criminal enterprises and adopt new skills, the statement is correct. However, when changes bring other perpetrators to the criminal playground, 'organised crime adapts' is no valid proposition. One can only say that new opportunities requiring new skills also attract another population of criminal entrepreneurs which subsequently changes the OC construction. Following the author's account of the variable Czech OC scene closely, we notice indeed that he presents a different population than the 'usual' one: a sophisticated and institutionalised class of entrepreneurs having found a comfortable place in the warm chambers of the better circles (Scheinost, 2013).

We find a very usual organised crime population, described by *Toine Spapens* in his chapter on Italian criminals in the Netherlands. Why this interest? This has long roots, going back to the late 1980s and 1990s when with the rising fear of organised crime, alarms were also raised about the mafia 'crossing the Alps' northward to the Netherlands. More than at present the official organised crime constructions were to a high degree fed by fear mongering, evoking emotions and threat images (Van Duyne,

2004). Nevertheless, it was not all fantasy: occasionally there were indications that members of the four Italian organised crime groups were in the country for other reasons than the Van Goch Museum: hiding for the Italian prosecution or planning new cocaine smuggling operations to Italy. To assess whether the Italian criminal presence should be considered a threat, particularly subverting the democratic rule of law in the Netherlands, the *Cerca Trova* team ("search and thou shall find") made an elaborate stock taking. And indeed, the team found indications of an Italian organised crime presence in the Netherlands: stretched over a time span of 25 years (1989-2014) there were 461 relevant observations mainly related to drugs trade (cocaine), and only 9 concerning extortion, in Italy the core business of OC groups. While some of the team jumped to an Italian OC presence with all the connected constructions, the author weighed the plausibility of long-term integrated Italian legal presence against the scarcity of typical OC (Camorra, 'Ndrangheta, etc.) information. He thought that finding odd: mafia presence needs to be recognised and 'respected' in order to have power. But to become respected implies to be seen, which is bound to come to the notice of the police. This did not happen. So yes, there are OC related Italians in the Netherlands, but this does not support the proposition of a subversive 'mafia threat'.

In the literature on organised crime and terrorism one can find many worrying constructions on the interconnectedness or 'nexus' of these two phenomena. This is assumed for terrorist financing, particularly regarding the acquisition of weapons. While sensational and speculative publications abound, empirical evidence is again scarce; at best anecdotal, such as in the Western Balkan during the 1990s (Prezelj, 2010). In a refreshing way, without allowing themselves to be burdened by speculative constructions *Niels van Wanrooij* and *Saraï Sapulete* undertook an inductive bottom-up investigation of the interconnectedness of organised crime and jihadi terrorist networks in the Netherlands. To that end they used the Social Network Analysis, and applied this to the 'raw' police data which had been filtered for 'firearm possession', 'firearm dealing' and (suspected) terrorism. From the resulting database of 40 persons relationships were mapped: five arm dealers, 15 suspected terrorists and 20 persons with a conviction related to fire arms. It was found that suspected terrorists had a one or two-step connection to the firearms dealers, confirming the link between criminal offenders and terrorism. But otherwise the findings did not reveal a coherent terrorist network in the Netherlands. There were interactions between criminals and terrorist suspects, some of whom also had a criminal record before their conversion to jihadism, but the authors could not qualify this finding as interconnectedness at a structural level. Though recent terrorist arrests demonstrate there are 'terrorist cells' in the country, the evidence is insufficient to justify an organised crime and terrorist nexus. Scientifically the chapter follows the rule of parsimony in deleting another speculative construction.

Corruption and integrity

Many criminal events occur as a fate, something sudden, not as a daily experience: the 'daily fate' is grammatically not wrong, but still sounds odd. But how should you construct a fateful reality which implies a daily criminal burden, mostly of a moderate nature but influencing your life nevertheless? That is the case when corruption has grown into a way of daily life, whether you like it or not: it has become a daily cost of getting various things done, from waving a parking ticket to getting your doctor degree. Of course, if you can compensate these corruption expenses by levying corruption fees yourself, you can in the end of the month or year determine whether you have succeeded to remain at the 'sunny' side of the corruption break-even point. So you can be a corrupt winner or a loser. As is the case with the legal economy, also at the social-economic bottom the corruption balance is negative: corruption rarely favours the underprivileged. No surprise that many people demonstrate an ambiguous attitude to corruption, as investigated by *Anna Markovska, Alexey Serdyuk, Petrus C. van Duyne* and *Konstantin Bugaychuk*. In their 2017 survey of citizens in Kharkiv, the second town of Ukraine, they found views, reflecting a similar ambiguity or even duplicity: condemning corruption goes side by side with condoning or even positive statements and confession of a willingness to offer bribes voluntary, without being solicited or extorted. (See for Bosnia, Datzer *et al.*, 2008). Small wonder that at higher political level there is not much political will to fight corruption. In fact, the institutional progress that has been made after 2014, was achieved under tough pressure of the international donors, threatening to withdraw funds if legislative and institutional reforms would not be implemented. It was a process of a drawn out foot-dragging as was the case with the new Anti-corruption Court, from the President downwards, obstructing and slowing down by every step.[5]

A large part of the public displays a clear resignation to the present corrupt landscape furthered by the opaque public administration with its closed windows and doors. This was also a characteristic of the police forces: an opaque and inward directed military organisation (*militsiya*), also considered highly corrupt. But after the Maidan Revolution (in which the police role was seriously criticised), a new police reform was carried out. Its most visual element was the introduction of a separate branch, the Patrol Police. Socio-psychologically, the most important element was citizen's confidence: police performance is supposed to be reflected in and measured by the confidence the public has in its police force. Naturally it is important to learn how the police reflect on their own role in this reform: what do they experience of this public trust? This part has been investigated by *Igor Sviatokum, Alexey Serdyuk* and *Petrus C. van Duyne* as presented in their chapter on police reform. Based on the responses of 479 officers the authors observe that the results are modest: between 40 and 50% of the respondents saw little change, with the exception of the Patrol Officers who thought the reform went into the right direction. In addition to the public trust perception, the research also asked the officers to assess the police organisation as a "fair employer". It appeared that the fairness scores for the employer were generally low, whether related to protection of officers in court, fair pay, care and support in sickness or otherwise officers in need of support. This is important for maintaining confidence and integrity in a law enforcement agency: this is no construction but a real-life basic condition.

How important such a trust is or the lack thereof, is not only apparent by the recent history of Ukraine, but is also borne out by a study in neighbouring country Moldova as described by *Petrus C. van Duyne* and *Brendan Quirke* in their chapter.

There are many reasons to compare the two countries for similarities and differences. The most important is their Corruption Perception Index:

---

5 Anastasia Krasnosilska: http://khpg.org/en/index.php?id=1529358373. This is not unique to Ukraine: Van Duyne and Stocco (2012) observed a similar lack of 'political will', rather personal attitude of a corrupt elite in Serbia.

30 for Ukraine and 31 for Moldova: the absolute bottom for Europe. Another similarity is that also in this country virtually no anti-corruption law would have been enacted or measure implemented if not accompanied by international (financial) 'arm twisting'. There is one interesting difference: in Ukraine there is still a plurality of oligarchs who more or less can balance each other (if they do not conspire) (Konończuk *et al.*, 2017). Such a 'democracy of oligarchs' is absent in Moldova: after a protracted political struggle the oligarch with the largest political and law enforcement clout, Plahotniuc, succeeded in getting his rival, Filat, indicted and convicted in 2016 to nine years imprisonment for the ill-famous one billion dollar fraud and laundering.[6] The principle accomplice in this scheme, Mr. Shor, was convicted to 7,5 years. Notwithstanding this conviction, Mr. Shor's sentence has thus far not been executed. He was allowed to remain at large, establish his own political party and succeeded in the February 2019 election to get a seat in Parliament. It is one of the most recent examples of 'capturing the state' by criminal oligarchs, in this case the only one left. By massive funding he 'owns' the Democratic Party, controls the majority of media outlets and influences legislation and judiciary nominations. Altogether Moldova represents an almost classical example of a 'captured state'. Are there no institutional guardians against corruption? Yes there are, such as the Anti-Corruption Prosecution Office, led by persons of questionable expertise, underfunded and burdened with small corruption cases that could also be delegated to a local prosecutor. These sub-modest efforts allow the government to state "We are on the right track", without moving much forward.

Policy and businesses in foggy constructions

Money laundering is one of the criminal law constructions that has become perceived as an entity in its own right. It shares this status with the adjacent concept of 'organised crime' with which it also shares a high degree of lack

[6] Though Filat denied any guilt, summer 2016, his son (22) arrived in the UK, and in a not too sophisticated laundering action paid £400.000 in rent upfront for a penthouse in Knightsbridge, spent £200.000 on a Bentley and received a recovery order of over nearly £500.000. https://www.theguardian.com/world/2019/feb/07/court-orders-son-moldova-former-pm-pay-466000

of clarity. Both also haunt us since the late 1980s (Van Duyne *et al.*, 2018). They are also classic examples of what impact a foggy concept can have on the apparatus of law enforcement. But money laundering encompasses an extra action circle: the whole financial industry and related non-financial sectors. This would not be so bad if clarity would have been served, which is not the case. This is one of the lessons the reader can learn from the chapter by *Brigitte Slot* and *Linette de Swart* about the attempt of the Financial Action Task Force (FATF) to evaluate the outcome of its policies, per country. Methodologically this is as ambitious as doing the Dakar Rally with an old 2-CV without mileometre and compass. Indeed, as the authors make it clear: the car is bound to run into the sand, if it can start at all. Basic methodological principles are violated: no concept clarity or proper operationalisation, no problem delineation and no zero measurement, to mention just four mortal methodological sins. This is not the whole story: we can observe a kind of real-life sociological experiment of collective make-belief: while before the start at Dakar the 2-CV stands already with its four wheels until its axes in the sand, all stakeholders around shout for joy that it is moving fantastically. A whole evaluation story is constructed: one after the other mutual evaluation report is stacked together with countries' national risk assessment, but we still cannot determine any outcome regarding the effectiveness of all these exploits, as also observed by Ferwerda (2018). The authors observe that the FATF outcomes are "predominantly the result of international negotiations, rather than strict analytical thinking", which is hidden behind the aplomb with which these are presented.

Another construction with undeniably clouding effects is elaborated in the final chapter of *Matjaž Jager, Ciril Keršmanc* and *Katja Šugman Stubbs*. It concerns 'corporate social responsibility', a construction of moral rules for the conduct of multi-national corporations. As such it has an inherent social acceptability, but, as the authors indicate in the title, it is rather used as a mask for various forms of corporal misconduct. Naturally there is a tension between the basic aims of the multinational: earning money and satisfying the shareholders on the one hand, and being morally accountable to the society on the other hand, if only by lip service to avoid criticism. But to what society? And where and who is the responsible legal person, when there is a mother company with daughters spread over multiple countries? All connected branches will have ethical codes of conduct which will be presented as tokens of corporate social responsibility. However, what happens behind this slick PR behaviour? The authors provide examples from the oil industry that clearly contradicts the tenets of its own social responsibility, particularly when they operate in countries with a flawed, corrupt governance. The authors even apply the analogy of the human psychopathy to the attitude and conduct of the corporate persons: deceptive, charming, rationally scouting for weaknesses, lack of sympathy for the victims, no remorse and, with an inflated ego, persistent in their claims of having done the best, pointing at philanthropic or ecological projects to 'greenwash' their corporate misbehaviour. Nevertheless, there is a silver lining. Like most constructions, once corporate social responsibility is consistently upheld by a large enough part of civil society, it will get a life of its own. That is good as it can be invoked to hold wrong-doers responsible, whether in court or in public.

So, although the world is shaped by constructions, some of them foggy mind projections, is does not mean that they cannot have a beneficial effect if actively invoked.

References

Datzer, D., A. Maljević, M. Budimlić and E. Muratbegović, Police corruption through eyes of bribers: The ambivalence of sinners. In: P.C. van Duyne *et al.*, *European crime-markets at cross-roads. Extended and extending criminal Europe*. Nijmegen, Wolf Legal Publishers, 2008.

Duyne, P.C. van, The creation of a threat image: Media, policy making and organised crime. In: P.C. van Duyne, M. Jager, K. von Lampe and J.L. Newell (eds.), *Threats and phantoms of organised crime, corruption and terrorism*. Nijmegen, Wolf Legal Publishers, 2004.

Duyne, P.C. van, J.H. Harvey and L.Y. Gelemerova, *The critical handbook of money laundering. Policy, analysis and myths*. London, Palgrave Macmillan, 2018.

Duyne, P.C. and E. Stocco, *Corruption in Serbia. From black box to transparent policy making*. Nijmegen, Wolf Legal Publishers, 2012.

Ferwerda, J., The effectiveness of anti-money laundering policy: a cost-benefit perspective. In: C. King, J. Gurulé and C. Walker (eds.), *The Palgrave handbook of criminal and terrorism financing law*. Cham Switzerland, Palgrave Macmillan, 2018.

Galeotti, M., *The vory*. New Haven, CT., Yale University Press, 2018.

Heather, P., *Empires and barbarians. Migration, development and the birth of Europe*. London, Macmillan, 2009.

Herkes, G., The Janus-faced victimisation in human smuggling and human trafficking. In P.C. van Duyne *et.al.*, *The Janus faces of cross-border crime in Europe*. Den Haag, Boom Uitgevers, 2018.

Kernteam Noord en Oost Nederland. *Algemene Criminaliteitsbeeldanalyse Oost-Europa, 2000-2001*, Zwolle, 2001.

Konończuk, W., D. Cenuşa and K. Kakachia, *Oligarchs in Ukraine, Moldova and Georgia as key obstacles to reforms*. 2017 www.3dcftas.eu/.

von Lampe, K., *Organised crime. Analysing illegal activities, criminal structures and extra-legal governance*. London, Sage Publications, 2016.

Norwich, J.J., *The popes. A history*. Amsterdam, Uitgeverij Bert Bakker, 2013.

Nguyen, T. and K. von Lampe, On the persistence of an open illegal market: Explaining the continued existence of street-vending of contraband cigarettes in Berlin since 1990. In P.C. van Duyne *et.al.*, *The Janus faces of cross-border crime in Europe*. Den Haag, Boom Uitgevers, 2018

Prezelj. I., (2010). The small arms and light weapons problem. In W. Benedek *et al.*, *Transnational terrorism, organised crime and peace building. Human security in the Western Balkans*. Houndmills, UK, Palgrave Macmillan, 2010.

Rawlinson, P., Mafia, media and myth. Representations of Russian organised crime. *The Howard Journal of Criminal Justice*, 1998, 4, 346-358.

Scheinost, M., Organised crime in the country of transition after twenty years. In P.C. van Duyne *et al.*, *Human dimensions in organised crime, money laundering and corruption*. Nijmegen, Wolf Legal Publishers, 2013.

Siegel, D., *Maffia, diamanten en Mozart*. Den Haag, Boom Juridische Uitgevers, 2010.

Constructing migrants as crime and public order problems

Comparing local press representations in two Italian cities

Anna Di Ronco and *Anita Lavorgna*[1]

Introduction

The presence of sanguinary civil wars and religious and separatist conflicts afflicting several countries in the Middle East and northern Africa has led, especially over the past five years, to what has been called in Europe as the 'refugee crisis', with southern European countries daily receiving increasing numbers of re-settlers. It was estimated that over one million people – refugees, displaced persons and other migrants – have made their way to the EU in 2015; more than 350.000 arrived via the Mediterranean Sea in 2016 alone, and about 60.000 in the first half of 2017 (European Commission, 2017; UNHCR, 2017). Those arriving via sea are split almost evenly between Italy and Greece, with smaller numbers arriving in Malta, Cyprus, and Spain (IOM, 2017).

The arrival of migrants in southern European countries and their relocation to other European Member States has often raised concerns and sparked the protests of sections of the population. As a result, in many EU countries tighter control systems have been introduced against the allegedly risk-posing 'non-citizens': namely undocumented migrants, asylum seekers and refugees. In Italy, these control systems have mostly relied on

1 Anna Di Ronco is Lecturer in Criminology at the University of Essex, UK. Anita Lavorgna is Associate Professor of Criminology at the University of Southampton, UK.

administrative, rather than on criminal, measures, and have been included in both security (public order) and migration control policies.

In Italy, right-wing political parties (particularly, but not limited to, the Northern League) have raised concerns over the arrival and presence of refugees and, more in general, migrants in Italian cities, often using a racist and xenophobic language that has legitimised 'local policies of exclusion' (Ambrosini and Caneva, 2012; Caneva, 2014). As will be detailed in the next section, these policies or *public order regulations* have been used by local authorities to administratively sanction and ban from public spaces all behaviour considered to be a 'threat' to the safety and security of citizens, including begging, illegal settlements in public spaces (Roma people), the selling and purchasing of alcoholic beverages and the presence of street prostitutes in certain city areas. In practice, however, these punitive regulations have mostly been applied against migrants (Caneva, 2014; Crocitti and Selmini, 2016), particularly Roma people and street sex workers (who in Italy are mostly migrants; for more see Di Ronco, 2017).

Research has highlighted that there are differences in the local enforcement of these public order regulations (Di Ronco, 2014, 2016) and that these differences are also related to the specific political parties entrusted with the local governance (Devroe *et al.*, 2016). The use of onerous administrative or civil measures, which substantially restrict individual's autonomy and de *facto* criminalise an individual's behaviour and exclude unwanted and already marginalised groups from public spaces (which has occurred not only in Italy but also in other European countries, see Peršak, 2017a), has been viewed as an example of popular punitiveness and protection of the public from feeling negative emotions (Peršak, 2017b). This misuse of measures has also been interpreted as a feature of the pre-crime society (Pleysier, 2015, 2017) and of Garland's (2001) 'culture of control' (Devroe, 2012; Devroe *et al.*, 2016).

Another broadly used control system (harshly criticised as contravening international human rights standards) is *administrative detention* – that is, the practice of detaining migrants for administrative purposes, such as to establish their identities, or to facilitate their immigration claims resolution or their removal (for a comparative study of the refugee detention systems in the US, UK, Italy, France and Germany, see Welch and Shuster, 2005). These detention systems have been studied in migration (Cinalli and El Hariri, 2011) and in the so-called 'crimmigration' literature (Guia *et al.*,

2011; Van der Woude *et al.*, 2017), and have been analysed through Garland's (2001) 'culture of control' and Simon's (2007) 'governing through crime' theoretical frameworks (see, among others, Welch and Shuster, 2005; Bosworth, 2008; Bosworth and Guild, 2008). Within the crimmigration literature, studies have emphasised the importance of the local context in the understanding of migration control and, consequently, the (informal) inclusion or exclusion of migrants by the action of criminal justice actors (Fabini, 2017).

National as well as local punitive policy responses towards unwanted minorities also depend on the *media representations* of the 'problems' to be addressed (Chibnall, 1977; Hall, 1982; Ericson *et al.*, 1991). According to a recent comparative study (Berry *et al.*, 2015), for instance, asylum seekers and refugees have been represented differently in Italian, Spanish, British and Swedish press outlets in 2014 and 2015. While the Swedish press has offered the most favourable and positive portrayal of asylum seekers and refugees, the British press has described them in the most negative terms: as a threat to the welfare and health systems ('bogus') and as criminals (Berry *et al.*, 2015). Labelling asylum seekers and refugees as bogus and illegal facilitated a vicious circle of criminalisation (leading, for example, to their detention and electronic monitoring – which helped to reaffirm the idea that migrants are criminals) (Cooper, 2009). In the study of Berry and colleagues (2015), the Italian press produced mixed results: it included humanitarian themes along with negative frames, which are to be explained through the hostility and anti-migrant sentiments that since long have been promoted by politicians through the media, also with the use of stigmatising language and labels such as 'clandestine', 'illegals' *etc.* (Montaly *et al.*, 2013; Quassoli, 2013).

These studies focused on the national press and offered, therefore, a national level of analysis. As suggested in the crimmigration literature, however, local approaches to (irregular) migrants may substantially vary across space and, in particular, in different local contexts. In addition to that, fear of crime and feelings of insecurity (which may, to an extent, be shared by people in Western societies and epitomise larger social anxieties) also very much vary in different local contexts (Girling *et al.*, 2000; Jewkes, 2015) and may reflect the ideologies and discourses of the political parties running the city. In other words, the extent to which national punitive regulations are implemented and enforced in a certain local context may reflect local (political) narratives on the "problems" posed by migrants, which are also voiced by local politicians (among other actors) through the local media.

The aim of this chapter is to inspect how the *local press* have framed the 'problems' associated with the increased presence of undocumented migrants, asylum seekers and refugees in two Italian cities, *Padova* and *Udine*, which have been run by different political parties: right-wing (Padova) and centre-left (Udine) parties. Ultimately, it aims to inspect whether there are similarities or differences in how the local press in these two cities has constructed the 'problems' posed by, and the solutions against, migrants at the local level.

Background: regulating asylum seekers and undocumented migrants in Italy

Before moving to the media analysis, it is necessary to provide a brief overview of the complex Italian hosting system and the asylum claim process, and of the two main administrative control systems available in Italy to deal with the so-called 'refugee crisis' – *i.e.*, administrative detention and public order measures (the latter take, in practice, the form of administrative fines).[2]

---

2 In late September 2018, the Italian government has approved a new "security Decree" (which has to be converted into law by the Parliament within 60 day to retain its legal validity). This Decree would reduce the possibilities of issuing residence permits to migrants for humanitarian reasons, and enlarge the types of crimes for which humanitarian protection is revoked or denied, leading to migrants' deportation. These crimes are, among others, intimidation of a public officer, serious physical violence, and theft and burglary aggravated by the use of weapons or by the use of drugs by the perpetrator. It worth noting that, according to the new legislation, when a person is merely prosecuted (not convicted or found guilty) for one of these crimes, the asylum application can be blocked and the person immediately repatriated. This provision, as many commenters have already suggested, is in breach of the presumption of innocence, which is crystallised in the Italian Constitution (art. 27). The Decree also revokes citizenship to people convicted for terrorism. In addition, it authorises the local police (usually unarmed) to use taser guns and the police to access data bases; allows urban DASPOs (see the section of this chapter on public order measures) to be applied in healthcare facilities, markets and public

The hosting system and the asylum claim process

Migrants and asylum seekers arriving it Italy are subject to a twofold hosting process. In the primary hosting phase ('*prima accoglienza*'), migrants are gathered in *Reception Centres* (CDAs) and *Hotspots*[3], where they are identified and divided into those who have to be repatriated as economic migrants and those with a right to apply for asylum. At least on paper, those with a right to apply for asylum should be tranferred to *Regional Hubs* (which since 2015 have replaced the so-called *Hosting Centres for Asylum Seekers* or CARAs). Those who have to be repatriated should be moved to the so-called *Identification and Expulsion Centres* (CIEs), soon to be renamed *Centers for Residence and Repatriation* (CPR, see below for further details).

The asylum claim starts in the primary hosting phase either with a request at the border police office, or with the formal registration (including fingerprinting and photographing) at the *Questura* (provincial Police station). Police authorities of the *Questura* ask the asylum seeker questions related to the Dublin III Regulation and then contact the Dublin Unit of the Ministry of the Interior to verify whether Italy is responsible for the examination of the asylum application. Police authorities cannot examine the merits of the asylum application, but they send the registration form and all the relevant documents to the *Territorial Commissions for International Protection*, which are competent for the substantive asylum interview.

In the secondary hosting phase ('*seconda accoglienza*'), refugees and asylum seekers are moved into the *Protection Systems for Asylum Seekers and Refugees* (SPRARs) while waiting for a decision on their claim. In the SPRARs, asylum seekers and refugees should benefit from ad-hoc programs to facilitate their integration (such as Italian language courses and vocational education programs). Unfortunately, SPRARs are often unable to provide sufficient room for the high numbers of applicants, so that many

---

events; and sanctions squatting more harshly (with detention to up to four years and an administrative fine to be determined by the judge).

3 The so-called 'hotspots', according to the approach developed by the EU Commission, are the facilities set up at the EU's external border in Italy (in Taranto, Trapani, Pozzallo and Lampedusa) and Greece for the initial reception, identification and registration of migrants coming by sea.

migrants are moved to the *Extra Hosting Centres* (CASs, similar to the Hubs) instead.

Administrative detention

In the Italian hosting system for migrants there are a number of administrative detention centres, originating from both Italian regulations and EU Directives that were only briefly mentioned in the previous section. This section aims at problematising the existence of the most controversial of these centers (those for identification and expulsion), and providing the necessary context to understand their development.

Immigration became an increasingly politicised issue from the late 1980s, when Italy (historically a country of emigration) started to become a country of immigration. In 1998, the 40/1998 Immigration Act ('Turco-Napolitano Act', after the names of the then Minister of Social Affairs Livia Turco and Minister of Interior Giorgio Napolitano) established, among others, an administrative immigration detention regime for irregular migrants who were to be identified before being expelled. The so-called Temporary Permanence Centres (CPTs), renamed in 2008 as *Identification and Expulsion Centres* (or CIEs) were regulated by the Prefectures (local divisions of the Ministry of Interior) and managed by private bodies funded with public money (initially, the Italian Red Cross and, currently, NGOs). CIEs, which were developed as an 'emergency' response, were criticised for grounds of unconstitutionality since their very inception, and especially after their regime was made harsher with the Immigration Act 189/2002 ('Bossi-Fini') under Silvio Berlusconi's right-wing coalition, and further amended by the so-called 'Security Package' (Law Decree 92/2008, converted into Law 125/2008), Act 94/2009 and Decree 129/2011 (implementing Directive 2008/115/EC on returning illegally staying third-country nationals) (Sabatini, 2002; Vassallo Paleologo, 2010; Commissione Straordinaria per la Tutela e la Promozione dei Diritti Umani, 2016).

Administrative detention and, essentially, penal restrictions in the CIEs were not based on the commission of a crime and imposed by a court at the end of a criminal proceeding (formally there are not 'inmates', but 'guests' [*sic*]). Rather, they were imposed by the *Questore* (the chief of the provincial Police) and validated by a specialised judge with a deportation order or with a refused entry (Colombo, 2013). However, not all migrants who were refused entry or were given a deportation order were detained in the CIEs, mostly because of their growing limited capacities. As contended by Colombo (2013), a crucial role in the decision on whether to detain a migrant in a CIE was played by the police: among the considered criteria, there were the availability of beds, the likelihood of being repatriated, and previous criminal convictions. Initially, there were 13 CIEs (hosting about 2.000 people), but were then formally reduced to five (in Roma, Caltanissetta, Bari, Torino, and Trapani), and could formally host a total of about 550 people. However, additional temporary CIEs were created to respond to specific crisis (such as in Libya) leading to increasing numbers of refugees, so that the actual number of CIEs swung often between 7 and 13, hosting about 1.000 people.

This legal framework for the regulation of asylum seekers and undocumented migrants was changed in 2017 by a governmental Decree – the so-called 'Minniti-Orlando', after the names of the then Ministry of the Interiors Marco Minniti and the Ministry of Justice Andrea Orlando, in Premier Paolo Gentiloni's cabinet – on immigration and asylum (DL 13/2017), approved by the Italian Parliament on 12 April 2017. The Decree had the explicit aim to hasten the appeal procedures for asylum seekers, whose number severely increased over the last couple of years, causing severe delays in the (already clogged) Italian court system. Unfortunately, the Decree left the previous legislative paradigm – international migration as an 'emergency' phenomenon to be repressed – unquestioned, and for this has been harshly criticised (Masera, 2017; Open Migration, 2017). In the name of simplifying judicial procedures and easing the burden of the reception system, asylum seekers will no longer have the chance to appeal in the second instance against the rejection of their claims. Furthermore, the examination phase changed from a summary proceeding to a full chamber proceeding, eliminating the need for a hearing; the judge will be now provided with a video recording of the asylum seeker's interview before the Territorial Commission, and will be able to hear the claimant in person only at his/her discretion. These procedural changes have been harshly criticised by the oppositions and civil society groups (Antigone, 2017; ASGI, 2017; Open Migration, 2017). In addition, specialised sections in courts will be dedicated to asylum claims and deportations.

The CIEs will be renamed *Centers for Residence and Repatriation* (CPRs); their number will be expanded from 4 to 20 throughout Italy, and their total capacity increased to 1.600 places. The CPRs will be smaller (not more than 100 persons each) and better managed than the CIEs, and they will have the clear purpose of repatriation (rather than reception). Some technical provisions of the Decree are expected to limit the right to asylum. For instance, the creation of a list of 'safe' origin and transit countries would probably imply that, if a person has transited through, or comes from, a 'safe' country (such as Turkey), the claimant has a very slim chance of being granted asylum (ASGI, 2017).

Public order measures

In 2008, when the so-called 'Security Package' (see above) was passed by the then Berlusconi government, local authorities have been allowed to sanction administratively any behaviour deemed to threaten public safety and security. Since then, local authorities, especially in the northern part of Italy (Cittalia, 2012), have substantially used this power to target a wide range of 'threatening' or, simply, uncivil behaviour, including begging, public drinking and drunkeness, vandalism, street prostitution (especially sex workers' 'indecent' clothing, see Di Ronco, 2017), littering, and noise nuisance (Cittalia, 2009, 2012). A recent study (Crocitti and Selmini, 2016) has suggested that, although not explicitly, these local regulations have mostly targeted migrants, as beggars, street sex workers, squeegee merchants *etc*. tend not to be of Italian nationality (see also Caneva, 2014).

The 'Security Package' and local security regulations have been negatively assessed by the Constitutional Court in one of its leading judgments of 2011 (of 7 April, No 115). In this ruling, the Court found that national and local security regulations breached a number of constitutional principles, including the principles of legality and proportionality. In essence, the prohibited conduct was not clearly identified by the law (in violation of the legality principle), thus allowing local actors to virtually penalise any behaviour considered problematic or threatening people's security with excessive measures (in breach of the proportionality principle). According to the Court, the penalisation of both harmful (and in many cases already criminalised behaviour, such as vandalism, which is often punished through the offence of criminal damage) and *harmless* conduct (such as the hanging about of young people on the streets, which may be harmless but considered as alarming by some powerful social groups) resulted in an excessive and disproportionate interference with the exercise of individual's rights. To realign the law to these fundamental constitutional principles, the Court 'corrected' the exercise of local public order powers: it allowed local authorities to adopt (temporary-limited) regulations only in exceptional cases of serious and concrete risks of harm to the public safety and security of people (Di Ronco and Peršak, 2014). Notwithstanding this judgment, local authorities have carried on issuing (illegitimate) local security orders (Caneva, 2014; Di Ronco and Peršak, 2014; Crocitti and Selmini, 2016).

To make things worse, broad local public order powers have recently been re-introduced by the Italian government through the recent Law Decree 14/ 2017, which has been approved on the same day as the 'Minniti-Orlando' decree referred to above and has the same nickname ('Minniti'). The Decree, which violates the Constitutional Court's ruling, allows municipalities to, among others, adopt orders to protect the 'decorum', the 'urban liveability' and the "peace and quiet of residents" (art. 8 co. 1 lett. a no 1), and to prevent behaviour that "favours the occurrence of criminal phenomena or illegality" (art. 8 co. 1 lett. B No 1). The use of very vague concepts in the Decree (such as 'decorum', 'liveability' *etc.*) may again lead to the penalisation of any possibly harmless yet unwanted behaviour, and, therefore, to excesses and abuses.

The Decree also gives the possibility to local authorities to ban people from certain city areas (mainly historical and touristic areas, and close to transport infrastructures) when they adopt behaviour that "impairs the access and use of those areas" by others (art. 9 co. 1). These orders are informally called 'urban DASPOs', as they resemble the bans from taking part to sport events (the "Divieto di Accedere alle manifestazioni Sportive" or DASPO) used to exclude hooligans from sports events. People can be banned from a certain area for 48 hours; however, their access in the area can be prohibited by the *Questore* to up to six months, when they reiterate the prohibited conduct and adopt a behaviour that "may cause a risk to security" (art. 10 co. 2). Of course, the risk carried by this ban is that it will mostly be applied against, and ultimately exclude, the most vulnerable segments of the population (Antigone, 2017).

This 'urban DASPO' is relevant to the scope of our analysis: suffice it to think that it was used in an operation that took place in the Milan Central

Station on 2 May 2017, when dozens of migrants who hover/live around the train station where dispersed and 52 of them were brought in the *Questura* for inspection. The operation was severely criticised by many (*e.g.*, activists from the civil society) but also praised by several politicians, such as Matteo Salvini of the Northern League (who thanked "God, the police, the *carabinieri* [for the] clean-up of this people we do not need [and who] every day infest [the station]") (*La Repubblica,* 2017b).

Methodology

In this study, we chose to focus on two Italian cities, *Padova* and *Udine*, which are two medium-size cities located in the northeast of Italy. Their districts are relatively comparable in terms of economies,[4] and they have a similar and rather high share of non-Italian residents compared to the total population.[5] In addition, both Padova and Udine have hosting centres in their territories and have also implemented a number of public order measures. In Padova, for instance, under Bitonci's administration, a number of public orders were issued in 2014, 2015 and 2016 to forbid, among others, rough sleeping on public benches, entering in certain recreation grounds without children, begging, soliciting of and procuring for prostitution; they have also been issued to limit the opening hours of 'Kebab shops' in certain areas of the city (Padovanet, 2017). Udine adopted a local regulation to protect the urban 'decorum' by mostly targeting street sex workers, homeless people, drunk people and graffiti writers relatively recently (on 20 December 2016).[6]

4 The average income (taxable income for the purpose of the personal income-tax surcharge) in these two districts is € 21.155 and € 22.568, respectively (data from 2015, retrieved from www.comuni-italiani.it).

5 In the Udine district migrants account to 7,5% of the total population (tot.: 533.282), whereas in the Padova district they are 10% of the total population (tot.: 936.887). See www.comuni-italiani.it, as above.

6 See: http://www.comune.udine.gov.it/files/amministrazione_trasparente/disposizioni_generali/atti/organizzazione/161219_regolamento_polizia_urbana.pdf.

Despite these similarities, these two cities strongly differ in terms of local politics. While Udine has firmly been under centre-left administrations since 2003, Padova has shifted over the last decade between centre-left and right wing (namely the regionalist and xenophobic Northern League) administrations; after the fall of the City Council ruled by Massimo Bitonci from the Northern League in November 2016, it has been ruled by a prefectorial commissioner until November 2009. New elections were held in Spring 2017 and won by a centre-left coalition led by Sergio Giordani (after a run-off with Bitonci). It will be interesting to see whether this will entail new patterns in the relationship between local politics and media representation of refugees and security issues.

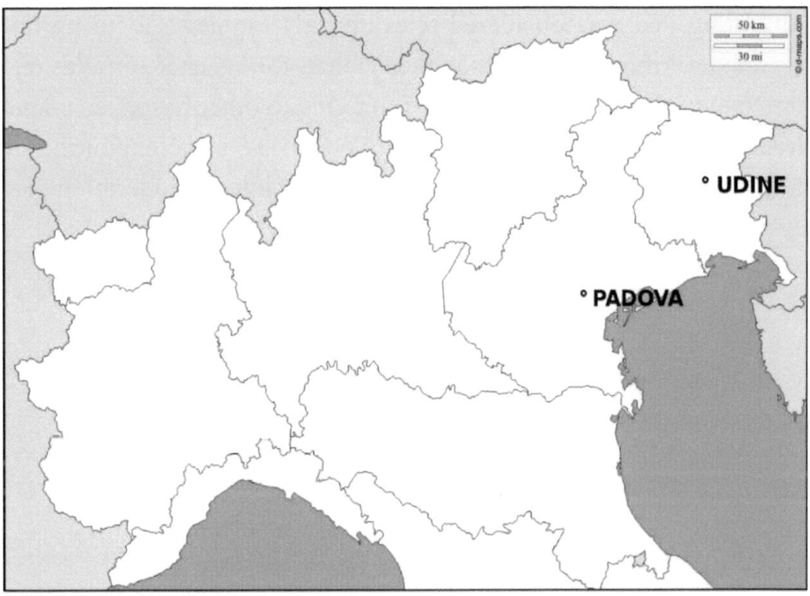

This study focuses on news articles published between 1 January, 2008 and 31 May, 2017. We decided to start our analysis in January 2008, the year of the 'Security Package', which introduces tough crimmigration and public disorder measures. The end date (31 May, 2017) is the latest possible date we could chose to complete the analysis.

The articles were extracted from the two most read newspapers in Padova and Udine, among the newspapers with a clear local focus which are *Il Mattino di Padova* and *Il Messaggero Veneto- Giornale del Friuli*, respectively.[7] Both newspapers used the same online platform for their digital archives, which allowed us to use the same keyword searches: "(rifugiato OR rifugiata OR rifugiati OR rifugiate OR profugo OR profuga OR profughe OR profughi) AND (sicurezza OR criminale OR illegale)". We considered articles published both online and on paper. Other keywords combinations could have been used. However, we carried out a pilot search and concluded that the selected searches provided a good balance between relevance and inclusiveness.

After having manually sorted the files to exclude non-relevant news and duplicates (see Tables 1 & 2), a final sample of 252 articles was obtained: 152 were retrieved from *Il Mattino di Padova* (henceforth: MP) and 100 from *Il Messaggero Veneto-Giornale del Friuli* (henceforth: MV). It is worth noting that we considered relevant only the news focusing on the local 'impact' of migrants (which means that, for instance, articles on migration in general, articles on refugees moving to other European countries such as Germany, or articles on events occurring in neighbouring cities such as Venezia or Pordenone were not taken into consideration for the analysis).

---

7 According to the data of Accreditamenti Diffusione Stampa [Press Diffusion Accreditation], retrievable from: http://www.adsnotizie.it/certif/index.php.

Tables 1 and 2 – Keyword searches

Il Mattino di Padova

	rifugiato (refugee – m)	rifugiata (refugee – f)	rifugiati (refugees – m)	rifugiate (refugees – f)	profugo (refugee – m)	profuga (refugee – f)	profughe (refugees – f)	profughi (refugees – m)
Sicurezza	133 (23 relevant)	17 (0)	314 (24 relevant after excluding duplicates	13(0)	91 (23 after excluding duplicates)	4 (1)	0(0)	1078 (72 after excluding duplicates)
criminal	24 (1)	1 (0)	27 (1)	1 (0)	4 (1)	2 (1)	0(0)	53 (1)
illegale	11 (2)	3 (0)	20 (0)	0(0)	15 (2)	0(0)	8(0)	62(0)

l Messaggero Veneto – Giornale del Friuli

	Rifugiato	Rifugiata	Rifugiati	Rifugiate	Profugo	Profuga	Profughe	profughi
sicurezza	232 (11)	38 (0)	867 (30)	8(0)	133 (6)	10 (0)	0(0)	2714 (39)
criminale	44 (0)	3(0)	88(1)	0(0)	11(0)	1(0)	0(0)	138 (4)
illegale	41(0)	2(0)	81(2)	1(0)	11(0)	0(0)	0(0)	210 (7)

The software NVivo was used for the computer-assisted qualitative and quantitative content analysis. Relevant passages in the text were categorised according to five main codes (‘Years’, ‘Actors speaking’, ‘Representations of migrants’, ‘Problems’, and ‘Solutions’) and 84 sub-codes. The use of NVivo allowed us to obtain descriptive statistics of the different codes and sub-codes: particularly, the number of references (that is, the number of text fragments within our sampled articles that have been coded with any code) provided us with insights into the recurrence of a certain theme in the press. The codes and sub-codes were also used to assist the qualitative part of the analysis, the results of which are presented in the following section.

Our methodological approach has limitations that need to be acknowledged, both in terms of the sources and the analytical approach adopted. First, media sources do not paint a true or complete picture of the social world: media representations necessarity consist of viewpoints that succeed in capturing the attention of the general public (Barak, 1994). Second, content analysis has the inherent limitation that it relies on the researchers' own categorisations and interpretation of the meaning of a text; as ambiguity is particularly frequent in media discourses and in sensitive topics, the replicability requirement is not clarly met (Krippendorff, 1980). Despite these limitations, media resources and content analysis are widely used in social sciences research, as they provide researchers with precious and rich information and representations of the social world.

Results and discussion

Years

The number of newspaper articles identified and analysed is overall rather scarce in the period of time stretching from 2008 to 2014, covering about one fifth of the total number of articles considered (N = 252). From 2015 onward, by contrast, relevant articles started to increase significantly and reached the highest number (86 references in total) in 2016. Please note that for the year 2017, when fifty news articles were sampled, only news released until 31 May were taken into consideration, thus suggesting that in 2017 the number of virtually all relevant items will likely surpass the number of relevant news sampled in 2016.

Actors speaking

The voices of political actors dominate the press discourse on migrants (50,7%). In particular, the press tends to cover the opinions of mayors (21,3%) and local politicians (17,3%), in addition to the regional (6,4%)

and national (5,3%) politicians. The voices of criminal justice actors – including the police (7,5%), the prefect (7,7%), the quaestor (3,3%) and judges (2.4%) – also substantially featured the local press debate on migrants (20,9%). In addition, residents and citizens are also given a voice (11,9%). Groups that speak infrequently in the news are religious representatives, groups and charities, who all try to get migrants integrated in the local communities (5,5%). Asylum seekers and refugees speak only in a very limited number of articles (1,75%) and, overall, less than their "victims" (or of the victims of crimes said to be committed by migrants) (2,6%). Experts' opinions are virtually absent in the debate, as their voices appear in only one article where a university professor speaks, in line with Berry and colleagues (2015).

Representations of migrants

Migrants are mostly represented as criminals (45%) and bogus (15,7%). In a much limited number of articles, they are described as 'illegal' ('*clandestini*') (5,9%), dangerous as they allegedly carry highly infectious diseases such as scabies (5,9%), and as terrorists (4,9%). Migrants are portrayed in positive terms, *i.e.* not as criminals but as people fleeing from civil wars, only in a very small minority of articles (6,4%). This partly contradicts the results of the recent study carried out by Berry and colleagues (2015), which suggest that the Italian (national) press has presented negative frames about migrants along with more positive (mostly humanitarian) themes. This difference may have to do with the fact that in the study of Berry *et al.* (2015) the sampled newspapers were national and not local as in the present research, and that the local newspapers may tend to give more coverage to local events and to the messages of the most vocal local politicians, who often belong to right-wing political parties.

Problems

Both the two selected press outlets are consistent in describing the 'refugee' problem as an 'emergency'. The emergency situation is particularly sensationalised in the news published in Udine: the Italian region of Friuli Venezia Giulia, where Udine is situated, is commonly referred to in the news as the 'Lampedusa of the North' (MV, 10 October 2015). This analogy is used to emphasise the high number of migrants who daily arrive in the region, either by crossing the Slovenian border or by being relocated by the central state (after landing in Lampedusa and reaching the Italian southern regions by sea).

In the substantial majority of the news (31,6%), national and local refugee hosting policies are questioned. For example, policies are problematised and criticised because of the limited capacities of municipalities, which only can offer limited places in the (often old and unsuitable) allocated reception centres to host asylum seekers and refugees, and of law enforcers to deal with the situation (10,6%). Hosting policies are also challenged because of the link between the arrival and acceptance of asylum seekers and the occurrence of social disorder and crime (5%) (*e.g.*, "These migrant flows increase delinquency", MV, 17 June 2015). The already (perceived) excessive number of asylum seekers and refugees in the locality is also considered very problematic (4,3%), along with the limited information provided by municipalities to the citizens in relation to the number of hosted migrants and hosting modalities (1,6%), the overall perceived ineptitude of local politicians in dealing with the refugee crisis (0,7%), and the utilisation of perceived unsuitable or "special" spaces (*e.g.*, with a cultural or historic relevance) as reception centres (0,5%). In addition, national policies are criticised as they are considered too 'open' and allow too many asylum seekers and refugees to be hosted in the country (3,2%). Refugee policies are also attacked as they are said to be serving individual's economic and political interests, at the expenses of the community (3,4%).

While the two press outlets offer a similar negative portrayal of national and local refugee hosting policies, they substantially differ in the way they frame the main problems associated with the arrival and stay of migrats in the local communities.

In Udine, for example, asylum seekers and refugees are mostly described in terms of *social* and *physical disorder* (in short, as decay or, in Italian, '*degrado*'). Especially the unregistered or 'irregular' ones (such as the individuals who enter – or are trafficked in – the country through the Slovenian border, and 'hang around' without filing the asylum request by the competent authorities) are considered as a problem as they sleep rough in public parks and close by the train station (8,6%), simply hang about

(5,2%), engage in fights among each other (4,7%), and 'pollute' the areas they occupy (4,3%) (*e.g.*, "They transformed the area into a latrine", MV, 31 December 2016). The emphasis on the link between migrants and physical disorder is well exemplified in the following fragment: "They do not annoy us, but they scare us and make [the area] dirty" (MV, 24 May 2015). More in general, the presence of migrants seems to alarm people as refugees and asylum seekers are said to adopt uncivil behaviour:

"There are reported fights, gatherings of refugees under the covered walkway and in front of the shop windows, and most of all drug dealing in the open-air. [. . .] All this has created a strong sense of fear. People feel impotent in front of others' rudeness. [. . .] This is a terrible defeat of [our] system of civilisation, law and order" (MV, 30 December 2016).

The representations of asylum seekers and refugees in Padova vary substantially, as they are mostly portrayed as *criminals* or as *bogus*. In many of the news, for example, asylum seekers and refugees are considered as 'fake' (MP, 9 August 2008): they are described as economic migrants, who are given more than what 'the others' – meaning the legitimate Italian citizens who pay taxes – get from the State. These representations are well exemplified in the fragment below, which describes migrants as fake, illegal, and welfare scroungers:

> "The welcoming of alleged asylum-seekers is up to those who are accomplices of this invasion, and who are at the Government. I perceive my role [as mayor, a.n.] as a family man and, as such, I need to defend my family and I won't use part of the scarce resources that the [national] Government leaves on our territory to support the illegal migrants who, according to Alfano and Renzi [national level politicians, a.n.], should make out a living on the shoulders and at the risk of our community. The pensioners and the pre-retired people trapped by the pension reform, the young couples, the unemployed, all the victims of the economic crisis and of three unelected governments, they all deserve security and respect" (MP, 15 April 2015).

When depicted as criminals (21% in total), migrants are mostly associated with drug dealing (6,3%), theft (2,1%), and, especially, with violence and sexual assault (7,5%), and sexual harassment (4,3%). When the press covers news on sexual harassment and assault (reporting a few episodes that have occurred in Padova), the victims (who are women) speak (*e.g.*, "We have been left alone at the mercy of a pervert", MP, 24 March 2017). Narratives on the importance of protecting women ("we see scared and worried women, who need to be listened to and protected", MP, 13 March 2017) and children ("But if they invade our streets and wander around to fill their time, it is difficult not to be worried. I have a daughter who does sport and she will have to spend time in public places, such as in the sports field", MP, 14 September 2016; "I am scared for my two little sisters", MP, 17 October 2015) are very typical.

In both press outlets, moreover, the presence of migrants is said to undermine the perceptions of safety of citizens (11%), who are "exasperated" (MV, 30 December 2016; MP, 14 September 2008) and "afraid" (MV, 1 October 2015; MP, 19 December 2016). In Padova, fears are sensationalised through the use of emotionally-laden adjectives such as feeling "under siege" (MP, 2 October. 2016), "angry and enraged" (MP, 10 August 2008), or "terrified" (MP, 26 September 2011).

Residents in both cities also describe urban neighbourhoods as becoming "of others" – not belonging to "them" anymore (4,1%). Consider, for instance, the following examples: "We are afraid to go out. We do not feel any longer masters in our own house", MV, 9 January 2017; "There is an attempt of these gangs of drug dealers, mostly Tunisians with residency permits in their pockets, to take control of some neighbourhoods at night, intimidating and frightening the citizens", MP, 26 September 2011; "The 'district' of asylum-seekers", MP, 25 March 2017; "The piazzas now are scary" MP, 25 June 2011; "They are invading our streets", MP, 14 September 2016; "We do not longer feel safe in our own homes", MP, 2 October 2016. This is said to have a negative impact especially on women and children: "The children can no longer play in the park as it became drug dealers' territory. The girls are harassed, denigrated or insulted when they pass by" (MV, 30 December 2016); "'They are all men, we – the women – do not feel safe', said the mums" (MV, 31 May 2015).

Only in a limited number of press news, the problem is associated with terrorism (2.1%) – as a potential crime committed by migrants – and with trafficking in human beings (2.1%) – and the migrants framed as victims.

Solutions

Mostly, the solutions that have been offered in the press in relation to the problem of migrants have to do with the enhanced presence of police officers, and even the army, on the streets (55,9%). In doing so, a sensationalistic and war-type rhetoric is used, as shown for instance by the following fragments:

> "We are barricaded in our houses, let the army intervene" (MV, 5 January 2017);
> "The station area is secured by dozens of squads" (MV, 15 August 2016);
> "It is now war on drug dealing" (MP, 8 September 2015);
> "Security emergency. The city has to be militarised" (MP, 28 December 2014).

Examples of successful and praised law enforcement actions are also offered by the news (31,9%):

> "The *questura*, since a long time, was organising ad-hoc services in the station area, with an impressive deployment of manpower. Even more: the questor Claudio Cracovia asked for, and obtained, the intervention of the [. . .] rapid response unit from the Padova police, with agents specialised in public order services, on the streets" (MV, 6 September 2016).
> "The other night, 40 law enforcement officers from the questura have hoovered up the hotspots of the city, and they brought 18 people to the questura, including 13 Tunisians, who are considered [as an ethnic group, a.n.] among the most dangerous ones as regards to drug dealing, thefts, and violence" (MP, 1 October 2011).

Typical solutions also include the arrest and conviction of 'criminal' migrants (6,7%), the adoption of punitive local regulations entrusting the police with sanctioning powers (6,2%), the shutting down of public spaces like subways and parks (*e.g.*, "The green areas are for the families, not for illegal migrants", MP, 24 September 2015) and private premises unsuitable for hosting migrants (5,3%), and the ejection and removal of 'bogus' and 'illegal' migrants (4%). In seven articles (1,7%), moreover, the emphasis is placed on the need to tighten the links between the citizens, the police and the municipality, with a view to establishing a new 'partnership in security' (so-called '*sicurezza partecipata*', MP, 19 Dec. 2015). Although these solutions are most common for Padova, they also feature in the press debate in Udine.

Responses to the problem of hosting an increasing number of migrants at the local level are the organisation of protests and marches (5,3%), and the transfer of migrants to other locations, including smaller towns (2,4%) and other EU countries (3,8%). Migrants are also to be hosted in dismissed army bases and other allocated places that ought to be refurbished and to comply with health and safety standards (4%), in buildings owned by the church or charities (1,2%), and in privately owned apartments (1%). Also the need for a greater EU intervention (1,4%) and better national coordination (1,4%) are mentioned as solutions.

Other solutions, which have mostly been offered in relation to the migration problem in Udine, are also linked to the redesign and revitalisation of certain city areas (10,8%). Among these measures, there are the installation of CCTV cameras (4,3%), the improvement of the street lightning during the night (2,9%), the amelioration of the street cleaning and of the urban architecture (2,2%), and neighbourhood regeneration (1,4%).

Alongside *criminal justice and administrative interventions*, therefore, the crime prevention policies promoted in the press news seems to be rooted in *situational* (Clarke, 1983) and *environmental* (Newman, 1972; Sorensen *et al.*, 1995) crime prevention. While the former are significantly present in both cities, the latter seems to be only present in Udine, a left-wing territory.

Community (Hope, 1995) crime prevention approaches, including education, integration and job opportunities for migrants, and the organisation of campaigns to sensitise citizens towards accepting and integrating migrants, are identified as solutions only in a minority of articles (5,7%). Perhaps unsurprisingly, considering who speaks in the news and the content of their messages, *developmental* crime prevention approaches (Tremblay and Craig, 1995), such as interventions for child migrants or second-generation asylum-seekers, are never addressed in the news.

Other solutions include the carrying out of health checks on asylum seekers and undocumented migrants (2,4%), and the fastening of the procedures that award them the refugee status (1,7%).

Concluding thoughts

The 'problem' of migrants in Italy has been constructed, both at the national and local levels, as a security problem and has been tackled with public order and 'crimmigration' measures. National legislations have been passed by both centre-right and centre-left coalitions mirroring the popular saying among politicians that "the issue of security is neither [a task] of the left nor of the right" (see Pighi, 2014). Security is, in fact, a very appealing topic that helps politicians – of any political colour – to tap into people's fears and anxieties and gain political consensus. For example, as explained by Colombo (2013), tough 'crimmigration' measures in Italy have been passed by both centre-right and centre-left coalitions. Similarly, enhanced security powers to local authorities have been introduced (through the so-called 'Security Package' mentioned above) by a centre-right coalition, and have been revamped in 2017 by a law decree (the 'Minniti' Decree) of the centre-left government run by PD, and more recently by a 'security decree' of the current populist government (a coalition between the 5 Star Movement and the right-wing party Northern League). The use of the banner of security as an electoral tool to gain political consensus has been pursued both by left- and right-wing political parties not only at the national level. At the local level, local authorities have, in practice, tended to enforce crimmigration measures, and to exercise (illegitimate) public order powers, to ultimately please the fearful electorate and maintain or gain political support.[8]

As emerges from our results, local politicians and law enforcers in Udine and Padova, the cities considered in this study and run by centre-left and right-wing (Northern League) political parties respectively, have con-

8 There are, of course, a few exceptions, for instance cases where people's fears have been addressed by local authorities with integration and community-led programmes rather than with more law enforcement. In Riace, a town in the southern region of Calabria, for example, the mayor Mimmo Lucano has introduced a welcoming system for migrants based on their integration in the community. However, with a contested decision occurring in a very difficult and polarized political contest, the mayor has been arrested in early October 2018 and charged with aiding and abetting illegal immigration.

structed the 'problems' of migrants in the local press in only slightly different terms: they have described them as disorderly, in Udine, and as criminal and bogus, in Padova – where a more sensationalistic and rhetoric tone has generally been used, also reflecting the political rhetoric of the populist party Northern League running the city. This notwithstanding, they have mainly proposed the same set of solutions: more law enforcement, including the deployment of the army. Since the study found that the local press tends mostly to cover the messages of local politicians and promote their problem-framing and solutions, its results seem to resonate the findings of a recent study of the representations of unauthorised migrants in the Dutch press, which has suggested that the press, rather than framing 'problems' and setting agendas for the policy-maker, tend to reflect and follow political debates fuelled by domestic politicians (Brower *et al.*, 2017).

We do not want in any way to downplay the problems that many Italian municipalities are currently facing when it comes to hosting (documented or undocumented) migrants in their territories, which are severe considering the number of migrants that daily arrive in Italy, both by sea and via land. In addition, very few cases of violent and sexual attacks committed by migrants against Italians have actually happened, particularly in Padova. However, such cases have been exploited by local politicians in the press and have been exaggerated/amplified, thus contributing to fuelling people's fears[9] and to constructing migrants as the 'dangerous other'. The local press construction of migrants as a security problem is worrying especially in light of the 2017 'Minniti' Decree, which allows municipalities to sanction individual's behaviour when it is deemed to impair the 'decorum', 'urban liveability' and the "peace and quiet of residents", and to ban people from certain city areas when their behaviour "impairs the access and use of those areas" by others (see above in the Background section).

Clearly, this Decree is based on very vague notions such as, 'decorum', 'liveability', 'peace and quiet', impairment to 'access and use' of city spaces by others, whose meaning is to be given by local authorities and can, in practice, be informed by arbitium (or, as already pointed out by the Constitutional Court in 2011, by not clearly pre-determined criteria valid

9 As pointed out by Lane and Meeker (2003), white people's fears are mostly affected by newspaper reporting (rather than TV viewing, which has been found to have no effect on fear of crime by Chadee and Ditton, 2005).

for all municipalities that ensure legal certainty). In essence, the simple presence of unwanted migrants in the streets, which may be considered alarming for some (although not actually causing any harm to people in an overwhelmingly majority of cases) can be penalised by local actors through public order and crimmigration measures, which may involve administrative sanctions as well as detention (especially in the case of undocumented migrants). This potentially leads to a net widening effect (Cohen, 1985), as certain individuals – for them belonging to a certain social group rather than for them committing (deviant or) criminal acts – are caught and retained in the net of the criminal justice system.

The local use of punitive measures to criminalise the (disorderly or criminal) migrant 'other' may be facilitated by the press coverage of the messages of politicians and law enforcers, who, with their negative portrayal of migrants, dominate the local press news as a kind of 'deviance-defining élite' (Erickson *et al.* in Jewkes, 2015). A very limited coverage is given, by contrast, to the voices of third sector associations, charities and religious groups, who can pass positive messages on migrants and examples of integration, and to the opinion of criminology and criminal justice experts, who can contribute to reframing the popular media constructions of the 'problem' and its solutions. Overall, media give very rigid representations of crimes committed by migrants, which is in line with previous research on Greek media (Antonopoulos and Papanicolaou, 2013). Third sector associations and experts – in an effort to enhance the presence of their views in the local press and ensure a greater pluralism in the content of media news – should aim at gaining access to the local press (and, more broadly, to the local media) and regularly make their voice heard on locally relevant news involving migrants. In particular, criminology and criminal justice experts willing to act as 'public criminologists' may, for example, benefit from the writings on 'newsmaking' (Barak, 1988, 2007) and public criminologies (see, *e.g.*, Loader and Sparks, 2010; Turner, 2013; Crépault, 2017), which may help them to better communicate through media outlets and, ultimately, to 'correct' biased or distorted images of 'criminal' groups. A more active newsmaking role of criminologist is desired especially considering the media interest in – and concern about –migration, which seems to be ever-growing (Spencer, 2008) and unlikely to decrease in the next years. This is the more important in view of the shared poor understanding of the issue by key stakeholders, including the (national and local) government(s), law enforcers and the media (Van Duyne, 2004a, 2004b).

References

Ambrosini, M., and E. Caneva, *Local policies of exclusion: the Italian case*. 2012. Available at:
http://cadmus.eui.eu/handle/1814/22317 (Accessed 1 May 2017).

Antigone, *Appello contro il decreto Minniti*. 2017. Available at:
http://www.associazioneantigone.it/news/antigone-news/3029-appello-contro-il-decreto-minniti (Accessed 1 May 2017).

Antonopoulos, G.A. and G. Papanicolaou, Migrants and 'Organised Crime' in the Greek Press (1991-2011): The Politics of Representing the 'Organised Criminal Other. In P. C. van Duyne, J. Harvey, G. A. Antonopoulos, K. von Lampe, A. Maljevic, & J. Spencer (eds.), *Human Dimensions in Organised Crime, Money Laundering, and Corruption*. Nijmegen, Wolf Legal Publishers, 2013.

ASGI (Lorenzo Trucco on the Minniti-Orlando Decree), *A wall of laws that limit the right to asylum*. 2017. Available at:
http://www.asgi.it/english/lorenzo-trucco-asgi-minniti-orlando-decree-not-reform-but-wall-of-laws-that-limit-the-right-to-asylum/ (Accessed 1 May 2017).

Barak, G. (ed.), *Media, process, and the social contruction of crime: studies in newsmaking criminology*. New York & London, Garland Publishing, 1994.

Barak, G., Newsmaking criminology: Reflections of the media, intellectuals and crime. *Justice Quarterly,* 1988, 5(4), 565–587.

Barak, G., Doing newsmaking criminology from within the academy. *Theoretical Criminology,* 2007, 11(2), 191–207.

Berry, M., I. Garcia-Blanco, and K. Moore, *Press coverage of the refugee and migrant crisis in the EU: a content analysis of five European countries* (December 2015). 2015. Available at:
http://www.unhcr.org/56bb369c9.pdf (Accessed 1 June 2017).

Bosworth, M., Border control and the limits of the sovereign state. *Social & Legal Studies*, 2008, 17(2), 199-215.
Bosworth, M. and M. Guild, Governing through migration control security and citizenship in Britain. *British Journal of Criminology*, 2008, 48(6), 703-719.
Brouwer, J., M. van der Woude and J. van der Leun, Framing migration and the process of crimmigration: a systematic analysis of the media representation of unauthorized immigrants in the Netherlands. *European Journal of Criminology*, 2017, 14(1), 100-119.
Caneva, E., Intolerant policies and discourses in northern Italian cities. *Journal of Immigant & Refugees Studies,* 2014, 12(4), 383-400.
Chadee, D., and J. Ditton, Fear of crime and the media: Assessing the lack of relationship. *Crime, Media, Culture*, 2005, 1(3), 322-332.
Chibnall, S., *Law-and-order news: an analysis of crime reporting in the British press.* London: Tavistock, 1977.
Cinalli, M. and A. El Hariri, Contentious opportunities: comparing metropolitan policymaking for immigrants in France and Italy. In E. Carmel, A. Cerami and T. Papadopoulos (eds.), *Migration and welfare in the new Europe: social protection and the challenges of integration*. Bristol: Policy Press, 2011.
Cittalia (Fondazione Anci Ricerche), *Oltre le ordinanze: i sindaci e la sicurezza urbana*. 2009. Available at: http://www.cittalia.it/images/file/Indagine_Oltre%20le%20ordinanze.pdf (Accesed 2 June 2017).
Cittalia (Fondazione Anci Ricerche), *Per una città sicura. Dalle ordinanze agli strumenti di pianificazione e regolamentazione*. 2012. Available at: http://www.cittalia.it/images/file/Cittalia_pubblicazione_Per%20una%20citta%20sicura(1).pdf (Accessed 2 June 2017).
Clarke, R.V., Situational crime prevention: its theoretical basis and practical scope. *Crime and Justice: An Annual Review of Research*, 1983, 4, 225-256.
Cohen, S., *Visions of social control: crime, punishment and classification*. Cambridge: Polity Press, 1985.
Colombo, A., Foreigners and immigrants in Italy's penal and administrative detention systems. *European Journal of Criminology*, 2013, 10(6), 746-759.

Commissione Straordinaria per la Tutela e la Promozione dei Diritti Umani, *Rapporto sui centri di identificazione ed espulsione – febbraio 2016. Senato della Repubblica, XVII Legislatura*. 2016. Available at: http://www.asylumineurope.org/sites/default/files/resources/senato_cie_report_2016.pdf (Accessed 2 July 2017).

Crépault, D., The rise of partisan pedagogy: how stakeholders outside of the academy are answering the call to public criminology. *British Journal of Criminology*, 2017, 57(4), 789-807.

Crocitti, S. and R. Selmini, Controlling immigrants: The latent function of Italian administrative orders. *European Journal on Criminal Policy and Research*, 2016, 1-16.

Devroe, E., A swelling culture of control: the genesis and application of the incivilities law in Belgium. In P. Ponsaers (ed.), *Social analysis of security: financial, economic and ecological crime, crime (in)security & distrust, public and private policing.* The Hague: Eleven International Publishing, 2012.

Devroe, E., G. Bruinsma and T. Vander Beken, An expanding culture of control? The municipal administrative sanctions act in Belgium. *European Journal on Criminal Policy and Research*, 2016, 1-18.

Di Ronco, A. Regulating street prostitution as a public nuisance in the "culture of consumption": a comparative analysis between Birmingham, Brussels and Milan. In N. Persak and G. Vermeulen (eds.), *Reframing prostitution : from discourse to description, from moralisation to normalisation?* Antwerp: Maklu, 2014

Di Ronco, A., Public drunkenness as a nuisance in Ghent (Belgium) and Trento (Italy). *Crime, Law and Social Change*, 2016, 66(1), 59-81

Di Ronco, A., Disorderly or simply ugly? Representations of the local regulation of street prostitution in the Italian press and their policy implications. *International Journal of Law, Crime and Justice*, 2017, doi: https://doi.org/10.1016/j.ijlcj.2017.09.004.

Di Ronco, A., and N. Peršak, Regulation of incivilities in the UK, Italy and Belgium: courts as potential safeguards against legislative vagueness and excessive use of penalising powers? *International Journal of Law, Crime and Justice*, 2014, 42(4), 340-365.

van Duyne, P.C., Fears, naming and knowing: an introductions. In P. C. van Duyne, M. Jager, K. von Lampe, and J. L. Newell (eds.), *Threats*

and Phantoms of Organised Crime, Corruption and Terrorism: Critical European perspectives. Nijmegen, Wolf Legal Publishers, 2004a.
van Duyne, P.C., The Creation of a Threat Image: Media, Policy Making and Organised Crime. In P.C. van Duyne, M. Jager, K. von Lampe and J.L. Newell (eds.), *Threats and Phantoms of Organised Crime, Corruption and Terrorism: Critical European perspectives*. Nijmegen, Wolf Legal Publishers, 2004b.
European Commission, *Refugee crisis in Europe*. 2017. Available at: http://ec.europa.eu/echo/refugee-crisis_en (Accessed 1 June 2017).
Ericson, R.V., P.M. Baranek and J.B. Chan, *Representing order: crime, law, and justice in the news media*. Milton Keynes: Open University Press, 1991.
Fabini, G., Managing illegality at the internal border: governing through "differential inclusion" in Italy. *European Journal of Criminology*, 2017, 14(1), 46-62.
Garland, D., *The culture of control: crime and social order in contemporary society*. Oxford: Clarendon Press, 2001.
Girling, E., I. Loader and R. Sparks, *Crime and social change in middle England: questions of order in an English town*. London: Routledge, 2000.
Hall, S., The rediscovery of ideology: return of the repressed in media studies. In T. Bennett, J. Curran and J. Woollacott (eds.), *Culture, society and the media*. London: Methuen, 1982.
Hope, T. Community Crime Prevention. In D. P. Farrington, and M. H. Tonry (eds.), *Building a safer society: strategic approaches to crime prevention (Crime and Justice)*. Chicago: University of Chicago Press, vol. 19, 1995.
Il Corriere, *Writer spagnoli bloccati in metrò. Scatta il primo "Daspo" urbano*. 2017. Available at: http://milano.corriere.it/notizie/cronaca/17_marzo_02/writer-spagnoli-bloccati-metro-daspo-urbano-divieto-avvicinarsi-stazione-f4f1ee2a-ff13-11e6-9d9a-77b6de6db49f.shtml (Accessed 1 July 2017).
IOM, *Mediterranean migrant arrivals top 363,348 in 2016; deaths at sea: 5,079*. 2017. Available at: www.iom.int/news/mediterranean-migrant-arrivals-top-363348-2016-deaths-sea-5079 (Accessed 1 July 2017).
Jewkes, Y., *Media & crime*. Third Ed. London: Sage, 2015

Krippendorff, K., *Content Analysis*. Newburn Park, CA, Sagem, 1980.
La Repubblica, *Firenze, arriva il primo daspo urbano per uno spacciatore*. 2017a. Available at: http://firenze.repubblica.it/cronaca/2017/03/15/news/firenze_arriva_il_primo_daspo_urbano_per_uno_spacciatore-160606305/?ref=search (Accessed 1 August 2017).
La Repubblica, *Migranti, maxi blitz in stazione Centrale a Milano: a decine identificati e portati in questura.* 2017b. Available at: http://milano.repubblica.it/cronaca/2017/05/02/news/migranti_milano_salvini_stazione_centrale-164448979/ (Accessed 23 August 2017).
Lane, J., and J.W. Meeker, Ethnicity, information sources and fear of crime. *Deviant Behaviour*, 2003, 24(1), 1-26.
Loader, I., & R. Sparks, *Public Criminology?* London: Routledge, 2010.
Masera, L., I centri di detenzione amministrativa cambiano nome ed aumentano di numero, e gli hotspot rimangono privi di base legale: le sconfortanti novità del Decreto Minniti. *Diritto Penale Contemporaneo*. 2017. Available at: http://www.penalecontemporaneo.it/d/5274-i-centri-di-detenzione-amministrativa-cambiano-nome-ed-aumentano-di-numero-e-gli-hotspot-rimangono (Accessed 1 August 2017).
Newman, O., *Defensible space: crime prevention through urban design*. New York: Macmillan, 1972.
Open Migration, *Why the new Italian law on immigration and asylum is not good news at all*. 2017. Available at: https://openmigration.org/en/analyses/why-the-new-italian-law-on-immigration-and-asylum-is-not-good-news/ (Accessed 1 August 2017).
Padovanet, *Archivio interventi straordinari e di emergenza a firma del Sindaco*. 2017. Available at: http://www.padovanet.it/informazione/archivio-interventi-straordinari-e-di-emergenza-firma-del-sindaco#22191 (Accessed 1 July 2017).
Peršak, N., *Regulation and social control of incivilities*. London: Routledge, 2017a.
Peršak, N., Criminalising through the back door: normative grounds and social accounts of incivilities regulations. In N. Peršak (*ed.*), *Regulation and social control of incivilities*. London: Routledge, 2017b.

Pighi, G., *La sicurezza urbana indivisibile: le politiche locali di prevenzione integrata*. Milano: Franco Angeli, 2014.

Pleysier, S., Local governance of safety and the normalization of behavior. *Crime, Law and Social Change*, 2015, 64(4-5), 305-317.

Pleysier, S., Normalisation of behaviour in public space: the construction and control of "public nuisance" in Belgium. In N. Peršak (*ed.*), *Regulation and social control of incivilities*. London: Routledge, 2017.

Quassoli, F., Clandestino": Institutional discourses and practices for the control and exclusion of migrants in contemporary Italy. *Journal of Language and Politics,* 2013, 12(2), 203-225.

Sabatini, S., *I centri di permanenza temporanea e la legge Bossi - Fini: cosa cambia*. 2002. Available at:
http://www.meltingpot.org/I-centri-di-permanenza-temporanea-e-la-legge-Bossi-Fini.html#.WSVsHk2QyUk (Accessed 1 June 2017).

Simon, J., *Governing through crime: how the war on crime transformed American democracy and created a culture of fear*. New York: Oxford University Press, 2007.

Sorensen, S., J.G. Hayes, E.W. Walsh, and M. Myhre, *Crime Prevention Through Environmental Design (CPTED): Workbook.* 1995. US Department of Housing and Urban Development, Community Safety and Conservation Division, Washington, D.

Spencer, J., Media constructing organised crime concepts in an extended criminal Europe. In van P. C. Duyne, J. Harvey, A. Maljevic, K. von Lampe, and M. Scheinost (eds), *European Crime-Markets at Crossroads*. Nijmegen, Wolf Legal Publishers, 2008.

Tremblay, R.E. and W.M. Craig, Developmental Crime Prevention. *Crime and Justice. Builiding a Safer Society: Approaches to Crime Prevention*, 1995, 19, 151-236.

Turner, E., Beyond 'facts' and 'values': rethinking some recent debates about the public role of criminology. *The British Journal of Criminology*, 2013, 53(1), 149-166.

UNHCR, *Operational portal. Refugees situation*. 2017. Available at: http://data2.unhcr.org/en/situations/mediterranean (Accessed 1 June 2017).

Van der Woude, M., V. Barker and J. van der Leun, J., Crimmigration in Europe. *European Journal of Criminology*, 2017, 14(1), 3-6.

Vassallo Paleologo, F., *Detenzione amministrativa - Uno storia di brutalità, violenze e violazioni*. 2010. Available at: http://www.meltingpot.org/Detenzione-amministrativa-Uno-storia-di-brutalita-violenze.html#.WSV_IE2QyUk (Accessed 2 June 2017).
Welch, M. and L. Schuster, Detention of asylum seekers in the US, UK, France, Germany, and Italy: A critical view of the globalizing culture of control. *Criminal Justice*, 2005, 5(4), 331-355.

Government-sponsored crime

The case of Vietnamese undocumented immigrants in Germany and the UK

Trang Nguyen[1]

Introduction

Undocumented Vietnamese immigrants have prominently been involved in two illegal markets in Europe: the selling of illegal cigarettes in Germany since the 1990s and, more recently, the cultivation of cannabis in indoor plantations in the UK. The German illegal cigarette market described in this study mainly refers to the Berlin large-scale black market which is publicly operated in continual existence since 1989 (Nguyen and von Lampe, 2018). Contraband cigarettes are sold at various locations in former East Berlin including train stations, supermarkets and shopping centres, and the vendors are exclusively Vietnamese. The cannabis cultivation in the UK is considered billion-worth market and it is widely acknowledged that the Vietnamese criminal networks play a significant role in this branch (ACPO, 2014; Bouchard, Alain and Nguyen, 2009; Bouchard and Nguyen, 2011; Daly, 2007; EMCDDA–Europol, 2016; Irasec and France terre d'asile, 2017; Schoenmakers, Bremmers and Kleemans, 2013; Schoenmakers, Bremmers and Wijik 2012; Silverstone and Brickell, 2017; Vy and Lauchs, 2013).

In this chapter, I seek to explore the common characteristics of the participants and the factors that have influenced their decision to join the illegal markets. My aim is to clarify the role of immigration agencies and brokers that are affiliated to the Vietnamese government and that provide logistical support to undocumented labour immigrants. It is important to note

1 Trang Nguyen is a PhD student at the Max Weber Kolleg, Erfurt, Germany.

that illegal immigration to Europe is widely recognized by Hanoi as a welcome solution to their unemployment problem and as a source of growing remittances.

The Berlin illegal cigarette market

Germany was the largest cigarette illicit market in the EU (KPMG, 2016) and Berlin had the highest prevalence of illicit cigarettes in the country (Transcrime, 2015). The history of the cigarette black market, in Germany in general and in Berlin in particular, dates back to the late 1980s and early 1990s during the German transition after the fall of the Berlin wall. When the visa obligation had been lifted for Polish citizens travelling to West Berlin in January of 1989, German smokers could go to street dealers for much cheaper contraband cigarettes from Poland instead of the highly taxed cigarettes sold in tobacco stores (von Lampe, 2005). However, this street vending in the Western part of the city did not last long under pressure from the public and it soon began to spread to the Eastern parts of the country after the currency unification in mid-1990 (von Lampe, 2002). This was happening at a perfect timing to an ethnic immigrant population in the former German Democratic Republic who had just been displaced from legitimate work during the period of economic reconstruction: the Vietnamese.

Interviewees recalled that some former Vietnamese guest workers had first begun by buying cigarettes from Polish travellers who would arrive at some train stations in Berlin with several cigarette cartons wrapped under their jackets or in a bag hidden in the train. This, however, quickly became an obsolete source. In early 1991, a large scale illegal cigarette trade in Germany run by Vietnamese people began, and cigarettes were transported in big trucks from Poland to Germany. Soon afterwards, some Vietnamese who could speak Russian started to connect with Russian military officers for the purpose of cigarette smuggling. This was believed to be the major supply source until 1994-1995 when the Russian troops completely withdrew from Berlin. Most Vietnamese guest workers were reported to have participated in the illegal selling of cigarettes at least once during this period.

In May 1993, the German authorities decided to provide legal residency to these former workers and subsequently this population gradually left the illegal business. However, the lucrative black market for cigarettes still appeared to be attractive to the criminal networks. Thousands of undocumented Vietnamese were quickly smuggled into the country in the 1990s and are believed to have eventually taken over the whole cigarette black market. After a massive attack launched by German police to crack down on the open market in 1996, the number of vending spots has decreased dramatically from about 1200 in the mid-1990s to about 200 in 2015 (Nguyen and von Lampe, 2018). Although the number of locations and sellers are way fewer compared to the early 1990s, the street sale of illegal cigarettes dominated by Vietnamese immigrants has demonstrated a resilient phenomenon in the Eastern part of the capital city.

The UK cannabis market

Cannabis is the most commonly used illicit drug and accounts for the largest share (38 %) of the EU illicit drug retail market (EMCDDA, 2018). In recent years, the EU cannabis market has appeared to experience considerable changes, partly explained by a move to more domestic production (EMCDDA 2017). The cannabis market in the UK – with an estimated value of up to € 6 billion per year (Atha and Davis, 2011; Prohibition Partners, 2018) – has not been an exception (Snowdon, 2018). In 2005, only 15 % of cannabis consumed in the UK was domestically grown (Thomson, 2010). However, from 2010, the proportion of cannabis farmed in the UK had increased to more than 90 % (Townsend, 2010). According to the UK Association of Chief Police Officers in 2012, the Vietnamese accounted for almost two-thirds of those being arrested for cannabis production (ACPO, 2012).

Since the mid-90s, Vietnamese criminal gangs have been known for their knowledge about how to grow cannabis in Vancouver, Canada. In 2004, The UK government reclassified cannabis from a Class B to a Class C drug, removing the threat of arrest for possession and reducing the risk of imprisonment for cultivation. Vietnamese criminal groups were believed to rapidly move from Canada to the UK and achieved dominance in Britain's marijuana business. They developed methods to turn networks of large houses into clandestine cannabis plantation farms (Luke, 2012). Information from Vietnamese-language online fora in the UK indicates that these houses are rented from housing agents using fraudulent or stolen identity papers. Set-up costs for an operation vary between £15.000 and £50.000 while annual profits from a single 'grow house' run from £200.000 to £500.000. According to interviewees and other media reports, Vietnamese-run cannabis farms are mainly located in the suburbs of London, Manchester and Birmingham.

Methods and samples

This chapter is primarily the result of formal and informal interviews with 63 participants related to or with knowledge about the illegal cigarette trade in Berlin, Germany. These individuals include 29 current illicit cigarette street-vendors, 9 retired vendors, 2 gang leaders, 3 former wholesalers, 1 former cigarette smuggler, 2 human smugglers, 2 academics, 2 journalists, 3 political activists, 1 former translator for guest workers, 2 business owners and 7 undocumented immigrants living in Berlin. Half of the participants and the current vendors were interviewed at least twice. The interviews were conducted on different occasions and as 'free-flowing conversations' between February 2015 and January 2018. Each took between 15 and 60 minutes.

Although I had no direct interviews with the gardeners in the UK, the Vietnamese cigarette vendors in Berlin appeared to have a tight connection with their national fellows in the cannabis industry in the UK. They showed great knowledge about the UK market as well as about the role of Vietnamese people in the business. That may be partly explained by the fact that the vast majority of the participants in both markets come from the same region in Vietnam and there is clear evidence showing the existence of a linkage between the two markets.

During the period from 2015 to 2018, I also collected data from the Vietnamese-language social media forums relating to human trafficking and job seeking of illegal Vietnamese immigrants in Germany and the UK.

The Vietnamese immigrants in Germany and the UK

Different waves of immigration

Germany is the home of about 163.000 Vietnamese (GIZ, 2015). The first group consists of almost 40.000 'boat people' and their families who left Vietnam after the end of the Vietnam war in 1975 and came to the Federal Republic of Germany (GIZ, 2007). They mostly fled from the political oppression of the Communist regime in the Southern part of the country.

The second wave of migration from Vietnam to Germany happened during the 1980s. Some 70.000 'contract workers' or 'guest workers', mainly from North Vietnam, were recruited by the German Democratic Republic through an agreement signed in 1980 (Bösch and Phi, 2018; GIZ, 2015).

When the communist regime collapsed in 1989, factories were shut down and thousands became jobless and dispossessed (Bilefsky, 2009; GIZ, 2015). Many returned to Vietnam. However, about 20.000 stayed behind in search of new sources of income (von Lampe, 2002). Only temporary stays were granted (GIZ 2015) and many of these Vietnamese temporarily turned to illegal cigarette trade to make their living. A social activist who had witnessed the period explained:

> "The workers lost their jobs suddenly; they were kicked out of the factory dormitories, having no paper, no status, even couldn't go back home because the Vietnamese government didn't want to take them. They were offered 3.200 DM to go home, but it was not much, so, many tried to stay. There were not many jobs and selling cigarettes was an easy choice for them." (Interviewee SA1)

The third significant wave of migration from Vietnam is the irregular immigrants who started coming to Germany in 1991 to seek better economic opportunities. This group of immigrants, mainly from the North Central Coast provinces of Vietnam including Nghe An, Quảng Binh, Thanh Hoa and Ha Tinh, is believed to have taken over the illegal cigarette market from the former contract workers in the first half of the 1990s, and has played the dominant role in the market until today. There are no definitive figures documenting the irregular Vietnamese population currently living in Germany, but vendors and smugglers mentioned the numbers between 1000 and 2000 individuals coming each year. In 2015, GIZ reported that some 4.000 migrants were deported to Vietnam from Berlin in a four year period. Nevertheless, Schmiz (2011) argued that the actual numbers of Vietnamese who are residing in Germany on an irregular basis are much higher.

Table 1:
Different waves of migration from Vietnam to Germany and to the UK

Period	In Germany	In the UK
1975-1990	Asylum seekers after the Vietnam war	Asylum seekers after the Vietnam war
During 1980s	Guest workers in the GDR	Family arrivals
1990s to early 2000s	Former guest workers from former Soviet bloc	Former guest workers from former Soviet bloc
1990s until now	New arrivals: the illegal migrants from Vietnam	
2000s until now		New arrivals: the illegal migrants from Vietnam

Source: Analysis of various sources, including data from interviews and media reports

The Vietnamese diaspora to the UK can be seen as constituted by three main waves (Silverstone and Savage 2010). The first migration of Vietnamese refugees to the UK happened at the end of the Vietnam War as part of a planned resettlement programme from South Vietnam. Many of them settled in London and the South East of England (Barber, 2018).

The Vietnamese population in the UK was enlarged by the second major migration wave which happened in the early 1990s. This phase consisted of undocumented Vietnamese migrants who were previously residing in the former Soviet Union, as well as other parts of Eastern Europe (Silverstone and Savage 2010). This also included a number of Vietnamese guest workers in former East Germany (IRASEC and France terre d'asile, 2017).

Finally, much like the situation in Germany, the third migration wave from Vietnam to the UK has also been known as the 'new arrivals' who illegally migrated due to economic reasons. It first included individuals smuggled from Northern provinces of Vietnam (Silverstone and Savage

2010) and then a further migration stream starting from the late 2000s from the same North Central Coast provinces (IRASEC and France terre d'asile, 2017). A study by Sims (2010) reported an estimate of some 20.000 undocumented Vietnamese living in the UK in 2007. BBC later cited police sources indicating a number of 35.000 in 2010.[2]

Administrative map of Vietnam

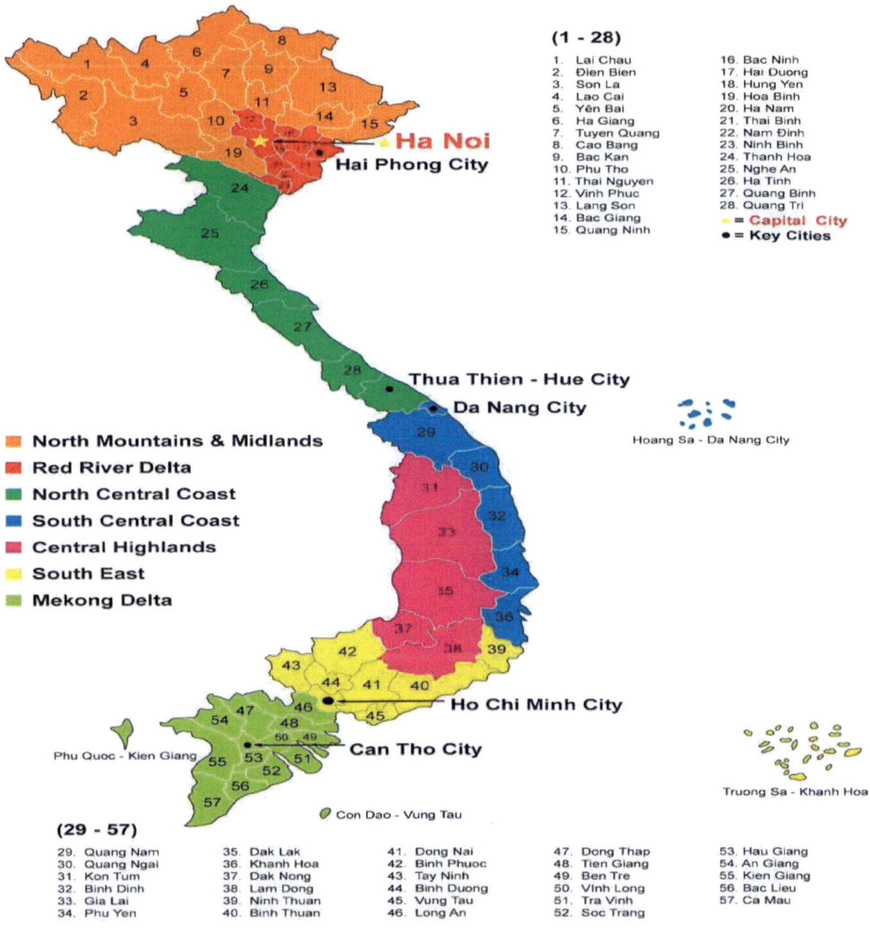

Source: www.ban-do.net

[2] https://www.bbc.com/news/10422480

The cigarette vendors and the cannabis gardeners

Today, both the cigarette black market in Berlin and the cannabis cultivation market in the UK are characterised by a constant influx of newly arriving Vietnamese migrants who mainly come from the North Central Coast Region. In Germany, this population is called "không quần áo" (English translation: no clothing) referring to their undocumented status. In the UK, these individuals are called "người rơm" (English translation: strawmen) indicating how easily they can be deported.[3] Many sell cigarettes or grow cannabis to repay the debts owed to human smugglers. According to the interviewees, these debts could amount to as much as € 35.000.

The majority of Vietnamese cigarette vendors in Berlin and the cannabis gardeners in the UK are men and boys (AAT, 2014; FCO, 2014; Nguyen and von Lampe, 2018), and most of them claimed to have no prior criminal records. Primarily, they come from rural areas and have low levels of education. Physical jobs such as fishermen, truck drivers, construction workers and farmers were commonly reported as their previous profession before coming to Germany. In 2014, AAT - an NGO who accompanied the return of 140 Vietnamese deportees – mainly from the cannabis industry – reported similar findings.

The typical image of a cigarette vendor in Berlin today is one Vietnamese-looking guy with a big cross-body bag, a cap and a pair of headphones, standing at a fixed location near an underground (U-Bahn) station, a suburban train (S-Bahn) station or a supermarket. They never carry lots of cigarettes with them, mostly 2-3 cartons, and the rest is stored nearby in a bush, inside an abandoned wall, or in a trash bin. Money is hidden in another place. If the vendor belongs to a gang, his employer remains invisible but within reach, collects money and supplies more cigarettes when requested.

In the UK, the newly arrived individuals from Vietnam are recruited to act as 'gardeners' maintaining indoor cannabis plantations (ACDM, 2008; IRASEC and France terre d'asile, 2017; Silverstone, 2010; Silverstone and Brickell, 2017). They are taught how to look after the plants, as well as the

---

3 The community uses the term "plasticmen" for those who have official documents, and "glassmen" for those who have obtained a green card in the UK.

method and timing of the collection of harvests. Most are locked up in the farm and work alone. Many claim to only have social contacts over the phone and rarely see their employer. Food is provided every few days. It is a common knowledge among the Vietnamese migrant population that cannabis gardeners face a high risk of being robbed by gangs from other ethnic groups.

An interviewee commented about the job of a gardener in the cannabis farm:

> "Many of them (gardeners) went to the UK and made a fortune, but came back not knowing a single English word. They probably did not even see the Big Ben tower, as they were locked up in the cannabis farm during the whole time in the UK". (Interviewee UM1)

The journey to Germany and the UK

Some Vietnamese were motivated to migrate as they had friends and family members already in Germany and the UK. However, there was also a significant number of claims about unscrupulous and fraudulent methods used by human smugglers. On online social media networks, there are plenty of posts and threads recruiting individuals by migration agencies and companies. Since most of the potential migrants come from rural and poor areas, they have to borrow money from relatives and friends or mortgage their land or house to obtain a loan.

Human smuggling chains operated between Vietnam and Europe include a sophisticated network with branches in Russia, Ukraine, Latvia, the Czech Republic, Poland, France, Germany, and the United Kingdom. Data from interviews show two main human smuggling methods are being used: The first option is that migrants are given false travel documents, fly from Viet Nam to Moscow and then walk and/or are transported by truck across Eastern Europe before they arrive in Germany. The service prices range between $ 12.000 and $ 20.000.

In the second method, smugglers offer a more expensive but more secure, asking between $ 16.000 and $ 25.000 for false documents and Schengen visa application papers, including a direct flight to one of the EU countries.

Table 2:
Smuggling service fees between Vietnam and Germany and the UK

Vietnam to Germany over Russia	$12.000 - $20.000
Vietnam to Germany over another EU country	$16.000 – $25.000
To the UK from Germany/or an EU country - *Economy service (cỏ)* - *Premium service (cỏ cao cấp)*	 £3.000 – £4.000 £10.000 – £15.000
To the UK directly from Vietnam	£25.000 – £30.000

Source: Data from interviews between 2015 and 2017

Some of the journeys were described as very "tough" and "dangerous" in the jungle, with high risks of getting caught by border guards and being put in jail for months. A few interviewees reported that the journey took much longer than a "few months" as had been promised by the smugglers. I came across cases in which interviewees spent about a year on the road, and a few cases lasted even longer due to time spent in prison in Russia, Lithuania or Latvia.

In order to continue to the UK, they travel to France and wait in a camp before proceeding to the UK. The most known camp is the one in Angres called 'the Vietnam city' which is located in a wood near the rest station of the A26 motorway. They then hide underneath the cargo of trucks travelling from France through the English Channel tunnel. The "cỏ" (English translation: weed) service is equivalent to an 'economy service', meaning they are shown the truck they would furtively get into without the driver's knowledge. They need to keep quiet and take care of their own escape upon arrival.

An undocumented Vietnamese who failed in attempting to enter the UK told his story:

> "From Germany, I went to France at night with Blabla car. I stayed with some people in a camp in a forest where there was no electricity. We were waiting. Then one night someone showed me a truck and told me to sneak in. It is the place where the truck drivers rest at night between France and the UK . . . No, the drivers didn't know. I had to be quiet, I

> couldn't move until the truck started to drive . . . Yes, they checked the truck. I was detected by police dogs. Then they put me in jail for some time. I went through 2 trials, they took my fingerprints and freed me coz I didn't have any paper with me . . . So finally they freed me and put me to another shelter in France. And I found my way back Germany". (Interviewee UM2)

A lot more expensive, the Premium service called "VIP" or "cỏ cao cấp" (English translation: fancy weed) offers them a place in a car or a truck agreed by the driver. This individual could be a Vietnamese or an European citizen. Another common method is to use false travel documents that smugglers rent from the Vietnamese who are EU-residents.

Irregular migration or human trafficking

Although many migrants were aware of what opportunities they could have in Germany and the UK, discussions in online fora and social networks of Vietnamese people living in the two countries revealed a great number of cases of people claiming to be deceived by smugglers and be left alone to fend for themselves. They fell into serious debt, and many are calling for help from the community. In Germany, about a third among newly arriving migrants interviewed did not really know what to expect when coming. Some realised that there was no job waiting for them, or the prospect of employment was exaggerated. There were cases of male interviewees being put into "really hard work condition" at construction sites. Many showed great disappointment on coming here. They referred the labour recruitment agencies in Vietnam as scams and expressed the bitter experiences of the "illegal life" in Germany.

Similar situations in the UK have also been well documented. According to AAT (2014), 75 out of 140 Vietnamese migrants (54%), said that they were promised by an agent that on arriving they would receive a job. In reality, 80% of respondents did not get their promised jobs when they arrived in the UK. In both countries, promised jobs often include positions in restaurants, nail workers, au pairs, room cleaners, kitchen-hands and construction workers.

The United Nations defines Trafficking in Persons as "the recruitment, transportation, transfer, harbouring or receipt of persons, by means of the threat or use of force or other forms of coercion, of abduction, of fraud, of deception, of the abuse of power or of a position of vulnerability or of the giving or receiving of payments or benefits to achieve the consent of a person having control over another person, for the purpose of exploitation".[4] Although most Vietnamese migrants make their decisions prior to their departure, in practice it is difficult to draw the distinction between human trafficking and illegal migration (Silverstone, 2017).

Joining the illegal markets

"You just need to obey the rules"

The days of the Vietnamese military-like hierarchy gangs strictly controlling their selling territory by exerting violence (von Lampe, 2001) in the Berlin cigarette black market are no longer in existence. Today, a Vietnamese may find it easy to enter the illegal selling, as long as he could afford to buy a vending spot, or rent it for a monthly fee. Over the past 20 years, the market appears to has shifted from 'pure extortion' in the 1990s in which the gangs only collected 'tax' in their territory but did not interfere in the daily business of the cigarette sellers (von Lampe 2002) to a self-regulated system (Nguyen and von Lampe, 2018). The term 'tax' is still being used to refer to the monthly rent of the vending place, but the gang structure appears to have broken apart and former extortion gangsters today simply have become the implicit 'owners' of specific vending places. This is the answer from one of the vendors when being asked how to become a vendor:

> "Vietnamese gangs collect "tax" from vendors, but the market is organised now, everyone who wants to participate in the retailing business just needs to follow the rules." (Interviewee V1).

---

4 Article 3, paragraph (a) of the Protocol to Prevent, Suppress and Punish Trafficking in Persons, United Nations

Prices of buying or renting a selling spot greatly vary according to locations, pedestrian flows, and possibilities to flee from police. Vendors claimed a price range of € 10.000 - 40.000 for a vending place for sale and of € 300 - 1.000 per month for rent. In both cases, the buyer and the renter become the exclusive beneficiary of the selling, irrespective of how lucrative it is.

Even easier, one can enter the market by being hired by someone who owns or rents one or more selling locations. The 'cigarette gang' functions as an entrepreneurial relationship between one employer and one or more vendors who work for him as labourers for specific tasks. The typical structure of a 2-3 member group is that the employer plays the role of the cigarette deliverer and money collector, while the employees take care the actual selling. Accommodation and food for employees are usually provided, yet not necessarily.

As described elsewhere, participants at the street level in the Berlin cigarette black market are not required to have special skills in order to join the market (Nguyen and von Lampe, 2018). The uniform price of € 2,2 plays a helpful role. In most cases, customers already know the price, money is prepared in their hand in advance, and once approaching a vendor, they only need to say the brand name and number of packs/cartons. Transactions happened in only a few seconds most times.

There is also evidence that joining the gardener team in the UK is not much more complex. Gardeners are not required to speak English and need only 1-2 month training until they can work alone at the farm. The job is described as "simple", "just a few hours a day", and "have time to stay online a lot". There is an unwritten rule that gardeners receive a third of the profit after a crop is harvested.

Cigarette vendors and cannabis gardeners are mainly recruited through networks of friends or acquaintances. Nevertheless, in both countries, there are also public announcements (in slang Vietnamese) recruiting vendors or gardeners at grocery shops and supermarkets of Vietnamese people, and on online communities.

Importantly, there is a notable trend of Vietnamese cigarette vendors in Berlin moving to the UK for the cannabis plantation. Four vendors had already left Berlin to go to the UK during the time I was researching, five others mentioned the same plan but claimed that it is costly. They would first need to make enough money by selling cigarettes.

Vulnerable immigrants are deliberately employed

Not only do Vietnamese find it easy to enter one of the two illegal markets, many Vietnamese end up joining the illegal cigarette vending team in Berlin, or a cannabis farm in the UK because they do not have many choices. The job market for Vietnamese as undocumented migrants in both countries is currently described as "not as good as before" . In Germany, since 2015, a judgement has made entrepreneurs liable to a fine up to €500.000 and 5 years of imprisonment in case of illegal recruitment. Likewise, business owners in the UK face a fine up to £20.000 per illegal worker. A greater number of job advertisements found on the online communities in both countries clearly state "có quần áo" ("having clothing") or "không tuyển người rơm" ("not hiring strawmen") as the first requirement. Being indebted and separated from family and support networks upon arrival, migrants become despondent and socially isolated, which increases their vulnerability to exploitation. A vendor bitterly explained what brought him to the illegal selling of cigarettes:

> "I thought I would have a job but they (human smugglers) just left me once I had arrived in Berlin. I didn't really have any relatives here. I found someone who let me stay when searching for a job and then someone else brought me to the cigarette selling. I wish I could go back but I can't, really I can't. I regret coming here but there is no way back now. I need money to pay the debts and send money to my family. I am thinking of going to the +44 (the UK) to grow "weed", but I first need money to do so . . . I have nothing to lose anymore." (Interviewee V2)

Interviewees mentioned the risks of losing their mortgaged property, or having their family in Vietnam receive threats from debt collectors if they were not able to pay back the debts. Many are eventually willing to accept any kind of job or any form of exploitation. Under a post on the online community in the UK, a gardener gave his opinion in a discussion about 'moral values' when joining the cannabis market:

> "*Some people see their friends or acquaintances sending money (from the UK) back home, they also borrow money to go. Once they arrive, they realize it is not as easy as they thought. But they are stuck in debt.*

Then they join the "weed" growing team. I mean, if I had to choose between growing "weed" and pushing my parents into the hands of the debt collectors, sorry but I can't think of those bullshit moral values". (OP1)

It is worth noting that the Vietnamese culture is largely constructed by Confusion values, meaning one is expected to remain loyal and submitted to his family. Furthermore, the presentation of an individual's image to the public is extremely important and is referred to as 'to keep face' in the Vietnamese culture. These may have led to the tendency that many Vietnamese migrants did not dare return after facing the reality upon arrival. While there are strong materialist aspirations that come from the evidence of wealth seen in the families of migrants who receive remittances, information about the difficulties incurred during the migration process is not wide-spread.

Prospect of making good money

The perception of selling illegal cigarettes in Germany and the possibility of growing cannabis in the UK without detection, and that good money that can be made from these businesses is common knowledge among the Vietnamese community. Like in many other illicit cigarette markets in Europe, vendors in Berlin face low risks of prosecution (Reuter and Majmundar, 2015). The general awareness among vendors is that illegal cigarette selling is a minor crime, and if arrested, they stand a good chance of quickly being set free again. In the case of the cannabis farmers in the UK, many believe they would receive 6-month imprisonment as the maximum penalty.

Sales profit from the illegal cigarette selling varies upon the location and nature of their 'ownership' to the selling spot. Four hired vendors claim to be paid around € 60 per day with provided accommodation. Another one claims to be paid € 1.000 per month with food and accommodation included. The vendors who own or rent a vending place sell between 8 and 20 cartons per day which make daily profit falls between € 50 and 100. Cigarette vendors, therefore, calculate an average time of 2 years to be able to free themselves from the smuggling debt.

In the UK's cannabis farms, crops are harvested every 2 months: each leaves the gardeners with £7.000 to £10.000 profit. There is common knowledge among the Vietnamese migrant population that if 2 out of 4 crops is not confiscated by the police or robbed by another gang, they will be able to pay their smuggling costs in half a year. A cigarette vendor in Berlin told me his plan:

> "I wanted to move to the UK, next year. A lot of people already went you know. They make a fortune in a year, a billion[5], with that you are out of (smuggling) debt in half a year . . . I am not afraid, they told me the worst case I get maximum 5-6 months in jail. They make good money and now send home every month already." (Interviewee V3)

The transmission of illegal remittances is carried out by an informal transfer system using Vietnamese businesses in Germany and the UK who have their partners in Vietnam. These businesses are often grocery shops, logistics companies, or translation agencies who receive foreign currencies from undocumented migrants and pass to Germany-based and the UK-based Vietnamese students or others whose family reach out to the system' partners in Vietnam to send money overseas.

Government-sponsored crime

Vietnam has recently been one of the fastest growing economies in the world, however, the distribution of wealth has been skewed towards urban areas (Kozel, 2014). This uneven distribution has contributed to a rising unemployment rate in rural areas (Nguyen *et al*, 2015). The Vietnamese Government addresses the issue by encouraging people to seek employment in overseas labour markets. For example, the Ministry of Labour of Vietnam set the target of exporting 105.000 migrant workers in 2017 and 110.000 in 2018.[6] The policy has resulted in Vietnam now being one of the top ten remittance recipients, receiving between $10 and $14 billion since 2012, accounting for 6-8% of its GDP (World Bank, 2018). The

5 Vietnamdong, equivalent to about USD 50.000

6 The Ministry of Labour of Vietnam, 2018

country's actual remittance including remittance via informal transfer system may be much higher.

While Hanoi views this as a scheme to bring great benefits to the economy, it does not properly regulate the labour agencies (Ishizuka, 2013). Rather, it appears reluctant to share preventive information on the unscrupulous and fraudulent methods used by perpetrators (USSD TiP report, 2015) and is unresponsive to workers' requests for assistance in situations of exploitation (USSD TiP report, 2016). These create opportunities for organised criminal networks to lure and traffic individuals and encourage the undocumented migrants to enter illegal markets. Most importantly, many among those migration agencies and labour recruiters are state-owned or stated-affiliated (Home Office, 2018; ILO, 2016; Miller, 2015; Silverstone and Brickell, 2017; USSD TiP report, 2016). The International Labour Organisation (2016) reported that 88% of Vietnamese migrants are sent by state-related recruitment agencies. These businesses are also believed to charge fees in excess of what is by determined by law (ILO, 2016; USSD human rights report, 2015), and provide fraudulent labour contracts in languages that migrants could not read (Bélanger, 2014).

The report on trafficking by America's State Department in 2011 stated that Vietnamese have among the highest debts of all Asian expatriate workers and they are "highly vulnerable" to forced labour and exploitation. More recently, a report from CSAGA (2013), a Vietnamese NGO found that nearly a third of over 350 interviewees who had returned felt they had been cheated, deceived or exploited.

Further than that, the Hanoi government did not report any investigations, prosecutions, or convictions of officials complicit in human trafficking offences (USSD TiP report, 2018). In 2011, Vietnam adopted specialised human trafficking legislation for the first time, and under international pressure, only in 2016, did Hanoi acknowledge that men and boys are being trafficked. Vietnam's constitution prohibits forced or compulsory labour. However, debt bondage is not included in the labour code's definition of forced labour. The penal code does not specifically criminalise labour trafficking, and the decree on administrative sanctions does not provide any penalty for violation of the labour code provisions prohibiting forced labour.

Although Germany and the UK do not rank among the most popular destinations for Vietnamese migrants, they are viewed as the top choices of migrants from Central North provinces including Nghe An and Quang Binh. The two are among the most deprived provinces in Vietnam, known for their poor natural resources and regular natural disasters. Nghe An, for example, has been widely reported by the Vietnamese media as the province that has most migrant workers aboard and more migration branches are being set up to recruit people. In recent years, many villages in the province are believed to have become wealthy relying on remittances. A former contract worker commented on how common it is for individuals from this province to move to Germany:

> "*Go to Yen Thanh and Dien Chau (2 districts in Nghe An province), you only see old people and children. Young males from these places are all over Europe. Here in Germany, there are thousands of them. They even have banks in the villages you know, specializing in lending money to people to pay the smugglers.*" (Interviewee FW1)

In 2012, *Tuoitre*, a known newspapers in Vietnam reported that there were about 10.000 individuals of Yen Thanh district illegally migrated to Europe. In 2018, another newspaper, *Baomoi*, cited the General Statistics Office of Yen Thanh district, reporting 15.278 workers abroad and an annual remittance of $200 million, via both formal and informal channels. The population of Yen Thanh district is about 275.000 in 2018.

Data from interviews and online communities of Vietnamese migrants in Germany and the UK indicate the involvement of the Vietnamese government in sponsoring the two illegal markets:

- Migration agencies/brokers in Vietnam (including state-licensed ones):
  a. Overstate or deceive about the reliability of their services and exaggerate the prospect of generating good income in the destination countries
  b. Leave workers with exorbitant debts and vulnerable to exploitation or illegal activities
- Human trafficking is facilitated by corruption, including:
  a. Approved fake documents such as birth certificates, marital status certificates, labour contracts, and education degrees, both at administration offices in Vietnam and Vietnamese Embassies in Europe;
  b. Bribed government officers at border crossings and checkpoints;
- Hanoi is reluctant to receive undocumented migrants back from Germany and the UK

A political activist noted:

> "Apparently, Vietnamese customs officers and police know that thousands of people are being smuggled from Vietnam to Germany and the UK annually, but they are all bribed by the criminal organisations. There is no reason 10-20 young guys each time, uneducated looking, coming from the countryside of Central Vietnam and have money and a reason to get a visa to fly to Russia or Europe. Go to Noi Bai airport, you will see, they have their own line and go through the customs checking quickly." (Interviewee PA1)

Another social activist also mentioned the role of the Vietnamese Embassy in Germany:

> "The Vietnamese Embassy in Germany has always known the existence of the illicit cigarette trade dominated by Vietnamese people in Germany but hides information and even gives support. They approve fake documents, even bring people here." (Interviewee SA2)

Irregular Vietnamese migration is an issue that has continued to feature high on the agenda of discussions between Vietnam and Germany and between Vietnam and the UK. However, it is the common knowledge among the Vietnamese migrant population that it is not easy for the host governments to deport Vietnamese migrants, since the Vietnamese government does not show much willingness in accepting these individuals (Hoangdanlambao 2018). A former cannabis farmer in the UK stated in an online discussion:

> "Usually, Vietnamese are deported when the Vietnamese and the UK governments have an official visit or meeting, and the UK government could offer some development aid in exchange for sending some migrants back to Vietnam. While few people can be deported since it is not easy to make the Vietnamese government identify them as Vietnamese, there are more and more coming each year." (OP2)

Conclusion

Despite Vietnam's economic prospects continuing to improve, opportunities for many in rural areas remain limited by under-employment and corruption. Every year, hundreds of thousands of Vietnamese leave the country in search for a better standard of living. The recent wave of irregular migration from Vietnam to Germany and to the UK has appeared to be the main source of supply of labour for the cigarette black market in Berlin and the cannabis cultivation industry in the UK. However, one should be cautious in making a direct link between human smuggling between Vietnam and Europe and the two black markets. The human smuggling networks – which largely include state-affiliated agencies – have been making huge profits from illegal migration, putting the migrants in danger while *en route* and leave them indebted and vulnerable to exploitation in the host country. Many turn to these illegal markets being the only choice available.

Illegal cigarette vendors in Berlin and cannabis growers in the UK today mainly come from the North Central Coast region of Vietnam where there is more poverty and unemployment rates are high. Although Vietnamese workers seek to migrate to many other countries, Germany and the UK rank as the top destinations in the region. Significant amounts of remittance generated by illegal activities received by the region have also been well-reported by the Vietnamese media.

The two illegal markets characterised by a constant influx of undocumented Vietnamese luck-seekers have existed for decades and changes are mainly skin-deep. The Vietnamese government continues to facilitate the two illegal markets because it has vital interests in remittances that result from these markets. They are willing to turn a blind eye to the darker side of illegal migration from Vietnam, which includes corrupted government officers being implicated in human trafficking for labour exploitation and illegal markets. As long as the economic and ethical positions of the Vietnamese government remain unchanged, the two illegal markets are likely to persist.

References

ACMD, *Cannabis: Classification and Public Health*, H. Office, Editor, Adivisory Council on the Misuse of Drugs (ACMD), London, 2008.

ACPO, *UK National Problem Profile: commercial cultivation of cannabis*, 2012

ACPO, *UK National Problem Profile: commercial cultivation of cannabis*, 2014.

Alliance Anti-Trafic (AAT), *Research report. Returnees in Nghe An*, 2014

Atha, M. and S. Davis, *Taxing the UK cannabis market*. Independent Drug Monitoring Unit, 2011. Available at https://s3.eu-west-2.amazonaws.com/assets. clear-uk.org/taxukcan.pdf

Barber, T., *The integration of Vietnamese refugees in London and the UK*. UNU-WIDER working paper, 2018.

Belanger, D., Labor migration and trafficking among Vietnamese migrants in Asia. *The Annals of the American Academy of Political and Social Science*, 2014.

Bilefsky, D., Crisis strands Vietnamese workers in a Czech limbo. *The New York Times Online*, 2009. Available at: http://www.nytimes.com/2009/06/05/world/europe/05iht-viet.html

Bösch, F. and Phi, Hong Su, *Invisible, successful, and divided: Vietnamese in Germany since the late 1970s*. UNU-WIDER working paper, 2018.

Bouchard, M. and H. Nguyen, Professional or amateur: Revisiting the notion of professional crime in the context of cannabis cultivation. In: *World Wide Weed: Global Trends in Cannabis Cultivation and Its Control*, London, U.K, 2011.

Bouchard, M., M. Alain and H. Nguyen, Convenient labour: The prevalence and nature of youth involvement in the cannabis cultivation industry. *International Journal of Drug Policy*, 2009.

CSAGA, *An exploratory research on the experiences and needs of returned Vietnamese overseas migrant workers*. Center for Studies and Applied Sciences in Gender, Family, Women and Adolescents, Hanoi, 2013.

Daly, M., Plant Warfare, In *Druglink*, London, 2007.

EMCDDA - European Monitoring Centre for Drugs and Drug Addiction and Europol, *EU Drug Markets Report: In-Depth Analysis*,

EMCDDA–Europol Joint publications, Publications Office of the European Union, Luxembourg, 2016. Available at http://www.emcdda.europa.eu/system/files/publications/.

EMCDDA - European Monitoring Centre for Drugs and Drug Addiction and Europol, *European Drug Report 2017: Trends and Developments*, Publications Office of the European Union, Luxembourg, 2017. Available at http://www.emcdda.europa.eu/system/files/publications/.

EMCDDA- European Monitoring Centre for Drugs and Drug Addiction, *European Drug Report 2018: Trends and Developments*, Publications Office of the European Union, Luxembourg, 2018. Available at http://www.emcdda.europa.eu/system/files/publications/

FCO, *Baseline research report: the current situations of Vietnamese returnees from the United Kingdom*, 2014.

GIZ, *The Vietnamese Diaspora in Germany*, 2007.

GIZ, *The Vietnamese diaspora in Germany*, 2015.

Hoang, T., người rơm Việt Nam và kỹ nghệ trồng cỏ tại Anh quốc, 2018, *thoibao*. Available at http://thoibao.com/nguoi-rom-viet-nam-va-ky-nghe-trong-co-tai-anh-quoc/

Home Office, *Report: Country Policy and Information Note* , Vietnam: Victims of trafficking Version 3.0, London, 2018

https://baomoi.com/hon-200-trieu-usd-gui-ve-huyen-lua-nghe-an-moi-nam/c/28335963.epi

https://tuoitre.vn/lam-giau-nho-chui-524831.htm

https://www.bbc.com/news/10422480

ILO, *Complaint mechanisms for Vietnamese migrant workers: an overview of law and practice*. Tripartite Action to Protect the Rights of Migrant Workers within and from the Greater Mekong Subregion, 2016

Irasec and France terre d'asile, *En route to the United Kingdom: A field survey of Vietnamese migrants*, Paris, 2017. Available at http://www.france-terre-asile.org/images/stories/publications/pdf/En

Ishizuka, F., *International Labor Migration in Vietnam and the Impact of Receiving remittances*, Institute of developing economies, Japan, 2013.

Kozel, V., Well begun but not yet done : progress and emerging challenges for poverty reduction, in *Vietnam*: *Equity and Development*. World Bank Group, Washington, 2014.

KPMG - Project Sun, *A study of the illicit cigarette market in the European Union, Norway and Switzerland-2016 results, 2017*. Available at: https://assets.kpmg/content/dam/kpmg/uk/pdf/2017/07/project-sun-2017-report.pdf.

Luck, A., Inside Britain's secret cannabis factories: how criminal gangs are turning our shuttered shops and disused warehouses into drug farms, *MailOnline*, 2012.

Nguyen, N.A., T.T. Nguyen, T.H. Nguyen, T.T.N. Trinh and V.T. Nguyen, *Labour market transitions of young women and men in Viet Nam*. International Labour Office, Youth Employment Programme, Employment Policy Department. Geneva: ILO, 2015.

Nguyen, T. and K. von Lampe, On the persistence of an open illegal market: Explaining the continued existence of street-vending of contraband cigarettes in Berlin since 1990, In: P.C. van Duyne *et al.* (eds.), *The Janus faces of cross-border crime in Europe*. Den Haag, Boom Uitgevers, 2018.

Prohibition Partners, *The European Cannabis Report, 2018*. Available at https://g8fip1kplyr33r3krz5b97d1-wpengine.netdna-ssl.com/wp-content/uploads/2018/11/TheEuropeanCannabisReportEdition3.pdf.

Reuter, P. and Malay Majmundar, *Understanding the U.S illicit tobacco market: characteristics, policy context, and lessons from international experiences*. The national Academy Press, Washington, D.C., 2015.

Schmiz, A., *Transnationalität als Ressource? Netzwerke Vietnamesischer Migrantinnen und Migranten zwischen Berlin und Vietnam*. Bielefeld, 2011.

Schoenmakers, Y., B. Bremmers and A. Wijk: *Vietnamese Cannabis Cultivation in the Netherlands: A research Summary*. Bureau Beke, 2012. Available at http://www.beke.nl/doc/2012/Vietnamese_Cannabis_cultivation_Netherlands.pdf.

Schoenmakers, Y., B. Bremmers and E. Kleemans, Strategic versus emergent crime groups: the case of Vietnamese cannabis cultivation in the Netherlands. *Global Crime*, 2013.

Silverstone D. and C. Brickell, *Combating modern slavery experienced by Vietnamese nationals en route to, and within, the UK*. Independent Anti-Slavery Commissioner, Vietnam report, 2017.

Silverstone, D., The policing of Vietnamese organized crime within the UK. *Policing*, 2010.

Silverstone, D. and S. Savage, Farmers, factories and funds: organised crime and illicit drugs cultivation within the British Vietnamese community. *Global Crime*, 2010.

Silverstone, D. Trafficked to grow cannabis: Vietnamese migrants are being exploited in Britain, *The conversation*, 2017. Available at https://theconversation.com/trafficked-to-grow-cannabis-vietnamese-migrants-are-being-exploited-in-britain-83738.

Sims, J.: *Vietnamese community in Great Britain: Thirty years on*, Runnymede Trust, London, 2007.

Snowdon, C.: *Estimating the size and potential of the UK cannabis market*. IEA Discussion Paper No.90, 2018.

SOCA, *United Kingdom Threat Assessment 2008/9*. Serious Organized Crime Agency (SOCA): London, U.K, 2009.

The U.S. Department of State, (USSD), *Trafficking in Persons (TiP) Report*, 2018.

The U.S. Department of State, (USSD), *Vietnam human rights report*, 2015.

The U.S., Department of State (USSD), *Trafficking in Persons (TiP)* Report, 2016.

The U.S., Department of State (USSD), *Trafficking in Persons (TiP)* Report, 2015.

The U.S., Department of State (USSD), *Trafficking in Persons (TiP)* Report, 2011.

Thomson, T., Untold profits fuel the violent gang world of London's cannabis farms, *Standard*, 2010. Avaliable at https://www.standard.co.uk/lifestyle/untold-profits-fuel-the-violent-gang-world-of-london-s-cannabis-farms-6509328.html.

Townsend, M., Britain's cannabis producers go global as factories multiply, *The Guardian*, 2010. Avaliable at https://www.theguardian.com/world/2010/aug/22/cannabis-factories-narcotics-europe

Transcrime, *European Outlook on the Illicit Trade in Tobacco Products*. Transcrime – Universita degli Studi di Trento, 2015. Availabe at http://www.transcrime.it/wp-content/uploads/2015/01/European-Outlook-on-the-ITTP.pdf

von Lampe, K., The trafficking in untaxed cigarettes in Germany: A case study of the social embeddedness of illegal markets. In P.C. van Duyne *et al.* (eds.), *Upperworld and Underworld in Cross-Border Crime*, Nijmegen, Wolf Legal Publishers, 2002.

von Lampe, Klaus, Explaining the emergence of the cigarette black market in Germany. In P.C. van Duyne *et al.* (eds.), *The organised crime economy: managing crime markets in Europe*. Nijmegen, The Netherlands: Wolf Legal Publishers, 2005.

Vy, L. and M. Lauchs., Models of South-East Asian organised crime drug operations in Queensland. *Asian Journal of Criminology*, 2013

World Bank, *Annual Remittances Data, updated as of December 2018*. Available at http://www.worldbank.org/en/news/press-release/2018/04/23/record-high-remittances-to-low-and-middle-income-countries-in-2017.

Transnational crime of Chinese origin in the EU: False flags and real concerns

Jurij Novak[1]

Introduction: attempt to define

This chapter examines three areas in which we could encounter transnational Chinese criminal activity in the European Union: traditional Chinese organised crime, also known as the Triads; Chinese criminal activity, encompassing sex trafficking and sexual exploitation; and Chinese criminal involvement in the Italian textile industry, which looks into the case of large-scale and rampant Chinese criminality in the city of Prato. While I attempt to de-mystify a number of assumptions about Chinese Triads and Chinese sex trafficking, concerns about criminal practices inside the textile industry are well supported by available evidence and this problem is therefore discussed in the following sections.

Defining 'Chinese' is not as clear as it seems. It can encompass citizens of the People's Republic of China (PRC), Republic of China (ROC, also known as Taiwan) and people of Chinese ethnicity abroad. All these can be perpetrators of crimes, active either in the EU (or in its relevant proximity) or targeting victims in the EU, regardless of the perpetrators' residence. The victims can also be people of Chinese ethnicity, who reside in the EU (legally or illegally), Chinese people abroad. It can also include EU citizens, companies, public services and even state institutions.

The link between the discussed topics lies in Chinese cultural features. It could be argued that a vast area of crimes by Chinese immigrants (*e.g.* human smuggling and labour trafficking, tax evasion, money laundering,

1 Jurij Novak, LLB, PhD Candidate, Institute of Criminology at the Faculty of Law, University of Ljubljana.

etc.) could be characterised as 'culturally specific', *i.e.* the cultural elements and specific traditions of the crimes in question are significant and should be considered when investigating any such crimes.

False Chinese transnational crime: the 'triad conspiracy' and Chinese sex trafficking

Chasing the phantom of Chinese Triads

Studies of organised and transnational crime are often burdened by speculative paradigms which have little, if any, basis in empirical evidence. They also fail to withstand even simple logical analyses. Such speculations often border on pure conjectures, political herd behaviour (Van Duyne and Nelemans, 2011) and even romantic fantasy.

The so-called Chinese Triads are probably the most illustrative example of such unfounded research paradigms (Petta, 2017). Indeed, many Chinese transnational crimes, including but not limited to human smuggling, sex trafficking and illicit drug trafficking, are attributed to Chinese Triads: "*an imaginary mystery of a centralised global crime super-organisation*" (*ibidem*). Since even the most avid fans of the triad conspiracy acknowledge that the Triads come only from Hong Kong and Macau, the application of the term "Chinese Triads" beyond these confines is grossly misleading. It would be equally erroneous to label Sicilian, Calabrian, and Neapolitan criminal traditions and OCGs as simply "Italian mafias". It would completely disregard a realistic assumption that each such traditional and related criminal group is quite probably a specific criminal universe of its own.

Nevertheless, the term Chinese Triads often serves as a synonym for all Chinese organised and transnational crime groups. Because there is serious discrepancy between Chinese scholars, sinologists, and historians of China on the one hand and organised crime scholars on the other hand, some short clarification is required.

Secret societies tend to exist in almost every place and era: they may be religious, political or simply criminal or some combination of the three. It should be of no surprise that a country as vast as the Chinese empire had a rich history of secret societies (the most legendary one is perhaps the White Lotus society that played an important part in organising a successful popular uprising against the Mongol Yuan dynasty in the 14th century) and clandestine brotherhoods. The latter were usually organised by migrants from the same area for mutual help. The most persistent of these societies were called *Societies of Heaven and Earth* (Chin. *tian di hui*), mentioned as early as 1761 (Murray, 1994) as a secret society of migrant workers from Fujian Province. These societies quickly developed a mythology about their founding, shrouded in mystery and obscure legends. They often assumed a political identity, one of secret rebels against Manchu conquerors who established the Qing dynasty. Quite often, they were also involved in criminal activities, mostly smuggling wheat and salt down rivers in defiance of state-imposed monopolies.

British colonial administrators in Shanghai and Hong Kong in the late 19th century who were, following the fashion of those times, often members of masonic lodges, interpreted the tradition of *tian di hui* through Western knowledge of masonic rituals, demonstrating little understanding for Chinese specifics. *Tian di hui* societies were viewed simply as an exotic parallel of masonic societies and hence named as 'the Triads' (Petta, 2017). The British colonialists, often paranoid of everything Chinese – going as far as being proudly ignorant of the Chinese language and culture – saw secret societies as a political threat and therefore outlawed all of them, interpreting them as inherently criminal in nature. However, most of the so-called triad societies had no criminal background. It is quite interesting to see these colonial attitudes towards Chinese criminality continuing into modern times.

New appearance

How should Chinese folklore and history be translated into the world of modern criminal Chinese Triads? It is not uncommon for criminal groups to develop their own mythology or to appropriate an existing one without any historical or even geographical relation to the group itself. The legends touting triad omnipotence exist even today and are believed by criminals, their victims, and by law enforcement alike. Therefore it is rather challenging to prove otherwise. Nevertheless, beliefs are not facts and should not be treated as such.

So far, the only comprehensive and empirical study of Hong Kong Triads available in English is the monograph *The Triads as Business* by Yiu Kong Chu (2002) which debunks almost all Western myths about these types of organisations and their criminal capabilities. Chu's research paints a picture of extremely local Organised Crime Groups (OCGs), limited to highly specific criminal activities (*e.g.* petty extortion of street vendors, tenant harassment aimed at vacating buildings, and night club protection) in Hong Kong and partially Macau. These criminal activities follow the specific environment of Hong Kong and Macau, characterised by high population density, coupled to the economic and cultural necessity of some services, such as illegal cheap labour and sex services. Hong Kong Triads are to some extent incorporated into the informal management of a large port city and show some similarities to the *modus operandi* of the Camorra clans in Naples or the organised crime families of the 'Ndrangheta (Sergi, 2015).

Hong Kong and Naples have a similar geographic configuration, *i.e.* both are port cities constructed on sloping terrain. This naturally leads to limited space in the city centres, while the suburbs (Secondigliano and Scampia in Naples, New Territories in Hong Kong) are far away, making them harder to govern. The Camorra gangs and the Hong Kong Triads are both involved in the profitable construction and real estate sector in various ways (persuading tenants to vacate premises marked for development, criminal activity related to public tenders, and supplying illegal workers), in smuggling and counterfeiting, in managing open-air illicit drug markets and in exploiting illegal immigrants (Chu, 2002; Behan, 2005; Saviano, 2006). However, according to official crime statistics, Hong Kong is one of the safest cities in the world (Broadhurst *et al.*, 2007; Hong Kong Monthly Digest of Statistics, 2016). Therefore we can conclude that the Triads exert much less influence on the local population and tend to be much less violent than the Camorra.[2] Also, since Hong Kong's political

2 According to the Hong Kong Monthly Digest of Statistics (2016), there were only 22 homicides in Hong Kong with a population of more than 7 million people. In Naples City, which has slightly less than a million people, there were 77 homicides (of which 38 were related to the Camorra) in 2016, a stark improvement when compared with the past (Beneduce, 2017). According to the only analysis of triad-related murders in Hong Kong (Lee at al., 2007) there were 124 such murders between 1989 and 1998. For comparison, there were

system remains firmly in the grip of Beijing, the political influence of the Triads, if any, is probably negligible. The absence of a political dimension to the Triads' activities is in stark contrast to the Camorra and even more so to the 'Ndrangheta (see Sergi, 2015).[3]

According to Chu, Hong Kong Triads lack the ability, knowledge, and resources to become even a 'mid-size player' in transnational criminal activities such as: large-scale smuggling of illicit drugs (heroin and methamphetamine from the Golden Triangle), human smuggling, cyber-crime, *etc.* Triad members also lack language skills (often not being able to speak even Mandarin Chinese), criminal skills (they are adept at street level crime but not capable of complex tax evasion and money laundering), and international connections to be successful outside of Hong Kong. Furthermore, there is no rational reason for them to leave Hong Kong to which they have adapted quite well. Of course, some triad members do sometimes smuggle drugs or people; however, there is no evidence to suggest that these activities are done on behalf of a larger organisation. Membership of a triad group does not prohibit members from engaging in (usually small scale) criminal projects of their own.

As far as the EU is concerned, there is supposedly a minor triad presence in the UK, limited mostly to petty extortion of Chinese shopkeepers (Silverstone, 2011). No affiliation with larger triad groups in Hong Kong has been proven so far, allowing for the possibility that some ordinary Chinese criminals assume a 'pseudo-triad' identity to be more successful, feared, and respected. In the continental EU, no triad presence has been detected. Since immigration from Hong Kong to the continental EU is negligible at best, we can safely assume that there is probably no triad presence of any kind.

---

311 Camorra-related murders in the province of Campania between the years 1999 and 2003 (Gazzetta del Mezzogiorno, 2005).

3 But the Triads might have found a new political niche in suppressing Hong Kong pro-democracy movements. In 2014, numerous members of the Umbrella movement were beaten by Triad-affiliated thugs-for-hire in the Mongkok area. See Varese and Wong, 2017.

The exotic allure of Chinese sex trafficking

This section discusses the alleged sex trafficking of Chinese young women in the EU and attempts to de-mystify some assumptions.

Sex trafficking is a form of human trafficking. Numerous definitions of human trafficking are perhaps best summed up by Spencer (2014) who defines it as "*exploiting human beings commercially in ways that involve degrading treatment*". According to Article 3, paragraph (a) of the United Nations Protocol to Prevent, Suppress and Punish Trafficking in Persons (Palermo Protocol), exploitation includes "*at a minimum, the exploitation of the prostitution of others or other forms of sexual exploitation, forced labour or services, slavery or practices similar to slavery, servitude or the removal of organs*".

It is obvious from the formulation of this provision that prostitution and other forms of sexual exploitation, *i.e.* sex trafficking, are considered the most important manifestations of human trafficking. If a person is involved in the sex business, consent to such activity or lack thereof are legally completely irrelevant, *i.e.* the Protocol goes so far that it considers a grown person, who is fully informed about going into sex business abroad and fully consents to it, is a victim of human trafficking (Hoyle *et al.*, 2011).[4]

If international law equates sex trafficking with voluntary prostitution of migrant women, it is hardly a surprise that the mass media follows suit. Indeed, sex trafficking has often been presented as one of the most heinous crimes and appalling social problems of the day (see home pages of NGOs Shared Hope International, Polaris, End Slavery Now, and others). A vast body of literature and countless NGOs and government agencies exist and are dedicated to 'eradicating' this problem.

However, there are numerous objections to such widespread representation. Several authors (Weitzer, 2005, 2007; Zhang, 2009; Gozdziak and Bump, 2008; Spencer, 2014) have offered serious criticisms of basic assumptions and typical narratives about sex trafficking and of flawed and unreliable research methods (*e.g.* the lack of random samples, very small

---

4 It seems that the legislators predicted that many victims would fake consent out of fear, but the main problem here is that the sex business often has no rigid roles, *i.e.* a prostitute might also act as a business intermediary (pimp) or even as a cashier. That means that her status as a victim or a victimiser may completely depend on temporary circumstances.

sample sizes, *etc.*). Critics also point to the lack of empirical research on the topic (especially Gozdziak and Bump, 2008). But we would also be remiss not to mention that the debate on human trafficking has become more balanced and nuanced during the last decade and that more attention has been paid to 'non-sex' trafficking (Alvarez and Alessi, 2011; Baker, 2015; Choi-Fitzpatrick, 2016).

Nevertheless, even the most liberal minded people acknowledge that forced prostitution and sexual slavery are a serious crime. However, the official statistics suggest that these also highly uncommon.[5] Isolated and extreme cases of forced prostitution, so-called 'atrocity tales' and are therefore used to argue against prostitution in every form, including voluntary and consensual sexual services for profit (again Weitzer, 2005, 2007; Zhang, 2009).

The sensationalist focus on examples of Chinese female immigrants, 'brutally enslaved' or by some other means coerced or at least tricked into prostitution (*e.g.* Sui, 2017), perpetuates racist stereotypes in a similar way as beliefs in triad-controlled Chinatown underworlds. Horror stories about Chinese prostitutes in seedy massage parlours often coincide with similar stories about brutal and sadistic triad-affiliated pimps and brothel owners.

However, as suggested by Chin (2014; Finckenauer and Chin, 2010) in his qualitative empirical research of 149 Chinese immigrant sex workers in South-East Asia, Los Angeles, and New York, the reality of Chinese sex workers overseas might be entirely different.

China has a long and colourful tradition of prostitution, perhaps best immortalised in the classic erotic novel *The Plum in the Golden Vase* from the late Ming dynasty. As soon as the Communist People's Republic of China instituted market-oriented reforms in the early 1980s, providing the population with some disposable income, thinly disguised brothels began to flourish again. Despite frequent crack-downs by police in mainland China, prostitution has remained a staple-element of Chinese nightlife and

---

[5] E.g. According to Eurostat report 'Trafficking in human beings' from 2013, 23.600 people were victims of human trafficking in the previous 3 years of which 62% were trafficked for sexual purposes. This calculation yields 14.632 victims of sex trafficking in 3 years or 4.877 victims a year on average. However, by way of comparison, according to Eurostat, there were 5.211 murders in 2012. Using official data, we can only conclude that murder is a slightly more common crime in the EU than sex trafficking. Moral panic cannot be justified by referencing official statistics. See Chappell, 2013.

traditional entertainment (Zheng, 2009). The number of prostitutes in the People's Republic of China is estimated to be in the range of 3 to 10 million women (Ebenstein and Sharygin, 2011).

Some of them also accept the risk and voluntarily become sex workers abroad so they can earn higher wages. Because of language barriers, Chinese brothels abroad are mostly frequented by Chinese immigrants, Chinese businessmen, and Chinese tourists. The relative isolation of Chinese prostitutes from the local population – typical for all low-skill blue collar Chinese immigrants, such as cooks, waiters, and vendors – serves only to fortify racist prejudices about Chinese patriarchal violence toward women. But according to Chin, almost all of the interviewed prostitutes knew themselves exactly what kind of work they were getting into abroad and were not tricked or coerced in any way. Some of them emigrated to work as masseuses but even they did not exclude sex work as a source of additional income. Contrary to the prevailing victim stereotype, the prostitutes in Chin's research (2014) often emerge as independent and strong-willed women with considerable business acumen. Extrapolating from research findings, which state that Chinese prostitutes were neither exploited nor mistreated in South-East Asian developing countries with notoriously corrupt or inept law enforcement or in the US, it is safe to assume they are normally not exploited or mistreated in the EU either except for serious cases of abuse which are made much of in the media.

Researching sex businesses (regardless of whether we focus on sex trafficking or other forms) should abstain from 'one-size-fits-all' assumptions and be more attentive to cultural nuances. As it will be demonstrated in the following section, immigrants usually do not adopt the business models of receiving countries, but rather transplant their own. There is no reason to believe that the same assumption does not apply to sex business. Chinese prostitution abroad is different from, say, the notoriously brutal treatment of Albanian prostitutes. According to Arsovska (2015), this often begins with kidnappings, selling daughters into forced marriages, rape, *etc.* in the Albanian countryside and might have its roots in warrior-like patriarchal traditional values (*ibidem*). Research of Chinese prostitution should thus probably begin with empirical research in China and be careful to recognize the cultural differences within China itself.

‘True’ Chinese transnational crime: immigrant crimes

1. Crimes of Chinese immigrants in continental EU

Background

China has had a long and rich immigrant tradition. In 2010, the Chinese diaspora included over 40,3 million people, making it the third most numerous and second only to the German and the Irish diaspora (Poston Jr and Wong, 2010). Most ‘overseas Chinese’ live in South-East Asia. In developed countries, the American Chinese community with more than 4 million people (10% of global Chinese diaspora) is undoubtedly the largest, followed by Chinese living in the EU – more than 2 million people (5% of the global diaspora) (Gui, 2011), roughly the entire population of Slovenia. The number of Chinese immigrants from the People's Republic of China (PRC) is much lower when considering only PRC-born immigrants (without their children): as of 2010, according to the UN estimates, there were 8,3 million PRC-born Chinese immigrants officially registered outside China, Hong Kong, Macau, and Taiwan in 2013, accounting for only 0,22% of the entire PRC population (Bofulin, 2014). The Chinese diaspora is growing at a rate of about 1,2% per year (Poston Jr and Wong, 2010).

However, saying ‘*Chinese person*’ can be vague and misleading. It could perhaps be argued that Europeans do not belong to a culture, as unified as the Chinese one, and therefore the adjective ‘European’ encompasses more variety than the adjective ‘Chinese’.

Out of the 1,4 billion people, less than 3% of Chinese have ever been tempted to emigrate from China in the last century. Most Chinese immigrants come from only three coastal provinces: Guangdong, Fujian, and Zhejiang. And then, even within one province, only a few counties, towns and cities provide the bulk of immigrants, whereas people from other places within the same province are not interested in leaving China at all. There is a subculture of immigration and even significant pressure on young people by their parents, relatives, and peers to emigrate and try their luck ‘overseas’.

In researching crimes by Chinese immigrants, it is therefore important to determine where in China the perpetrators and victims come from.

Chinese immigration happened in three waves (Ding, 2010). The first wave started in the mid-19th century and ended around 1950. Chinese people from Guangdong (Cantonese people) and Fujian province moved to South-East Asia and to the US.

The second wave, which lasted from 1950 to 1980, included Chinese people from Hong Kong, Macau, and Taiwan who emigrated to the US, UK, Canada, Australia, New Zealand and Japan.

The third wave began after the Reform and Opening Up Policy in the People's Republic of China in 1978, gaining increasing momentum in the 1990s. Its main targets were the EU and its neighbouring states. These Chinese immigrants also established a strong presence in Africa and Latin America. The third wave has been dominated by immigrants from Zhejiang province, especially from the coastal city of Wenzhou and its rural surroundings. The correct term for these immigrants would be Wenzhounese.

In recent years, there has also been a significant rise of mostly female immigrants from Manchuria (the Heilongjiang, Jilin, and Liaoning provinces). These women are drawn to France, where they work in the service industry. Their number is already estimated to be around 15.000.

2. Origins of Chinese migrants in the EU and their characteristics

According to 2011 estimates (Latham and Wu, 2011), the EU member states with the highest number of Chinese immigrants are: the United Kingdom – 630.000; France – 540.000; Italy – 330.000; Spain – 170.000; Germany – 170.000; and the Netherlands – 160.000 immigrants. The number of Chinese immigrants in the continental EU (excluding the UK) is estimated to be around 1,75 million. It should be noted that most of these immigrants were born in the PRC, meaning Chinese immigrants in the EU represent a formidable 20 to 25% of the all the 8,3 million individuals that came to the continent during the third wave. Most of them are of Wenzhounese origin. Among the Wenzhounese, the immigrants from Qingtian are especially significant.

The Wenzhou prefecture (Chin. *Wenzhou shi*) of Zhejiang province is located 450 km south of Shanghai. Outside Wenzhou City, a large and modern industrial port, the region is a fragmented coastal area with a mountainous rural hinterland, difficult to access even in times of modern transport. Agricultural yields are modest and the population has embraced the practice of running small family businesses since the early 19th century.[6] The tradition persisted underground even during the Cultural Revolution. Coastal towns and villages in the Wenzhou prefecture have long been notorious for smuggling and even for petty piracy during periods of social instability. All this is criminologically relevant, because the Wenzhounese people have historically developed an attitude which sees any state power as an obstacle to their business goals or simply as a predator.

The rural element infuses the local Wenzhounese culture with a great deal of deep-rooted traditions and superstitions. People rely on resilient social networks of clans, fraternities, and old friends. The strength of these networks seems to be much more formidable than even traditional Chinese social connections called *guanxi*.[7] Distrust of any and all outsiders is typical of the Chinese psyche (Bo, 1991) and Wenzhounese people are suspicious of every other Chinese. Finally, the Wenzhounese speak a very difficult and untypical dialect of Chinese, incomprehensible even in neighbouring towns and villages. In short, Wenzhou prefecture is *mutatis mutandis* culturally somewhat similar to 'scofflaw' (lawless) areas' in Europe, such as South Italy and Albania.

Within a larger Wenzhounese immigrant community, we find a significant group from Qingtian County (Chin. *Qing tian xian*), located 50 km from Wenzhou City. The Qingtianese maintain a separate but very strong

---

6 The area has been known for its stone carving prowess since ancient times. During colonisation by foreign super-powers in the beginning of the 20th century, the stone merchants established contacts with the first foreigners and started to emigrate to sell small stone figurines, first to Japan and then to France. There was a vibrant community of Wenzhounese merchants in Paris as early as the 1920s (Bofulin, 2014).

7 Without going into too much nuances of the definition, *guanxi* (loosely translated as *connections*; the term with the same Chinese characters is also used in Japanese as *kankei*) are the Chinese cultural equivalent to Western notions of networking and social capital. They have some cultural specifics and yet it is doubtful to assume that such a *modus operandi* is uniquely Chinese, as argued by some Chinese scholars (see Wang, 2014). As the concept of *guanxi* is applied all over China, it alone cannot explain the economic successes of some areas. As Studwell (2010) points out, *guanxi* in China often do not work and can be highly unreliable, but *guanxi* networks are very efficient within the Chinese diaspora in South-East Asia.

identity. As of 2010, the official statistics of Qingtian County give a population count of 336.500 people, 230.000 of which live abroad as immigrants (Bofulin, 2014). The remaining population is more or less concentrated in Qingtian Town which has grown from 20.000 to more than 100.000 people.

Far from being a typical backwater town in the Chinese countryside, Qingtian Town is incredibly prosperous and cosmopolitan, even earning the nickname of 'little Hong Kong'. Its immigrant community is of vital importance for the local economic development as official statistics for 2009 state an income of $ *2.137 million* (sic!) from migrant remittances alone (Bofulin, *ibidem*). If the estimate of 230.000 migrants is correct, that would mean that the average Qingtianese abroad remits more than $ 9.000 annually. The Qingtianese group is generally present in Italy, Spain, and France. They also speak a specific dialect which is so different from Wenzhounese that the dialect speakers cannot understand each other. However, most Qingtianese people are also fluent in Wenzhounese, giving them the upper hand in collaborating with immigrant business circles from Wenzhou.

3. Predicting typical crimes of Chinese immigrants

To avoid prejudices and racist hysteria, it should be emphasised that Chinese migrants' crime rate all over the world is very low, especially for violent crimes. In most countries, including the US and Canada (Rumbaut *et al.*, 2007) (but not Japan), the crime rate of Chinese immigrants is in fact lower than the crime rate of the domestic majority population.

Furthermore, crimes of Chinese immigrants – when they occur – are mostly harmful to the Chinese community itself and not to the local population. The Chinese are not only the perpetrators of these crimes, they also comprise the bulk of the victims. Researching, predicting, preventing and punishing crimes of Chinese immigrants would thus primarily benefit Chinese immigrants themselves. Typical crimes connected with Chinese immigrants are:

- 'Low skill' crimes, which do not require expertise: smuggling (*e.g.* meat) and avoiding customs taxes and duties; importing or manufacturing counterfeit goods (especially textile and leather); human smuggling and clandestine immigration, usually for the purpose of illegal and undocumented labour.

- 'High skill' white-collar crimes which require special expertise: tax evasion, tax fraud, business fraud, investment visa fraud[8], establishing fake 'strawman' companies to smuggle workers into the EU, and exploitation of migrant labour.

Regretfully, the exploitation of Chinese migrant labour is pervasive in numerous industries where Chinese migrants are traditionally employed, either legally or illegally. Chinese owners of laundromats and restaurants consider this completely normal. It is especially common in the Italian textile industry (Calleri, 2016). Chinese workers are underpaid, work overtime without compensation, are excluded from social security, denied leave, *etc.* In worse cases, they must also live and sleep in the factory, are denied freedom to leave the premises and face dangerous, even lethal working conditions, thus becoming slaves in all but name. This problem deserves to be explored in more detail.

4. Economic incentives for illegal labour exploitation: the Wenzhou model

Wenzhou City has been repeatedly declared "the most enterprising city in China". It is the Chinese unofficial centre of shadow banking, land grabbing, and the monopolisation of light industries. *E.g.* 70% of plastic lighters in the world are made in Wenzhou (Ramzy, 2011). Its businessmen have repeatedly demonstrated vast experience with avoiding and corrupting law enforcement and bending the rules to their advantage. In China, they enjoy a reputation for dishonesty, trickery and an uncanny ability to haggle.[9]

---

8 In cases where investment in real estate is a prerequisite for getting an investor's visa, it is not uncommon to sell the same real estate numerous times to many consecutive Chinese investors. Visas, issued for planned business projects which are supposed to create a certain number of new jobs, lend themselves to fraud even more easily. As the newest case of massive visa fraud in the US reveals, the investors proposed construction projects which were never built. The US were defrauded in the excess of $ 50 million in subsidies for construction projects (Bukhari, 2017).

9 Such a reputation might not be entirely deserved and could also be the result of envy as Wenzhounese people are allegedly the most common group among

The Wenzhounese are well versed in aggressively creating efficient low-cost, labour-intensive businesses in unsophisticated, 'brute force' ways. Their most typical tactic involves clusters of small family businesses which are located in the same area where they mutually cooperate to the detriment of local competition (Bongardt and Neves, 2007). Where small and medium enterprises (SMEs) in the West are often hindered by inheritance procedures (the company must be divided among heirs or the oldest heir must pay the others their shares), this obstacle does not apply to a Wenzhou company. When the owner of the business passes away, the business is not divided among heirs into smaller units but instead continues to be managed collectively by surviving family members.

Nevertheless, in spite of all its obvious advantages, the so-called *Wenzhou business model* is self-defeating overseas. The greatest weakness of Wenzhounese businessmen lies in two aspects of their business culture: (a) *cost-cutting mentality* (paying workers very low wages and producing low quality goods) and (b) an utter *lack of formal education* (often attending only primary school). In China, it is often said that Wenzhounese people never attempt a business that the owner or the investor cannot understand; so their entrepreneurial complexity remains low. Investment into high tech gadgets, software, media, the internet and other goods and services with high added value is therefore discouraged. Due to the lack of education, the Wenzhounese are often also powerless to surmount language and cultural barriers when faced with an international context.

In times of economic growth, when a group of Wenzhounese accumulates enough capital to potentially upgrade their SME business to a large modern corporation, they are often simply incapable of coping with such sophistication. Their deep distrust of all outsiders also more or less excludes services from experts, such as lawyers, accountants, managers, consultants and even interpreters. The cost-cutting mentality also prevents them from hiring skilled workers. Complex business ventures with international elements are therefore hobbled from the start and remain quite rare. Large profits, often in cash, can be invested only into real estate or

China's *nouveaux riches*. They often buy the best real estate in large cities, (out-pricing the local population), while they lack and even intentionally ignore formal education which is the unquestionable pillar of Chinese traditional values, reinforcing existing prejudices and fears.

into similar business ventures (restaurants, shops, and hotels), inevitably leading to saturation and stagnation.

In times of recession when demand is low, the Wenzhou model is bound to lead quickly to collapse because their source of income is based on producing huge amounts of cheap goods with a very low profit margin. If costs cannot be controlled anymore by cutting, the business fails to generate a profit and is forced to close down or at least downsize.

Overall, the very economic essence of the Wenzhou model lies in aggressive cost-cutting in various areas (labour, materials, taxes and other duties, administrative costs). Such a mentality inevitably produces strong incentives for various (cost-cutting) crimes: smuggling, tax evasion and tax fraud, and above all – labour exploitation and the violation of workers' rights.

5. Estimating the costs of illegal Chinese immigration

It is not difficult to logically deduce the reasons why illegal migration is preferred to the legal alternative. Illegal migration can be: (1) cheaper; (2) quicker; (3) more convenient and 'user friendly' (less bureaucracy and red tape), and (4) 'safer' – from the point of view of an illegal immigrant who lacks access to information and legal knowledge.

There can be very few arguments against the fact that in the increasingly bureaucratic modern world, illegal immigration is often quicker and more convenient. Furthermore, even if illegal immigrants are caught by the authorities, the same bureaucracy provides them with many options and opportunities (applying for asylum, government amnesties, *etc.*) to prolong their stay for many months, even years.

As for safety, the situation is objectively speaking quite the opposite, since many illegal immigrants fall victim to various kinds of abuse or even die on the way. It should, however, be emphasized that illegal immigrants have little to no knowledge about the country to which they intend to immigrate and do not speak the language of that country. Fear of everything foreign, which in the case of Chinese illegal immigrants often borders on paranoia, compels illegal immigrants to trust human smugglers and illegal employers of their community because they at least provide an illusion of protection against the hostile outside world.

The only enigma remaining is the price of illegal immigration. Estimates range from 10.000 to 75.000 or even 100.000 US dollars for smuggling a single Chinese illegal immigrant into a developed Western country. This information does not seem credible in the case of Wenzhounese and Qingtianese immigrants. By using other available information, it is possible to make a more realistic estimate.

The Wenzhounese immigration to the EU is strictly for economic reasons, *i.e.* the opportunity to earn much higher wages than at home. We should therefore assume that the costs of immigration, legal or illegal, are a matter of rational economic calculation. If the immigrants immigrate for political (escaping state repression or religious persecution) or socio-economic reasons (relocating abroad indefinitely in search of a better life for themselves and their children), they often accept very high, even unbearable costs. However, the immigration costs for Wenzhounese should only be considered as an investment to be returned to the investor over a certain period of time.

According to Qingtian County official estimates, an average Qingtianese immigrant remits $ 9.000 annually. Assuming that remittances from legal and illegal immigrants are of a similar amount, we can deduce that the yearly remittance should cover the immigration costs in a short time span, *i.e.* from one to three years. It is likewise well known that the most notorious Chinese human smuggler in the US, Chen Chui Ping alias Sister Ping, used a standard tariff of $ 18.000 per smuggled person. The standard price was such common knowledge among Chinese Americans that wives of illegal immigrants were nicknamed *wan ba sao*, 'Ladies Eighteen Thousand' (Zhang, 2007). From this information, we can deduce that the price of smuggling a single Chinese immigrant should be roughly equal to an average of two-year remittance: somewhere between 15.000 and 20.000 dollars or euros.[10]

This price is highly competitive and can in fact be cheaper than the cheapest options available for legal immigration to the EU, *i.e.* establishing

10 This estimate is confirmed by the case of the Xiang (Hsiang) crime family which smuggled hundreds of illegal labourers into Prato and subsequently terrorised them with ever increasing extortion demands. The initial fee was 17.000 Euros, paid in three instalments. The criminal network of Xiang family was successfully broken by the Anti-mafia Investigative Division. See Calleri (2016).

a limited liability company in East Europe. For Chinese immigrants interested in the Italian, Austrian, and German markets, we can make an appropriate comparison with immigration costs to Slovenia. Slovenia is located the inside Schengen area, providing hassle-free access to Italy and Central Europe.

Establishing a limited liability company requires € 7.500 of initial capital and the ability to pay some notary and legal costs, immigration consultants, consular fees, as well as the cost of travelling to the Slovenian consulate in Peking or Shanghai. All together this puts the final price tag at roughly € 10.000. However, in this case the residence permit must be prolonged every year. The priority immigration procedure, which guarantees an automatic three-year residence permit with only one extension necessary for 5 years requires an investment of € 30.000 investment (including € 7.500 of initial capital) and at least € 3.000 for other expenses, putting the final price tag at a hefty € 33.000. Because this is one of the cheapest options for the EU, it is unsurprising to see illegal Chinese immigration continue.

City of Prato as an example of Chinese immigrant crimes on a massive scale

Prato is a city in Tuscany, located close to Florence. At least 30.000 to 40.000 of its 191.000 inhabitants are estimated to be Chinese migrants (Latham and Wu, 2013). As of 31 December 2013, only 16.182 Chinese residents are legally registered (Johansen *et al.*, 2015). Prato has been the heart of the Italian textile industry for decades. The first Chinese migrants from Wenzhou began to arrive in the 1990s and started working in small, family-owned textile factories. Slowly, the Wenzhounese community in Prato expanded as their companies started to increasingly monopolise the so-called fast fashion segment (Italian: *pronto moda*).

Nowadays, the Chinese businesses, mostly owned by Wenzhounese and Qingtianese families, directly or indirectly control approximately one third of the entire garment and textile turnover worth around € 4,5 billion annually and an additional 2,5 billion Euros in exports. Chinese businesses are therefore expected to earn an aggregate income of more than 2 billion Euros. The orders for textile and garment production were outsourced to Prato from textile giants (Zhang, 2015), producing affordable and fashionable clothing (*e.g.* Zara and many others).

To remain competitive, *i.e.* cheaper and quicker than Italian companies and even production facilities overseas (China, Vietnam, Bangladesh), some Chinese textile businessmen have developed and perfected, as numerous investigations by Italian law enforcement have revealed, increasingly illegal and criminal business tactics. For the local textile industry, however, Prato did not represent a threat, but rather an opportunity of "outsourcing to China without going to China" (Cipriani, 2016). Cheap Chinese fabrics were imported and often smuggled from China, while the final work was done by the meagrely paid Chinese workers themselves.

The city has the largest Chinatown in the entire EU. In proportion to its population roughly one fourth of the inhabitants are Chinese; since 2009, more than half of new-borns have been Chinese (Bressan and Krause, 2014). Prato has in the last decade attracted considerable attention from scholars in migration, multi-culturalism, ethnography, Chinese studies, business models and business networks, public spaces, *etc*. (see Ceccagno, 2003, 2012; Ottati, 2009, 2014; Santini et al., 2011; Chang, 2012; Nielsen et al., 2012; Barbu et al., 2013; Lan and Zhu, 2014; Lombardi and Sforzi, 2016; Lazzeretti and Capone, 2017). However, virtually all of these analyses remain in the 'politically correct area' and fail to mention that the district of Prato also suffers from inordinate levels of crime. According to a recent Transcrime analysis (Riccardi, 2017), Prato has comparable levels of organised crime infiltration to traditional '*mafia* strongholds' in the South of Italy: Campania, Calabria, and Sicily.

The Antonino Caponnetto Anti-mafia foundation has identified three types of Chinese immigrant criminal associations in Prato and its surroundings (Calleri, 2016):

1. A *mafia-type association*, according to the definition given in Article 416 bis of the Italian Penal Code, mostly involved in human smuggling, extortion of prostitutes and to a lesser degree in illicit drug trafficking;
2. Gangs of young Chinese delinquents, mostly involved in robberies and violent crime;
3. So-called *nuova mafia borghese*, new bourgeois criminal groups of Chinese businessmen and entrepreneurs.

Contrary to expectation, the crimes of Chinese mafia-type associations and Chinese gangs are completely dwarfed in comparison to *bourgeois* criminal groups as demonstrated below.

In 2009, the Italian authorities conducted their first major operation against Chinese criminal entrepreneurs. Operation *Economia Sicura* saw the Italian Financial Guard (*Guardia di Finanza*) seize 50.000 counterfeit bags and discover hundreds of meters of fabrics used to make Louis Vuitton and Gucci fashion accessories. When a team of labour inspectors raided a textile factory near Florence and discovered 70 illegal Chinese workers, living and working underground with their entire families, sharing same beds during their shifts, the team had to be assisted by the military (Calleri, 2016).

This operation was followed by the most successful investigation so far. Codenamed *Money2Money* and once again conducted by the Financial Guard, it was finalised in July 2010 and resulted in the arrest and indictment of 158 people, the confiscation of 181 pieces of real estate (many of them expensive villas) and 166 luxury cars, the majority being the Porsche brand, the freezing of 300 bank accounts, and the seizure of 73 companies. The value of seized assets was estimated to be around € 80 million. Money transfers, made by the indicted individuals to China, was always done in small amounts (so-called *smurfing*), but they amounted together to more than € 2,7 billion between 2006 and 2010 (Calleri, 2016).

It is quite probable that criminal Chinese entrepreneurs have been highly adept at avoiding Italian law enforcement. Therefore, a vast dark number of unreported crime continues to exist. But even if we ignore this assumption, simply comparing the amount of unrecorded income, wired to China (€ 700 million), identified by various investigations, with the amount of the entire turnover of the Chinese textile businesses in Prato (€ 2 billion) we get a disturbing picture of the deeply entrenched illegality. That means a third of the Chinese textile corporate income in Prato was illegally diverted.

Obviously, this is tax fraud on a massive scale, but tax crimes might be just the tip of the iceberg, since the main question is just how such high earnings were achieved in the first place? Even in times of the global financial crisis when Italian businesses were struggling with the high costs of labour and materials, Chinese businesses managed to be immensely profitable. It is therefore possible to suspect other (economic) crimes to raise profits: the illegal exploitation of Chinese workers, paying them much below the Italian minimum wage, avoiding social security contributions, buying materials on the black market or smuggling them from China.

Of course, it is almost impossible to give a final estimate of the proportion of Chinese businesses in Prato which routinely and systematically engage in illegal practices. Some commentaries (*e.g.* Cipriani, 2016) even state that only a minority of Chinese businesses work in compliance with Italian laws and regulations, as law compliance would make them uncompetitive. In Prato, it is well known that most Chinese-owned companies are established for a very short time span (Ceccagno, 2012). If the company closes because of shrinking profits, this is referred to as 'natural death'. The opposite, 'unnatural death', happens if the company gets in trouble with the authorities and must pay hefty fines and taxes. Such a company files for bankruptcy and a new company emerges on the same address or nearby, like mushrooms from an underground mycelium (the Chinese poetically refer to it as 'phoenix from the ashes'). There is also a widespread tactic of 'name lending', *i.e.* elderly Chinese or immigrants who intend to return to China simply lend their name as *de iure* owners of companies. When trouble arises, the name lender is nowhere to be found and the *de facto* owner simply 'resets' the business with another name lender.

Some intermediate conclusions about Chinese crime in Prato

The Chinatown in Prato and its garment and textile businesses have been and will continue to be an interesting and highly complex phenomenon with no simple, 'quick fix' solutions in sight. Its model of integration for Chinese immigrants has been highly praised by numerous observers as well as denounced as an abject failure where a few unscrupulous immigrant businessmen ruthlessly exploit their own countrymen and pay no taxes nor social contributions to the Italian state. The victims of such a system have mostly been the Chinese immigrants themselves, while many Italian locals – often assuming the role of the 'victims' in the local right-wing populist media – have substantially profited from the Chinese: as landlords, outsourcing companies, notaries, and attorneys. The situation is further complicated by the observation that many of the Chinese exploited illegal workers do not see themselves as victims[11] but only as pursuers of the 'European dream' (higher income) stuck in temporary hardship. Prato used to have the highest percentage of business owners among its Chinese population, because literate people sometimes succeeded in working their way up to owning a small company. This implies that hope of a better life were not as far-fetched in the near past as they might seem today. What is more, the ideology of cultural relativism (*e.g.* "it is in the Chinese nature to work hard and patiently suffer") has spread from scholars to the Chinese community itself. Once adopted it has been quite skilfully applied by its leaders who claim that Chinese migrants are victims of systematic discrimination, such that even Italian citizens of Chinese descent are treated as second class. They state that Chinese businesses should more or less be left alone in their self-imposed isolation from the dominant Italian population. These claims often carry a lot of truth and therefore cannot simply be dismissed as entirely unfounded. However, the culture and tradition of a certain group of immigrants, however ancient and rich it may be, does not guarantee any immunity from local laws and regulations. Finally, in spite of rampant illegality in Prato's Chinatown, a significant number of Chinese businesses have nevertheless managed to respect laws, pay taxes, and remain competitive. Such positive examples should lead the way in combating unethical and criminal business practices.

Conclusion: phantoms of Chinese transnational crime, real crime and new areas of research

The distinction between real and mostly exaggerated transnational crime is not purely academic but has negative practical implications as well. Chasing criminal phantoms such as the Chinese Triads and fighting against overestimated social ills, such as sex trafficking, has logical consequences:

[11] A factory of workers who were toiling 12 to 14 hours a day had no locks on the doors, meaning that the workers were free to leave at any time and therefore their exploitation cannot be regarded as forced labour. Indeed, nobody left. See documentary "*Sirene: Indagine mafia cinese della Guardia di Finanza a Prato*", available on YouTube website: https://www.youtube.com/watch?v=8rZraoVPWkk.

true problems, often persisting in plain sight, are neglected. Typical example would involve the police "liberate" voluntary prostitutes, all the while the exploitation of underpaid illegal labour in Chinese-owned restaurants and textile factories continues unhindered.

It is therefore unsurprising that the case of Prato as the largest 'Criminal enterprise' perpetrated by Chinese immigrants in the entire EU, is much rarely covered by international media and even by scholars focusing on Chinese organised crime. Since Chinese immigrants tend to continue their isolation from mainstream society sometimes even into the 3rd generation, empirical criminological research and field work, conducted together with language and culture specialists are much needed.

However, it should be emphasised that transnational crime of Chinese origin also occurs in areas with no connection to Chinese immigrants. So far, we can mention three important examples.

The first one, which is gaining considerable media attention, is cybercrimes perpetrated by Chinese hackers. These often seem to be state-sponsored, but as freelancer attacks are becoming increasingly 'popular' as well.[12]

The second example is the manufacture of synthetic opiates, new psychoactive substances (NPS), and precursor chemicals by Chinese chemists (see US Department of the Treasury, 2014; United Nations Office on Drugs and Crime, 2016; Riggs, 2017). Even though hard evidence is very difficult to obtain, numerous incidents point out that quite a few people and companies inside Chinese chemical and pharmaceutical industry are skilfully exploiting loopholes in the global prohibition regime without facing any serious response from the Chinese government. These problems deserve to be investigated in more depth and detail by scholars of organised crime.

Both of the aforementioned categories of crimes cannot be characterised as 'culturally specific' as their *modus operandi* is more or less unrelated to the perpetrators' cultural environment. It therefore makes no significant difference whether NPS are manufactured by the Chinese or by any other nationality. A Chinese cultural background is moreover mostly

---

[12] The most recent worldwide attack was perpetrated using the WannaCry ransom ware crypto worm. Linguistic analysis of the ransom ware message suggests Chinese speaking authors (Condra *et al.*, 2017).

irrelevant when investigating hacking attacks, since they could also be perpetrated by people from many other countries or even by international groups of cyber-criminals.

The last and very recent example of Chinese transnational crime are fraudulent call centres, mostly operated by Taiwanese nationals. So far it is unclear whether these call centres could also be considered 'culturally specific' (like the Nigerian "419" fraud, see Glickman, 2005) or whether the perpetrators simply copied successful fraud tactics and scripts from other countries. Surprisingly, even in criminally rather uneventful Slovenia, such a call centre was discovered and a vast criminal investigation, involving 150 policemen, followed (Pečarič, 2018). As the majority of the callers is stating that they were forced to call potential fraud victims, only six ring leaders have been arrested and are currently under investigation. Other callers are being assisted by the Slovenian Ministry of Interior as alleged victims of human trafficking. Interestingly, the representatives of the People's Republic of China insist that this is a completely false claim and that the callers are only trying to abuse loopholes in the unclear human trafficking legislation.

Many of the discussed cases clearly illustrate the contradictions between Western and Chinese cultural understanding of victims and victimizers. If Chin's empirical research (2014) is correct, Chinese prostitutes in the EU are not victims, however they are treated as such. If they also temporarily work as pimps or cashiers, they can suddenly turn into victimizers. Quasi-slaves, working in Prato underground textile factories, are without doubt victims, but as, to paraphrase Buddhist thought, "prisoners of their own mind" they do not see themselves as being condemned to years or even decades of misery and debt slavery. Workers in fraudulent call centres simply declared themselves victims and were believed.

These complex cases are challenging established paradigms and narratives of human trafficking (including sex trafficking). Obviously, there is a great need for empirical and more objective research of immigrant criminality with less reliance on generalised assumptions.

References

"A Napoli record di omicidi", *Gazzetta del Mezzogiorno*, 28 January 2005. Available at: http://www.lagazzettadelmezzogiorno.it/news/notizie-nascoste/28296/a-napoli-record-di-omicidi.html.

Alvarez, M.B. and E.J. Alessi, Human trafficking is more than sex trafficking and prostitution: Implications for social work. *Affilia* 2012, 27, no. 2: 142-152.

Arsovska, J., *Decoding Albanian organized crime: Culture, politics, and globalization*. Oakland, Ca.: University of California Press, 2015.

Baker, C.N., An examination of some central debates on sex trafficking in research and public policy in the United States." *Journal of Human Trafficking,* 2015, 1, no. 3: 191-208.

Barbu, M., M. Dunford, and L. Weidong, Employment, entrepreneurship, and citizenship in a globalised economy: the Chinese in Prato." *Environment and Planning* A, 2013, 45, no. 10: 2420-2441.

Behan, T., *The Camorra: Political Criminality in Italy*. Routledge, 2005.

Beneduce, T., Napoli, nel 2016 omicidi in aumento «Le stese sono il nostro terrorismo». *Corriere della Sera*, 28 January 2017. Available at: http://corrieredelmezzogiorno.corriere.it/napoli/cronaca/.

Bo, Y., *The ugly Chinaman and the crisis of Chinese culture*. Allen & Unwin, Sydney, 1992.

Bofulin, M. (2014), Sodobni migracijski procesi v Ljudski republiki Kitajski / People's Republic of China's Contemporary Migration Processes. *Časopis za kritiko znanosti,* 2014, 258, 125–136.

Bongardt, A., and M. Santos Neves, *The role of overseas Chinese in Europe in making China global: The case of Portugal*. No. 44. Departamento de Economia, Gestão e Engenharia Industrial, Universidade de Aveiro, 2007.

Bressan, M., and E.L. Krause, Ho un luogo dove lavoro e un luogo dove abito. Diversità e separazione in un distretto industriale in transizione. *Mondi migranti,* 2014.

Broadhurst, R., K.W. Lee, and C.Y. Chan, Crime trends. Understanding criminal justice in Hong Kong: 45-68, 2008.

Bukhari, J., Feds Raid a Suspected Green Card Fraud Ring for Wealthy Chinese Investors", *Fortune*, 6 April 2017. Available at:

http://fortune.com/2017/04/06/green-card-fraud-chinese-investors/.
Calleri, S., *Criminalità Cinese a Prato, Firenze e dintorni rapporto 2016*, Fondazione Antonino Caponnetto, 2016. Available at: https://stopmafia.blogspot.ru/2016/07/criminalita-cinese-report-2016.html.
Ceccagno, A., New Chinese migrants in Italy. *International Migration,* 2003, 41, no. 3, 187-213.
Ceccagno, A., The hidden crisis: the Prato industrial district and the once thriving Chinese garment industry. *Revue européenne des migrations internationales,* 2012, 28, no. 4, 43-65.
Chang, A., 20th century Chinese migration to Italy: The Chinese diaspora presence within European international migration. *History Compass,* 2012, 10, no. 2: 179-190.
Chappell, B., *European Union Report Details Growth Of Human Trafficking*. NPR, 15 April, 2013. Available at: http://www.npr.org/sections/thetwo-way/2013/04/15/177326963/european-union-report-details-growth-of-human-trafficking.
Chin, K.L. *Going Down to the Sea: Chinese Sex Workers Abroad*. Silkworm Books, 2014.
Choi-Fitzpatrick, A., The good, the bad, the ugly: Human rights violators in comparative perspective." *Journal of Human Trafficking,* 2016, 2, no. 1: 1-14.
Chu, Y.K., *The Triads as business*. Routledge, 2002.
Cipriani, S., This is China, not Italy. *The Huffington Post*. 2016. Available at:www.huffingtonpost.com/simone-cipriani/.
Condra, J., *et al*., Attribution of the WannaCry ransomware to Chinese speakers. 2017. Available at: https://www.flashpoint-intel.com/blog/linguistic-analysis-wannacry-ransomware/.
Ding, S., Sons of the Yellow Emperor go online: The state of the Chinese digital diaspora. *Global Migration and Transnational Politics*, Working Paper No. 13, July 2010. Available at: http://gmtp.gmu.edu/publications/gmtpwp/gmtp_wp_13.pdf.
Ebenstein, A., and E.J. Sharygin, Demographic change, prostitution, and sexually transmitted infection rates in China. In *The Oxford Handbook of the Economics of Prostitution,* 2012.

Finckenauer, J.O., and K. Chin., Sex trafficking: a target for situational crime prevention? In *Situational Prevention of Organised Crimes*, pp. 58-80, Karen Bullock, Ronald V. Clarke, and Nick Tilley, eds., 2010.

Glickman, H., The Nigerian "419" advance fee scams: prank or peril? *Canadian Journal of African Studies/La Revue Canadienne Des Études Africaines,* 2005, 39.3, 460-489.

Gozdziak E. and M.N. Bump, *Data and Research on Human Trafficking: Bibliography of Research-Based Literature, A Final Report to NIJ Grant 2007-VT-BX-K002*. Washington, DC: Institute for the Study of International Migration, Georgetown University, 2008.

Gui, S., "The Contribution of Overseas Chinese to China´s Developement", in Qu, Zhang Lou and Li (eds), *Annual Report on Overseas Chinese Studies*, Beijing: Social Sciences Academic Press, 2011.

Hong Kong Monthly Digest of Statistics, *Crime Statistics in 2015*, Census and Statistics Department, The Government of the Hong Kong Special Administrative Region, Hong Kong, 2016.

Hoyle, C., M. Bosworth and M. Dempsey, Labelling the victims of sex trafficking: Exploring the borderland between rhetoric and reality." *Social & Legal Studies,* 2011, 20, no. 3, 313-329.

Johanson, G., N. McAuliffe and M. Bressan, *Chinese migration to Europe: Prato, Italy, and beyond*. Springer, 2015.

Lan, T., and S. Zhu, Chinese apparel value chains in Europe: low-end fast fashion, regionalization, and transnational entrepreneurship in Prato, Italy. *Eurasian Geography and Economics,* 2014, 55, no. 2, 156-174.

Latham, K., and B. Wu, *Chinese immigration into the EU: New trends, dynamics and implications*. London: Europe China Research and Advice Network, 2013.

Lazzeretti, L., and F. Capone, The transformation of the Prato industrial district: an organisational ecology analysis of the co-evolution of Italian and Chinese firms. *The Annals of Regional Science,* 2017, 58, no. 1, 135-158.

Lee, K.-W., R.G. Broadhurst, and P.S.L. Beh., Triad-related homicides in Hong Kong." *Forensic science international,* 2006, 162, no. 1-3, 183-190.

Lombardi, S., and F. Sforzi. "Chinese manufacturing entrepreneurship capital: evidence from Italian industrial districts." *European Planning Studies,* 2016, 24, no. 6, 1118-1132.

Murray, D.H., and B. Qin, *The origins of the Tiandihui: the Chinese triads in legend and history.* Stanford University Press, 1994.

Nielsen, I., O. Paritski, and R. Smyth, A minority-status perspective on intergroup relations: A study of an ethnic Chinese population in a small Italian town. *Urban Studies,* 2012, 49, no. 2, 307-318.

Ottati, G.D., An industrial district facing the challenges of globalization: Prato today. *European Planning Studies,* 2009, 17, no. 12, 1817-1835.

Ottati, G. D., A transnational fast fashion industrial district: an analysis of the Chinese businesses in Prato. *Cambridge Journal of Economics,* 2014, 38, no. 5: 1247-1274.

Pečarič, J., Obsežne kriminalistične preiskave trgovine z ljudmi", *Delo,* January 18, 2018. Available at: www.delo.si/novice/kronika/neuradno-obsezne-kriminalisticne-preiskave-financnih-goljufij.html.

Petta, D.L., As tríades e as sociedades secretas na China: entre o mito e a desmistifição. *Revista Brasileira De Ciencias Sociais,* 2017, vol.32, n.93. Available at: www.scielo.br/pdf/rbcsoc/v32n93/0102-6909-rbcsoc-3293092017.pdf.

Poston Jr, D.L., and J.H. Wong, The Chinese diaspora: The current distribution of the overseas Chinese population. *Chinese Journal of Sociology,* 2016, 2, no. 3, 348-373.

Ramzy, A. "When Wenzhou Sneezes", *Time*, November 28, 2011. Available at: http://content.time.com/time/magazine/article/.

Riccardi, M. *et al., Assessing the risk of money laundering in Europe. Final report of project IARM*. Milano: Transcrime, 2017.

Rumbaut, R.G., *et al.*, Debunking the myth of immigrant criminality: imprisonment among first- and second-generation young men. *Migration Information Source*, 1 June 2006. Available at: https://www.migrationpolicy.org/article/.

Santini, C., S. Rabino, and L. Zanni, Chinese immigrants socio-economic enclave in an Italian industrial district: the case of Prato. *World Review of Entrepreneurship, Management and Sustainable Development,* 2011, 7, no. 1, 30-51.

Saviano, R., *Gomorra: viaggio nell'impero economico della camorra.* Milano: Mondadori, 2006.

Sergi, A., Mafia and politics as concurrent governance actors. In P.C. van Duyne, A. Maljevic, G.A. Antonopoulos, J. Harvey, and K. von Lampe, (eds.) *The relativity of wrongdoing*. (pp.43-70) Oisterwijk: Wolf Legal Publishers, 2015.

Silverstone, D., From Triads to snakeheads: organised crime and illegal migration within Britain's Chinese community". *Global Crime,* 2011, 12, no. 2, 93-111.

Spencer, J.R., International Law, People Trafficking and the Power to Stay Criminal Proceedings for Abuse of Process. *The Cambridge Law Journal,* 2014, 73, no. 1, 11.

Studwell, J., *Asian godfathers: money and power in Hong Kong and South East Asia*. Profile Books, 2010.

Sui, C., Film exposes London's sex industry underworld", *BBC News*, 23 June, 2017. Available at: http://www.bbc.com/news/world-asia-40363513.

Varese, F. and R.WY Wong, Resurgent Triads? Democratic mobilization and organized crime in Hong Kong. *Australian & New Zealand Journal of Criminology*, 2017, DOI: 0004865817698191.

Wang, P., Extra-legal protection in China: How guanxi distorts China's legal system and facilitates the rise of unlawful protectors. *British Journal of Criminology,* 2014, 54, no. 5, 809-830.

Weitzer, R. New directions in research on prostitution. *Crime, Law and Social Change,* 2005, 43, no. 4, 211-235.

Weitzer, R., The social construction of sex trafficking: Ideology and institutionalization of a moral crusade. *Politics & Society,* 2007, 35, no. 3, 447-475.

Zhang, G., 'Made in Italy' by Chinese in Prato: the "carrot and stick" policy and Chinese migrants in Italy, *The Online Journal of the China Policy Institute*, November, 2010. Available at: https://cpianalysis.org/2015/10/22/.

Zhang, S.X., *Smuggling and trafficking in human beings: all roads lead to America*. Greenwood Publishing Group, 2007.

Zhang, S.X., Beyond the 'Natasha'story–a review and critique of current research on sex trafficking. *Global Crime,* 2009, 10, no. 3, 178-195.

Zheng, T., *Ethnographies of prostitution in contemporary China: Gender relations, HIV/AIDS, and nationalism*. Springer, 2009.

Human smuggling reconsidered: the case of Lesbos

Dina Siegel[1]

Human smuggling – a complicated phenomenon

Article 3(a) of the United Nations Smuggling Protocol defines migrant smuggling as a crime involving "the procurement, in order to obtain, directly or indirectly, a financial or other material benefit, of the illegal entry of a person into a State Party of which the person is not a national or a permanent resident". This definition underlines that human smuggling is a transnational crime, but the emphasis here is on economic gain, not on violence or other harm to the smuggled person's life, health or property. In the academic literature various authors have tried to narrow down the definition of the phenomenon. Kyle and Koslowski, for example, put forward the following definition of human smuggling: "an individual's crossing of a state's international border without that state's authorization and with the assistance of paid smugglers" (2011:4). Here again, no clear, direct victims are identified as an element in the definition. Attempts to clarify exactly what kind of crime is being committed in terms of victims, offenders and harm have rarely been successful. Human smuggling is still often linked to and confused with human trafficking, even though it is the aspect of exploitation that distinguishes the two phenomena.

In-depth historical and anthropological studies characterise human smuggling as a consensus between someone who, for a variety of reasons, cannot leave his or her country and/or enter another country on a regular basis and seeks help to be brought from one country to another; someone who is able to provide this type of assistance in return for payment, and/or someone (or several people) who can guarantee payment. The practice of

1 The author is Professor of criminology at the Willem Pompe Institute, Utrecht University, the Netherlands.

human smuggling is also directly related to the practice of 'beating' the existing migration system. All over the world irregular border crossing or other forms of illegal migration have been a response to restrictive migration policies and the obstacles created by policy-makers and law enforcement.

Although we now know much more about the global practice of people smuggling, some authors maintain that empirical research on this phenomenon and the actors involved has remained scant (Zhang *et al.*, 2018: 10), in contrast to the number of government reports and media stories on this crime of mobility. Many academic researchers and analysts have published critical studies on migration policies (Andreas, 2011) or on the morality of human smuggling (Aloyo and Cusumano, 2018), but these studies are mostly based on government data and media stories. Many ethnographers, on the other hand, have provided information on the root causes of migration and migrants' travel experiences, but not specifically on people smuggling (Spencer, 2004: 302).

This chapter will provide empirical knowledge on human smuggling by analysing my ethnographic data on the smuggling of migrants from Turkey to the Greek island of Lesbos and by giving a voice to the people who underwent the process. This will offer some food for thought with respect to the prevailing views on human smuggling in the academic and public debate.

Methodology

I spent the summer of 2017, from the end of May until the middle of September, on Lesbos to study the consequences of the so-called refugee crisis as experienced by migrants, local islanders, NGO representatives and EU officials. My ethnographic research methods included participant observation and 66 open interviews with asylum seekers, local islanders and representatives of government organisations, NGOs and law enforcement. Human smuggling, the focus of the present chapter, was only one aspect of a larger study I completed in 2019, titled *Dynamics of solidarity - consequences of the 'refugee crisis' on Lesbos* (Siegel, 2019).

The extended case method was used to collect information from various sources (multi-site and multi-level ethnography) and it included different sub-cases which provided many pieces of the puzzle needed to compose a complete picture of the situation in all its complexity (Marx, 1976). Human smuggling was one of these pieces and it raised a number of questions about the meaning of crimes of mobility.

Research question

During the 'refugee crisis' of 2015-2017, Lesbos, an island in the Aegean Sea close to Turkey, became the most-discussed migrant destination in the international media. Lesbos is one of the EU's 'hotspots', where migrants are identified and given the opportunity to apply for asylum in Europe. The island's infamous camp, Moria, where thousands of migrant are currently living in precarious conditions, has become a symbol of the EU's failing migration policy (Siegel, 2018; Siegel, 2019).

Reading media and government reports on the mass migration to Lesbos made me wonder why so many migrants were apparently willing to pay thousands of Euros to members of organised crime networks (*i.e.* human smugglers) to organise their trip from Turkey to Lesbos, only 12 km away. Why did they come at all, knowing that they ran the risk of either drowning in the stormy sea or being caught by the Turkish Coast Guard and forcibly returned? Why did these people keep trying to make the crossing to Lesbos while being aware – as they must have been – of the conditions in reception centres such as camp Moria, whose inhabitants were lacking basic needs and were suffering from illnesses, a general lack of hygiene and internal fights between different ethnic groups of migrants? They also must have known that it could take months or even years for a decision to be reached on their asylum application and that it was more than likely that they would be denied entrance to Europe. What was the role of people smugglers in their 'adventures' and how did these migrants and their helpers experience the practice of human smuggling?

People smugglers in the public discourse

There are significant differences between law enforcement sources and empirical research on the phenomenon of human smuggling with respect to organised crime activities, the brutality of criminal smugglers and the vulnerability of migrant victims. Governmental and EU reports are often contradicted by ethnographic studies drawing attention to individual initiatives, community assistance and the agency of migrants themselves. The stereotype of smuggled persons as 'victims' of organised crime depicted in official reports is countered by stories (documented in academic publications) of the 'winners' who made it to their desired destination. The image of people smugglers, on the other hand, is a lot less clear-cut.

Smugglers as criminals

Most official documents tend to portray human smugglers as criminals who "exploit the desperation and vulnerability of migrants" (Europol, 2016). On the basis of this assumption, Europol launched the European Migrant Smuggling Centre to "pro-actively support EU Member States in dismantling criminal networks involved in organizing migrant smuggling". Official reports on human smuggling indicate that "in 2015 alone, criminal networks involved in migrant smuggling are estimated to have had a turnover of between EUR 3-6 billion. This turnover is set to double or triple if the scale of the current migration crisis persists in the upcoming year" (Europol, 2016:2). And "more than 90% of migrants are facilitated to the EU, mostly by criminal networks" (*ibid*: 4). Europol predicted that these criminals would continue to expand their activities, using vulnerable migrants for sexual and labour exploitation in the coming years "unless decisive action is taken" (*ibid*:13). Human smuggling is hereby equated to human trafficking, with the emphasis on the exploitation and victimhood of migrants. In the same line, the United States State Department refers to smuggled people as being ". . . extremely vulnerable to human trafficking, abuse and other crimes, as they are illegally present in the country of destination and often owe large debts to their smugglers" (U.S. State Department, 2017:1). In this document the line between smuggling and trafficking is not only blurred, but practically obliterated.

The European Commission's starting point is that "ruthless criminal networks organise the journeys of large numbers of migrants desperate to reach the EU. They make substantial gains while putting the migrants' lives at risk" (European Commission, 2015:1). These smugglers allegedly treat migrants not as human beings, but as goods, similar to the drugs and firearms that are transported along the same routes. Although the document's authors admit that there are no data on the profits human smugglers around the world are making with their criminal activities, "isolated cases show that these are substantial" (*ibid*). One of the recommendations in the EU Action Plan against human smuggling 2015-2020 is to raise awareness of the risks of human smuggling to prevent potential victims from embarking on a dangerous journey and putting their trust in cruel and deceitful smugglers who have approached them through social media (*ibid*: 6).

Similar 'facts' are presented on the official website of the United Nations Office of Drugs and Crime (UNODC), which explains that human smuggling is a transnational crime, in the course of which migrants are subjected to grave human rights abuses. The criminals have "tremendous power, while the migrants are left vulnerable" (UNODC, 2019). The potential risks are specified: even if the journey is consensual, it can still turn into a nightmare. "During the trip, people might be squeezed into exceptionally small spaces in trucks or onto unseaworthy boats in order for smugglers to maximize their 'cargo'. Migrants might be raped or beaten *en route* or left to die in the desert. Once they reach their destination, many find that they (or their families) are the victims of blackmail or debt bondage. The latter can involve migrants paying huge sums of money to criminals in order to settle near-impossible levels of debt out of fear of violence or fear of being deported by the authorities, which can result in them becoming victims of human trafficking" (*ibid*). People smuggling can also fuel corruption and organised crime. "There is evidence suggesting that, with the ever-growing interdependence of the global economy, the involvement of criminal groups in the smuggling of migrants is on the rise" (*ibid*). However, no concrete empirical data or references to this 'evidence' are provided and the links in the text all refer to other UNODC reports.

This image of the smuggler does not only appear in official reports. Various researchers have reinforced the negative stereotype of human smugglers as violent, evil men (Kyle and Scarcelli, 2009) who have no qualms about letting their victims/customers suffer or even die (Human

Rights Watch's Dispatches, 2014). Human smugglers are often presented as members of criminal organisations (Kaizen and Nonnema, 2007; Narli, 2006; Saha, 2007; Schloenhardt, 2002; UNODC 2015; Sciopi and Ionescu, 2016), as kidnappers (Walser, Baker McNeill and Zuckerman, 2011) and/or as synonymous with human traffickers (Aronowitz, 2001; Bilecen, 2009; Lintner, 2002).

In the Oxford Handbook of Organised Crime (Paoli, 2014), the categories of human trafficking and human smuggling are discussed in one breath (Kleemans and Smit, 2014). Fortunately, the authors acknowledge that a distinction must be made and that there is growing concern about the opposing views on the difference between the two phenomena, as this creates obstacles for empirical research (*ibid*: 397). However, the real problem is not with the research, as in most cases criminologists know (or are expected to know) how to conduct independent, unbiased research. The real problem is with the application of the incorrect and generalised conclusions of some of the above-mentioned reports to policy-making, as this may lead to stigmatisation, wrongful accusations and damage to the interests and humanitarian protection of migrants (Tazzioli, 2016).

The positive image of a smuggler

Instead of recycling law enforcement data and the findings of so-called migration experts, empirical criminological research has focused in recent years on the activities and business organisation of people smuggling around the world, based on interviews with those involved in it (DiNicola and Musumeci, 2014; Staring, 2012; Zhang, 2008; Van Liempt, 2010; Bilger, Hofmann and Jandl, 2006).

Traditionally the phenomenon of irregular migration is deeply rooted and embedded in communities (Zhang, 2008) where social ties and trust relationships exist as these aspects are crucial to its success. In many communities, relatives, close friends, neighbours and co-villagers all make a vital contribution to facilitating the journey and guaranteeing payment. Zhang and Chin showed in their studies how entire villages in China were involved in planning and supporting smuggling operations (Zhang and Chin, 2002). Majid emphasised that community and family ties are key factors in the smuggling of people from Afghanistan and Somalia (Majid,

2018). Baird shows that trust is the basis of the relationship between migrants and smugglers in Turkey (Bairda, 2016) and Sanchez shows in her research how trust is based on 'socially cemented ties' in Mexico (2015:17). The social embeddedness of human smuggling as a collective practice is emphasised by Mengiste (2018) in the context of Eritrean and Ethiopian migrants. According to Achilli, the relationships between smugglers and migrants are "rich in solidarity and reciprocity and grounded in local notions of morality" (Achilli, 2018: 77). Chinese migrants in the US even consider their smugglers as philanthropists (Zhang, 2007: 89).

The image of the smuggler that emerges from these empirical studies is that of a family member, a friend or an acquaintance who can arrange a migrant's journey and make their dream come true. Maher describes how in Senegal the smuggler is considered as a friend, protector and guide (Maher, 2018). He is a member of the community, someone who enjoys the respect and trust of other migrants. Trust, reputation and personal relationships are thus key factors in understanding migrant smuggling.

Members of the community usually consider people smuggling as a legitimate enterprise rather than a criminal activity and regard smugglers as well-connected and knowledgeable entrepreneurs. They view illegal people smuggling as a strictly rational business with its own specific risks, just like any other business, and they 'silence morality' (Bauman, 2000: 29). Not all smugglers appear to be equally experienced and successful and sometimes they fail to complete their mission or make serious and even fatal mistakes during the trip. But in many cases, mainly those that are not registered in police statistics and do not attract media attention, the smuggling operations are successful. These successes reinforce the smuggler's positive image and function as an informal advertisement for recruiting new clients.

The smuggler as an information and service provider is also often mentioned in the literature. Austrian research revealed that smugglers gave migrants information about the legal situation in the destination country and practicalities on how to deal with the authorities, even though this information was not always correct (Bilger, Hofmann and Jandl, 2006). In his research on smuggling along the Mexico-US border, David Spener introduced the term 'coyote', meaning professional service providers who help migrants to cross the border (2004). These *coyotes* appear to 'make sure that disasters do not befall the migrants they transport' (Spencer, 2004:

310). Migrants usually choose *coyotes* who have already proven that they are capable of organising a trip by safely transporting other family or community members (*ibid*: 311). Migrants perceive their know-how and value it as a guarantee for the success of the operation.

One of the main reasons why human smugglers are presented as criminals in the media and the public debate is that they profit from those who use their services. The question is whether this should be considered a problem. As Castells and Portes (1989) argue, the migrant smuggler is an actor engaged in the informal economy, something that usually happens when state institutions fail to provide regulations. Other authors have similarly emphasised that human smuggling is a market and smugglers are economic actors filling a niche that governments cannot provide or regulate (Di Nicola and Musumeci, 2014; Zhang, 2008). Achilli (2018) takes this a step further in his analysis, arguing that smugglers are not driven solely by profit, but mainly by morality and religious duties, when they become involved in this illicit enterprise.

This type of smuggler appears to contradict the image of smugglers as cruel, rapacious criminals who knowingly send people to their death on the open seas that is propagated by the media and in the public and political debate. This discrepancy in the representation of human smuggler in public debate is persistent. Perhaps anti-smuggling officials are turning a blind eye to the narratives in the academic literature, or maybe the researchers are misinterpreting what they see and hear during their research. The only way to understand this discrepancy is to go to the field and communicate with the actors involved in human smuggling.

Human smuggling on Lesbos

I found the same discrepancy between positive and negative views on human smuggling during my fieldwork on Lesbos. During this period there were reports in the local media that several smugglers had been arrested. It was striking that these smugglers were not bringing migrants from Turkey to Lesbos, but had been trying to smuggle migrants from the island to the mainland or even back to Turkey on private boats or the ferry. One attempt, widely reported in the local media, involved a person who was arrested while trying to smuggle four migrants onto the ferry on his motorcycle

(Lesvosnews.net, 24 July, 2017). There were, however, no reports of human smuggling from Turkey to Lesbos, as there had been in previous years. In 2015-2017 human smuggling activities to Lesbos were frequently mentioned in local and social media and police reports. In this period this mainly involved the smuggling of migrants from Turkey to Lesbos.

During my fieldwork I could distinguish three types of human smuggling. Firstly, activities shifted from smuggling people from Turkey to Lesbos to smuggling them from the island to the Greek mainland. Migrants arriving on Lesbos became 'locked' there, as according to the Dublin regulation they have to be registered in the first EU country in which they arrive, which was Greece in this case. They had to apply for asylum there, even though their real destination was usually somewhere else in Europe. Those who did not want to apply for asylum on Lesbos tried to disappear into illegality (a difficult feat on an island) and escape to mainland Greece, from where they hoped to continue their journey to West Europe illegally on land.

Secondly, migrants who had already applied for asylum on Lesbos and realised that they had no chance of getting it, or who could no longer tolerate the long wait for an asylum decision, especially in view of the difficult conditions in the camps, tried to return to Turkey with the help of smugglers in order to look for other possibilities for reaching Europe. In principle, they could tell the authorities that they wanted to be voluntarily deported back to Turkey, but the deportation process (bureaucratic and physical preparations) could take a long time, which obviously they did not want to waste. Approaching smugglers to bring them back was a much swifter solution.

Last, but not least, there were the still regular arrivals of boats carrying migrants to Lesbos. The smugglers who had arranged their trip did not travel with them, remaining in Turkey and issuing instructions by phone or text. Usually their boats were found by Frontex, the Hellenic Coast Guard or activist ships (such as Sea Watch), who rescued them and brought them ashore.

On the basis of police and Frontex information and stories of migrants, activists and academic researchers (all personal communication in the summer of 2017), human smugglers on Lesbos could be divided into several categories.

The local police mainly mentioned *organised crime networks*, especially Turkish and Albanian smuggling groups. These groups appeared to be particularly active at the start of the 'refugee crisis'. According to police sources, these violent criminal smugglers had no compunction about sending migrants out to sea on defective rubber boats without providing them with usable life jackets. In the north of Lesbos, the 'cemetery' of thousands of abandoned life-jackets, many in children's sizes and some with visible warnings in different languages that they should not be used for swimming, still serves as a grim reminder of the dangers of the migrants' journey. Another cemetery, not far from the capital Mytilene, where the 'unknown' migrants are buried whose bodies were washed ashore on the island, is held up as proof by politicians and media for the involvement of ruthless criminal smuggling gangs who are only focused on their own profits and do not care for the safety of their clients.

A second category consisted of *immigrants from the same country of origin*, especially Syrians, Afghans and Iraqis, who were smuggling their compatriots and were usually mentioned by migrants themselves.

According to Frontex, local police and some migrants, the third category consists of so-called '*guest-smugglers*' who had come to Turkey from other countries, such Russia, Georgia and Bulgaria, and successfully obtained the contacts and know-how needed to conduct their operations.

Members of non-governmental organisations and other charity groups were also considered as human smugglers, mainly by the local police and residents. 'Occasional smugglers' included tourists and fishermen was also mentioned by police and local islanders.

All these categories can be considered as human smugglers if one applies the UN or EU definition. Some were involved in the entire process, from planning and organising to facilitating the journey. Others, such as 'guest-smugglers', were brokers, who connected migrants with 'real' smugglers, or arranged false documents. Others, such as members of NGOs or tourists or local islanders facilitated some parts of the journey by providing migrants with transport, food or shelter. The latter aspect of smuggling will be discussed later in this article as an example of crimes of solidarity.

Making profits on migrants?

According to a Hellenic Police respondent: "*In the last few years, a lot of smugglers were caught. There is still smuggling going on this summer, but less*". He attributed the decline in the arrests of smugglers to the fact that smuggling had become less profitable: "*the prices are very low now, between 300-500 euros*". He explained that the prices had gone down because there were fewer migrants who wanted to be smuggled than in the previous years, especially in 2015, when the crisis was at its peak and thousands of people arrived on the island.

The *modus operandi* had also changed: "*The smugglers do not accompany the refugees; they teach them how to operate a boat and send them out alone. The smugglers are mostly Turkish, but also Syrian, Moroccan and Algerian. The problem of fake documents is huge, especially for minors. The people who make them are their own nationals*".

This information about smugglers provided by a police officer, shows a typical business-oriented operation method: prices are fixed according to the demand and opportunities created by migration. The decrease in demand for their services means a decrease in the profits. This observation definitely contradicts the prevailing idea that human smugglers make huge profits on migrants, or that they force them to pay exorbitant prices.

It is not human smuggling, but migration in general that can create an opportunity for local people to earn sometimes large amounts of money. One example of such an opportunity is that of the taxi drivers on Lesbos in 2015, when thousands of migrants who had landed on the north of the island needed transport to the south-east port of Mytilene in order to continue their journey. The local authorities refused to arrange bus services for the newcomers and this provided the taxi drivers with a golden opportunity to charge excessive rates (around 300-400 euros) for a 70 km trip. In 2015-16, the price of daily goods and services, such as food, drinks, using the toilet or charging your telephone battery was hiked up by local restaurant owners and ordinary islanders, who saw an opportunity to earn money from the daily needs of newly arrived migrants. They, however, were not viewed as human smugglers: they were just trying to make a bit out of these migrants. The latter were victims of a rip off by locals, not by some bad ruthless smuggler as the policy papers depict.

The good smuggler?

All of my migrant respondents told me that they had used the services of smugglers and were convinced that they would not have been able to reach Europe without them. The relationship between smugglers and migrants was primarily based on a financial agreement, but often it involved more than just money. One respondent told me that his smuggler had tried to transport him four times: three times the boat had been caught by the Turkish Coast Guard and returned to the Turkish shore. The smuggler never asked for more money, even when the boats were confiscated each time they were caught and he actually lost money on the venture. Instead he kept trying to smuggle the migrants until he succeeded. According to my respondent: "*he promised to bring me to Greece and he kept his promise*". According to another respondent, his smuggler knew that he could not afford to pay him much, so he agreed to smuggle him for less money than the others and his two young children for free.

Another migrant trusted one specific smuggler because of the positive experiences his brother and his family had had with him earlier that month. Successes serve as a positive advertisement and personal recommendations by family members or friends can enhance a smuggler's reputation. This smuggler was careful and delayed the boat's departure several times because of bad weather conditions.

In these stories, the smuggler came across not as a callous money-making machine but as a helpful and understanding person, who was considerate of individual problems and committed to bringing people to the next stop of their destination.

I also heard several times that smugglers helped migrants to decide on a better destination for their customers. When stories about the overcrowded camps on Lesbos started to dominate media headlines, smugglers advised migrants to travel to other islands, such as Kos or Samos. One respondent told me that his smuggler advised him to travel to Chios as there were fewer migrants there, meaning shorter waiting times for the asylum decision. When my respondent refused because he wanted to reunite with his wife and children on Lesbos, the smuggler sent him there. According to my respondent, the smuggler "*was thinking what would be better for me, but I was the one who decided where to go, and he did what I asked*". This example at least is at odds with the stereotype of victimized migrants who have no 'agency' and are manipulated by smugglers.

Human smuggling out of solidarity

Although facilitating irregular migration is not included in the definition of human smuggling, it is often associated with it. Article 1 of the 'Facilitators Package', composed of Directive 2002/90/EC, establishes a common definition of the offence of facilitating unauthorized entry, transit and residence, as does Framework Decision 2002/946/JHA on the strengthening of the penal framework to prevent the facilitation of unauthorised entry, transit and residence (European Commission, 2015). Although no financial profit is mentioned in this legislation, it includes a so-called '*délit de solidarité*'. Many Europeans have been accused of this delict during the migrant crisis, according to the media reports.

Rozakou (2016) described how people were arrested on Lesbos for assisting migrants. The most dramatic case was in January 2016, when the Greek police pressed charges carrying prison sentences of up to 10 years against a group of Spanish lifeguards for towing a stranded dinghy with 51 refugees on it near Lesbos (*Ekathimerini.com*, January 14, 2016).

According to local police officers, several NGOs intended in recent years to facilitate the smuggling of migrants to Lesbos and there was evidence of contact between smugglers and NGOs, whereby the latter were given the precise location of the boats and other information so that they could meet migrants before the Greek Coast Guard found them. This was denied by my respondents from NGOs, who argued that they had no links with smugglers and were "operating only out of humanitarian purposes". The NGO members claimed that these accusations are part of a political campaign aimed at getting rid of NGOs on the island. Supposedly, NGOs are no longer needed as the 'refuge crisis' officially came to an end in March 2016 when the EU-Turkish agreement was signed and the authorities assumed control of migrants on the Aegean islands. In 2016-2017 various NGOs in other countries were accused in the media of cooperating with criminal human smuggling networks. Members of *Médecins Sans Frontières,* for example, were accused by Frontex of colluding with criminals and being "responsible for more deaths at sea" (Sigona, 2017).

Most of my respondents were not aware that they were committing a crime by helping migrants; they had never heard of these EU laws and they could not identify themselves with criminal human smugglers and members of organised crime who harm their victims or exploit them for profit.

Both international volunteers helping migrants on Lesbos and local people giving migrants food and dry clothes were faced with a dilemma as their desire to help the needy was in direct contravention of their duty to obey the law, which forbade any such assistance. As a local resident explained to me:

> "These poor people need my help, and I want to help, but my government prohibits me from doing this. What shall I do: follow my heart or follow my brain, because I don't want to go to prison?"

Human smuggling reconsidered

When there is such a huge discrepancy between official reports and accounts given by respondents in different studies on smuggling, including the present one, the effect of criminalising human smuggling in order to combat 'organised crime' must be doubted. It can harm individuals who facilitate illicit travel, and sometimes the punishments may seem highly disproportionate (Weber and Grewcock, 2012). Continuing to consider human smuggling as a crime cannot solve the more important problems of the recent migration. Human smugglers, labelled as criminals, have become scapegoats for inefficient migration policies around the world. It is they who are blamed for all the misery at sea, not the EU officials who are failing to look for root causes and solutions in the migrants' countries of origin and who are neither willing nor able to give them a decent reception in Europe. However, as many empirical studies have shown, 'cracking down on smugglers' does not deter migrants from trying to reach Europe. Human smuggling is a response to the increase in border controls and restrictive legislation. In the recent crisis in migration policies in the EU when hundreds of thousands of people were fleeing war, ethnic conflict or economic misery, human smuggling was unavoidable. Humanitarian assistance is also an old and unavoidable phenomenon, as there have always been people prepared to break the law in order to save the lives of others.

The criminalisation of both human smuggling and facilitating irregular migration must therefore be reconsidered. Empirical research from all over the world has revealed plenty of negative consequences of such criminalisation.

The idea of reconsidering human smuggling as a criminal activity is not new. Smuggling is already being discussed in academic literature as a 'travel business' with 'service providers' (Zhang, 2007), and as a transnational service industry' (Bilger, Hofmann, and Jandl, 2006) with specific tasks assigned to 'brokers', 'fixers', or 'pushers' (Berg and Tamagno, 2013; Gammeltoft-Hansen and Sorensen, 2013; Lucht, 2013). This brokerage can be viewed as a business with customers to "shape transactions between migrants and smugglers in ways that are highly pronounced in travel and transit" (Ahmad, 2011, p. 7).

Regulation and acceptance of the historical fact that people have always been moving from one place to another in order to escape misery, be it political, social or economic and to search for better perspectives and opportunities could provide a real alternative to the failing struggle against alleged 'organised networks' of human smugglers. The prevailing stereotypes of cruel and greedy criminals sending their victims to their deaths continues to persist: it is such a convenient and politically accepted concept in policy papers, certainly if combined with 'organised crime'. The tragic media images of accidents at sea, the governmental reports and often exaggerated estimations of harm and victims in addition to the statements issued by moral entrepreneurs who have never talked to either smugglers or migrants make it more difficult for policy-makers to open their mind and search for better definitions and legislation for this phenomenon.

At the beginning of this chapter, I asked why people use the services of criminals. During my fieldwork I realised that human smugglers to Lesbos were not considered as criminals, at least not by the migrants who had been smuggled. On the contrary, the smugglers were seen as important helpers who had made it possible for them to fulfil their dream of reaching Europe. I also realised that there are many types of smugglers, ranging from the stereotypical images of organised criminals, as they are perceived by the police, to friends, compatriots, and even members of NGOs. Generalising these types and groups does not help us to understand or respond to this phenomenon. Political decision making must never rest upon abstract, imprecise knowledge. Empirical research, therefore, is vital for decision makers. Human smuggling (including crimes of solidarity) should be regulated, de-criminalised and recognised as an important factor facilitating migration.

References

Achilli, L., The "good" smuggler: The ethics and morals of human smuggling among Syrians. In: *Migrant smuggling as a collective strategy and insurance policy: views from the margins.* The ANNALS of the American Academy of Political and Social Science, 2018, 676 (1), p. 77-97.

Ahmad, A.N., *Masculinity, Sexuality and Illegal Migration: Human Smuggling from Pakistan to Europe*. Farnham, UK and Burlington, VT: Ashgate, 2011.

Aloyo, E. and E. Cusumano, Morally evaluating human smuggling: the case of migration to Europe, in: *Critical Review of International Social and Political Philosophy*, 2018, on: www.tandfonline.com/doi/full/10.1080/13698230.2018.1525118

Andreas, P., The transformation of migrant smuggling across the US-Mexican border. In D. Kyle and R. Koslowski (eds.) *Global human smuggling. comparative perspectives*. Baltimore: The John Hopkins University Press, pp.107-25, 2011.

Aronowitz, A., Smuggling and trafficking in human beings: the phenomenon, the markets that drive it and the organisations that promote it. *European Journal on Criminal Policy and Research*, 2001, vol. 9, No. 2.

Baird, Th., *Human smuggling in the Eastern Mediterranean*. London: Routledge, 2016.

Bauman, Z., *Modernity and the Holocaust.* Ithaca: Cornell University Press, 2000.

Bilecen, B., *Human smuggling networks operating between Middle East and the European Union: evidence from Iranian, Iraqi and Afghani migrants in the Netherlands*. COMCAD Working Paper No. 62. Bielefeld: Centre on Migration, Citizenship and Development, 2009.

European Commission, *Communication from the commission to the European Parliament, the Council, the European Economic and Social Committee and the Committee of the regions EU Action Plan against migrant smuggling (2015 - 2020),* Brussels, 27.5.2015 COM(2015).

Human Rights Watch Dispatches, J. Sunderland, 'A heinous act, more deaths on the high seas' (September 16), 2014 on: https://www.hrw.org/news/2014/09/16/dispatches-heinous-act-more-deaths-high-seas.

Kaizen, J. and W. Nonnema, Irregular migration in Belgium and organised crime: an overview. *International Migration*, 2007, vol. 45, no. 2.

Kleemans, E. and M. Smit, Human smuggling, human trafficking, and the exploitation of sex industry. In L. Paoli, (ed.) *The Oxford Handbook of Organised Crime*, Oxford: Oxford University Press, pp. 381- 401, 2014.

Kyle, D. and R. Koslowski (eds.), *Global human smuggling. comparative perspectives*. Baltimore: The John Hopkins University Press, 2011.

Kyle, D. and M. Scarcelli, Migrant smuggling and the violence question: evolving illicit migration markets for Cuban and Haitian refugees. *Crime, Law and Social Change*, 2009, vol. 52, No. 3.

Lintner, B., Illegal aliens smuggling to and through Southeast Asia's Golden Triangle. In: Nyiri. P and I. Rostislavovich (eds.) *Globalizing Chinese Migration: Trends in Europe and Asia*, Aldershot, Hampshire: Ashgate, 2002.

Maher, S., Out of the West Africa: Human smuggling as a social enterprise. In: S. Zhang, G. Sanchez and L. Achilli (eds.) *Migrant smuggling as a collective strategy and insurance policy: views from the margins.* The ANNALS of the American Academy of Political and Social Science, 2018, 676 (1), pp. 36-56.

Majid, N., Community dimensions of smuggling: the case of Afghanistan and Somalia. In: S. Zhang, G. Sanchez and L. Achilli (eds.) *Migrant smuggling as a collective strategy and insurance policy: views from the margins.* The ANNALS of the American Academy of Political and Social Science, 2018, 676 (1), pp. 97-113.

Marx, E., *The Social Context of violent Behaviour. A Social Anthropological Study in an Israeli Immigrant Town*. London, Henley and Boston: Routledge & Kegan Paul, 1976.

Mengiste, T.A., Refugee protections from below: Smuggling in the Eritrea-Ethiopia context. In: S. Zhang, G. Sanchez and L. Achilli (eds.) *Migrant smuggling as a collective strategy and insurance policy: views from the margins,* The ANNALS of the American Academy of Political and Social Science, 2018, 676 (1), pp. 57-76.

Narli, N., Human trafficking and smuggling: the process, the actors and the victim profile. In N. Narli, (ed.) *Trafficking in persons in South East Europe—a threat to human security*, Vienna: National Defence Academy; Istanbul, Center for Strategic Research, 2006

Paoli, L. (ed.), *The Oxford Handbook of Organised Crime.* Oxford: Oxford University Press, 2014.

Rozakou, K., Crafting the volunteer: volunteer associations and the reformation of sociality. *Journal of Modern Greek Studies*, 2016, vol. 34, no.1, pp. 79-102.

Saha, K.C. Smuggling of Indian citizens: preliminary findings. *Journal of Immigrant and Refugee Studies*, 2007, vol. 5, No. 1.

Sanchez, G.. *Human smuggling and border crossings*. London: Routledge, 2015.

Schloenhardt, A., *Organised crime and migrant smuggling: Australia and the Asia-Pacific,* Research and public policy series, No. 44. Canberra: Australian Institute of Criminology, 2002, on: www.aic.gov.au/en/publications/current%20series/rpp/41-60/

Sciopi, O. and A. Ionescu, Migrants' smuggling is knocking at the danube's door. Threats at the Romanian state border. *Journal of Danubian Studies and Research*, 2016, vol. 5. No.2, pp. 320-332.

Siegel, D., Crimes of solidarity in times of a migrant crisis. In D. Siegel and V. Nagy (eds.), *The migration crisis? Criminalization, security and survival.* The Hague: Eleven International Publishing, pp. 243-264, 2018.

Siegel, D., *Dynamics of Solidarity. Consequences of the 'refugee crisis' on Lesbos*, The Hague: Eleven International Publishing, 2019.

Siegel, D. and V. Nagy (eds.), *The Migration Crisis? Criminalization, security and survival.* The Hague: Eleven International Publishing, 2018.

Sigona, N., NGO's under attack for saving too many lives in the Mediterranean. *The Conversation,* March 29, 2017.

Spener, D., Mexican migrant-smuggling: a cross-border cottage industry. *Journal of International Migration and Integration / Revue de*

l'intégration et de la migration international, 2004, Vol. 5 (3), pp. 295-320.
Spener, D., Global Apartheid, *Coyotaje,* and the Discourse of Clandestine Migration: Distinction between Personal, Structural and Cultural Violence. In: Kyle, D. and R. Koslowski (eds.), *Global Human Smuggling. Comparative Perspectives*. Baltimore: The John Hopkins University Press, pp. 157-185, 2011.
Tazzioli, M., Border displacements. Challenging the politics of rescue between Mare Nostrum and Triton. *Migration Studies*, 2016, 4(1), pp. 1–19.
UNODC, *Transnational crime. Human smuggling*, 2019, on: https://www.unodc.org/toc/en/crimes/migrant-smuggling.html
U.S. State Department, *Human trafficking and human smuggling. Understanding the difference*, Washington, DC: Office to Monitor and Combat Trafficking in Persons, U.S. State Department, 2017.
Walser, R., J. Baker McNeill, J. Zuckerman, The human tragedy of illegal immigration: greater efforts needed to combat smuggling and violence. *Backgrounder,* 2011, No. 2568 June 22, pp. 1-18.
Zhang, S., *Smuggling and trafficking in human beings: All roads lead to America*. Westport, CT: Praeger, 2007.
Zhang, S., G. Sanchez and L. Achilli (eds.). *Migrant smuggling as a collective strategy and insurance policy: views from the margins.* The Annals of the American Academy of Political and Social Science, 2018, 676 (1).

Market dynamics of harm and labour exploitation

Jonathan Davies[1]

Introduction

During the last twenty years, there has been a significant increase in the attention given to issues associated with 'modern slavery', human trafficking and forced labour (Anderson, 2015; FRA, 2015; Gadd and Broad, 2018). A range of public, political, and academic attention (within and beyond criminology) has led to significant developments of the ways in which these issues are conceptualised and enforced against (GLA, 2015; HM Government, 2015). However, the anti-trafficking framework tends to consist of the so-called '3Ps' – prevention, protection and prosecution, referring to the need to address root causes, improve victim protection, and to hold perpetrators criminally accountable (Ollus, 2015). While this emphasis has arguably improved overall awareness of the issues and led to some policy improvements, it tends to oversimplify the problems by blaming individuals as the key drivers of exploitation (LeBaron *et al.*, 2015). This is a concern because it neglects the role of the state as being responsible for facilitating exploitation through its regulation of labour markets, border controls, immigration policy, and social policy more widely – rather than simply being a neutral or benign actor that 'rescues' victims from exploitation (LeBaron, 2015).

The purpose of this chapter is to move beyond the traditional anti-trafficking agenda, and instead pay greater emphasis to the role of legitimate businesses, supply chains and markets, as well as the way they are regulated, thereby facilitating exploitation and harm. In doing so, it adopts a criminological lens of harm, which asserts that a large number of actions and omissions associated with corporations are neither criminalised nor

1 Research Fellow, Faculty of Law, Tel Aviv University, Israel.

prosecuted. From a worker perspective, this lack of accountability does not make the harm they experience any less important. This chapter contains a number of sections in order to elaborate on the role of businesses and markets, along with the harm that can emerge from them. First, an outline of harm in relation to criminology is provided. Second, key issues related to human trafficking are explored. Third, some underlying explanations for harmful labour practices are signposted, including the role of businesses, supply chains, and the regulatory context. It seeks to address the key question of 'how do some supply chains facilitate harmful labour practices?', drawing on supporting examples where appropriate. The intention here is not to provide a full account of these challenges, but to illustrate recent key developments within the topic areas.

Crime and harm in the workplace

When considering the workplace, workers are subject to a number of vulnerabilities that may result in labour exploitation or harm. While this chapter focuses primarily on workers, a broader range of harms against businesses, employers, consumers, animals, and the environment may emerge from deviant actions within the workplace. These wider concerns are well grounded in previous work on corporate, organisational and white-collar crime, such as food fraud (Lord *et al.*, 2017), toxic oil spills (Slapper and Tombs, 1999), and the Libor scandal (van Erp *et al.*, 2015). The purpose of this section is to examine the notions of crime and harm, especially with regards to actions or omissions that have consequences in the workplace.

The terms 'labour exploitation' and 'harm' are complex and require some unpacking for the purposes of this discussion. While there is no universally accepted definition of labour exploitation, 'severe exploitation' is typically understood as criminalised actions or processes, including human trafficking and forced labour (FRA, 2015) – increasingly referred to as modern slavery. Other forms of non-criminalised exploitation such as underpayment or unfair dismissal may be covered by regulatory or civil law – sometimes referred to as 'labour abuse' or routine exploitation (Davies, 2018; France, 2016). If taking a broader sociological or even a Marxist view, exploitation can be understood as occurring beyond the scope of criminal and civil law – in the absence of formal sanctions (Scott, 2017).

Terms such as 'lawful but awful' and '3D' (dirty, difficult, dangerous) work are used to refer to issues such as long working hours in low-paid work, physical exhaustion, and degrading treatment by employers. These practices are more controversial since they arguably occur in most occupations in some form, and lack any formal legal sanction. Rather than trying to resolve the tension between these competing definitions, this chapter acknowledges the spectrum of exploitation alluded to above, but refers to a broader criminological perspective of 'harm' as a means to frame the discussion.

Like labour exploitation, harm is a problematic concept. While harm is a well-grounded subject in disciplines such as law and philosophy, it has only recently gained significant attention within criminology (Hillyard *et al.*, 2004; Paoli and Greenfield, 2015; Pemberton, 2015). Greenfield and Paoli (2013: 864) define harm as 'breaches of stakeholders' legitimate interests', referring to functional (physical and psychological), material, reputational, and privacy harms. As part of their typology, harm can (i) range from minor, rare, and momentary occurrences to severe, frequent, and long-lasting consequences; (ii) affect individuals, private and public sector entities, as well as the environment (physical and social) (Greenfield and Paoli, 2013).

Alternatively, some critical criminologists assert that criminology is limited when addressing 'harm' that is not state defined, *i.e.* harm that frequently occurs beyond the scope of criminal justice systems and formal sanctions, such as air pollution and poverty. They argue that 'social harm' or 'zemiology'[2] should be a discipline in its own right in order to study a wider range of harms – therefore beyond the confines of criminology (Pemberton, 2015). While non-criminalised responses to certain incidents (*e.g.* high levels of air pollution, poor health and safety practices) may be intended to minimise the number of new criminal-legal court cases, the social harm perspective intends to make such cases the focal point of analysis, arguing that it is precisely these issues that risk being overlooked by society, despite the role that corporations and states have in facilitating them. For instance, an employer who violates safety standards that results in a workplace death or severe injury may be regarded by employers and

2 Zemiology originates from the Greek word 'zēmía', meaning harm.

the wider public as an 'accident' whereby 'lessons need to be learned', rather than a criminal action deserving guilt and punishment.

The purpose of this chapter is not to resolve these tensions between crime and harm – indeed, it is recognised here that such a resolution is highly unlikely regardless of how much attention is paid to them. The definition adopted for the purposes of this chapter is based on Greenfield and Paoli's (2013) work, who as noted above, define harm as breaches of stakeholders' legitimate interests. Stakeholders, according to their definition, may consist of individuals, businesses, other institutions, as well as the physical and social environment (Greenfield and Paoli, 2013). This chapter does not argue for 'abandoning' criminology, albeit it recognises the value of a social harm approach in drawing attention to wrongdoing that frequently occurs.

Having problematised the theoretical notion of harm, it is important to consider how this may be applied to the context of the workplace. In using Greenfield and Paoli's (2013) framework of harm, it is possible to consider harm to individuals, private and public sector entities, as well as the environment (physical and social). Although this chapter does not conduct a systematic harm 'assessment' in line with Greenfield and Paoli's research due to the lack of empirical evidence, harms can be identified from existing research and developments from the harm agenda. Here, harms affecting workers, businesses, the government, and physical environment are discussed. This discussion is certainly not exhaustive, but provides some illustrative examples of how different groups with potentially competing interests can be harmed.

Workers are subject to numerous harms within the workplace, including labour exploitation and forms of 'modern slavery' (discussed further in the next section), health and safety problems, and in extreme cases, death. Tombs and Whyte (2007) assert that the blame for workplace injuries is frequently placed on workers, or presented as unavoidable accidents; whereas in many cases, blame arguably lies with employers and are preventable incidents. The result is that responsibility tends to be pinned on individual workers, rather than being seen as an organisational problem where employers are not ensuring appropriate safety standards. Regulatory bodies, while they tend to build up specific expertise, they may lack the resources and remit to effectively hold businesses accountable for preventing and reacting to workplace injuries – at least in the UK context. For instance, the Gangmasters and Labour Abuse Authority (GLAA) can only licence labour providers in the agri-food sector, which excludes other vulnerable sectors such as construction and social care.

An issue that is increasingly on the public agenda is that of sexual harassment in the workplace, with UK estimates suggesting that approximately 40% of women are affected by unwanted sexual advances while at work (House of Commons, 2018: 7). This can be particularly problematic if the advances are from senior colleagues who have the authority to dismiss or promote workers, or at least make their working lives more difficult for them. The issues of workplace injuries and sexual harassment, then, both suggest forms of physical and psychological harm to individuals in line with Greenfield and Paoli's definition.

Shifts from modern slavery to labour exploitation

The issues of labour exploitation and 'modern slavery' have received a significant increase in attention during the last 20 years, especially since the UN Convention against Transnational Organised Crime (UNTOC) was adopted. The UNTOC provides a contemporary framework for member states who ratify it to develop their responses to human trafficking. Although there were initiatives and international agreements pre-dating UNTOC, such as the 1926 Slavery Convention, UNTOC represented a shift in emphasis from regarding human trafficking as solely a human rights issue, towards the sphere of transnational organised crime. In recent years, legislation has increased on the issues of human trafficking and 'modern slavery', including the California Transparency in Supply Chains Act of 2012, the UK's Modern Slavery Act 2015, as well as an increasing number of specialist NGOs, charities and other interest groups. However, there are a number of concerns with regards to the 'modern slavery' agenda, both in definitional scope and with the practical issues of implementation and responses.

Modern slavery is commonly accepted as an umbrella term for severe and (usually) criminalised forms of sexual and/or labour exploitation, including human trafficking, forced labour, and domestic servitude (FRA, 2015; GLA, 2015). Most national and supranational governments have integrated these offences into their domestic criminal-legal codes, either as stand-alone offences, or as part of broader legislation. However, modern slavery represents just the 'tip of the iceberg' of the exploitation continuum, since not all manifestations experienced in the workplace count as 'slavery', or are even severe enough to be subject to criminal prosecution. There are numerous practices which do not meet such high thresholds, but which could still be considered as exploitative in some form. It is here where definitional (and legal) problems of 'labour exploitation' begin to emerge: labour exploitation has no universally agreed definition, either at the national or international level. While 'modern slavery' also has no internationally agreed definition, its subsets of human trafficking and forced labour (among others) tend to be referred to as severe exploitation (FRA, 2015).

As a means to find some balance between the narrowly defined forms of severe exploitation on the one extreme, and the Marxist 'omnipresence' of exploitation on the other, Scott (2017) has advanced a definition of exploitation that consists of excessive workplace 'control'. While acknowledging that some form of workplace control is necessary and helpful to an extent, he argues that when this becomes excessive, labour exploitation and so harmful consequences result. 'Excessive' control is categorised into three key areas – direct, indirect, and exogenous controls, broadly referring to interpersonal (inter)actions, processes occurring at the organisational level, and dynamics of societal factors respectively (Scott, 2017). These controls are now unpacked further for the sake of clarity.

Direct controls, which could otherwise be loosely referred to as 'micro' factors, refer to individual interactions in the workplace, primarily between employers, managers and employees, that could facilitate harm. For instance, airline cabin crews have reported concerns that their employers have pressured them into working longer hours than stipulated in their contracts without appropriate pay to compensate, as well as charging recruits for their uniforms (Boyle et al., 2017). These practices are also likely to be found in manual, low-wage work such as agriculture, food processing, and construction, due to the fast-moving nature of these industries (EHRC, 2010).

Indirect controls, alternatively viewed as the 'meso' level factors, refer primarily to processes that occur at the organisational level, including workplace culture and decision-making procedures. There is a significant literature that discusses how decisions are made within organisations (*e.g.*

Braithwaite, 2017; Gobert, 1994; Passas, 2005), many of which can have adverse consequences on workers. On the one hand, individual managers or employers may pursue rogue actions that are outside the scope of the law – or at the very least, actions that are morally 'dubious'. On the other, structures within an organisation or even the entire industry may shape individual perceptions and actions. Individual employees may consider actions that others in similar positions have taken in order to inform their own decisions (Gobert and Punch, 2003). For example, new businesses in the UK construction sector continue to encourage workers to register as self-employed, which is a widespread industry practice, despite this being linked to harmful labour practices such as underpayment (FLEX, 2018).

Exogenous or 'macro' controls refer to broader societal factors associated with markets, as well as political, economic, and legal structures, including immigration and welfare regimes. In the case of undocumented migrant workers, for example, it is possible that strict border controls and a lack of opportunities to enter a destination country by legal means resulted in them seeking entry via irregular means. A consequence of this irregularity is that they have no official documentation, which encourages them to remain 'under the radar' by working without a contract, being paid in cash, and potentially relying on others for help with accommodation – all of which make workers more vulnerable to exploitation and harm. Other examples of exogenous controls may refer to the dynamics of product and labour supply chains/networks, which are discussed in the next section.

While Scott's (2017) definition of labour exploitation begins to move beyond the confines of the legal system. This is done in the spirit of the social harm agenda discussed in the previous section, which allows criminologists to examine harms that are not part of criminal law state definitions as represented through legal interventions. The risk of pursuing such a loose 'harm' agenda that moves beyond the confines of formal sanctions is that advocates are accused of 'moralising' or at the very least, adopting a less scientific approach (Tappan, 1947). Nevertheless, a harm approach provides the opportunity for criminology to remain relevant in 'grey areas' where demarcations between legal, illegal and criminal actions are not clear-cut, amid accusations that it is limited when addressing 'non-criminal' harms (Scott, 2017).

As part of this emphasis on the full spectrum of exploitation, there are a number of limitations with the modern slavery agenda which risk overlooking a number of key factors. For instance, it is usually only the most severe, 'newsworthy' and 'outrageous' cases of exploitation that are portrayed in the media, rather than the more mundane, repetitive, and less severe exploitation.

There are a number of caveats to this, since public bodies and the media have recently been paying greater attention to standard business practices which may be harmful to workers, including the 'gig economy' and zero hours contracts, which are both associated with insecure, flexible work (Taylor, 2017).

It is common to identify individuals who are responsible for patterns of criminal and harmful behaviour. In cases of modern slavery and labour exploitation, it may be relatively straightforward to identify individual perpetrators, especially in the more sensationalist cases. As part of this, there is a particular emphasis on 'rescuing' victims from these malicious perpetrators, thereby potentially generating an incomplete depiction of the problem. Instead, the notion of 'victims, villains, and rescuers' is easy to understand and has popular appeal (Anderson, 2015), whereby a malicious perpetrator causes harm to an innocent (female/child) victim; hence, the state intervenes in order to rescue the victim and punish the perpetrator. This is not to deny that there are malicious individuals who deliberately set out to exploit people for the sake of financial gain. However, such discourse has potentially damaging consequences for the way in which exploitation and its resulting harm is addressed. For instance, O'Connell Davidson (2005: 420) asserts that the archetypal victim of human trafficking is depicted as a woman or girl (child) who is being sexually exploited by an individual with links to organised crime. In the 2000s especially, such a discourse on 'ideal victims' limited the attention on other abuses such as labour exploitation and the role of legitimate actors.

There are well-grounded reasons that pinning the blame on a small number of individuals for heinous crimes diverts attention from broader societal factors, including immigration and border controls, supply chains, and the political-legal context (LeBaron, 2015; Tombs and Whyte, 2015). In other words, while the state may indeed 'rescue' some victims from severe exploitation, it is arguably contributing to the underpinning social conditions that lead to exploitation in the first place, through its immigration controls and fragmented labour market regulation. For example, the UK has 13 different regulatory bodies that deal with different aspects of labour market enforcement, which is confusing for workers (Citizens Advice, 2017). In severe instances, once victims have been officially recognised as victims of trafficking (through the National Referral Mechanism in the UK, for instance), the level of support provided to victims has a mixed track record (Home Office, 2014), to the extent that 're-trafficking'is a significant concern in the event of limited support for victims. Re-trafficking refers to someone who escapes, is 'rescued', or otherwise detaches themselves from the trafficking process, and ends up in similar vulnerable positions that expose them to the same process a second time, frequently due to a lack of support from the destination country or their country of origin (Jobe, 2010). It is on this basis that researchers across disciplines have paid a strong level of attention to the role of businesses, supply chains and their oversight (*e.g.* Barrientos, 2013; EHRC, 2010; Potter and Hamilton, 2014) in order to develop more nuanced depictions of the problem.

The role of businesses, supply chains and markets

As noted in the previous section, focusing exclusively on individual perpetrators may be helpful in the most extreme cases of labour exploitation where individuals are more easily identified. However, shifting the focus onto the role of businesses, their supply chains, and the otherwise legitimate markets in which they operate, arguably provide a more comprehensive explanation for how exploitation and harm occurs. Supply chains can be defined as a system of suppliers, manufacturers, distributors, buyers (retailers) and customers, where materials feed forward from suppliers to customers, and demand feeds back from customers and buyers (Stevens, 1989). In the agri-food industry, such an example can be seen with how growers purchase tomato seeds, before, planting, growing, and eventually picking the tomatoes. The products are then packed, transported to wholesalers or buyers, before consumers purchase them from supermarkets, smaller grocers, or restaurants *etc.*

However, in the case of food production, Croall (2012) argues that the economic context of the global food system is criminogenic, since it encourages a culture where profits are prioritised to the extent that deviant corporate behaviour is normalised. For instance, the research of Lord *et al.* (2017) found in the drinks industry that internal market actors played a key role in facilitating the tampering of labels (i.e. 'best before' dates), rather than being an exclusive problem of external criminal actors. Similarly, the 2017 Grenfell Tower incident in London, where 72 people died in a fire that engulfed the building, highlighted serious concerns regarding corporations prioritising profit over appropriate building safety standards (BBC News, 2018). According to Ruhs and Anderson (2010), workers, far from being passive victims, may sometimes benefit from deviant corporate practices by colluding with employers. Their research found that migrant workers who were legally resident in the UK colluded with employers to exceed employment restrictions associated with their immigration status in order to earn more money, whereby the lack of oversight in the supply chain helped to facilitate this (Ruhs and Anderson, 2010).

By focusing on broader market and business factors, rather than just criminality, the issues under consideration begin to move beyond the traditional confines of criminology and the criminal justice system, which integrates well with a harm-based approach in order to more fully understand how and why labour exploitation occurs. This section begins by considering some key issues in relation to increasingly standard business practices, including precarious work and subcontracting, while examining important economic sectors where these processes have resulted in harm, including agriculture, food production, education, healthcare, and hand car washes.

Corporations and organisations more broadly have frequently been identified as hotspots for deviant and criminal activity by critical criminologists (*e.g.* Box, 1984; Gobert and Punch, 2003; Tombs and Whyte, 2015). According to this body of work, organisations provide the motivation, the opportunity, and the means for deviant behaviour that can harm employees, the interests of the organisation, consumers, the public, as well as the environment. This is frequently conceptualised and applied to case studies within the areas of organised crime, state-corporate crime, white-collar crime, and green criminology (Gray and Hinch, 2018; Paoli, 2014). Incidents ranging from oil spills, faulty car manufacturing, food production, consumer fraud, air pollution, and more recently, harm to non-human animals, have all been important focal points in these spheres of interest. For example, the impacts of climate change on farming and sustainable production have recently been a subject of focus for researchers (e.g. White and Yeates, 2018). In terms of labour conditions, there have been important developments, especially since the 1970s, that have shaped increasingly common workplace practices.

Many economic sectors, especially in Europe and North America, have been affected by various developments associated with neoliberalism. Neoliberalism is strongly associated with privatisation of industries, deregulation (or a lack of regulation), flexible working conditions, stricter immigration and welfare regimes (LeBaron, 2015), as well as a stronger emphasis on individual responsibility. Part of this process is sometimes referred to as Fordism and 'post-Fordism' (Melossi, 2003), whereby the former represented an era of mass industrial production, full employment, and stable work. The latter tends to represent post-industrial production that is in decline and fragmented across numerous countries, as well as precarious and flexible employment that does not guarantee a stable income or ability for workers to plan their lives in the long term.

Interlinked with these post-Fordist conditions is the rise of globalisation, where supply chains and networks have significantly expanded and become more complex (Barrientos, 2013). As part of this process, farmers and producers at the beginning of the chain, who are frequently (though not exclusively) in the Global South, have faced increasing price pressure and deterioration of profits due to the buying power of larger, multi-national corporations who buy their products for distribution and sale in the Global North (LeBaron et al., 2018). Such dynamics are particularly apparent in agriculture and food production, whereby farmers have seen a 'race to the bottom' in terms of wages and general working conditions (Scott, 2017) due to the bargaining power of global firms that dominate the industry who increasingly price out smaller scale producers.

While some multi-national corporations have developed strategies to tackle the issue of modern slavery and ethical initiatives (New, 2015), not only have these approaches been criticised as superficial, but large buyers such as retailers may be several steps away from where exploitation and harm occurs at the bottom-end of supply networks, therefore arguably do not fully understand the consequences of their decisions. For instance, decisions made at the top-end of supply networks may be made with the best economic intentions in mind for the business and shareholders, without regard to the impact that these decisions can have on workers who are frequently based in other countries and occupy low-wage positions. An example is the garment industry in Bangladesh, where the Rana Plaza collapsed in 2013 due to poor safety standards and a lack of oversight, killing 1,100 people and injuring 2,500 (CIOB, 2018: 8).

Despite some international bodies and movements, including the International Labour Organization (ILO) and the International Trade Union Confederation (ITUC) advocating improved working conditions across global supply chains/networks, these bodies have little formal authority. This remains largely with national states and regulatory frameworks, who have struggled to keep up with global developments in terms of their responses. Simply put, it is highly problematic for national governments to regulate global supply networks by themselves, due to the number of jurisdictions that products may pass through from production to consumer shelves. However, aside from a small number of supranational frameworks, such as the Council of Europe Convention on Trafficking, most states implement their own legislation in order to tackle labour abuse, which can vary widely between the confines of civil and criminal law. These regulatory concerns and forms of oversight are explored further in the next section.

Workplace and industrial relationships

Alongside the business and supply chain practices identified above, these have been accompanied by a gradual shift from collective organisation and bargaining to individual employment rights/contracts, in part due to the decline of labour movements since the late 1970s (Turner *et al.*, 2014). In the UK context, trade union membership has gradually declined from almost 14 million to little more than 6 million between the late 1970s and 2017 (BEIS, 2018). This has harmful impacts on workers, since they are less able to negotiate better working conditions as with individual employers. Thus, if workers are not part of trade union movements, which potentially serve as a bulwark against exploitative workplace practices, then workers are potentially less influential in improving their day-to-day work conditions. Such issues are prevalent in transport/taxi firms, as well as people who work for (food) delivery companies, and construction workers, who are routinely denied full working rights due to their self-employed status (FLEX, 2017).

Third, and partly as a consequence of reduced trade unionisation, the growth of 'atypical' or 'non-standard' employment has increased during the last decade (Hipp *et al.*, 2015). These concepts refer to work that is not full time, permanent, and not accompanied with various employment benefits such as sick pay, holiday pay, and pension plans. Non-standard employment, therefore, consists of flexible, part time, temporary or seasonal work, often with very few or no employment benefits, especially if workers are employed through agencies or other labour market intermediaries. Some workers are even pressured to register as self-employed as a way for firms to avoid paying appropriate levels of tax and/or providing employment benefits such as paid sick leave (FLEX, 2017). Figures suggest that in the UK, this 'precarious' work has increased to affect up to 10 million workers (GMB Union, 2017). Hence, atypical and non-standard work is becoming increasingly typical and standard within labour markets. Has a new proletariat emerged?

While businesses (and governments) may cite the benefits of flexible contracts, including many workers 'choosing' flexible work, and demonstrating that their companies can respond flexibly to ever changing market dynamics, such employment conditions can be associated with exploitation and harm. For example, workers who are employed on flexible contracts can be more easily dismissed than permanent employees, which potentially gives a greater degree of control to businesses, by denying workers rest breaks or toilet breaks, or 'encouraging' them to work harder and faster under the threat of dismissal should they fail to comply (EHRC, 2010). This issue integrates with the notion of labour subcontracting, whereby a business may hire workers from an agency on a temporary basis, in order to meet peaks in demand. Businesses can then easily discard these workers back into the 'reserve labour pool' once the peak of demand falls again, since they are not permanent employees of the business and so do not have to provide full employment benefits. Having said that, such issues are not new – van Duyne and Houtzager (2005: 165) point out that business sectors such as construction, garment manufacturing, and horticulture have frequently relied on cheap labour in order to manage the demands of volatile market conditions.

Fourth, there is a heavy reliance on migrant labour in key economic sectors. It should be stressed that, in the author's view, increased migrant labour is not the cause of increased modern slavery or exploitation; nor is exploitation the cause of further migrant labour. Arguably, the post-Fordist conditions that have been building up over recent decades have far more to do with the issue of labour exploitation and harm than increased migration flows to destination countries, since these conditions affect all workers, especially those who occupy low-wage positions, not just migrants. Therefore, while the issues of migration and labour exploitation are certainly connected and overlap: one does not cause the other.

Regulatory oversight of labour exploitation and harm

The question of how to tackle labour exploitation and modern slavery has long been a focal point for researchers, both in national and international contexts (LeBaron *et al.*, 2018; Ollus, 2016). Arguably, single intervention will serve as a 'silver bullet' for exploitative practices; this point seems to be especially valid when addressing severe exploitation and labour abuse (France, 2016). Traditionally, there has been a focus on the 'three Ps', referring to prevention, protection and prosecution, which has had mixed results in terms of addressing root causes, victim protection, and offender prosecution respectively. However, these approaches potentially neglect the role of the state and businesses in facilitating exploitation, through (lack of) regulation of markets and business activities. A discourse of 'rescuers, victims and villains' is the result, which was alluded to above as a critique of the anti-trafficking framework. More recently, however, there has been a greater emphasis on alternative forms of oversight, including state regulation, labour inspections/audits, corporate social responsibility, and labour or trade union movements (Scott, 2017; Tombs and Whyte, 2015). While all these issues cannot be covered with the rigour that they deserve here, a discussion of some key issues in terms of regulatory oversight is presented, with a particular focus on the UK context.

Within and beyond criminology, there is an assumption that regulation and enforcement against deviant behaviour is difficult to 'do well' (Braithwaite, 2008: 62) due to the number of actors and processes that may be involved in given situations. Ayres and Braithwaite (1992: 35) develop a regulatory 'pyramid' in order to conceptualise different responses to criminal activity, especially in relation to businesses.

At the bottom-end of this pyramid, oversight is based on persuasion and negotiation between regulators and businesses, whereby responses gradually get harsher towards the top-end, progressing from warning letters to civil and criminal law intervention. As Almond and van Erp (2018) argue, it is here that interdisciplinary problems are apparent, because criminology tends to emphasise only the 'top-end' of this regulatory pyramid by focusing on criminal law responses to deviance. On the other extreme, regulation tends to focus on the 'bottom-end' by emphasising meditation rather than punishment as the most constructive way forward. These points concerning the regulatory pyramid relate to harmful labour practices, since criminology tends to focus on 'top-down' criminal law and criminal justice system responses to the most severe harm, while potentially overlooking other forms of 'bottom-up' intervention. These tensions are outlined for the rest of this section.

Police and criminal law involvement are clearly necessary, and sometimes lacking, in many cases of exploitation. Even in relatively well-publicised cases that have identifiable individual perpetrators, this does not guarantee a criminal prosecution or conviction. A useful example in the UK is the DJ Houghton case, where a group of Lithuanian workers were transported to the UK and subject to severe forms of exploitation while working across different UK farms, including substandard accommodation, sleep deprivation, and withholding of payment (The Guardian, 2016). Although there was an initial police investigation into the employers (the Houghtons) and their associates, no criminal charges materialised, which resulted in the workers eventually securing financial redress through the civil courts, based on breaches of employment law. While the reason for the lack of a criminal charge was not explicit, there are suggestions that there was a lack of evidence to proceed, especially since one of the suspects could not be traced (The Guardian, 2016). In many respects his case gets to the heart of debate in terms of whether such events should be considered as 'crimes' in the absence of criminal convictions (Sutherland, 1941; Tappan, 1947). While it could be argued that the Lithuanian workers in this case were subject to exploitation and suffered harmful consequences, labelling the business owners as 'criminals' or their actions as 'criminal' is dubious, at least in legal terms.

Given the severity of the DJ Houghton case, this suggests that even where individual perpetrators seem to have a strong role in facilitating exploitation, securing a criminal conviction is far from a foregone conclusion. Proving intent and linking the accused to specific actions beyond reasonable doubt has long been an issue within the sphere of enforcing against corporate and white-collar crime (Gobert and Punch, 2003). Therefore, when considering the spectrum of exploitation and the 'grey areas' in between decent work and severe exploitation, involvement from the criminal justice system is even less likely (France, 2016). Instead, responses from civil law or specialist regulatory bodies may take a more prominent role, assuming that concerns of exploitation are reported in the first place. It is therefore possible that police and prosecution authorities are reluctant to press charges, especially if they lack the financial resources and legal expertise that are available to larger corporations.

Regulatory agencies are usually quasi-governmental bodies that have the authority and, especially over time, develop an area of specialism in order to investigate and potentially prosecute deviant behaviour within organisations and businesses. Given the problems associated with achieving criminal prosecutions, primarily around high thresholds of evidence and proving guilt beyond reasonable doubt, regulatory sanctions or investigations could be seen as an alternative, albeit less severe, form of accountability. However, such regulatory bodies may lack resources and 'teeth' in order to hold businesses accountable for harmful actions or omissions (Balch, 2012). This criticism is broadly directed at states who provide the remit and funding to these regulatory bodies, rather than taking care of the quality of work that such bodies do (although the former inevitably influences the latter to some extent).

Beyond the UK context, other countries present a mixed picture with regards to labour market enforcement. According to International Labour Organisation (ILO) recommendations, developed market economies (i.e. developed countries) should contain one labour inspector per 10.000 workers (Weil, 2008: 351). However, many European countries fall short of this standard, with the Netherlands and Poland having 0,5 and 0,8 inspectors per 10.000 workers respectively (FLEX, 2017: 24). Norway, in contrast, has 1,3 inspectors per 10.000 workers, which suggests significantly differing approaches towards labour market enforcement – although there are EU proposals to introduce a European Labour Authority in order to replace or reorganise existing regulatory structures (Kiss, 2018). These issues of inspection are problematic to examine in developing countries, some of which do not keep data on labour inspections or regulatory issues more widely (ILO, 2019).

Some countries have a more fragmented regulatory picture than others. The UK, for instance, does not have a single authority or 'labour inspectorate' that is responsible for regulating against exploitation. Instead, a number of fragmented organisations adopt specific roles, some of which may seem to overlap. The UK's Gangmasters and Labour Abuse Authority (GLAA) regulate labour market intermediaries, traditionally in the agricultural and food industries. The Employment Agency Standards Inspectorate (EASI) oversees employment agencies. In addition, the National Minimum Wage (NMW) team within HM Revenue & Customs oversee financial issues related to contracts, such as tax payments and National Insurance contributions. There have been some efforts to reconcile these numerous agencies, each of which have different priorities and functions, by developing a common strategy, as seen with the Director of Labour Market Enforcement (HM Government, 2018), who works closely with the GLAA, EASI, and the NMW team. Such a fragmented regulatory context therefore arguably has advantages and disadvantages, through the specialism gained from focusing on a limited number of areas, but at the expense of a unitary authority with a single set of goals.

Other countries have a less fragmented regulatory regime. Finland, for instance, has the Occupational Safety and Health Administration (OSHA), which is the main authority responsible for monitoring work conditions, as well as health and safety (EU-OSHA, 2019). Therefore, countries that contain a national unitary 'labour inspectorate' may find it easier to develop labour market enforcement strategies, rather than having multiple organisations who each have responsibility either for particular stages of labour use (*e.g.* recruitment), or for particular sectors (*e.g.* agri-food).

Given the limits of criminal law and state regulation, the notion of corporate social responsibility (CSR) as a form of 'self-regulation' has emerged as an alternative to the traditional binary 'regulator-regulated' relationship. Since organisations are in a prime position to facilitate but also resolve harmful workplace practices, there is a question of to what extent they should be permitted to regulate themselves, and what consequences this has on accountability when harm occurs. However, as is well discussed in other literature (New, 2015; Tombs and Whyte, 2015), the key counter-argument to CSR is that businesses will tend to prioritise profit over ethical social practices if they are unable to do both. Given that businesses are legally obligated to maximise profits for their shareholders (Fauset, 2006), this generates significant tension – and from a harm perspective, the material interests of shareholders could be harmed if the business chooses to pursue a more expensive social-ethics programme. However, the issue of labour exploitation is increasingly becoming a high-profile issue across many countries and sectors, which means that businesses risk significant reputational damage (and even criminal charges) if they are seen to neglect responsible practices in their supply chains (CIOB, 2018: 6). This is by no means a fool-proof protection, but represents one example of the important role that businesses have in addressing exploitation in their supply chains.

With the development of modern slavery and labour exploitation, and the role that businesses can play in facilitating these practices, a large number of businesses have been keen to emphasise the role that they can have in preventing such practices. Most large companies have some form of labour ethics statements that are publicly available, and more recently in the UK, now publish an annual 'transparency in supply chains' document, in line with the requirements of the Modern Slavery Act 2015. This annual publication sets out the measures businesses have taken to identify 'slavery' in their supply chains, and what they are doing to resolve the problem. However, such legislation applies only to larger businesses whose annual turnover exceeds £36 million which means that smaller companies are excluded from this remit, even though significant exploitation may occur in these smaller companies. In addition, the legislation focuses exclusively on severe forms of exploitation, including human trafficking and forced labour, while neglecting 'less severe' abuses that fall into the grey area between 'decent work' and violations of criminal-legal codes.

Aside from CSR, there are numerous labour movements and workers' rights advocates groups who aim to encourage workers to be more proactive in challenging workplace conditions through mutual support. As noted in the previous section, trade union membership has been in decline for some time (BEIS, 2018), and the efficacy of unions in the workplace has been questioned (Potter and Hamilton, 2014). The likelihood of increasing union membership in the context of flexible work practices and transient working populations remains a significant uncertainty in this area. However, the number of charities and similar groups in the UK has expanded in recent years – many of them adopt the 'anti-trafficking' agenda and tend to focus on improving victim's rights and protection. These 'bottom-up' approaches towards improving workplace conditions are fragmented, localised, and focus on particular groups, but in the long term, such community-based responses may be constructive ways forward as part of a broader package involving stronger state regulation in order to oversee organisations.

Conclusion

This chapter has argued that scrutiny of workplace and supply chain contexts that place workers in vulnerable positions result in a wide range of harmful practices. As Anderson (2010: 313) notes, it is important to understand such practices not just as a product of rogue employers, but also of the markets in which they operate. This begins to move away from discussing harm as a problem of individuals to one of businesses, supply chains, markets, and the political-legal contexts in which they operate (Scott, 2017). In order to make such a move, the value of a harm approach is a helpful lens through which to view harmful practices that are neither criminalised nor prosecuted, since numerous harms occur that are hidden within organisations or market relationships. While labelling all these practices as criminal is problematic, there are grounds to assert that they can be harmful to workers and wider society.

Through this lens of harm, it is critical to focus on the full spectrum of labour exploitation, rather than the most severe forms usually categorised as human trafficking, forced labour, and modern slavery (Davies, 2018; France, 2016). More subtle cases and 'grey areas' that fall in between the notions of 'decent work' and severe exploitation are neglected, yet these arguably merit attention, especially if working conditions deteriorate and encourage further exploitation to occur. Part of this process involves shifting attention from rogue employers and human 'traffickers' towards a more rigorous understanding of how decisions are made and overseen in contemporary industries.

In some cases, decisions made within businesses may not be intended to cause exploitation or harm to others; instead, they are likely doing what they think is right for their business within the context of competitive environments. However, decisions to subcontract labour or to use flexible employment contracts frequently have unintended consequences, such as confusion for workers whom to report concerns to. Workers who are easily hired and fired tend to be less willing or able to speak up against unfair treatment. More complex supply chains that extend over numerous countries may also make oversight and regulation problematic. Where there is oversight, there are contradictions and limitations associated with top-down responses such as criminal law, as well as bottom-up responses including trade union and labour movements.

Regarding future impacts in the European context especially, estimating the full impacts of Brexit would be highly speculative at this stage, and may not be known for a number of years – signposting these issues may serve as a springboard for further work in future. In particular, concerns around migrant workers' rights, work shortages in migrant dependent sectors such as agriculture, and labour market enforcement, are all subject to ongoing debate (France, 2017). However, if EU-wide enforcement bodies such as the European Labour Authority come into existence, aligning the regulatory systems of different countries may prove challenging, especially given significant approaches towards labour inspection.

These issues all point to a large amount of complexity with regards to the features, organisation and control of harmful labour exploitation. There are a number of disciplines that examine these issues in the context of local, national and global supply chains. However, criminology is perhaps 'guilty' of overly focusing on state based and criminal justice system interventions, while neglecting a broader range of harms that occur within and beyond the workplace. Although this chapter does not advocate 'abandoning' criminology in favour of a social harm discipline, it is clear that a more rigorous assessment of supply chains and business practices within the dominant capitalist system would provide advantages to the discipline in terms of broadening its approach and developing contemporary solutions.

References

Almond, P., and J. van Erp, Regulation and governance versus criminology: disciplinary divides, intersections, and opportunities. *Regulation & Governance*, 2018. Epub ahead of print: doi:10.1111/rego.12202.

Alvesalo, A. and D. Whyte, Eyes wide shut: the police investigation of safety crimes. *Crime, Law and Social Change*, 2007, no. 48(1-2), 57-72.

Anderson, B., Migrant domestic workers: good workers, poor slaves, new connections. *Social Politics*, 2015, no. 22(4), 636-652.

Anderson, B., Migration, immigration controls and the fashioning of precarious workers. *Work, Employment and Society*, 2010, no. 24(2), 300-317.

Ayres, I. and J. Braithwaite, *Responsive regulation: transcending the deregulation debate*. New York, Oxford University Press, 1992.

Balch, A., *regulation and enforcement to tackle forced labour in the UK: a systematic response?* York, Joseph Rowntree Foundation, 2012.

Barrientos, S., 'Labour chains': analysing the role of labour contractors in global production networks. *The Journal of Development Studies*, 2013, no. 49(8), 1058-1071.

BBC News, *How the tragedy unfolded at Grenfell Tower* [online] available from<https://www.bbc.com/news/uk-england-london-40272168> [28th January, 2019], 2018.

BEIS, *Trade Union Membership 2017. Statistical Bulletin*. London, Department for Business, Energy & Industrial Strategy, 2018.

Box, S., *Power, crime, and mystification*. London, Routledge, 1984.

Boyle, S., G. Keogh, and P. Bentley, *How Ryanair cabin crew work five extra hours a day for no pay* [online] available from <https://www.dailymail.co.uk/news/article-5188899/ [25 January 2019], 2017.

Braithwaite, J., *Regulatory capitalism. How it works, ideas for making it work better*. Cheltenham, Edward Elgar Publishing Limited, 2008.

Braithwaite, V., Closing the gap between regulation and the community. In *Regulatory Theory: Foundations and Applications*. In P. Drahos (ed.). Acton, ANU Press, pp.25-42, 2017.

CIOB, *Building a fairer system: tackling modern slavery in construction supply chains*. Bracknell: CIOB, 2018.

Citizens Advice, *Employment rights are only as strong as your ability to enforce them* [online] available from https://wearecitizensad-vice.org.uk/ 28th January 2019], 2017.

Davies, J., From severe to routine labour exploitation: the case of migrant workers in the UK food industry. *Criminology & Criminal Justice*, 2018, Epub ahead of print, 10 March 2018. DOI: 10.1177/.

De Giorgi, A., Immigration control, post-fordism, and less eligibility. *Punishment & Society*, 2010, no. 12(2), 147-167.

Drahos, P. and M. Krygier, Regulation, institutions and networks. In *Regulatory Theory: Foundations and Applications*. P. Drahos (ed.) Acton, ANU Press, pp.1-22, 2017.

EHRC, *Inquiry into recruitment in the meat and poultry processing sector: report of the findings and recommendations*. London, Equality and Human Rights Commission, 2010.

EU-OSHA, *Finland* [online] available from <https://osha.europa.eu/en/about-eu-osha/national-focal-points/finland> [28th January 2019], 2019.

Fauset, C., *What's wrong with corporate social responsibility?* Oxford: Corporate Watch, 2006.

Fisse, B., and J. Braithwaite, The allocation of responsibility for corporate crime: individualism, collectivism and accountability. *Sydney Law Review*, 1988, 11(3), 468-513.

FLEX, *Shaky foundations: labour exploitation in London's construction sector*. London: FLEX, 2018.

FLEX, *Risky business: tackling exploitation in the UK labour market*. London: FLEX, 2017.

FRA, *Severe labour exploitation*. Vienna, European Union Agency for Fundamental Rights, 2015.

France, B., *Lost in transition: Brexit & labour exploitation*. London, Labour Exploitation Advisory Group, 2017.

France, B., *Labour compliance to exploitation and the abuses in-between*. London, Labour Exploitation Advisory Group, 2016.

Gadd, D. and R. Broad, Troubling recognitions in British responses to modern slavery. *British Journal of Criminology*, 2018, 58(6), 1440-1461.

GLA, *Labour exploitation: spotting the signs*. Nottingham, Gangmasters Licensing Authority, 2015.

GMB Union, *Up to 10 million insecure workers* [online] available from www.gmb.org.uk/newsroom/millions-insecure-work. Accessed 22 June 2017.

Gobert, J., Corporate criminality: four modes of fault'. *Legal Studies*, 1994, no. 14(3), 393-410.

Gobert, J. and M. Punch, *Rethinking corporate crime*. Cambridge, Cambridge University Press, 2003.

Greenfield, V.A., and L. Paoli, A framework to assess the harms of crimes. *British Journal of Criminology*, 2013, no. 53(5): 864-885.

Hillyard, P., and S. Tombs, From "crime" to social harm? *Crime, Law and Social Change*, 2007, no. 48(1), 9-25.

Hillyard, P., C. Pantazis, S. Tombs and G. Gordon (eds.), *Beyond Criminology: Taking Harm Seriously*. London, Pluto Press , 2004.

Hipp, L., J. Bernhardt, and J. Allmendinger, Institutions and the prevalence of nonstandard employment. *Socio-Economic Review*, 2015, no. 13(2), 351-377.

HM Government, *Transparency in supply chains*. London, HM Government, 2015.

Home Office, *Review of the National Referral Mechanism for victims of human trafficking*. London: Home Office, 2014.

House of Commons, *Sexual harassment in the workplace*. House of Commons, Women and Equalities Committee, London, 2018.

ILO, *Figures and statistics on labour inspection systems* [online] available from www.ilo.org/labadmin/info/WCMS_141079/lang--en/index.htm. 28 January 2019.

Jobe, A., *The causes and consequences of re-trafficking: evidence from the IOM Human Trafficking Database*. Geneva: IOM, 2010.

Kiss, M., *European Labour Authority*. Brussels: European Parliament, 2018.

LeBaron, G., N. Howard, C. Thibos and P. Kyritsis, *Confronting root causes: forced labour in global supply chains*. Sheffield, Sheffield Political Economy Research Institute, 2018.

LeBaron, G., Unfree labour beyond binaries: insecurity, social hierarchy and labour market restructuring. *International Feminist Journal of Politics*, 2015, no. 17 (1), 1-19.

Lloyd, A., *The harms of work: an ultra-realist account of the service economy*. Bristol, Bristol University Press, 2018.

Lord, N., C.F. Elizondo and J. Spencer, The dynamics of food fraud: the interactions between criminal opportunity and market (dys)functionality in legitimate business. *Criminology and Criminal Justice*, 2017, no. 17(5), 605-623.

Melossi, D., 'In a peaceful life': migration and the crime of modernity in Europe/Italy'. *Punishment & Society*, 2003, no. 5(4), 371-397.

New, S., Modern Slavery and the supply chain: the limits of corporate social responsibility? *Supply Chain Management*, 2015, no. 20(6), 697-707.

O'Connell Davidson, J. *Children in the Global Sex Trade*. Cambridge: Polity, 2005.

Ollus, N., Forced flexibility and exploitation: experiences of migrant workers in the cleaning industry. *Nordic Journal of Working Life Studies*, 2016, no. 6(1), 25-45.

Paoli, L. (ed.), *The Oxford Handbook of Organized Crime*. Oxford, Oxford University Press, 2014.

Paoli, L. and V.A. Greenfield, Starting from the end: a plea for focusing on the consequences of crime. *European Journal of Crime, Criminal Law and Criminal Justice*, 2015, no. 23(2), 87-100.

Passas, N., Lawful but awful: 'legal corporate crimes'. *The Journal of Socio-Economics*, 2005, no. 34, 771-786.

Pemberton, S., *Harmful societies: understanding social harm*. Bristol: Policy Press, 2015.

Potter, M., and J. Hamilton, Picking on vulnerable migrants: precarity and the mushroom industry in Northern Ireland. *Work, Employment and Society*, 2014, no. 28(3), 390-406.

Ruhs M. and B. Anderson, (2010), 'Semi-compliance and illegality in migrant labour markets: an analysis of migrants, employers and the state in the UK'. *Population, Space and Place* 16(3): 195-211, 2010.

Scott, S., *Labour exploitation and work-based harm*. Bristol, Policy Press, 2017.

Slapper, G. and S. Tombs, *Corporate crime*. Essex: Pearson, 1999.

Snider, L. and S. Bittle, The challenges of regulating powerful economic actors. In *European Developments in Corporate Criminal Liability*. Ed. J. Gobert and A. Pascal, Abingdon, Routledge, 53-69, 2014.
Stevens, G.C., Integrating the supply chain. *International Journal of Physical Distribution & Materials Management* 19(8): 3-8, 1989.
Sutherland, E.H., Crime and business. *Annals of the American Academy of Political and Social Science*, 1941, no. 217(5), 112-118.
Sutherland, E.H., White-collar criminality. *American Sociological Review*, 1940, no. 5(1), 1-12.
Tappan, P.W., Who is the criminal?. *American Sociological Review*, 1947, no. 12(1), 96-102.
Taylor, M., *Good work: the Taylor review of modern working practices*. London, HM Government, 2017.
Thiemann, I. (2016), Villains and victims, but no workers: why a prosecution-focussed approach to human trafficking fails trafficked persons. *Anti-Trafficking Review*, no. 6, 126-129.
Tombs, S., and D. Whyte (2015), *The corporate criminal: why corporations must be abolished*. Abingdon: Routledge.
Tombs, S. and D. Whyte (2007), *Safety crimes*. Cullompton, Willan.
Turner, T., C. Cross and M. O'Sullivan (2014), Does Union membership benefit immigrant workers in 'hard times'? *Journal of Industrial Relations*, no. 56(5), 611-630.
Van Duyne, P.C., and M.J. Houtzager (2005), 'Criminal sub-contracting in the Netherlands: the Dutch 'koppelbaas' as crime-entrepeneur'. In *The Organised Crime Economy: Managing Crime Markets in Europe*. Ed. by P.C. van Duyne, K. von Lampe, M. van Dijck and J.L. Newell. Nijmegen: Wolf Legal Publishers, pp.163-188.
van Erp, J., W. Huisman and G. Vande Walle, *The routledge handbook of white-collar and corporate crime in Europe*. London: Routledge, 2015.
Weil, D., 'A strategic approach to labour inspection'. *International Labour Review* 147(4), 349-375, 2008.
White, R., and J. Yeates, 'Farming and climate change'. In *A Handbook of Food Crime*. Ed. by Gray, A., and R. Hinch. Bristol: Bristol University Press, pp.315-330, 2018.

From harmless incivilities to not-so serious organised crime activities

The expanded realm of European crime prevention and some suggestions on how to limit it

Anna Di Ronco and *Anna Sergi*[1]

Introduction

People in Europe – as in many other parts of the world – fear about their personal safety and feel rather insecure. According to Eurobarometer (2017), although the large majority of Europeans tend to feel quite secure in their immediate city and neighbourhood, they tend to be less convinced about their country and much less so about the European Union in comparison to previous years. Among others, people in Europe tend to regard challenges to the internal security of the EU as important, particularly terrorism and organised crime. Factors that may have influenced the security feelings of EU citizens may have to do with the 'recent' refugee 'crisis' (for a critical account of the refugee 'crisis' see Siegel and Nagy, 2018), the terror 'threat' and recent attacks carried out by terror groups (or simply isolated individuals) in many EU cities, along with more general late modern fears, also linked to the effects of the 2007 financial crisis, which have often translated in governmental cuts in spending, especially affecting social policy.

The diffuse concerns about individual and social security, which have resulted from changes in the late modern society in which we live (see, *e.g.*, Bauman, 1987; Young, 1973, 1999; Waquant, 2008; Ponsaers, 2012), have led many European countries in recent years to intensify state intervention in

[1] Anna Di Ronco is a Lecturer in Criminology at the University of Essex (UK). Anna Sergi is a Senior Lecturer in Criminology at the University of Essex (UK).

the area of security and public order. To quickly respond to widespread fears and anxieties over the problem of safety and of physical and psychological integrity, which are often amplified by the media reporting on certain crime-related events or issues (Reiner, 2002), politicians and policy makers in many EU countries have adopted punitive security measures targeting both incivilities (nuisance, disorder, anti-social behaviour) and more 'serious' forms of crime regarded as organised crime or terrorism, with several negative implications for individuals' liberties, social inclusion and integration.

On the one hand, punitive measures (not only 'proper' criminal justice measures, but also measures that are civil or administrative in their form yet punitive or criminal in their nature; Van Duyne and Van der Vorm, 2017) have been used against 'incivilities', or any behaviour or even social group considered a 'nuisance', 'unsightly' or annoying for powerful majorities despite not necessarily causing harm to others.[2] These measures have often been grounded on the assumed link between social and physical disorder with more serious forms of criminality. The underlying conviction is that if not tackled from its root 'causes' (disorder or incivilities) 'serious' crime would otherwise thrive in the city or city areas (for the example of England see, *e.g.*, Burney, 2005; Innes and Jones, 2006; Squires, 2008). On the other hand, some threats, perceived as increasingly serious and potentially very harmful due to their reach – national or transnational – or their impact on different communities, have been "securitised".

This means that the realm of security – and especially national security – has enlarged to comprehend also crime issues (Farrand & Carrapico, 2012). This has certainly been the case with organised crime (Campbell, 2014) and cybercrime (Lavorgna and Sergi, 2016). While both are umbrella terms that include different types of misconducts, the potential harm associated to the

2 Some of the conducts generally considered 'anti-social' or a 'nuisance' are or can be, to be sure, harmful and seriously offensive to people, at least at times. Arson, vandalism and physical assault do cause serious harm to others; however, these conducts tend to be already punished by criminal law proper and are often not in need of being re-regulated by other legal systems (*e.g.*, civil or administrative). By the same token, certain behaviour that is included in and punished through security policies is certainly harmless, as the case of young people hanging about in public spaces, which may be considered as causing 'distress' to certain dominant social groups and thus be penalised.

'transnationality' of organised crime and the ubiquity of cybercrime have elevated their *seriousness* for the national system and therefore subsumed both concepts within the national security context alongside threats of terrorism and concerns over border safety (Sergi, 2017).

These two processes have been observed both at state levels and in regional agendas and often intertwine. At the EU level, for example, EU institutions have given recognition to the importance of people's (in)securities and fears, which may be engendered by both organised crime and disorder/petty crimes. Local crime and disorder (including incivilities like graffiti, vandalism, noise nuisance and unruly or aggressive behaviour) have been included in the EU crime prevention (henceforth: CP) strategy for them engendering fear and insecurities among Europeans. Most importantly, they are considered as being conducive to more serious forms of transnational and organised criminality (Crawford, 2002; Di Ronco, 2016) – regardless of their actual 'seriousness' or proven cross-border dimension.[3] This reasoning, which has justified the granting of EU funding to national and local CP initiatives targeting low-level crime and disorder (Di Ronco, 2016), obviously resonates with the Broken Windows rationale (Wilson and Kelling, 1982). Thereby it supports its argued causal link between disorder, fear and crime, which has long been discredited in the literature (see, *e.g.* Sampson and Raudenbush, 2004; Sampson, 2009).

Organised crime, on its part, is considered a phenomenon that 'undermines the values and prosperity of our open societies' (EU Council, 2010: 2). Consequently, it is seen as a serious threat to the EU. As the EU Council states: 'people have the right to expect the European Union to address the threat to their freedom and legal rights posed by serious crime' (EU Council 2000: 1).

3 For example, in two policy documents of the European Commission (2000) and Council (2001), where they proposed (in the former) and deliberated (in the latter) the establishment of the European Crime Prevention Network (EUCPN), crime has been defined as any 'anti-social conduct which, without necessarily being a criminal offence, can by its cumulative effect generate a climate of tension and insecurity' (European Commission, 2000), and crime prevention as a group of 'measures that are intended to reduce or otherwise contribute to reducing crime and citizens' feeling of insecurity' (Council of the European Union, 2001). As put it by Crawford (2002: 44), the logic behind these policies – and the importance they place on insecurities and fears – lies in the 'perceived interconnectedness of transnational developments and highly localised activities'.

However, as it has already been observed (Carrapico, 2014), the approximation of the organised crime concept at the EU level has led to an enlargement of the anti-organised crime strategy, which has come to include both the protection of the single market and the protection of citizens due to the perceived increase of the threat and its seriousness for the EU. Most of EU criminal law actually comes from the need to tackle some sort of serious and/or organised crime. After the Lisbon Treaty, in fact, 'seriousness' is embedded in the rationale of EU criminal law, in the recognition that the EU can and should intervene to maintain citizens safe and borders secure from crime and criminals. This trend is also visible in the enhancement of the mandate of Europol, which originally required that there had to be "factual indications that an organised criminal structure [was] involved".[4] But in 2009, this was broadened to cover "serious crime affecting two or more member states".[5] Thus by inserting the feature 'serious', Europol is effectively involved whenever a serious crime – also not organised in its nature – is committed with a cross-border dimension, even in cases when Mutual Legal Assistance and bilateral agreements would suffice. In other words, the recognition of the seriousness in itself and organised crime types pushes the necessity for the EU and EU-wide institutions to take a more forceful step in the criminalisation and the prevention of such crimes.

Drawing on the crime prevention and organised crime literature, and on examples taken from the authors' previous research, this chapter discusses the implications of an expanded realm of CP to behaviour that – independently from its seriousness – is considered to be conducive to further criminality (as in the case of incivilities) and/or to involve an organised crime group. In essence, we argue that two processes occurring at the same time are expanding the remit and reach of CP:

---

4 Convention based on Article K.3 of the Treaty on European Union, on the establishment of a European Police Office (Europol Convention) – Official Journal C 316, 27/11/1995 P. 0002 –0032 – http://eur-lex.europa.eu/LexUriServ/LexUriServ.do?uri=CELEX:41995A1127(01):EN:HTML.

5 Council Decision of 6 April 2009 establishing the European Police Office (Europol) OJ L 121,15.5.2009 – http://eur-lex.europa.eu/legal-content/EN/ALL/?uri=CELEX:32009D0371.

1. the increasing fears and insecurities among people have called for the application of prevention mechanisms also via criminalisation from below, in light of the connection between local disorder with (more serious forms of) crime;
2. the securitisation of certain concepts – such as organised crime – increases the perceptions of the *seriousness* of certain conducts and crimes and leads to excessive responses against them.

This chapter will also question whether – given its limited competence in CP – the EU has the potential to influence national and local ways of doing CP, at least through soft law mechanisms including the circulation of best practices by some of its bodies and networks.

Expanded Crime Prevention: its object, agencies and limits (in theory)

The (liberal) critical criminological literature is quite unanimous in arguing that roughly in the last thirty years we have witnessed a reconfiguration of security and its modes of governance (Jones, 2012) and, therefore, a change in the CP complex. Particularly, a change has occurred, among others, to the 'criminal' *behaviour* that is subject to criminalisation. This applies in particularly to criminal justice and other punitive measures, which have often included behaviour that is harmless and had previously been tolerated. A change has also affected the number and nature of the local, national and EU *agencies* that are competent for the prevention, prosecution and punishment of 'crime, including 'serious' crime. These agencies have expanded up to including partnerships, citizens involvement, private security firms etc. This expansion in CP has resulted in policies and practices that have often exceeded the *limits* set out by our constitutional systems and theorised by criminal law theorists and philosophers, and dangerously eroded individual's exercise of civil liberties.

Object

The expansion in CP has been reflected in its goals, which, as put it by Garland (2001: 16-17), have broadened to include "prevention, security, harm-reduction, loss-reduction, fear-reduction—that are quite different from the traditional goals of prosecution, punishment, and 'criminal justice'". According to social theorists of risk, CP is currently dominated by an anticipatory logic (Zedner, 2007; Pleysier, 2015, 2017), which emphasises the importance of preventing the public from future harms and protecting it from 'risk' (Beck, 1992). In contemporary actuarial justice (Freely and Simon, 1994), individual and collective assessments of what constitutes a 'risk group' may largely be affected by public perceptions and fears, also fuelled by the media and contingent 'moral panics' (for a case of fears shaping the national security policy and its reliance on 'risk profiles', see van Swaaningen, 2005).[6] Fears and a more generalised sense of 'ontological insecurity' (Giddens, 1991) are caused, among others, by the growing social polarisation and economic inequality, and the fragmentation and individualisation of society. All these developments have contributed to the contemporary heightened fear of the 'other' (Furedi, 1997, 2004) and to the adoption by many countries and cities of public reassurance initiatives. These cover a broad behavioural field, including anti-social behaviour legislations (Waiton, 2008a, 2008b) that aim at protecting the public from feeling negative emotions including fear (Peršak, 2017).

As put quite eloquently by Crawford (2009: 15), contemporary CP has put its "emphasis on wider social problems, including public perceptions and fear of crime, quality of life, broadly defined harms, incivilities and disorder". To enhance people's 'quality of life' and reduce fears and perceived 'risks', crime control at the local level has also intertwined with urban revitalisation projects – what is known as 'gentrification' – in many European cities (Peršak and Di Ronco, 2018).

The importance of protecting public spaces through urban design and revitalisation has also been emphasised at the EU level. In two of its recent communications, for example, the Commission has suggested a number of

6 Risks can be assessed through a probabilities calculus or, in the post-risk society, through the principle of 'precaution' – a response to uncertainty that operates by imagining worse case scenarios of possible inaction. This is what O'Malley (2017) called 'speculative pre-emption': "[i]f it can be imagined, it must be governed".

measures intended to support member states and local authorities within them in their efforts to reduce the vulnerability of public spaces, in particular against terrorist attacks. These measures include the allocation of funding, and the organisation of initiatives aimed at bringing together relevant stakeholders (including private actors or 'operators', local and national authorities, practitioners etc.) and at sharing information and best practices between them (European Commission, 2017, 2018a).

Scholars from many disciplines, including not only criminology and sociology, but also urban planning, urban studies, and critical geography, have warned against the negative and exclusionary effects that spatial 'cleansing' or spatial 'purification' have on the 'undeserving minorities' (the poor, young people, ethnic minorities etc.) (see, *e.g.,* Atkinson and Helms, 2007; Bannister *et al*., 2006; Belina and Helms, 2003; Sibley, 1995; Smith, 2005). The spatial and social exclusion of these minorities is often accomplished through gentrification, which tends to drive up the housing prices. In gentrified urban spaces, moreover, individual's behaviour is also controlled and punished through regulations and particular policing styles (*e.g.,* zero tolerance policing). For example, place bans, administrative and civil measures and fines mainly target behaviour or social groups that are considered a 'nuisance', 'unsightly' or annoying for dominant majorities despite not necessarily causing harm to others. These coercive regulations and measures have been adopted not only in the UK with the New Labour's infamous ASBOs starting from the 1990s (see e.g. Burney, 2005, and Squires, 2008), but also in many other European countries (Peršak, 2017) and cities (Di Ronco, 2014, 2016), despite the negative evaluation of many national supreme courts (Di Ronco and Peršak, 2014).

The expansion of CP has not only occurred 'downwards', towards low level crime – if we can talk about 'crime' at all. As pointed out by Hörnqvist (2004), the 'security mentality' that dominates current criminal justice has 'ruptured the law' – and compromised its legal protections – both upwards and downwards, *i.e*., by erasing the line between crime and acts of war (as in the case of terrorism) and between crime and incivilities, respectively.

In a similar vein, in Europe the security mentality (legitimised by the too often invoked state of 'emergency') has justified the use of crime control measures – including incarceration – against asylum seekers and refugees from war zones in the Middle East and northern Africa. These victims of acts of war have often been assessed as 'risk groups' and framed in some countries as ‘criminals’ and ‘terrorist’ (see Berry et al., 2015). The practice of detaining migrants for administrative purposes has been critically analysed in “crimmigration” studies (*e.g.*, Guia *et al.*, 2011; van der Woude *et al.*, 2017). Such detention is said to be required to establish their identities, or to facilitate their immigration claims resolution or their removal. However, they are de facto incarcerated, often without them having committed a crime. This has been much problematised in the light of excessive interference with individual’s rights (see *e.g.* Welch and Shuster, 2005).

Agencies

In his work, the French philosopher Michael Foucault understood and conceptualised power not as an exclusive prerogative of the state, but as something dispersed throughout the social field and used by institutions as diverse as the family, the church, schools, prisons etc. to control individuals and their behaviour. Working within the Foucauldian tradition of ‘governmentality’ (which, as put by Newburn (2007: 325), focuses not only on the state but also on the “nature and rationalities of certain social and political *practices*”), governmentality theorists have discussed how governmental power and control, including crime control, are dispersed in the social field. Agencies of social control have expanded much beyond the police, which is only one of the actors responsible for the prevention and control of crime. In addition to the military – deployed at least occasionally or in some EU countries, including France, Belgium and Italy, after the 2015-2017 terror attacks – also private actors share competences in CP (Garland, 2001): individuals, community groups (neighbour watch or warden schemes), private security actors, various local agents, and private-public partnerships. This ‘dispersal of discipline’ (Cohen, 1985) produced what Stan Cohen described, using his famous fishing metaphor, the ‘widening of the net’ and ‘thinning of the mesh’ of the criminal justice system. In practice, this results in more people being ‘captured’ and retained in the criminal justice ‘net’ for behaviour that had previously been accepted or tolerated. Obviously this pushes towards more serious responses to those forms of conduct already criminalised. Because of the need to justify the enlarging justice net for previously accepted/tolerated behaviours, low-level and mid-level offences rise to more serious ranks and attract more severe sentences. An example of this is in the UK Public Order Act 1986, which now recognises the offence of 'Affray' as triable-either-way depending on 'the seriousness of the effect that the behaviour of the accused has on members of the public who may have been put in fear'[7].

The expansion of the penal sphere throughout society has much been problematized by critical scholars, who have also linked it to the sharpening of insecurities and anxieties, to the reduced tolerance towards low level crime and incivilities, and to greater public demands for security (*e.g.,* Tonry, 2004).

Law enforcement agencies operating in the crime prevention field have multiplied at the EU level as well (during a relatively long process and not without resistance of member states, see *e.g.* Baker, 2010). They are especially directed at tackling the so-called 'EU crimes', or particularly serious crimes with a cross-border dimension such as terrorism, trafficking in human beings and sexual exploitation of women and children, illicit drug trafficking, illicit arms trafficking, money laundering, corruption, counterfeiting of means of payment, computer crime and 'organised crime'. Since the 2009 Treaty of Lisbon, indeed, the EU Parliament and Council have been given the power to legislate in criminal matters (articles 82 and 83 TFEU). In short, following the ordinary legislative procedure, the Parliament and Council can establish minimum rules:

i. to the extent necessary to facilitate mutual recognition of judgments and judicial decisions and police and judicial cooperation in criminal matters having a cross-border dimension; and
ii. to approximate definitions of particularly serious crimes with a cross-border dimension and their sanctions.

---

7 Affray is an offence under section 3 of the Public Order Act 1986 and is triable-either-way. The maximum penalty on conviction on indictment is 3 years' imprisonment and/or a fine of unlimited amount. On summary conviction the maximum penalty is 6 months' imprisonment and/or a fine not exceeding level 5. Under section 3 of the Act, it must be proved that a person has used or threatened: unlawful violence towards another and his conduct is such as would cause a person of reasonable firmness present at the scene to fear for his personal safety. - See Crown Prosecution Service's Legal Guidance on Public Order Offences Incorporating Charging Standards at https://www.cps.gov.uk/legal-guidance/public-order-offences-incorporating-charging-standard.

Article 87 (2) TFEU also enables the EU to establish measures on police co-operation involving all the member states' competent authorities (including police, customs and other specialised law enforcement services), in particular concerning the collection, storage and exchange of information relevant for the prevention, detection and investigation of criminal offences (letter a) and common investigation techniques in relation to the detection of serious forms of organised crime (letter b), in particular through enhanced operational powers of Europol. For example, in April 2018, the European Commission put forward a proposal for laying down the rules facilitating the use of financial and other information for the prevention, detection, investigation or prosecution of certain criminal offences, including serious and organised crime, as required by the European Agenda on Security adopted in April 2015 (European Commission, 2015) and its follow up Action Plan on strengthening the fight against terrorist financing (European Commission, 2016). As the European Commission (2018b: 3-4) states, CP is at the core of the criminal law framework against serious and organised crime.

This proposal complements and builds on the preventive side of the Money Laundering Directive[8] and reinforces the legal framework from the point of view of police cooperation. Furthermore, this proposal for a Directive reinforces and builds the Union criminal law framework with regard to the fight against serious offences, in particular Regulation (EU) 2016/794 on the European Union Agency for Law Enforcement Cooperation (Europol).

Limits

Expanding the ambit and agencies of CP carries, however, dangerous implications for civil liberties. Modern democracies are based in their core on the liberal idea of individual autonomy, which is predicated on a limited and exceptional use of (criminal) measures restricting individual's rights. In other

[8] Directive (EU) 2015/849 of the European Parliament and of the Council of 20 May 2015 on the prevention of the use of the financial system for the purposes of money laundering or terrorist financing, amending Regulation (EU) No 648/2012 of the European Parliament and of the Council and repealing Directive 2005/60/EC of the European Parliament and of the Council and Commission Directive 2006/70/EC (OJ L 141 of 5.6.2015, p. 73) – as amended in December 2017 (5th Anti-Money Laundering Directive).

words, the criminal law – and punitive measures alike – is considered exceptional or a last resort (*extrema ratio*), and is thus only allowed for the most severe violations of constitutionally protected "goods" (values or interests). "Substantive" (Peršak, 2007) reasons for criminalisation instruct the legislator on the content of the criminal law or on which behaviour it can legitimately criminalise. The most accepted and recognised grounds for criminalisation are the harm and offence principles (see Feinberg, 1984; Jareborg, 2004; Peršak, 2007; Simester and von Hirsch, 2006, 2011). In addition to these substantive reasons, there are also formal principles that the policy-maker ought to follow to properly criminalise human behaviour (Peršak, 2007). Such formal principles are, for example, the principles of legality and proportionality.[9] Because of the EU accession to the ECHR and the adoption of the Charter of Fundamental Rights of the European Union (henceforth: the Charter), which have both occurred with the entry into force of the Treaty of Lisbon, the EU has also given recognition to these two formal principles of criminalisation. Particularly, at article 52(1)[10] the Charter crystalises the principle of proportionality:

> Any limitation on the exercise of the rights and freedoms recognised by this Charter must be provided for by law and respect the essence of those rights and freedoms. Subject to the principle of proportionality, limitations may be made only if they are necessary and genuinely meet objectives of general interest recognised by the Union or the need to protect the rights and freedoms of others.

These formal principles – and particularly, to our purposes, the proportionality principle – appear, for example, in the European Agenda on Security, where

---

9 Of course, one important principle that limits EU competence in criminal law is the subsidiarity principle. According to this principle, the EU (excluding the areas that fall within its exclusive competence) can legislate only if the objectives of the proposed action cannot be reached more effectively at the national, regional or local levels, but are better achieved at the EU level because of the scale and effects of the proposed action. According to the proportionality principle, the content and form of the EU proposed action should also not exceed what is necessary to achieve the objectives of the Treaties (see article 5 of the Treaty on the European Union as amended by the Treaty of Lisbon).

10 The proportionality principle has also been laid down at art. 49 par. 3 of the Charter, which stipulates that the severity of the penalties must not be disproportionate to the criminal offence.

the European Commission (2015) places great emphasis on the need not to interfere with fundamental rights while protecting the security of citizens.[11] More in detail, the first of five key principles is to 'ensure full compliance [of EU CP/security measures] with fundamental rights'. As put it by the Commission:

> "All security measures must comply with the principles of necessity, proportionality and legality, with appropriate safeguards to ensure accountability and judicial redress. The Commission will strictly test that any security measure fully complies with fundamental rights whilst effectively delivering its objectives. The impact of any new initiative on free movement and the protection of personal data must be fully in line with the proportionality principle, and fundamental rights."

The proportionality test and the harm principle[12] both support the development of criminal law – and the creation and implementation of security measures – at the EU as well as at national levels. In particular, when it comes to the criminalisation of organised crime, the characterisation of the harm is fundamental to understand the conceptualisation of organised crime in a given country. While for example in Italy organised crime is harmful against public order, in the UK it is a national security threat – which implies different degrees of the seriousness of the offence as well as different responses to such seriousness (Sergi, 2017).

The downwards and upwards spirals of crime prevention

As said, behaviours targeted by national and local CP measures are not always harmful, 'serious' or 'so-serious'. Yet, they can engender fear – also in light of their (close or remote or probable, if any) connection with more serious forms of crime like organised crime – among other emotional responses. Al-

11 In the Joint declaration on the EU legislative priorities for 2018-9, this appears as the first priority area (out of seven). See https://ec.europa.eu/commission/publications/joint-declaration-eus-legislative-priorities-2018_en.

12 For the importance of the harm principle in EU criminal law, see Peršak (2018).

though these emotional responses ought to be taken into serious consideration, not all of them are deserving of protection by criminal law or punitive interventions.

Is the inclusion of harmless, or 'deviant' or 'not-so-serious' behaviour within the field of CP – often involving punitive measures – always legitimate and/or desirable? If we consider this matter from the point of view of national and local politicians, the answer would most likely be affirmative: punitive measures are often an easy and effective way to tap onto individual and collective fears and ensure (re)election. A different response comes from criminal law scholars: criminal law – and punitive measures in general – can only be used for certain substantive reasons (mostly, harm and offence, as above) and following specific formal principles – particularly the proportionality principle – lest being too intrusive of individual's liberties. In the next sections, we will draw on examples to investigate cases where member states have *excessively* regulated behaviour that is not necessarily harmful or so-serious, yet considered as conducive to further criminality, or 'serious', because being committed by an 'organised crime group'. In the final concluding sections, we will reflect on the possible soft-law/watchdog role for EU, particularly for the EUCPN in cooperation with other relevant EU bodies in the flagging of excessive national and local CP measures.

Harmless Incivilities

In Italy, as well as in other European countries (Peršak, 2017), punitive security measures have been put in place to target a wide range of behaviour considered a threat to public safety and urban security, or simply distressing or annoying to (at least, some) people. Starting from the 1990s, when insecurity feelings and fear of crime and disorder became a major concern in Italy, also in light of the increased presence of migrants (Pavarini, 2006; Melossi and Selmini, 2009), local authorities have been pressured to provide responses to crime and disorder at the local level. These pressures led them to apply administrative sanctions against "uncivil" people (including, *e.g.*, prostitutes' clients), mostly for violations of road traffic, and public health and safety regulations.

The 2008 "Security Package" (Pacchetto Sicurezza or decree No 92 of 23 May 2008) of the then Berlusconi government, legitimised and further broadened the public order competences of local authorities. Through this law decree, local authorities have been given the power to sanction through administrative fines any conduct considered a threat to the safety and security of citizens. More concretely, municipalities have used these powers to sanction – and *de facto* criminalise – not only already criminalised behaviour (such as vandalism and drug dealing) but also rather harmless and long tolerated behaviour, including (among others) soliciting of prostitution, being drunk in public, begging, and littering. The end result has been the production of a scattered regulatory scenario, whereby different behaviours have unevenly been regulated in different localities according to the wish of the ruling coalitions (and their interpretation of people's fears and perceptions of the 'problem(s)'). Since the Security Package, moreover, local authorities have also been authorised to request the presence of the *military* on their municipal territory, particularly to monitor sensible targets (such as the *Identification and Expulsion Centres* for migrants), and patrol city areas in conjunction with the (state and municipal) police. This operation, called 'Safe Streets' (Strade Sicure), which currently deploys 7.100 soldiers across the national territory, is described as the "most onerous task of the military in terms of soldiers, resources and materials" – *i.e.*, more onerous than the operations on which the Italian army is deployed on foreign territories.[13]

The exercise of these sanctioning powers has, however, been found illegitimate by the Constitutional Court in one of its famous judgments in 2011. In this judgement it normatively assessed the legality of local security regulations and measures on the basis of the constitutional principles of legality and proportionality. In essence, local regulations have been found in breach of the legality principle as they prohibited *any behaviour* considered by local authorities (upon their discretion) a "threat to public safety and security" – rather than a conduct whose defining traits had been identified by law and made known and predictable to people before its adoption. Local regulation and measures have also been found in violation of the proportionality principle as they resulted in an excessive state intervention and intrusion into individual's

---

13 See http://www.esercito.difesa.it/operazioni/operazioni_nazionali/Pagine/Operazione-Strade-Sicure.aspx.

exercise of fundamental rights and freedoms, such as the right to associate, to free movement and speech.

In overt opposition to this judgment, local authorities have not stopped from issuing (*illegitimate*) orders and applying punitive administrative sanctions, particularly against homeless people, street vendors and prostitutes, who in Italy are mostly migrants (Crocitti and Selmini, 2017). Public order powers against incivilities have also been recently re-introduced by the Gentiloni government through the so-called "Minniti Decree" (law decree No 17 of 20 February 2017), which borrows its name from the then Minister of the Interior Marco Minniti. According to this decree, municipalities are entrusted with adopting orders that aim at protecting the "decorum", "urban liveability" and the "peace and quietness of residents" (art. 8 co. 1 lett. a no 1), and at preventing "situations that favour the occurrence of criminal phenomena or illegality, such as drug dealing, the exploitation of prostitution, begging with the aid of minors and disabled people, the illicit occupation of public space [*e.g.*, by unauthorised street vendors], and violent behaviour, also linked to alcohol or substance abuse" (art. 8 co. 1 lett. b No 1). In short, according to this decree local measures can target behaviour that falls within the pre-crime stage (Pleysier, 2015, 2017), for it favouring or being conducive to 'serious' crime, such as drug dealing, violence and the exploitation of prostitution.

The decree also allows local authorities to punish the behaviour of people that "impair[..] the free access and use" (art. 9 co. 1) of "special areas" (mostly, areas that have a touristic destination, or are green areas like public parks, see art. 9 co. 3) and areas of transit (e.g., train and bus stations) by others in two different ways: by applying an administrative fine (up to € 300) and by banning them from that space for 48 hours (art. 9 co. 1 and art 10. co. 1). The length of the ban can be further extended by the police chief (questore) to up to six months (or two years, for a person who in the past five years had been found guilty of an offence against the person or property), if the banned person reiterates the prohibited conduct and providing that such a behaviour "may lead to a threat to security" (art. 10 co. 2).[14]

---

14 According to media accounts, many bans have so far seemingly been used against asylum seekers and refugees. See e.g. https://www.fanpage.it/a-genova-il-decreto-minniti-divide-contro-i-bivacchi-arrivano-i-dissuasori-di-seduta/.

Clearly, all these provisions of the "Minniti decree" are based on very vague concepts (such as the ones of "decorum" and "liveability") and on nebulous definitions of the proscribed behaviour, which include: "situations that favour the occurrence of criminal phenomena or illegality", and "behaviours that impair the free access and use" of specific and special areas by others "that may lead to a threat to security". Similarly to the 2008 Security Package, also the legislative vagueness of this more recent decree opens up possibilities for abuses and for a quite arbitrary exclusion of unwanted people from public spaces by local authorities.

This legislative framework is (at least partly) the result of dominant representations of 'problems' and solutions, which have been presented by relevant actors (such as politicians) in the media overtime, in particular against migrants. For example, a longitudinal study that has analysed media representations of the local regulation of street prostitution in the national press from 2008 (the year of the adoption of the Security Package) until 2017 (Di Ronco, 2017), suggested that the 'problem' of street prostitution has been amplified in much of the news through the link with other "problems". These are particularly connected to other cases of social disorder (*e.g.*, public drunkenness, rowdy behaviour), physical disorder (*e.g.*, littering), and crime proper (*e.g.*, drug dealing, physical assault). All these 'problems' have been deemed to contribute to the decay of neighbourhoods attended by middle class families, especially residential areas, city centres, areas of transit and of summer vacation. To overcome the 'emergence' and revitalise 'degenerating' districts, politicians in the press – mostly using a sensationalistic rhetoric – have invoked the need to increase the presence of police officers. This presence was made grim by a militarised appearance with heavy weapons, which are usually not carried by the police in Italy, and by the military. In addition, reference was made to the need of enhancing the public order powers of local authorities (including through administrative fines against both sex workers and clients).

Similar results emerge from a longitudinal study conducted over a similar period of time (from 2007 until the end of May 2017), which explored the representations of migrants (particularly, asylum seekers and refugees) in the local press of two different cities run by different political coalitions (centre-left in Udine and right in Padova) (Di Ronco and Lavorgna, in this volume). Either because of their association with social and physical disorder (in Udine) or with crime proper (in Padova, where crime has mostly consisted of sexual assaults, and gangs-related criminal activities such as drug dealing and violence), migrants in both cities have been identified as a 'problem' enhancing citizens' fears and making urban living 'unbearable'. Once more, politicians in both cities have advocated the use of the military, the enhanced presence of the police and of the use of administrative fines, as the ideal solutions to the 'problem'. This was presented as the key strategies to regaining control of areas that have been 'invaded' by unwanted migrants (Di Ronco and Lavorgna, in this volume).

In short, in Italy punitive and excessive measures (so judged by the national constitutional court) have been adopted by local authorities mostly against migrants (Crocitti and Selmini, 2017), who sometimes (for instance in the case of homeless and street sex workers) have been penalised for their mere unwanted presence in certain areas and their easy association with disorder and crime. This penalisation (and the granting of enhanced public order powers to local authorities by the national legislator) has been fed by the need of responding to the increasing fears and anxieties felt among Italian citizens, who seem to be particularly concerned about the perceived worsening standards of living (in terms of increased levels of disorder, crime, and social diversity) in 'their' neighbourhoods.

Not so serious Organised Crime

In the UK, the current system regulating gang injunctions provides a good example of both upwards and downwards spirals of crime prevention. In essence, on one side the seriousness of organised crime absorbs gang-related crimes, and on the other side, the aim of prevention of gang-related activity leads to more punitive responses for both adults and teenagers deemed to be involved in "gangs" (for a critical account of the gang label, see Alexander, 2008).

Gang injunctions are civil orders that have first been introduced by the Policing and Crime Act 2009; they are aimed at preventing gang-related violence and criminal activity. Terms imposed can (for example) prevent or restrict association with other gang members, prohibit travel to certain areas, prevent the congregation of people in groups of three or restrict individuals from possessing more than one mobile telephone. It can also prevent the promotion of gang related activity on social networking sites. With the Crime and Security Act 2010 and the Crime and Courts Act 2013 these provisions have been applied to 14 to 17 year olds with the involvement of Youth Court and Youth Offending Teams. Research shows that there has been violence reduction associated to locations where gang injunctions have been used (Carr, Slothower and Parkinson, 2017). However, the Serious Crime Act 2015 amended the statutory definition of what comprises a 'gang' to make it less restrictive and expanded the scope of the activity, to include groups involved in drug activity.

Currently, a gang under revised section 34 of the Policing and Crime Act 2009 (a) consists of at least three people; (b) has one or more characteristics that enable its members to be identified by others as a group and; (c) engages in gang-related violence or is involved in the illegal drug market. The identifying characteristics of a gang may, but need not, relate to any of the following: (a) the use by the group of a common name, emblem or colour; The group's leadership or command structure; (b) the group's association with a particular area; (c) the group's involvement with a particular unlawful activity. Crucially, this definition and the inclusion of illegal drugs as an element for requesting an injunction, substantially homologates gangs with organised crime groups. There remains one difference: the local level focus of the gangs and the expectation that the latter could have national or international reach.

Differently from the highly contested Anti-Social Behaviour Orders (ASBOs), whose breach consisted in a criminal offence, the consequences of breaching a gang injunction are not criminal per se. Breaching of a gang injunction amounts to civil content of court - even though arrest, remand in custody, followed by a prison sentence are still possibilities depending on the nature of the breach. The main issue with these injunctions, therefore, is not in the technicality of the provision, but rather in the overlapping between concepts and norms of gangs and concepts and norms of organised crime groups. The language of gangs – both adult and youth gangs – and organised crime constantly intersects across UK policy and law enforcement approaches (Sergi, 2017). Similarly, competences of institutions and agencies tackling both tend to overlap too. In fact, even though local police forces and local authorities are the ones to initiate an application for a gang injunction, the National Crime Agency's (NCA), which is the agency leading the fight against organised crime, is often involved in investigations of gangs at local level. This is because the NCA focuses on illegal drugs markets and trends and therefore monitors both both organised crime groups as well as local gangs – as a division is in practice quite impossible. The NCA also considers gangs a pathway into drug criminality at a more sophisticated level. As the NCA (2018: 10) notices:

> "Young people brought up in deprived neighbourhoods by fragmented families are more susceptible to members of commodity-based OCGs or street gangs looking to recruit. Initially these young people can become involved in anti-social behaviour and petty crime before progressing into more significant criminality".

As the NCA's mandate is on serious and organised crime, local gang activities involving drug smuggling – which would often not pass the threshold of seriousness – are essentially included de facto within the agency's mandate. Moreover, as the Home Office has been promoting local partnerships to fight organised crime, the cross-over between the NCA's activities and those of local police forces against drug markets is a well-known consequence (Home Office, 2013). Further proof of this is the function the NCA has assumed within the Home Office's programme "Ending Gang Violence and Exploitation (EGVE)" re-launched in 2016. The NCA carries out assessments of county lines – which is the phenomenon of gangs moving into drug markets outside urban areas where they usually operate. As vulnerable and young local people are groomed and/or coerced into moving or selling drugs, and the homes of vulnerable adults can be taken over as a base from which drugs are sold, the NCA has to step in. It provides an assessment of the situation, the nature and scale of the problem, and leads the national response together with local policing. In practice this means that the NCA – a national security and intelligence-led agency – is using its intrusive powers against less serious forms of organised crime irrespective of the proportionality principle. Therefore, this also translates in a downward spiral of crime prevention. That a national intelligence and security agency influences, more or less directly, the policing of street crime in the form of (youth) gangs – which might be, but not necessarily are, 'serious' forms of criminality according to the legal framework – means essentially securitising policing work, *i.e.* making traditional policing an instrument to deliver national security. This, in practice, results in the justification of special measures of prevention and disruption, which might be asked of police forces in the name of national security.

At the same time, in an upward spiral of crime prevention, gangs and organised crime groups are increasingly becoming interchangeable concepts – even though the harm they pose to communities is quite different – thus elevating the status of gang criminality to national security levels. In essence, a too big (legal) hammer is used for a small social nail risks causing more harm than the one that it tries to reduce in the first place.

Discussion –

Is there a role for the EU in ensuring that national and local CP policy and practice are not excessive?

Many EU countries have expanded the remit and reach of their CP complex. In this chapter, we have used the cases of Italy and the UK to illustrate the expansion in CP both downwards and upwards. In Italy, 'unwanted' people like migrants have been targeted with punitive measures (mostly administrative fines and location bans). People's fears have played a key role here: white middle-class Italians tend to feel rather uncomfortable and unsafe, also in the light of the association (rather unproblematised yet reinforced by politicians also through the media) of migrants with disorder and crime. In the UK, individuals may experience severe restrictions of their fundamental rights (including their rights to free movement, and to associate and assemble in public spaces) because of their alleged membership of, or participation in, a "gang" – a concept that is very vaguely defined by the relevant legislation and policies. In addition, gang-related activities, in particular when involving drugs, are equated with organised crime activities and are thus tackled by the NCA.[15] CP measures as these are often excessive in their scope, especially if the harm

[15] Another example is provided by 2003 Act Furthering Integrity of Decisions by Public Administration (or Bibob Act) in The Netherlands, which gives local authorities the power to decide on applications for licences and to reject or withdraw them in case infiltration of serious and organised crime groups is detected or seriously suspected. According to van Duyne and van der Vorm (2015), this power has essentially been used not that much to target organised crime, but nuisance and public order disturbances (particularly, pub violation of closing times, noise levels and public nuisance rules, dirty restaurants etc.) with great repercussions on people's privacy and other fundamental freedoms.

(if any) they aim at preventing is compared to the effect they have on individuals, their liberties, possibilities of integration, and social opportunities.

Crime prevention – and especially, within it, the power to legislate in criminal matters – has historically been considered a national competence and has belonged to the sovereignty of member states. The European Council's meetings in Tampere, The Hague and Stockholm, have progressively paved the way for the Treaty of Lisbon and, therefore, to an EU expanded competence in CP matters. This competence was justified by the shared interest to create an Area of Freedom Security and Justice (AFSJ). Going beyond that was the aim of combating crime having a cross-border dimension, including OC and terrorism along with other 'Euro-crimes'. This relative long process, which has resulted into the broadening of the EU CP competences, has not been met without resistance from the member states (Baker, 2010).[16]

As a result, the EU competence in CP is anything but broad. As seen above, although the proportionality and legality principles in CP or security measures have been given legal recognition at the EU level (particularly, in the Charter), their violations by member states are not enforceable by EU bodies – unless they involve the implementation of EU law. In short, the EU has little to no power to 'tell off' member states for their eventual excessive use of CP measures. This notwithstanding, the EU has a number of bodies that can act as watchdog against excessively punitive CP measures against harmless incivilities (mainly, discriminatory practices against specific social groups) and non-so serious crime, which has yet been subsumed into the area of organised crime.

The European Crime Prevention Network (EUCPN), for example, is an EU body that has been established in 2001 with the specific mandate of supporting CP initiatives and activities at the national and local levels. The network has in the past few years worked towards the promotion of cooperation between member states as well as between local authorities. It has mainly pursued this

16 The EU competence in criminal law, for example, is limited, among others, by the principles of subsidiarity and proportionality. According to the former principle, the EU can only legislate in criminal matters if the goal cannot be reached more effectively with measures at the national, regional or local levels. In light of the latter principle, the EU ability to harmonise criminal law should not exceed what is necessary to achieve the objectives of the Treaties.

aim by making available through its online knowledge centre[17] information regarding best practices in national and local CP, which have been collected through its national contact points.

In the past few years, there have been proposals to enhance the powers of the network. In the Stockholm Programme,[18] for example, the Council suggested converting it into the Observatory for the Prevention of Crime. The European Commission (2012) suggested providing it with a better resourced Secretariat instead (EUCPN+ and observatory type of functions). These proposals have led in 2015 to the project entitled "the development of the observatory function of the European Centre of Expertise in the Prevention of Crime within the EUCPN" (EUCPN, 2015a, p. 14), which has strengthened the work of the EUCPN Secretariat around five 'pillars' (EUCPN, 2015a). Two of these 'pillars' are based on the goals to support and assist national and local policy makers as well as practitioners in their daily CP work and to disseminate qualitative knowledge on CP (EUCPN, 2015c). The goals of disseminating qualitative knowledge on crime prevention and of supporting crime prevention activities at national and local level both with knowledge (including evaluations) and assistance in funding applications, have also been reiterated in one of the network's most recent Working Programmes (EUCPN, 2018) and in its Multiannual Strategy 2016-2020 (EUCPN, 2015b).

In sum, the EUCPN seems to be the best placed to provide guidance to member states and local authorities in their CP efforts. This ideal advisory role of the network is reinforced both by the increased competences and resources of its Secretariat (as reflected in its goals and plans of action),[19] and by the EU focus on protecting individual's fundamental rights while adopting and implementing CP measures at the EU, national and local levels. At a practical level, this means that, especially when requested by national and local authorities, the network should be able to warn them against possible violations of fundamental EU-principles, such as the legality and proportionality principles. In addition, it should also advise them against the adoption of 'bad' practices, and share with them the best ones, *i.e.* those that deliver security with the least

---

17 See eucpn.org/knowledge-center.

18 OJ C 115 of 4 May 2010.

19 For the increased funding and personnel available to the EUCPN, see https://eucpn.org/about/network?language=24.

compression of individual's freedoms. The EUCPN can do so also by partnering up with other relevant EU bodies, including: the European Network on the Administrative Approach tackling serious and organised crime (ENAA), which is already embedded in the EUCPN; the Agency for Fundamental Rights (FRA); the European Forum for Urban Safety (EFUS); Eurojust, and Europol.

Concluding thoughts

This chapter has used the two case studies of the Italian security regulation and of the UK gang legislation to illustrate how CP in European member states has often expanded both upwards and downwards. It did so by equating incivilities to crime and not-so serious crime to organised crime. But in both directions this erodes individual's rights and violates the proportionality principle. Expanded CP is also mushrooming a multitude of bodies and agencies that are competent in CP at the local, national and European levels. At the EU level, this has occurred more substantially from the 2009 Treaty of Lisbon onwards, when the EU has been given competences to (among others) approximate definitions of and sanctions for 'Euro Crimes' and facilitate and promote police and judicial cooperation in criminal matters between member states mainly through EU bodies such as Europol and Eurojust. This extension of CP powers at the EU level has, however, come along with the recognition of the need to respect people's rights while delivering security and, therefore, with the duty for the Union, its member states and local authorities within them, of not imposing measures that have a disproportionate effect on individual's autonomy. We have suggested that the EU – particularly through the EUCPN and other 'soft law' bodies and networks – could play a role in facilitating the compliance of national and local CP measures with the proportionality principle. This does not mean, however, that this role will be taken up by the EU and its networks, or that – if exercised – it will be effective in persuading member states and local authorities not to adopt excessive CP measures. In the end, we cannot ignore the fact that the field of CP is very much politicised and that crime and fear of crime – and discourses around them – have proven in recent years to be crucial to decide elections and positions of political power. The urge of showing to the electorate that 'problems' and 'serious threats' are being handled – and preferably handled with a firm hand – by the relevant institutions and bodies, may ultimately frustrate (as has certainly done so in the past) the need to balance security with the safeguarding of fundamental rights.

References

Alexander, C., Rethinking "gangs"'. Runnymede Trust https://www.runnymedetrust.org/uploads/publications/pdfs/Rethinking-Gangs-2008.pdf), 2008.

Atkinson, R. and G. Helms, *Securing an urban renaissance*. The Policy Press, Bristol, 2007.

Bannister, J., N. Fyfe and A. Kearns, Respectable or respectful? (In) civility and the city. *Urban Studies*, vol. 43, no. 5-6, 2006; p. 919-937.

Bauman, Z. *Legislators and interpreters. On modernity, post-modernity and intellectuals.* Cambridge: Polity Press, 1987.

Baker, E., Governing through crime—the case of the European Union. *European Journal of Criminology*, 2010, vol. 7, no. 3, pp. 187-213.

Beck, U., *Risk society: towards a new modernity*. Sage, London, 1992.

Belina, B. and G. Helms, Zero tolerance for the industrial past and other threats: policing and urban entrepreneurialism in Britain and Germany. *Urban Studies*, 2003, vol. 40, no. 9, pp. 1845-1867.

Berry, M., I. Garcia-Blanco and K. Moore, *Press coverage of the refugee and migrant crisis in the EU: a content analysis of five European countries* (December 2015). 2015. Available at: http://www.unhcr.org/56bb369c9.pdf (Accessed 1 June 2017).

Burney, E., *Making people behave: anti-social behaviour, politics and policy*. Routledge, London, 2005.

Campbell L., Organized crime and national security: A dubious connection? *New Criminal Law Review: An International and Interdisciplinary Journal,* vol. 17 issue 2, pp. 220–251.

Carr, R., M. Slothower and J. Parkinson, Do gang injunctions reduce violent crime? Four tests in Merseyside, UK, *Cambridge Journal of Evidence-Based Policing*, vol. 1, issue 4, pp. 195-210, 2017.

Carrapico, H., Analysing the European Union's responses to organized crime through different securitization lenses, *European Security*, 2014, vol. 23 issue 4, pp. 601-661.

Cohen, S., *Visions of social control: crime, punishment and classification*. Polity Press, Cambridge, 1985.

Council of the European Union (EU Council), *The Prevention and Control of Organized Crime. A European Union Strategy for the beginning of the New Millennium*. Official Journal C124/1- 124/33. 3rd May 2000.

Council of the European Union (EU Council), *Draft Council Conclusions on the creation and implementation of a EU policy cycle for organised crime and serious international crime*. 15358/10. 25th October 2010.

Crocitti, S., and R. Selmini, Controlling immigrants: the latent function of Italian administrative orders. *European Journal on Criminal Policy and Research*, 2017, vol. 23, no. 1, pp. 99-114.

Di Ronco, A., Regulating street prostitution as a public nuisance in the 'culture of consumption': a comparative analysis between Birmingham, Brussels and Milan. In: N. Persak and G. Vermeulen, (eds.), *Rethinking prostitution: from discourse to description, from moralisation to normalisation?* Maklu, Antwerp, 2014 (pp. 145-171).

Di Ronco, A., Disorderly or simply ugly? Representations of the local regulation of street prostitution in the Italian press and their policy implications. *International Journal of Law, Crime and Justice*, 2017, vol. 52, pp. 10-22.

Di Ronco, A., and N. Peršak, Regulation of incivilities in the UK, Italy and Belgium: courts as potential safeguards against legislative vagueness and excessive use of penalising powers? *International Journal of Law, Crime and Justice*, 2014, vol. 42, no. 4, pp. 340-365.

EUCPN, *Annual Report of activities in 2014* (\http://eucpn.org/sites/default/files/content/download/files/eucpn_annual_report_2014.pdf), 2015a.

EUCPN, *Multiannual strategy for the European Crime Prevention Network*

http://eucpn.org/sites/default/files/content/download/files/mas_2016-2020_final_version.pdf), 2015b.
EUCPN, *Work Programme 2015* (https://eucpn.org/sites/default/files/content/download/files/work_programme_2015.pdf), 2015c.
EUCPN, *Work Programme 2018* https://eucpn.org/sites/default/files/content/download/files/work_programme_2018.pdf), 2018.
Eurobarometer, *Special Eurobarometer 464b. Report. Europeans' attitudes towards security*. file:///C:/Users/ad16315/Downloads/ebs_464b_en.pdf), 2017
European Commission, *Report from the Commission to the Council. Evaluation report on the European Union Crime Prevention Network*, COM(2012) 717 final, Brussels, 2012.
European Commission, *Communication from the Commission to the European Parliament, the Council, the Council, the European Economic and Social Committee and the Committee of the Regions. The European Agenda on Security*, COM(2015) 185 final, Brussels, 2015.
European Commission, *Communication from the Commission to the European Parliament and the Council, on an Action Plan for strengthening the fight against terrorist financing,* COM(2016) 50 final, 2016.
European Commission, *Communication from the Commission to the European Parliament, the Council, the European Economic and Social Committee and the Committee of the Regions. Action Plan to support the protection of public spaces,* COM(2017) 612 final, Brussels, 2017.
European Commission, *Communication from the Commission to the European Parliament, the Council, the European Council and the Council. Thirteenth progress report towards an effective and genuine Security Union,* COM(2018) 46 final, Brussels, 2018a.
European Commission, *Proposal for a Directive of the European Parliament and of the Council laying down rules facilitating the use of financial and other information for the prevention, detection, investigation or prosecution of certain criminal offences and repealing Council Decision 2000/642/JHA*, COM(2018) 213 final, 2018b.
Farrand, B., and H. Carrapico, Copyright law as a matter of (inter)national security? The attempt to securitise commercial infringement and its spill

over onto individual liability. *Crime Law Social Change*, 2012, vol. 57 issue 4, pp. 373–401.
Feinberg, J., *Harm to others*. Oxford University Press, New York, 1984
Freely, M., and J. Simon, Actuarial justice: The emerging new criminal law. In: D. Nelken (ed.), *The Futures of Criminology*. Sage, London, 1994.
Furedi, F., *Culture of fear: risk taking and the morality of low expectation*. Cassell, London, 1997.
Furedi, F., *Therapy culture: cultivating vulnerability in an uncertain age*. Routledge, London, 2004.
Garland, D., *The culture of control: crime and social order in contemporary society*. Oxford University Press, Oxford, 2001.
Giddens, A., *Modernity and self-identity: self and society in the late modern age*. Polity Press, Cambridge, 1991.
Guia, M.J., M.A.H. van der Woude, and J. van der Leun, *Social control and justice: crimmigration in the age of fear*. Eleven International Publishing, The Hague, 2011.
Home Office, *Serious and organised crime strategy*, London, The Stationery Office, 2013.
Hörnqvist, M., Risk assessments and public order disturbances: new European guidelines for the use of force?. *Journal of Scandinavian Studies in Criminology and Crime Prevention*, 2004, vol. 5, no. 1, pp. 4-26.
Innes, M., and V. Jones, *Neighbourhood Security and Urban Change*. Joseph Rowntree Foundation, London, 2006.
Jareborg, N., Criminalization as last resort (Ultima Ratio). *Ohio State Journal of Criminal Law*, 2004, vol. 2, no. 2, pp. 521-534.
Jones, T., Governing security: pluralisation, privatisation, and polarisation in crime control and practice. In: M. Maguire, R. Morgan, and R. Reiner (eds.), *The Oxford handbook of criminology*. Oxford University Press, Oxford, 2012.
Lavorgna, A. and A. Sergi, Serious, therefore organised? A critique of the emerging 'cyber organised crime' rhetoric in the United Kingdom. *International Journal of Cyber Criminology*, 2016, vol. 10 issue 2, pp. 170–187.
Melossi, D. and R. Selmini, Modernisation of institutions of social and penal control in Europe: the 'New' crime prevention. In: A. Crawford (ed.),

Crime Prevention Policies in Comparative Perspective. Cullompton, Willan, 2009, pp. 153-176.
National Crime Agency (NCA), *National Strategic Assessment of Serious and Organised Crime*, London, The Stationery Office, 2018.
Newburn, T., *Criminology*. Abingdon, Willan Publishing, 2007.
O'Malley, P., Crime and risk. In: P. Carlen and L.A. França (eds.), *Alternative criminologies*. London, Routledge, 2018.
Pavarini, M., *L'Amministrazione locale della paura. Ricerche Tematiche Sulle Politiche di Sicurezza Urbana in Italia*. Carocci, Roma, 2006.
Peršak, N., *Criminalising harmful conduct: the harm principle, its limits and continental counterparts*. Springer, New York, 2007.
Peršak, N., *Regulation and social control of incivilities*. Routledge, Abingdon, 2017.
Peršak, N., EU criminal law and its legitimation: in search for a substantive principle of criminalisation. *European Journal of Crime, Criminal Law and Criminal Justice*, 2018, vol. 26, no. 1, pp. 20-39.
Peršak, N., and A. Di Ronco, Urban space and the social control of incivilities: perceptions of space influencing the regulation of anti-social behaviour. *Crime, Law and Social Change*, 2018, vol. 69, no. 3, pp. 329-347.
Pleysier, S., Local governance of safety and the normalization of behavior. *Crime, Law and Social Change*, 2015, vol. 64, no. 4-5, pp. 305-317.
Pleysier, S., Normalisation of behaviour in public space: the construction and control of "public nuisance" in Belgium. In N. Peršak (ed.), *Regulation and social control of incivilities*. Routledge, London, 2017 (pp. 95-107).
Ponsaers, P., *Social analysis of security. financial, economic and ecological crime – crime (in)security and distrust – public and private policing*. Eleven International Publishing, The Hague, 2012.
Reiner, R., Media made criminality: The representation of crime in the mass media. In: M. Maguire, R. Morgan and R. Reiner (Eds.), *The Oxford handbook of criminology*. Oxford University Press, Oxford, 2002; p. 302–340).
Sampson, R.J. and S.W. Raudenbush, Seeing disorder: neighborhood stigma and the social construction of "broken windows". *Social Psychology Quarterly*, 2004, vol. 67, no. 4, p. 319-342.
Sampson, R.J., Disparity and diversity in the contemporary city: Social (dis)order revisited. *The British Journal of Sociology*, 2009, vol. 60, no. 1, p. 1-31.

Sergi, A., *From mafia to organised crime. A comparative analysis of policing models*, London, Palgrave Macmillan, 2017.
Siegel, D. and V. Nagy, *The migration crisis? Criminalization, security and survival.* Eleven International Publishing, The Hague, 2018.
Sibley, D., *Geographies of exclusion: society and difference in the west.* Routledge, London, 1995.
Simester, A.P. and von Hirsch, A., *Incivilities: regulating offensive behaviour.* Hart Publishing, Oxford, 2006.
Simester, A.P. and von Hirsch, A., *Crimes, harms, and wrongs: on the principles of criminalisation.* Hart Publishing, Oxford, 2011.
Smith, N., *The new urban frontier: Gentrification and the revanchist city.* Routledge, London, 2005.
Squires, P., *ASBO Nation: The criminalisation of nuisance.* The Policy Press, Bristol, 2008.
Tonry, M., *Punishment and politics: evidence and emulation in the making of English crime control policy.* Willan, Cullompton, 2004.
van der Woude, M., V. Barker and J. van der Leun, Crimmigration in Europe. *European Journal of Criminology*, 2017, vol. 14, no. 1, pp. 3-6.
van Duyne, P.C. and B. van der Vorm, From organised crime threat to nuisance control. In: P.C. van Duyne, A. Maljević, G.A. Antonopoulos, J. Harvey and K. von Lampe (eds.), *The relativity of wrongdoing: Corruption, organised crime, fraud and money laundering in perspective.* Wolf Legal Publishers, Oisterwijk, 2015 (pp. 127-158).
Waiton, S., Asocial not anti-social: The 'Respect Agenda' and the 'therapeutic me'. In: P. Squires (ed.), *ASBO Nation: The criminalisation of nuisance.* The Policy Press, Bristol, 2008a (pp. 337- 357).
Waiton, S., *The politics of antisocial behaviour: amoral panics.* Routledge, London, 2008b.
Welch, M. and L. Schuster, Detention of asylum seekers in the US, UK, France, Germany, and Italy: A critical view of the globalizing culture of control. *Criminal Justice*, 2005, vol. 5, no. 4, pp. 331-355.
Wilson, J.Q. and G. Kelling, The police and neighborhood safety: broken windows. *Atlantic Monthly*, 1982, vol. 127, pp. 29-38..
Young, J., *The amplification of drug use. The manufacture of news: social problems, deviance and the mass media.* Constable, London, 1973.

Young, J., *The exclusive society: social Exclusion, crime and difference in late modernity*. Sage, London, 1999.
Zedner, L., Pre-crime and post-criminology? *Theoretical Criminology*, 2007, vol. 11, no. 2, pp. 261-281.

How well established is research on organised crime in Germany?

Klaus von Lampe and *Susanne Knickmeier*[1]

Introduction

The study of organised crime has developed into a distinct academic (sub)-discipline over the past two or three decades. However, there are considerable variations across countries. In some places, such as the Netherlands, research on organised crime is well established, while in other places it appears to be a much more marginalised endeavour, at least when assessed on contributions to the international scholarly debate. Germany is a case in point. For example, a cursory review of the programs of the annual meetings of the American Society of Criminology (ASC) and European Society of Criminology (ESC) reveals that presentations by criminologists from Germany relating to the topic of organised crime are rare although otherwise there is a strong German presence at these conferences. Similarly, there are only few organised crime-related contributions by German-based scholars to journals such as *Crime, Law and Social Change*, *Global Crime*, and *Trends in Organised Crime*. For example, for every contribution from Germany between 2008 and 2017 there were five times more contributions from scholars based in the Netherlands. In *Crime, Law and Social Change*, no organised crime-related articles by German-based scholars can be found in this 10-year period at all compared to 12 organised crime-related articles by authors from the Netherlands. In *Global Crime*, there was one organised crime-related contribution from Germany and seven from the Netherlands, and in *Trends in Organised Crime*, German-based authors accounted for only seven articles compared to 22 articles authored by Dutch-based authors.

---

1 Klaus von Lampe is professor of criminology at the Berlin School of Economics and Law, Berlin, Germany. Susanne Knickmeier is researcher at the Max Planck Institute for Foreign and International Criminal Law, Freiburg, Germany.

The purpose of this chapter is to assess the state of organised crime research in Germany and to examine whether the impression of a general neglect of the study of organised crime is a misconception.

This chapter is divided into two main parts. The first part provides a brief overview of the situation of organised crime in Germany as it presents itself in official and media accounts. As it becomes evident, Germany has very good reasons for being concerned about the organisation of crimes and criminals within its borders, so the lack of research on organised crime cannot be explained by the absence of appropriate objects of study. The second part describes findings of a systematic analysis of the output of researchers based in Germany who study organised crime. This includes an inventory of research projects, dissertation projects and academic publications on issues relating to organised crime over a period of some ten years. The focus is on the continuity and consistency of lines of research rather than on questions of quality or content. The aim is to illustrate how well the study of organised crime is established institutionally, namely with regard to specific academic disciplines and institutions, and with a view to its funding. No attempt is made to systematically review the substance of the research and to elucidate what it might reveal about the situation of organised crime in Germany. The reason for this omission is twofold. First, a considerable share of the pertinent scholarship does not address the situation in Germany but rather the situation elsewhere in the world, and second, as will be shown in more detail below, the study of organised crime in Germany is far too fragmented to present an even remotely coherent picture. Against this backdrop, this chapter concludes with a discussion of how organised crime research in Germany can potentially be strengthened and how scholars based in Germany can achieve a greater impact on the international academic debate on organised crime.

The current situation of organised crime in Germany

Law enforcement agencies and the media in Germany regularly report on manifestations of organised crime, broadly defined. One focus is on organised criminal activities and illegal markets. Another focus is on criminal groups and networks. A third major concern is with criminal milieus that reportedly have come under the influence of powerful underworld figures and underworld alliances.

Organised criminal activities

If organised crime is understood in terms of organised criminal activities, two broad areas have to be distinguished: illegal markets characterised by seller-buyer relations, and the organised commission of predatory crimes involving perpetrators and victims. Not least because of a large and growing population (82,79 million in 2017),[2] Germany is an important market place for illegal goods and services. This is particularly true for the illegal drug trade, although in terms of per-capita consumption, Germany tends to rank only in the middle or towards the bottom among European countries (EMCDDA, 2017).

Most of the drugs consumed in Germany (cannabis, cocaine, heroin and amphetamine) originate from other European and non-European countries. The country also functions as a transit country for drug smuggling (Europol 2013). In addition, Germany is the leading European country by sales volume in the distribution of drugs via the darknet (EMCDDA, 2017: 20). With respect to the production of drugs, however, Germany is only of marginal relevance, with small shares in the manufacturing of amphetamines and the cultivation of cannabis (Bundeskriminalamt, 2016: 5-6).

Apart from illegal drugs, Germany ranks high among consumer countries for illegal cigarettes. In terms of overall volume, Germany is in fourth place behind France, Poland, and the UK. However, according to a study sponsored by the tobacco industry, the consumption of smuggled and counterfeit cigarettes has declined considerably in recent years, dropping from a share of 11,5% of the overall cigarette market in 2012 to only 5,2% in 2016 (KPMG, 2017: 76).

Other illegal markets that have repeatedly been mentioned in connection with organised crime and the crime situation in Germany include the trade in counterfeit brand products, counterfeit medicine, protected species, protected cultural artefacts, and guns, human trafficking and human smuggling, as well as illegal gambling, in particular illegal sports betting.

---

2 https://de.statista.com/statistik/daten/studie/2861/umfrage/entwicklung-der-gesamtbevoelkerung-deutschlands/ (7 February 2019)

Finally, Germany is considered a hotbed for money laundering (Bülles, 2013, p. 249).

The supply of illegal goods and services is not the only facet of the organised crime landscape in Germany. In fact, a lot of attention in the German debate on organised crime has been paid to predatory crimes, including such offences as motor vehicle theft (Bundeskriminalamt, 2017), serial residential burglary (Backes *et al.*, 2016) and pickpocketing (Gögelein, 2017). A substantial part of these crimes is attributed to transnationally mobile offender groups from Eastern Europe (Winter, 2015). Other areas of organised predatory crimes with a remarkable extent of damages, estimated at several billion Euros annually, include, for example, cybercrime (Berg and Maaßen, 2017) and fraud against the welfare system (Dowideit, 2017).

Offender structures

Referring to the organisation of crimes it cannot automatically be considered that the respective perpetrators are also 'organised'. For example, the existence of illegal markets implies a web of buyer-seller relations across different levels of the illicit supply chain. However, it remains an open question to what extent more integrated and coherent offender structures are involved. This open question applies, on one hand, to the presence of foreign criminal organisations on German soil, and on the other hand, to indigenous criminal structures (Kamstra, 2014; Paulus, 2015; Schulz, 2012).

The federal German police agency Bundeskriminalamt (BKA) prepares an annual organised crime situation report which includes an assessment of the degree of organisation of offender groups under investigation by German law enforcement agencies at the state and federal levels. For each offender group, a score ("organised crime potential") on a scale from 0 to 100 is calculated based on a weighted list of 50 indicators which range in value from 1,17 to 4,35. The highest ranked indicators are 'hierarchical structure', followed by 'international', 'an at first glance inexplicable relation of dependence or authority between several suspects', 'payment of bribes', and 'measures to launder money', while the lowest ranked indicators include 'assumed names', 're-admittance after release from prison', 'work on demand', 'disappearance of formerly available witnesses', and 'use of relatively expensive or difficult to implement scientific means and findings' (von Lampe, 2004: 92). The limitations of the use of such a composite index aside, it is remarkable that only few of the detected offender groups achieve a high score. In 2017, the average organised crime potential was only 40,9 out of 100 points referring to 572 investigations (Bundeskriminalamt, 2018: 5). This is consistent with results of early research on the level of organisation of offender groups in Germany from the 1970s and 1980s. These pioneering studies concluded that the German underworld is predominantly populated by loose, network-like offender structures (Kerner, 1973; Rebscher and Vahlenkamp, 1988; Weschke and Heine-Heiß, 1990).

Illegal governance

The exposure of illegal markets, predatory crimes, and the illegal businesses running these various schemes is relatively straightforward police business. In contrast, it is much more challenging for law enforcement agencies to detect and to investigate underlying criminal *power structures*, given that these structures tend to be elusive and rest primarily on the perceptions and beliefs of those that are governed. However, that is difficult to determine. Accordingly, organised crime situation reports neither contain information on the territoriality and spheres of influence of criminal groups, nor on the details of how criminal power is exercised.

What can be gleaned from the annual organised crime situation reports is the small share of cases attributed to members of Italian criminal associations. In 2017, only 14 out of 572 organised crime investigations were directed against Italian mafia-type associations, including seven involving 'Ndrangheta, three pertaining to the Sicilian Cosa Nostra, and two against the Camorra (BKA, 2018: 20). Contrary to their cliché, these organisations do not automatically attain positions of power when establishing a presence abroad, but they have shown an ability to acquire territorial control at least under certain circumstances (Varese, 2011). Nevertheless, according to a recent assessment provided by the German federal government, Italian criminal associations do not occupy prominent positions in the ethnically diverse criminal landscape of Germany (Bundesregierung, 2017).

The fact that the annual situation reports remain inconclusive regarding the existence of underworld power structures does not mean that such structures do not exist. In fact, there are numerous indicators, documented in official and media sources, which point to a consolidation and concentration of power in the German underworld, partly in the course of a historical process of the rise and fall of influential groups and alliances (see Behr, 1989; Gülay and Kuhn, 2009). At the centre of attention in the current debate on criminal power structures are so-called *Arab clans*. The term is applied to various large 'blood families' that originate from the Turkish-Kurdish-Arabic region and have settled in Germany since the 1980s. Many of the male members of these family clans have been implicated in criminal activities including theft, robbery, extortion, illegal prostitution and drug trafficking. In certain urban areas, namely Berlin, Bremen and the Ruhr region, they allegedly control entire neighbourhoods and illegal markets. If conflicts arise between different clans, self-proclaimed underworld magistrates provide dispute resolution services (Ghadban, 2018; Henninger, 2002; Wöhrle, 2017).

Sometimes, a dominating role in criminal milieus is also attributed to outlaw motorcycle clubs, for example by collecting protection payments from drug dealers (Adelsberger, 2012: 574). Against this backdrop, frequent conflicts between biker clubs are interpreted as struggles over spheres of influence and control over criminal activities (Bader, 2010; Jäger, 2012; Ziercke, 2010).

There are also claims that the influence of groups such as family clans or biker clubs extend to the legal spheres of society. This pertains primarily to the red-light sector and, more generally, the nightlife economy. Thereby, fluid boundaries appear between pure extortion, the provision of protection through illegal means, and the operation of legal security firms owned by underworld figures (Henninger and Susebach, 2005). However, there is no evidence that criminal influence has reached further to, for example, the construction sector (see Bundesregierung, 2017), in a way similar to the control acquired by Southern Italian Mafiosi in Northern Italy (Varese, 2011).

Taking stock of output of scholars based in Germany

From even the most cursory review of official and media accounts of the crime situation in Germany it becomes clear that students of organised crime have plenty to examine and many unanswered questions. Of course, one would exaggerate and overly dramatize things by drawing parallels between Germany and, say, Italy, the United States, Russia or Mexico with respect to the scale of the problem and the degree to which underworld and upperworld are intertwined. Yet, in essence all facets of the problem of organised crime can be observed in Germany, be they in a nascent state, emerging, or fully developed. In addition, Germany provides an important research site for studies of organised crime by its crime-geographic position. When seeking to understand the major trafficking routes that start, end or transect Europe, it is difficult to ignore Germany's role. For all these reasons, one would expect to find a well-developed German tradition of research into the organisation of crimes and criminals. Indeed, in the 1970s and 1980s, Germany was at the forefront in Western Europe when it came to criminological research on organised crime, just as it was pioneering the debate on the conceptualization of organised crime (Kerner, 1973; Mack and Kerner, 1975; Rebscher and Vahlenkamp, 1988; Weschke and Heine-Heiß, 1990). But what is the state of organised crime research in Germany today?

Methodology

The aim of the present analysis is to provide a rough overview of the study of organised crime in Germany over the past ten years with a view to such aspects as the volume of scholarly work, thematic foci, methodological approaches, and funding. Because of limited resources, it was not possible to extend the scope of the analysis to an in-depth, critical review of the research activities and scholarly literature. One line of inquiry relates to the scientific work, for example to what extent there is a clustering of research around specific topics and research questions, certain theoretical and conceptual approaches, or the usage of specific types of data. Another issue that is being addressed here pertains to the institutional context within which research on organised crime is carried out, namely regarding the academic and non-academic institutions and academic disciplines involved, and the sources of funding that are available.

This chapter is based on a project commissioned by the Forschungsforum Öffentliche Sicherheit (Research Forum Public Security) at Freie Universität Berlin, Germany.[3] The project entailed taking stock of the projects pursued and publications published by scholars based in Germany between 1 January 2008 and 1 September 2017. In an effort to identify all relevant scholarly activities, a number of literature databases and internet platforms (Deutsche Nationalbibliothek, Google Scholar, Google Books, KrimDok) were searched using various terms including "organisierte Kriminalität" (organised crime), "organised crime" + "Germany," "Kriminalität" (crime), "Mafia," "Schmuggel" (smuggling), "Drogenhandel" (drug trade), "Menschenhandel" (human trafficking), and "illegal" + "Handel" (trade).

Given that the purpose of the study was to assess the state of organised crime research in Germany, only projects and publications of those scholars were included who were based in Germany at the time the project was carried out, respectively, at the time of the publication. This excludes two groups of scholars, first, German scholars based abroad,[4] and, second, non-German scholars based outside of Germany doing research on, and writing about organised crime in Germany. The determination of the geographical location presented no methodological problems in the case of research and dissertation projects, as these tend to be clearly attached to specific institutions, and thus to specific places. It was much more challenging ascertain where authors were based at a particular point in time. Since it is not unusual for scholars to move from one academic institution to another throughout their careers, while institutional websites and other sources of information about academic affiliations are not necessarily always up-to-date. In some instances, the inclusion or exclusion of a publication rested on a determination of the most likely scenario based on available information.

---

3 See von Lampe and Knickmeier (2018).

4 This also applies to the first author who was based in Germany for only the first seven months of the study period, and accordingly only three of his solo-authored publications are included in the present analysis.

The assessment of the scholarly output of researchers based in Germany encompasses a total of 285 items, including 32 research projects, 38 doctoral dissertations, and 215 academic publications. These categories are not mutually exclusive in the sense that research and dissertation projects often (but not always) lead to other academic publications.

Research Projects

For the time period under study, a total of 32 completed or ongoing research projects could be identified (see von Lampe and Knickmeier, 2018: 32-37). In this context, research projects are defined as formal research endeavours undertaken by (academic or non-academic) institutions with a defined purpose and a set time frame, irrespective of the source of funding. In other words, the analysis covers externally funded projects as well as self-funded, respectively non-funded research. PhD-dissertation projects, however, are excluded here, and included in a separate category discussed further below.

In identifying pertinent research projects, we drew, first of all, on our literature review. In addition, we searched databases and websites of research funding institutions such as the European Commission, the German Federal Ministry of Education and Research (BMBF) and the German Research Foundation (DFG) as well as the websites of research institutions that potentially carry out or participate in studies related to organised crime. These latter institutions included the Criminological Research Institute Lower-Saxony (KfN), the Centre for Criminology (KrimZ), the National Centre for Crime Prevention (NZK), the German Police University (DHPol), and the Max Planck Institute for Foreign and International Criminal Law (MPICC). Further information of completed and ongoing research projects was obtained from a review of media sources.

When examining the 32 research projects and their respective time frames it becomes immediately apparent that there has been a marked upward trend in the number of projects pursued in a given year over the past 10 years. While between 2008 and 2013 only up to seven projects were initiated, continued or completed in a given year, this number jumped to 17 in 2014 and 24 in 2015. This sharp increase can partly be explained by a new line of funding launched by the federal government (BMBF) in 2013 under the title *Civil Security: Protection against Organised Crime*. On the basis of this research program eight projects have been financed since 2014 (von Lampe and Knickmeier, 2018: 37).

Figure 1.
Research projects related to organised crime, 2008-2017*:
Thematic focus

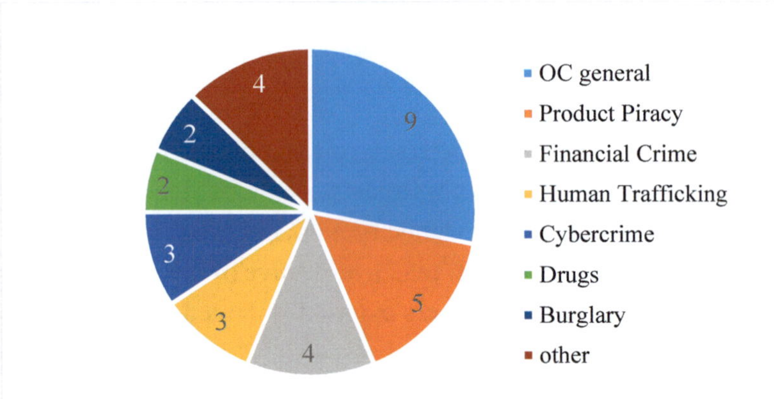

* Started, continued or completed in a given year;
2017 = 1 January – 1 September 2017

The research projects vary greatly with respect to their thematic focus (Figure 1). Nine out of 32 projects relate to organised crime in general, five cover product piracy including fraud in connection with pharmaceuticals, four relate to financial crimes including money laundering, three projects, respectively, deal with human trafficking and cybercrime, although criminal activities on the internet are also taken into account by other projects. Two studies investigate residential burglary and four deal with other areas of crime. Among these latter four, there are two studies addressing issues that have been at the centre of public attention in recent years and investigated by Mathias Rohe and Mahmoud Jaraba (2015) in their research project commissioned by the city government of Berlin, investigated the so-called *parallel justice* system among Arabic Clans, where disputes are settled in a subcultural system of conflict resolution in a way that undermines the legitimate criminal justice system. The other project aimed at a comprehensive analysis of the outlaw biker scene in Germany. It was launched in 2017 by the KfN with a grant from the European Union.

The thematic focus is not necessarily indicative of the degree to which a project aims to investigate the phenomenon proper. In many cases, the main emphasis is on prevention and countermeasures, rather than on the description, measurement, explanation or prediction of manifestations of organised crime. The spectrum of projects is manifold with respect to how directly they are concerned with the nature and development of empirical phenomena. At one end of the spectrum is a project on the structure of illegal markets by the Max Planck Institute for the Study of Societies. In this project, prevention or policy implications were of only secondary importance. At the other end of the spectrum is the project "Securestamp" coordinated by the Fraunhofer Institute for Physical Measurement Techniques, which dealt with new technologies for the forgery-proof printing of train tickets. Between these extremes are projects that comprise individual modules with an empirical focus on organised crime phenomena. For example, the European project "ALICA RAP" (Addiction and Lifestyles in Contemporary Europe Reframing Addictions Project) which otherwise had no direct focus on organised crime, but contained a work package that dealt with the careers of drug dealers.

Projects with an empirical component draw on a broad range of data sources and mostly collect data from more than one source. The most widely used methods of data collection are expert interviews (13 projects), analysis of open sources (11 projects), analysis of police and justice data (8 projects), interviews with incarcerated offenders (4 projects), and interviews with victims of crime (4 projects). An example for an interview-based study with a broad range of subjects is the above-mentioned study by Rohe and Jaraba on parallel justice. This study drew on interviews with 93 members of Arabic-Kurdish family clans or the Muslim communities in Berlin more generally, as well as on expert interviews with, for example, police officers, prosecutors and judges (Rohe and Jaraba, 2015, p. 31).

A large share (75 %) of the projects received grants from one of only two institutions, the European Commission (41 %) and the BMBF (34%), both of which have a clear preference for applied research. In contrast, there was no support for research related to organised crime from institutions that otherwise play a major role in the funding of social science research in Germany, such as the German Research Foundation (DFG) and the Volkswagen Foundation. It is also remarkable that 15 out of the 32 identified projects are international in nature, including 13 multi-country projects funded by the European Commission and two German-Austrian projects funded in part by the BMBF. In addition, two national-level projects by the KfN received funding from the EU.

Among the numerous academic institutions that participated in research on organised crime, there are only two that stand out in quantitative terms with the KfN involved in four projects and the University of Münster involved in three. However, their importance pales in comparison to the federal police agency Bundeskriminalamt (BKA) which in varying roles and with differing units participated in a total of 13 out of the 32 projects. This includes participation in the EU-project "Cyber-OC" and coordination of the EU-funded "Research Network on Organised Crime" by the Criminalistic Institute of the BKA (Töttel, Bulanova-Hristova and Flach, 2016).

Doctoral Dissertation Projects

The 38 dissertation projects with topics relating to organised crime that were completed since 2008 do not follow a clear trend similar to the sharp increase in other research projects from 2014 onwards. If anything, there is a development in the opposite direction. 30 out of the 38 dissertations were completed by 2013, which could suggest that organised crime has become significantly less attractive as a dissertation topic in the past few years (von Lampe and Knickmeier, 2018: 41-46; Figure 2).

In contrast to the research projects reviewed above, the dissertations also differ thematically with a clear preference for one specific phenomenon (Figure 3). While only 10 % (3 out of 32) of the research projects deal with human trafficking, the share is much higher with 39 % (10 out of 38) among doctoral dissertations. There is no similar thematic concentration with regard to any other phenomenon. Only financial crime, including money laundering, with three (8 %) dissertations is noteworthy in this respect. 39 % of the dissertations are not focused on specific areas of crime. This includes a number of theses that examine various aspects of the organisation of criminals, for instance, a comparative analysis of terrorist and criminal offender structures, taking the Albanian Mafia and the Jemaah Islamiyha as an example (Florack, 2010), a study of the communication between competing criminal groups (Bossert, 2010), and a study applying different structural models to organised crime in Russia (Abasov, 2016). It is also important to point out that a large share (24 out of 38; 63%) of the completed dissertations with reference to organised crime are legal treatises, including 18 (47%) with an exclusive focus on legal doctrine. Overall, the doctoral dissertations are mainly concerned with measures against organised crime, not with understanding the underlying empirical phenomena.

Figure 2.
Completed doctoral dissertations related to organised crime: 2008-2017*

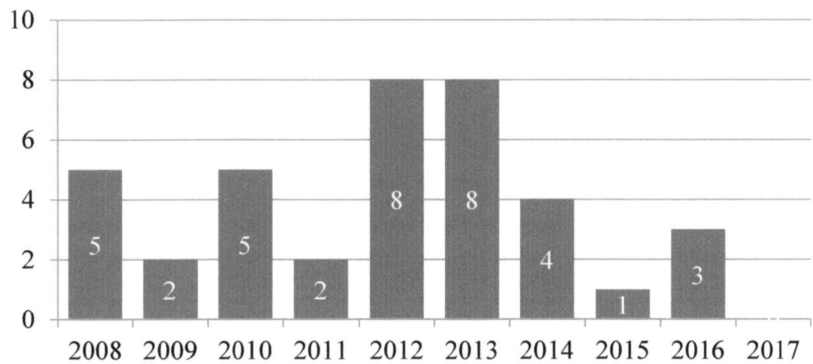

* 2017 = 1 January – 1 September 2017

Among the doctoral dissertations that are based on empirical research, open sources are the preferred source for data (9 theses). Three dissertations include interviews with non-incarcerated offenders; three dissertations draw on interviews with victims; two dissertations are based on expert interviews; and another two dissertations conduct interviews with incarcerated offenders, including one (Filter, 2010) which investigates drug dealing inside the prison. It is remarkable that in all dissertation projects relying on field research, including the interviewing and observation of non-incarcerated offenders, the data were collected outside of Germany. This includes, for example, Annette Hübschle's (2016) study of the illegal rhino horn trade with field research carried out in Southern Africa, a region that would appear to pose much higher risks for field researchers than any part of Germany.

Another interesting difference between the doctoral dissertations and the previously discussed research projects relates to the concentration on specific institutions. The three universities with the highest number of organised crime related dissertations (Humboldt University Berlin: 5, Goethe University Frankfurt: 3, Cologne University: 3) otherwise do not play a prominent role in connection with research on organised crime. This creates the impression of a rather fragmented research landscape. This impression is compounded by the review of the pertinent academic publications from the time under consideration.

Figure 3.
Completed doctoral dissertations related to organised crime 2008-2017*: Thematic focus

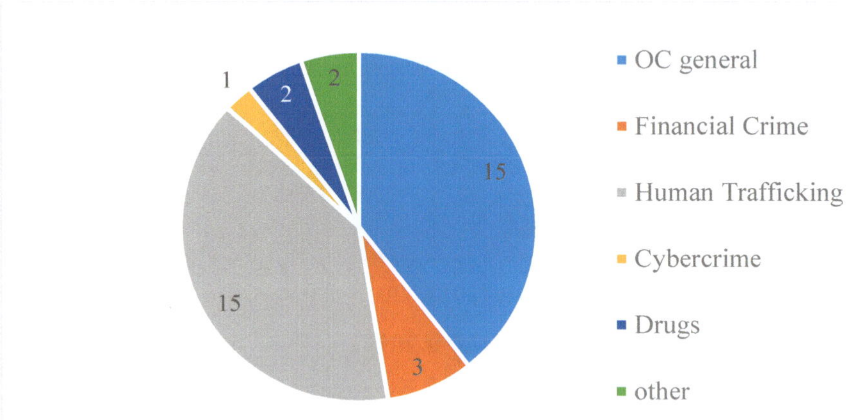

* 2017=1 January – 1 September 2017

Academic Publications

215 academic publications with reference to organised crime, authored by scholars based in Germany, could be identified for the period 1 January 2008 until 1 September 2017 (von Lampe und Knickmeier, 2018: 50-69; Fig. 5). This set of publications comprises journal articles, book chapters, books (including dissertations published as books), as well as working papers published on the internet. Anthologies (co-)edited by scholars based in Germany were not included as such, but only the pertinent individual chapters contained therein. Seminar papers, bachelor theses and master theses were not included in the analysis, even if they were available on the internet.

At times it proved difficult to decide if a publication was academic. For the purpose of the present analysis, publications were classified as academic when they were written with scholarly aspirations and in scholarly form by academics for an academic audience. When in doubt, these criteria were applied rather leniently and not in the sense of quality standards. Consequently, some poorly researched and written academic papers were included, while highly informative publications authored, for example, by journalists or by active or retired police officers based on their investigative work, were not.

Figure 4.
Academic publications relating to organised crime, 2008-2017*

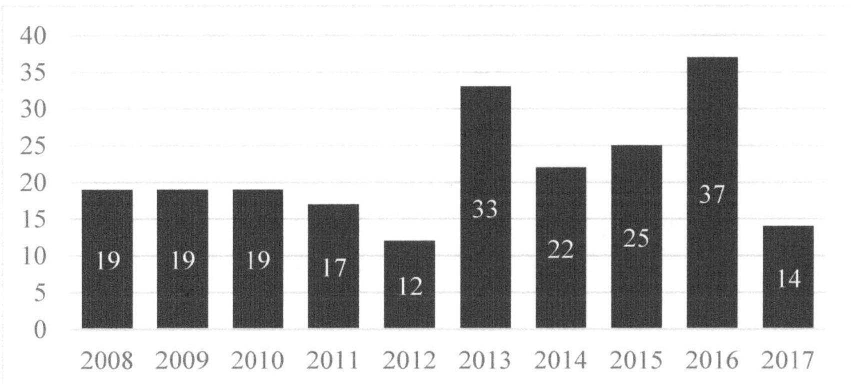

* 2017=1 January – 1 September 2017

The classification of a publication as academic does not imply that it is based on original empirical research. Only a relatively small portion (22%) of the identified publications fall in this category. 17% of the publications are legal treatises and another 6% can be classified as theoretical works. 5% of the publications cannot be placed in a specific category. By far the largest share (50 %) of the identified academic publications qualify as review essays in a broad sense. They essentially summarise previously published material, although at times paired with novel ideas.

In quantitative terms, the academic publications follow a trend similar to that of the research projects. In both cases there is an increase in number during the second half of the study period. Whereas for the years 2008 to 2012 an average of 17 publications per year could be identified, the number rose to 29 for the period 2013 to 2016 (Figure 4). These numbers are somewhat skewed by edited volumes with numerous chapters relating to organised crime. For example, for the year 2016 eleven out of 37 identified publications are included in the Handbook "International Law and Transnational Organised Crime," edited by Pierre Hauck and Sven Petarske (2016).

As with the research projects, the academic publications are thematically clustered around specific areas of crime (Figure 5). About half of the publications fall into this category, including 36 (16,7%) on human trafficking and 23 (10,7%) on drug trafficking. Other areas of crime comprise the illegal trade in cultural artefacts (8; 3,7%), cybercrime (7; 3,3%), environmental crime (6; 2,8 %) and product piracy (5; 2,3%). 56 (26%) publications are broad in scope and address organised crime in a general sense. Another 20 (9,3%) publications deal specifically with transnational organised crime.

Figure 5.
Academic publications related to organised crime 2008-2017*: Thematic focus

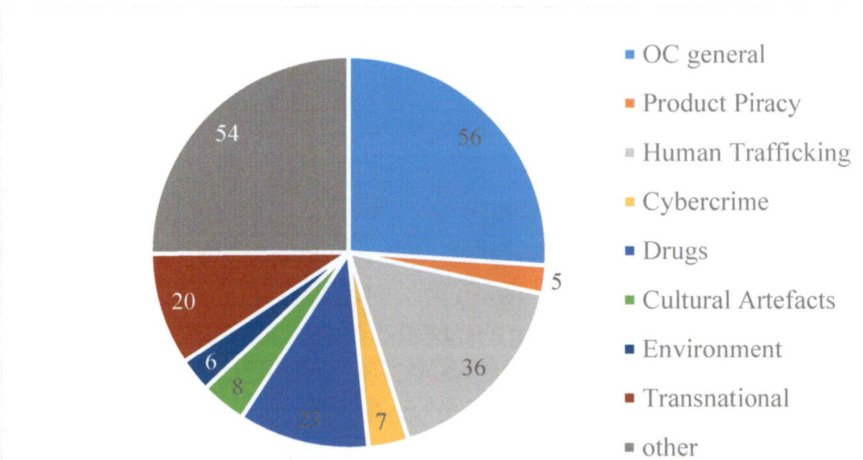

* 2017=1 January – 1 September 2017

Many of the publications that are focused on specific areas of crime also raise questions regarding the organisation of criminals. However, offender structures are only rarely at the centre of attention. Apart from discussions of legal doctrine regarding the criminalisation of participation in criminal groups there are only a few publications that provide overviews of offender structures (Hartmann, 2009; Paul and Schwalb, 2012) or address issues of criminal organisation in abstract terms, for example with respect to the resilience of criminal networks (Lotzmann and Neumann, 2016). In addition, there is limited literature on particular offender structures. 10 (4,7 %) publications deal with Italian mafia-type associations. Some papers, by discussing protection racketeering by mafia organisations (see Troitzsch, 2017), could also be placed in a category of publications focusing on illegal governance.

Besides showing a preference for certain areas of crime, the 215 identified academic publications are noteworthy for their limited interest in the situation in Germany. Only 45 (21%) focus exclusively on organised crime in Germany. Half of these 45 publications are legal treatises, where the focus on Germany results from the discussion of national law. A larger portion (24 %) of the publications deals exclusively with organised crime in countries other than Germany. The other half (55%) address the situation in Germany and other countries or, most often, discuss organised crime at the international level.

Similar to the research projects and similar to the doctoral dissertations, the pertinent academic publications give the impression that manifestations of organised crime in Germany are of only limited interest to German-based scholars. Only 18 publications (8,4%) are specifically concerned with current manifestations of organised crime within Germany and are based on original research. This includes: five works on drug trafficking; three on human trafficking; three on residential burglary; and two on outlaw biker groups. Interestingly, four out of these 18 publications are focused primarily or exclusively on crimes and criminals inside of German penitentiaries. There are no studies that seek to provide a comprehensive picture of organised crime in the tradition of the early research carried out by Hans-Jürgen Kerner (1973) and others, that would contrast and complement the annual organised crime situation reports by the BKA. Accordingly, there are only few empirical findings that would shed light on the current situation in Germany, and would permit a judgment on how organised crime has developed over the past two to three decades. Overall, the available research data do not enable a deeper understanding of offender structures. For example, an analysis of 2403 investigative files on residential burglaries produced no evidence of a dominance of organised groups of offenders (Dreißigacker, Baier, Wollinger and Bartsch, 2015).

With regard to outlaw biker groups it is on one hand suggested that traditional organisational structures are falling apart, while on the other hand illegal criminal activities are said to have become more widespread and more diversified in the outlaw biker subculture (Bley, 2016).

No clear picture emerges from the literature review regarding the disciplinary and institutional embeddedness of organised crime research. While the BKA, the KfN, and the University of Münster figure prominently with respect to research projects, and Humboldt University Berlin, Goethe University Frankfurt and Cologne University rank highest in the number of organised-crime related doctoral dissertations, yet other institutions have the highest output of pertinent academic publications.

There are 226 German-based authors behind the 215 identified academic publications. They belong to a large number of academic and non-academic institutions and represent a variety of academic disciplines, ranging from the humanities and social sciences to the natural sciences and computer science. Most authors (178; 78,8%) are linked to just a single publication. This is also true for the authors of doctoral dissertations, which means that in most cases dissertations do not lead to a longer-term occupation with the topic of organised crime.

Only twelve authors (5,6%) have produced three or more pertinent publications, with Michael Müller-Karpe, a researcher at the Romano-German Central Museum in Mainz, and Arndt Sinn, a law professor at the University of Osnabrück, taking the lead with six publications each. The twelve most productive authors account for 49 of the 215 publications, which represents a share of 22,8%. To put these numbers into perspective, Edward Kleemans, one of the leading Dutch organised crime scholars, authored or co-authored 50 publications relating to organised crime within the same time period.

Two of the most productive German-based authors, Martin Neumann and Klaus G. Troitzsch, have participated in the EU-project "GLODERS" at the University of Koblenz, which resulted in a number of journal articles and book chapters. Two other authors, Daniel Brombacher and Judith Vorrath, have been affiliated with the German Institute for International and

Security Affairs in Berlin. The remaining authors with at least three pertinent publications have not been clustered at one institution.

Interestingly, among the twelve authors with the highest output there are only two criminologists, even though it has to be considered that the classification as criminologist is not always obvious given the typical incorporation of criminology into law faculties. In addition to the two criminologists there are three legal scholars, three political scientists, three sociologists and with Michael Müller-Karpe one archaeologist.

Discussion and conclusion

From the review of pertinent research projects, doctoral dissertations, and academic publications emerges no coherent picture of the landscape of organised crime research in Germany. The topic of organised crime seems to have gained some degree of popularity, but it is remaining unclear how sustained the scholarly interest really is. While institutionally based research projects and publications show a more or less pronounced numeric upward trend between 2008 and 2017, the attractiveness of organised crime related issues for dissertation projects seems to have declined in recent years. The thematic focus tends to lie on specific criminal activities, such as human trafficking, whereas offender structures only receive limited attention, and illegal governance is hardly ever an object of study. Moreover, there is a certain preference for the study of organised crime phenomena in countries other than Germany. This is especially true for studies including field research. At the same time, there is little tangible interest in those manifestations of organised crime that have been at the centre of public attention in Germany, such as the so-called Arabic Clans, outlaw biker groups, and phenomena such as organised residential burglary. To what extent recently launched studies into these thematic areas will lead to more than just sporadic, short-lived research efforts remains to be seen.

Overall, there is a striking discrepancy between a relatively large number of pertinent publications and the scarcity of empirical research. The existing research also appears to be highly insular. On one hand, there are no studies in the tradition of the comprehensive analyses of the situation of organised crime produced in earlier decades. The annual organised crime situation reports prepared by the BKA are no appropriate replacement even though they do have their value. What would be needed is a regular in-depth assessment of the situation, perhaps along the lines of the "Monitor georganiseerde criminaliteit" in the Netherlands (Kleemans, 2014).

On the other hand, studies seldom build on each other, and thus contribute little to a cumulative body of knowledge. Without having examined the staffing of projects in any detail, a severe problem seems to be that in particular funded research tends to involve researchers that are only hired for a specific project. They naturally have little time to immerse themselves in the relevant scholarly literature and move on to other subject matters at the conclusion of a project without being able to appropriately digest and disseminate findings.

A major reason for the scarcity of empirical research arguably lies in the politics of research funding. Most of the available grants are earmarked for applied science, not for basic research. This means, first of all, that projects have to operate on the basis of untested and quite likely unfounded assumptions about the nature and dynamics of organised crime phenomena, unless insights from international research are applicable and, importantly, taken into consideration. The lack of funding for basic research also means that scholars based in Germany have relatively little to contribute to the international academic literature and to the debates centred on essential research questions regarding the nature and dynamics of organised crime. This does not necessarily mean that organised crime research in Germany is internationally isolated. There are numerous links between the German and the international research landscape. This is evidenced by the large share of international research projects and by the fact that about one third of the pertinent academic publications by German-based authors are English-language publications. However, scholars based in Germany are obviously under-represented in the international scholarly debate on organised crime. This becomes apparent in a review of the programs of major criminological conferences where international organised crime scholars congregate with little participation from Germany, and from a review of international journals that have a thematic focus on organised crime, where likewise contributions from scholars based in Germany are rare.

The main problem for organised crime research in Germany arguably lies in the fact that institutional embeddedness is weak and fragmented. Although some academic institutions make valuable contributions to the study of organised crime, there are no true centres of organised crime research with a more or less continuous flow of research projects, doctoral dissertations and academic publications. This may have to do with the interdisciplinary nature of the study of organised crime which makes integration into existing academic structures difficult and puts organised crime researchers in a disadvantage when it comes to applying for research grants and advancing one's academic career. Arguably, there is also a lack of political will to take organised crime seriously as an object of study when it comes to the weak institutional support for organised crime researchers.

A better institutionalisation of the study of organised crime would have a number of advantages. Having one or even several research centres in Germany would ensure greater continuity in the study of organised crime, which in turn would facilitate the networking among researchers in Germany and abroad, and it would make it easier for researchers in Germany to establish links to law enforcement agencies and also to victim populations, NGOs and into criminal milieus for better data access. Reliable access to data, in turn, is of course the key to obtaining funding for empirical research and to being able to participate in international projects that involve the coordinated collection and analysis of data.

References

Abasov, R., *Organisierte Kriminalität in Russland: Entwicklung und wissenschaftliche Erfassung vor dem Hintergrund unterschiedlicher Strukturmodelle*. Baden-Baden: Nomos, 2016.

Adelsberger, F., Kriminalität von Rockern im Land Brandenburg. *Kriminalistik*, 2012, 66(10), 569-576.

Backes, L., M. Bartsch, M. Baumgärtner, J. Diehl, J. Jüttner, C. Neumann, J. Schindler, A. Ulrich, W. Wiedmann-Schmidt, Nicht zu fassen. *Der Spiegel*, 2016, Nr. 21, 12-21.

Bader, J., Outlaw Motorcycle Clubs. *Kriminalistik*, 2011, 65(4), 227-234.

Behr, H.-G., *Organisiertes Verbrechen*. Frankfurt am Main: Ullstein, 1987.

Berg, A., Maaßen, H.-G., *Wirtschaftsschutz in der digitalen Welt*. Bitkom, 2017. https://www.bitkom.org/sites/default/files/pdf/Presse/Anhaenge-an-PIs/2017/07-Juli/Bitkom-Charts-Wirtschaftsschutz-in-der-digitalen-Welt-21-07-2017.pdf (last accessed 7 February 2019)

Bley, R., Strukturen und Entwicklungen im kriminellen Rockermilieu. *der kriminalist*, 2016, 48(10), 26-31.

Bossert, O., *Die Kommunikation konkurrierender Gruppierungen der organisierten Kriminalität*. Frankfurt am Main: Verlag für Polizeiwissenschaft, 2010.

Bundeskriminalamt. *Rauschgiftkriminalität: Bundeslagebild 2015*. Wiesbaden: BKA, 2016.

Bundeskriminalamt. *Kfz-Kriminalität: Bundeslagebild 2016*. Wiesbaden: BKA, 2017.

Bundeskriminalamt. *Organisierte Kriminalität: Bundeslagebild 2017*. Wiesbaden: BKA, 2018.

Bundesregierung. Antwort der Bundesregierung auf die Kleine Anfrage der Abgeordneten Irene Mihalic, Dr. Gerhard Schick, Volker Beck (Köln), weiterer Abgeordneter und der Fraktion BÜNDNIS 90/DIE GRÜNEN: Entwicklung der italienischen Mafiakriminalität in Deutschland seit dem Mordanschlag von Duisburg 2007. *Deutscher Bundestag Drucksache* 18/13320, 15.08.2017.

Bülles, E. *Deutschland Verbrecherland? Mein Einsatz gegen die organisierte Kriminalität*. Berlin: Econ, 2013.

Dowideit, A. Das Netz der Pflegemafia. *Die Welt*, 30 May 2017, p. 9.

Dreißigacker, A., D. Baier, G.R. Wollinger und T. Bartsch, Die Täter des Wohnungseinbruchs: Sind es die „Osteuropäer", die „professionellen Banden" oder die „Drogenabhängigen"? *Kriminalistik*, 2015, 69(5), 307-311.

EMCDDA. *Europäischer Drogenbericht: Trends und Entwicklungen*. Luxemburg: Amt für Veröffentlichungen der Europäischen Union, 2017.

Europol. *EU Drug Markets Report: A Strategic Analysis*. The Hague: Europol, 2013.

Filter, I. *Beschaffung, Handel und Konsum illegaler Drogen im Strafvollzug: Eine Situationsanalyse*. Doctoral dissertation. Universität Bremen, 2010.

Florack, N. *Transnationale kriminelle und terroristische Netzwerke: ein Vergleich der Netzwerkstruktur der albanischen Mafia mit der Jemaah Islamiyah*. Berlin: Köster, 2010.

Ghadban, R. *Arabische Clans: Die unterschätzte Gefahr*. Berlin: Econ, 2018.

Gögelein, M. Taschendiebstahl-Lappalie oder schwere Kriminalität? *Kriminalistik*, 2017, 71(2), 129-136.

Gülay, C., Kuhn, H., *Türken-Sam: Eine deutsche Gangsterkarriere*. München: Deutscher Taschenbuch Verlag, 2009.

Hartmann, A., Delinquenz in der Gruppe. In: H.-L. Kröber, D. Dölling, N. Leygraf, H. Sass (eds.), *Handbuch der Forensischen Psychiatrie* (pp. 209-235). Frankfurt am Main: Steinkopff, 2009.

Hauck, P., S. Petarske, (eds.), *International Law and Transnational Organised Crime*. Oxford: Oxford University Press, 2016.

Henninger, M., 'Importierte Kriminalität' und deren Etablierung. *Kriminalistik*, 2002, 56(12), 714–729.

Henninger, M., T. Susebach, Die Berliner "Türsteherszene". *Kriminalistik*, 2005, 59(7), 395-407.

Hübschle, A., *A game of horns: transnational flows of rhino horn*. Cologne: International Max Planck Research School on the Social and Political Constitution of the Economy, 2016.

Jäger, S., Strategische Aspekte der Bekämpfung der Rockerkriminalität. *Kriminalistik*, 2012, 66(8-9), 495-501.

Kamstra, S., Berlin im Griff der OK? *der kriminalist*, 2014, 46(7-8), 18-26.

Kerner, H.-J., *Professionelles und organisiertes Verbrechen*. Wiesbaden: Bundeskriminalamt, 1973.

Kleemans, E., Organised crime research: challenging assumptions and informing policy. In: E. Cockbain and J. Knutsson (eds.), *Applied Police Research: Challenges and Opportunities* (pp. 57-67). New York: Routledge, 2014.

KPMG, *Project Sun: A study of the illicit cigarette market in the European Union, Norway and Switzerland*. 2017 https://assets.kpmg.com/content/dam/kpmg/uk/pdf/2017/07/project-sun-2017-report.pdf (last accessed 15 September 2017)

Lotzmann, U. and M. Neumann, A simulation model of intra-organisational conflict regulation in the crime world. In: C. Elsenbroich, D.

Anzola and N. Gilbert (eds.), *Social dimensions of organised crime: modelling the dynamics of extortion rackets.* (pp. 177-213). Cham: Springer, 2016.

Mack, J., H-J. Kerner, *The crime industry*. Westmead: Saxon House, 1975.

Paul, A. and B. Schwalb, Kriminelle Organisationen. In: M. Apelt and V. Tacke (eds.), *Handbuch Organisationstypen* (pp. 327-344). Wiesbaden: Springer VS, 2012.

Paulus, M., Ignoriert, toleriert und verkannt? Die albanische Mafia im bundesdeutschen Rotlichtmilieu. *der Kriminalist*, 2015, 47(2), 18-25.

Rebscher, E. and W. Vahlenkamp, *Organisierte Kriminalität in der Bundesrepublik Deutschland*. Wiesbaden: Bundeskriminalamt, 1988.

Rohe, M. and M. Jaraba, *Paralleljustiz: Eine Studie im Auftrag des Landes Berlin, vertreten durch die Senatsverwaltung für Justiz und Verbraucherschutz*. 2015. https://www.berlin.de/sen/justva/_assets/gesamtstudie-paralleljustiz.pdf *(last accessed 12 September 2017)*

Schulz, A., Rocker, Mafia, Geldwäscher - Deutschland fest im Griff der Organisierten Kriminalität? *der kriminalist,* 2012, 44(3), 13-15.

Töttel, U., G. Bulanova-Hristova and G. Flach (eds.), *Research Conferences on Organised Crime at the Bundeskriminalamt in Germany, Vol. III, Transnational Organised Crime, 2013-2015*. Wiesbaden: Bundeskriminalamt, 2016.

Troitzsch, K., Can agent-based simulation models replicate organised crime? *Trends in Organised Crime*, 2017, 20(1-2), 100-119.

Varese, F., *Mafias on the move*. Princeton: Princeton University Press, 2011.

von Lampe, K., Measuring organised crime: A critique of current approaches. In: P. van Duyne, M. Jager, K. von Lampe, J. Newell (eds.), *Threats and phantoms of organised crime, corruption and terrorism: Critical European perspectives* (pp. 85-116). Nijmegen, the Netherlands: Wolf Legal Publishers, 2004.

von Lampe, K. and S. Knickmeier, *Organisierte Kriminalität: Die aktuelle Forschung in Deutschland*. Schriftenreihe Forschungsforum Öffentliche Sicherheit, no. 24. Berlin: Freie Universität Berlin, 2018.

Weschke, E. and K. Heine-Heiß, *Organisierte Kriminalität als Netzstrukturkriminalität Teil 1*. Berlin: Fachhochschule für Verwaltung und Rechtspflege, 1990.

Winter, M., Osteuropäische Einbrecherbanden auf Beutezug durch die Republik. *Kriminalistik*, 2015, 69(10), 572-575.
Wöhrle, C., Ehrenwerte Familien: Libanesische Clans in Deutschland. *Focus* , 2017, 16, 24 April.
Ziercke, J., Aktuelles Lagebild und Entwicklung der Gewaltkriminalität. *Kriminalistik*, 2010, 64(12), 697-703.

Hierarchy, strategic assets and distinctive capabilities in Scottish organised crime

Kenneth Murray[1]

Introduction

This chapter considers the significance of hierarchy in Scottish organised crime: the evidence that supports its existence and the conditions that are necessary for its occurrence. In doing so the chapter examines how Serious Organised Crime Groups ('SOCGs') in Scotland compete in their principal markets, both criminal and legitimate, focussing on the market factors and dynamics that are necessary for survival, endurance and dominance. On this basis, a platform for analysis is proposed which is designed to assist in identifying the distinctive capabilities of dominant SOCGs and how these have enabled the development of the strategic assets form the basis of their hierarchical strength. A practical application of this approach is proposed to enable SOCG vulnerabilities to be identified such that their activities and influence, not least in legitimate markets, can be curtailed, or at least more effectively constrained.

Tackling organised crime in Scotland

The official approach to tackling serious organised crime in Scotland is set by a Scottish Government body known as the 'Serious Organised Crime Task Force' ('SOCTF'). SOCTF uses a thematic strategy known as the 4 'D's (Detect, Disrupt, Divert and Deter), which emphasises awareness raising and partnership working, as well as traditional law enforcement

1 The author is Head of Forensic Accountancy at Police Scotland. The views expressed here are his own and should not be read as being those of Police Scotland.

measures, in an effort to demonstrate that Scotland is a hostile environment for organised crime. Within law enforcement, the principal operational decisions about how resources should be deployed in this context are set by a mapping process, known as Serious Organised Crime Mapping ('SOCM'). This process collates all available relevant intelligence relating to serious organised crime ('SOC') and ranks SOCGs in accordance with how they score on a harm matrix. This scoring process explicitly identifies and defines these groups according to structures of hierarchy: SOCGs are essentially discerned by means of tracked hierarchical relationships between individual SOCG players (known as 'nominals') within them.

The SOCM process provided much of the source material for a recent Scottish Government study entitled 'Serious Organised Crime in Scotland: A Summary of the Evidence' (Scottish Government, 2017). In considering what it referred to as 'the evidence' about serious organised crime in Scotland, this document augmented interpretations of mapping data with a review of academic literature. It drew the conclusion that "*in order to disrupt and weaken SOC activity, a fuller understanding of the structure, operation and behaviour of SOC groups is required.*" On this foundation the report assessed:

> ". . . it is important to recognise that while SOC groups are often very hierarchical and highly structured, SOC groups come in a variety of shapes and forms, which also includes very loose networks of criminal actors . . . Recognising the diverse structures and compositions of SOC groups is critical to understanding how SOC can be tackled." (pp. 16-17).

It is one thing to observe that a garden is full of many different flowers (or maybe we should say weeds) but another to explain how they actually grow. What do they need to grow? Why do some, if they are allowed to, appear to take over the whole allotment? The 'social construct' conception of organised crime, whereby all the various kinds of collective criminality that might attract the 'OC' label are collected under an 'umbrella' (Von Lampe, 2016 a and b), provides a suitable basis for describing the many facets of organised crime, but its value as a guide to SOC dynamics is limited. Recognising diversity of SOC type in itself does little to assist in devising strategies of tackling its harms. What is required is a way of understanding SOCGs primarily in terms of what they do rather than how they can be described or classified.

Hierarchy versus network – a false dichotomy

Re-focussing on what SOCGs do serves some way to providing clarity on the vexed question of whether SOC can be best conceived in terms of a market/hierarchy framework or a network structure (Campana, 2016b). In simple terms: SOCGs are formed because some crimes requiring a measure of organising to carry them out. One-off crimes may only require temporary arrangements which can dissolve when the crime is complete. Where there is a profit to be made from repeat activity, then a mode of association that might be described as organisation starts to form. It might of course be argued that there are other formational influences on organised crime groups than the market, but the Finckenauer assertion that "*making a profit is in fact the primary goal of organised crime groups*" (Finckenauer, 2005: 66) is a difficult one to refute. This is not the same as saying all organised crime groups have been formed in response to market opportunities. But it does imply that, whatever their provenance, they have to adapt to the markets they participate in to survive, or otherwise they fail. The market imposes an organisational conduct. The question is how do SOC players engaged in criminal markets associate in order to accommodate the conditions that they face?

There is a tradition in the academic literature which posits a contrast between SOC conceived in terms of 'mafias' or hierarches, and conceptions based on networks. Morselli described a 'debate' between law enforcement treatments of SOC and network based treatments favoured by academics.

> "The debate in brief is whether the organisation of the distribution of illegal drugs is more likely an orthodox pyramid-based governance structure regulated by strong-hand criminal dictators, or the 'arms-length' transactional process (Naylor, 1997) that so resembles dealings in legitimate cross border business" (Morselli, 1999: 27). This point of view was given further amplification by Dick Hobbs: "the notion of crime groups as tightly organised hierarchical entities whose tentacles

reach around the globe is not supported by the evidence, and this market should be understood as one that is populated by networks or partnerships of independent traders or brokers." (Hobbs, 2013: 156)

In Hobbs' view, associating 'mafia's' with territorial domination is no longer valid, SOC markets are more accurately characterised as "*different kinds of brokerage and ever-mutating, interlocking networks featuring a variety of links with similar entities in other neighbourhoods*." (Hobbs, 2013: 218).

So, why does hierarchy continue to have relevance in Scottish SOC? The Scottish Government report clearly accepts that structured hierarchical SOCGs still exist, something that will be evidenced in more detail below. The Scottish SOC theatre, especially in the Central Belt, continues to demonstrate the existence of dominant territorial influences, although it is fair to say from current practitioner experience the foundations for dominance may be moving away from territory to ability to access supply routes and specialist services. The SOCM process on the other hand is based on understanding the associative links that connect SOC in Scotland across a network. The SOC challenge in Scotland therefore involves modes of association within illegal markets that are both hierarchical and which involve networks. This would appear to chime with Campana's assertion that in order to capture the reality of SOC, an instrumental approach to networks is needed which is able to elucidate the continuum that exists between market conduct and hierarchic operating in its various forms (Campana, 2016b). Any meaningful analysis of Scottish SOC therefore has to accommodate both types of association. There is a continuing need to articulate how hierarchical influence continues to arises and flourish in SOC and how this influence interacts with, and is expressed through, network forms of association.

Transactional dynamics in understanding SOC

What are the key factors or characteristics that account for economic success in organised crime? Answering this satisfactorily requires an understanding of the dynamic forces that form, nurture, create and destroy SOCGs. Categorisations in accordance with type, shape, form, or other defining factors such as ethnicity, inform in terms of describing groups of participants engaged in SOC, but descriptions in themselves don't tell us enough about how or why SOCGs succeed or fail; what factors are at play in determining these outcomes, and also the many partial successes and failures that lie between them.

All SOCs transact. They all deal in criminal markets and most above a certain level deal in legitimate markets too. Analysis of the attributes and characteristics that enable SOCs to transact successfully in these markets can answer many of the questions that arise in relation to them: for example those relating to identity, purpose, character, method, vulnerabilities and weaknesses. It follows that a better understanding of the constituent factors that make SOCs successful in transacting with others will in turn provide better understanding of the forces that influence the *development* of SOC structure. For example, in terms of understanding how *hierarchical* structures interact with *network structures*, and why hierarchical structures continue to be suited to market dynamics at the top end of markets and why networks are more suited to the bottom end, where they are the dominant form of association.

Illegal drug markets rely on longitudinal interfaces *between* hierarchical and network modes of structure which have to function together. High value importations and street corner retail are two ends of the same business process, and the part played by an SOCG in that process is determined by what they are able to contribute to it. In most cases this refers to what they are *allowed* to do in these markets in accordance with whatever hierarchical influences they are subject to. The influence of hierarchy in other words is not a concept that is best considered in opposition to network forms of association, but rather, in the context of SOC, an influence that is present and part of the networks, both relevant to all serious SOC markets. Because of this, the existence of hierarchical influence in these markets provides a door of analysis through which the networks they interact with can be understood too.

The Serious Organised Crime Mapping Process ('SOCM')

It is on the basis of identifying hierarchical relationships that the SOCM process approaches its challenge of identifying and prioritising SOC threats and where they come from. Using intelligence data sweeps from all relevant intelligence sources throughout Scotland, this process categorises featured players in the relevant intelligence disseminations as principals, members, associates and rivals. The network analysis applied to the relevant intelligence considers the suitability of each nominal to these classifications (using a variety of sources, such as telephone billings and surveillance logs). Using conventional network analysis tools, the process assesses connectedness of nominals, or nodes, and these are differentiated in terms of degree and between-ness centrality (essentially in the same way as Morselli discusses in his analysis of Canadian Hell's Angels) (Morselli, 2010). High degree centrality counts the number of connections, whereas between-ness centrality assesses the strategic importance of connections between otherwise disconnected others.

The base objective of this stage in the SOCM process is to establish what the hierarchical relationships are (as defined on this basis). These are then used to build an understanding of group structure. In this regard, the nominals identified as 'principals' and 'members' are of most importance. 'Associates' often demonstrate a high degree of centrality, but may flit from 'group' to 'group' or influence to influence. In strategic terms, however, these nominals may be important enablers, providing specialist services to a number of groups or centre of influence. The data sweep is then used to develop an understanding of the activities and capabilities of each group through the compilation of a harm matrix. This generates a threat score supported by a justification document. The organised crime groups are ranked in accordance with their threat score and this is fed into the tasking process, which determines how resources are to be deployed operationally.

The latest available mapping report at the time of writing[2] provides the following profile of organised crime groups and connections:

- 132 Serious Organised Crime Groups (SOCGs) were mapped;
- 89 of these SOCGs contained a total of 335 individuals who had connections to multiple groups; the most connected individuals (*i.e.* those individuals with links to more than 7 SOCGs) were all principals of their own group and each had links to at least 9 groups including their own;
- the 13 most connected nominals were linked to a total of 37 SOCGs;
- of 84 nominals identified as specialists, one quarter were identified as being connected to more than one group.
- 70% of SOCGs (104) were involved in 'quasi-legitimate' enterprises involving 674 identified companies.

SOCM provides an indicator of what harm SOCs threaten most as conveyed by historic intelligence. The quality of that intelligence is therefore crucial to the value of the SOCM output. Over the past five years, there has been a concerted effort within Police Scotland to broaden the base of the intelligence captured, and financial and business intelligence is now given an emphasis commensurate with the more traditional areas of law enforcement intelligence gathering.

SOCM relies on establishing group identity through identification of hierarchical relationships between individuals (known as 'nominals'). While this can enable hierarchical relationships between SOC groups to be discerned, it cannot on its own provide an analysis of the market and transactional dynamics that underpin hierarchical intra group relationships. SOCM in other words identifies which SOCGs are most active and possess most threat, but requires this further mode of analysis to determine *why* these SOCGs are prominent in the rankings. What are the factors that got them there and keep them there? The incorporation of transactional dynamics into the picture, therefore, requires a further mode of analysis in order to complete the picture when it comes to understanding hierarchy. That mode of analysis must be capable of providing a dynamic dimension

2 The source is the Scottish Organised Crime Group Mapping Report (SOGM) 2017/19 Q4 and Year End April 2018, which is a classified document and is not included in the list of references provided below

to the periodic snapshot pictures provided by SOCM. Recent law enforcement successes in Operation Escalade provided an outstanding field opportunity to study the foundations of hierarchy in Scottish SOC.

Operation Escalade

In 2017, the Escalade SOCG was ranked number one not only in the Scottish mapping rankings, but also those relating to the UK as a whole. Of particular significance in the context of examining hierarchical influence, a number of other high-ranking Scottish SOCGs (i.e. within the top ten in the SOCM rankings) were also the Escalade SOCGs customers.
In December 2017, nine individuals connected with the Escalade SOCG were convicted for a variety of organised crime offences. Each of these individuals was identified by the SOCM as a 'serious organised crime' player. At the relevant High Court hearing, prosecuting counsel, Alex Prentice QC, described the relevant SOCG group as follows:

> "The Organised Crime Group is the most sophisticated group encountered by Police Scotland. Their operation centres on the importation of vast quantities of cocaine. Their role is as wholesalers to other organised crime groups. They are the top of the chain in terms of drugs transactions in Scotland and the United Kingdom as a whole. The amount of cash and firearms recovered in this case was indicative of an international operation." (Daily Record, 2017b)

The picture painted by Mr Prentice for the court was designed to convey how serious the crimes were and how worthy the convicted individuals were of substantial sentences. The individuals convicted, however, were not the principals of that group, but essentially constituted its core operational management in Scotland. The lead principals of the SOCG were other nominals identified in SOCM, whose methods of delegation and displacement enabled them, up to that point (at the time of writing it is an ongoing operation), to protect themselves from direct evidential connection with the crimes for which the operatives who worked for them were convicted. In February 2019, these lead individuals were identified publicly as Barry and James Gillespie (Sunday Mail, 2019), and they remain at large at the time of writing.

The size of the cash hauls involved from Operation Escalade disclosed at trial amounted to some £1,6 million, a signifier of the operational importance of the convicted individuals to the SOCG. In terms of the estimated profits earned by the SOCG, this amount was estimated to be roughly equivalent to the revenues it earned across the UK in one week. The circumstances leading to their arrest and conviction directly related to the debt enforcement methods they used when seeking payment for supply of imported cocaine. The press reports provided lurid detail of these methods, which included extended torture of a victim debtor including chain whippings, treating his open wounds with bleach, shooting him in both knee caps and rolling him down a hill close to his home. The drug debt owed by the victim concerned was only £30.000; in the course of his ordeal, however, he was advised by one of his tormentors that: "*It wasn't the money, it was the principle*". The need to be seen to exert discipline in respect of a relatively low debt indicated the importance accorded by the SOCG to its reputation, one which still persists. The ability to dispense violence by itself, however, does not explain how the Escalade SOCG managed to acquire such a degree of dominance. Most SOCGs in Scotland are well capable of violence. So the exceptional success and market dominance of the Escalade SOCG requires some further explanation.

As indicated, the business of the Escalade SOCG was the supply of high purity drugs to high level customers, for the most part other high ranking SOCGs. The Escalade SOCG was a primary importer of Class A drugs into Scotland, and also managed and controlled supply lines into London, Liverpool and Manchester. The key attribute that enabled the SOCG to attain this position was the *direct supply contacts* it had established with producer cartels in South America, enabling it to control the importation and transport of commodity across Europe and in the UK itself, and bypassing more established European channels of supply. The Escalade SOCG instead developed its own supply chain by creating an extensive network of logistics and physical storage assets across Western Europe, extending in particular into the Iberian Peninsula. Through a network of warehouses and transport vehicles it was able to co-ordinate transports of imported commodity from their landing points, mainly on the Iberian coast, to locations in the Netherlands. Stock piles of commodity were accumulated in Dutch warehouses to form a 'mother-load' from which wholesale shipments could be dispensed to the UK. In this way, the SOCG was able to control and maintain desired wholesale price levels on the British mainland. Once imported, the management of supply to major UK distributors was achieved through a network of warehouses and transactional relationships with high ranking Scottish SOCGs, each of whom were able to exert their own regional dominance in order to exert the necessary discipline and control of widely dispersed local distribution networks.

All distributors supplied with Escalade commodity were subject to detailed oversight and scrutiny through the monitoring of activity and financial accounts – an effort supported, where and when required, by enforcement techniques characterised by extreme violence, including murder, abduction, torture, firearms and the use of bladed weapons. In some cases, this has led to tensions developing with some of the other major SOCG nominals in Scotland, or the businesses they are/were associated with. (Daily Record, 2017b)

The character of the Escalade SOCG's transactional relations (as disclosed by SOCM), together with the hierarchical traits characteristic of many of their customers, underpin the assertion that hierarchy is still a prominent feature in Scottish SOC. Given the apparently dominant influence these SOCGs have in Scotland, particularly in the area covered by its high population density, the 'central belt' between Glasgow and Edinburgh, the roots of that dominance are to be analysed in terms of the particular capabilities necessary to achieve and sustain their hierarchical positions. The most obvious way to examine how such hierarchical relationships form and relate to each other is to consider how they exert themselves in what are still the principal criminal markets: those of Class A drug supply. Examining the process through this door enables exploration of the relationships between SOCGs, and how they interact with looser retail networks further down the chain.

The shape of supply lines - the 'class A' drugs market in Scotland

Intelligence disseminations relating to the principal SOCGs involvement in Class A drugs markets indicate the following outline profile of the relevant supply chains:

The structure presented at the next page, appears consistent with the generic view of Scottish SOC taken in the Scottish Government paper (Scottish Government, 2017), in that the top end is characterised by hierarchical structures and the bottom end by looser network structures. Given the illegal nature of the activity, it is not a surprise this should be so. At the top end, importation requires access to significant resources, not least financial, to participate in the relevant transactions. At the bottom end, visible street level retail transactions require the deployment of expendable human assets where the linkages to controlling forces have to be obscured. A further feature of significance is that *cash management* is a separate process from drug distribution management, with the detail of cash collection mechanisms closely guarded.

Figure 1
Scheme of supply chains between organised crime groups

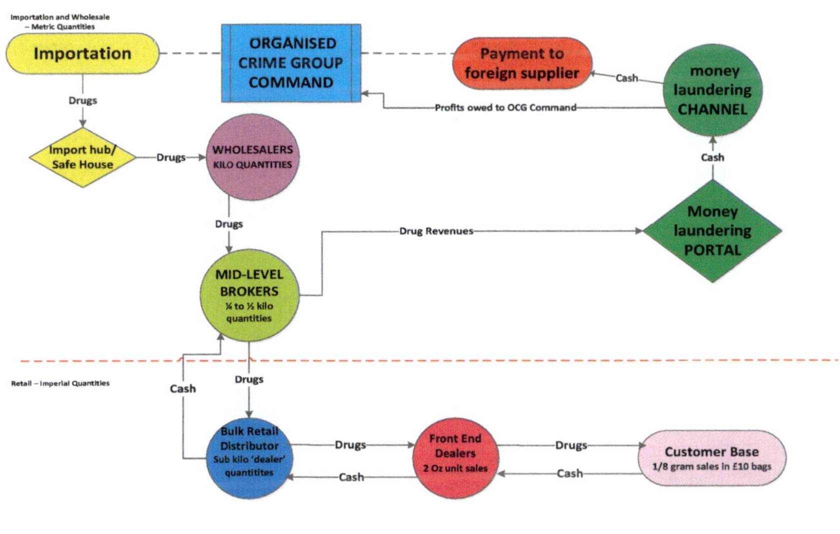

The key frontier is the level at which the controlling influences interface with the local distribution and retail networks. This is represented above by the red dotted line. There is a simple way to ascertain where an individual stands in relation to this frontier in Scotland: above this dotted line, the consignments are dealt in kilos or fractions of kilos; below this dotted line, the units are dealt in imperial measure: principally ounces or fractions thereof (although, confusingly, some retail bag amounts for sale at street level are measured in grams).

The size of the financial commitment involved at the top of the scale, at the importation level, can be gauged from the major drug seizure in the spring of 2016 in the North Sea by the NCA, working with Police Scotland, in Operation Screenplay (The Herald, 2016). A Turkish trawler, MV Hamsun, was intercepted in the North Sea off the east coast of Scotland. The NCA 'deep rummage' team were called in to examine and search the impounded vessel. After an extensive and very probing search, an extensive illicit cargo of cocaine was found: it amounted to a haul of 3,2 tonnes. Translated into street prices, the value of the haul was in excess of £500 million.

As Reuter (2004) has pointed out the use of street prices to value an intercepted cargo is not really justified, in that it doesn't reflect the true value of the commodity in the place and condition where it is found, the cost value relevant to these preferred parameters indicated a value of this drugs consignment of £80 million plus. MV Hamsun was transporting a multi-million pound investment of which a sizeable economic return would be expected: likely to be between 50% and 100%[3] (Gash, 2016). The return expected from this level of investment would have to be realised from a revenue stream (*i.e.* an actual cash stream) sourced from physically dirty cash revenues earned at the retail end of the chain, and which involved their subsequent collection, secretion, and distribution to investors. The processes required to achieve these functions, and thus realise the economic return from the multi-million pound investment, would also involve the deployment of specific service attributes at various levels of the structure to enable the revenue to be secured and realised.

---

3 Gash (2016) uses an estimate of 69%, for example.

The set of required arrangements to harvest the money is almost always quite separate from the various co-ordinating arrangements relevant to distribution of the actual commodity. Again, there is a critical interface to be discerned at the level of the red dotted line: the amounts collected from the distribution networks below the line represent the accumulated cash resource (*e.g.* the £1,6. million seized in Operation Escalade) that requires to be secreted into a company or a bank account through a professionally managed laundering process. In some cases this is achieved by physical transportation of the cash abroad; in others money is secreted in a network of legitimate businesses controlled by specialist financial controllers who serve a number of different SOCG clients.

Empirical studies of the constituent elements of the chain are often limited in their scope to those aspects of it that are visible *i.e.* the local warehousing and street retain elements. At these levels, a degree of physical contiguousness exists between the commodity and the revenue it generates that is not present elsewhere in the chain. If, however, the process arrangements relating to how the required financial return reaches the importers, and indeed the investors standing behind the importers, are not properly understood – that is, the parts of the process which are usually kept separate from the commodity – then the relevant structures may appear to be flatter than is actually the case.[4]

The missing elements of the picture derive to a large extent from the traditional law enforcement bias that favours commodity as the focus of attention, as opposed to the revenue it earns. Given that the players with the most power in the relevant governing structures will generally not go anywhere near the commodity, this implies that one of the prizes for seniority in this industry is protection, if not immunity, from prosecution. In addition, the players at this level must maintain the ability to enjoy access to criminal revenue streams.

The oft expressed need to do more about 'high end money laundering' (Financial Times, 2015) is a reflection of the extent to which this problem has proved elusive to traditionally equipped law enforcement agencies. This is at least partly due to a lack of understanding of what the relevant business processes are which secure that revenue. This may also be read as

4 See Gash (2016) for an example of this line of argument, which is based on Reuter (2004), and also conversations with him.

a testament to the effectiveness of the design of these processes, or at least how jealously they are protected. It is an important gap, which counts against a proper understanding of the ways SOCGs relate to each other and the markets they participate being obtained.

A related but equally important challenge, however, is to find ways of properly visualising, or conceptualising, the attributes necessary to be able to exert the necessary control and influence in these realms. If these attributes can be properly identified, the prospect opens up of being able to identify and exploit, from a law enforcement point of view, structural weaknesses and vulnerabilities. Understanding the factors necessary for the formation of established hierarchies, therefore, provides an entry point for considering the factors which influence all capabilities relevant to participating in SOC, since hierarchies have to engage with network forms of association to profitably participate in these markets.

Understanding how those relationships work requires the formulation of a suitably based theoretical framework. The objective from a law enforcement point of view of developing such a framework would be to develop a practical template that would enable the relevant capabilities to be properly identified, so that they can be turned into vulnerabilities that can be targeted for law enforcement action.

The formation of firms and the importance of transaction costs in both legal and illegal markets

The first step to achieving this understanding is to analyse the dynamics that lie behind the relevant transactional relationships. The source of wealth and competitive success of any entity, including SOCGs, lies with its ability to successfully manage transactions. The entity, or 'firm', can essentially be defined in terms of the arrangements it engages in to achieve that.

In Ronald Coase's analysis (1937; see also Coase, 1960), firms are formed where functions and services cannot be accessed from the external market at a price which more than compensates for the increased transaction costs associated with dealing with an external supplier. The performing of these functions and services in-house become specialisations managed internally through hierarchical instructions. Different specialisations by different firms form the basis for the exchange of goods and services upon which a market economy is based. The Coase analysis relies heavily on the classic assumptions of efficient allocation of resources achieved through a properly functioning price mechanism, but the analysis still has contemporary relevance to the characteristics of the so called 'gig' economy, which has arisen in many instances as a consequence of the collapse of transaction costs across a number of service sectors. Firms are incentivised to outsource more and more functions as a result and reduce their own internal operations to core specialisations.

In the field of SOC, it is obvious that the natural discipline of the market will not reflect all of the relevant factors at play when determining whether or not to transact with another party. Illegal markets confer a number of different conditions: the threat of law enforcement; the extent to which a trading partner can be trusted in an unregulated environment; the threat of violence and so on. These are all factors likely to affect and distort the purely economic parameters relating to the relevant trading relationships. The theorising necessary to accommodate these features needs therefore to be able to accommodate the relevant non-market based features of transactions which can affect transactional outcomes.

Drawing on the Coase insights on firm formation, Oliver Williamson (1979) constructed a theory of economic activity based on a more detailed analysis of the costs and conditions relevant to economic transacting. This emphasised that economic organising could be essentially considered a problem of contracting, with the 'critical dimensions' of transacting being those of uncertainty, frequency, and a factor termed 'asset specificity.' This construct provides insights not only in respect of normal trading in legal markets between legal participants, but also SOCG trading in illegal markets too.

There are uncertainties about outcomes in both legal and illegal markets. Contracts cannot cover all contingencies, however well drawn. Other factors have to come into play in terms of the decision to transact with another party, the most obvious relating to the critical dimensions of 'uncertainty' and 'frequency'. For example, in terms of 'uncertainty', there are always natural boundaries of knowledge (or 'bounded rationality') which limit the number of possible counterparties that can be engaged with and the range of activities it is possible to engage in. Also, the dimension of 'frequency' in transacting is bound up in notions of trust. In situations where a new contracting party is identified, particularly in the highly cynical environment of SOC, certain questions arise, such as: am I going to be taken advantage of by this person – perhaps even in the same way that I, given the same opportunity, might very well take advantage of him? As with legal markets, the frequency and recurrence of transacting in illegal markets is contingent on the establishment of a suitable measure of trust between the transacting parties, and this tends to evolve and develop through repeated transacting. Transactions therefore occur in an environment of constant reputational evaluation and re-appraisal.

The Coase/Williamson analyses were both founded on the insight that firms and markets were alternative ways to organise transactions, with the decision as to which option was taken informed by evaluation of all the relevant transaction costs. The corollary of this is that firms tend to evolve in a way that encourages specialisms which are managed internally through hierarchical corporate structures and application of related cost and knowhow advantages exploited in the market place. The firm, as conceived by Williamson, is essentially characterised by these 'extra-market' specialisations; the ability to exploit and deploy advantage derived from being able to do certain things better than anyone else in that time and space. In the case of SOCGs, this state of affairs, where achieved, is partly because controllable conditions have been engineered to ensure this is the case, and will continue to be the case so long as the advantages conveyed by these specialisations prevail.

The establishment of these specialisms and their subsequent exploitation in the context of SOC have a particular relation to the formation of the third Williamson dimension, namely 'asset specificity,' which, in a paper entitled 'Hierarchy and Markets' (Williamson, 1973), he identified as the major indicator of hierarchy formation. It is the way in which SOC relates to this concept of 'asset specificity' that provides the key to understanding why SOC hierarchies form, and identifying the factors that enable them to form.

The significance of 'Asset Specificity' in explaining hierarchy formation

'Asset specificity' can be defined as the extent to which investments made to support a particular transaction have a higher value to the firm than doing anything else. According to Klaus von Lampe, it means that, "*certain resources such as specialised skills and machinery cannot be flexibly used for a variety of purposes*." (Von Lampe, 2016: 149). This is asset specificity explained as if it is a limitation, as if it is a problem to be overcome. According to Von Lampe, organisations respond to this asset specificity problem in two ways: incorporation of specific skills into the organisation, and then backwards and forwards integration of sourcing or raw materials and distribution of finished product or service.

In SOC, however, asset specificity is not so much a challenge to be overcome as a condition to be engineered and then exploited. The principal reason for this is that the conditions of asset specificity enable the extraction of what are referred to as 'quasi-rents'. The successful organised crime boss looks to engineer conditions which enable control of a particular service capability, or control over a geographical area or key transit channel. The key characteristic of such an advantage is that use of the asset of capability is in demand from other users, thus conferring the ability to extract quasi-rents and sustain economic power and influence.

The two essential characteristics expressed in formal terms, as further elucidated by Per Bylund (2011), arc *high complementarity* - the extent to which the relevant assets or commodities traded have utility value to a broad range of other firms; and *low substitutability* – the limited scope for other firms to access these assets or commodities from another source. Where these characteristics are present in respect of an asset, or a traded commodity, or a channel through which a commodity is traded, the achieved asset specificity conditions are transformed into what is referred to as a *strategic asset.*

The asset specificity conditions required to achieve such a strategic asset relate not only to the complementarity and substitutability variants indigenous to the transaction, but also the time and space in which the trade is conducted. Within these variables lie the reasons why certain players and groups in SOC exert a lasting influence, whereas others do not. Those able to engineer large scale shipments across borders and sea barriers, for example, are able to have an influence over the nature of the commodity supplied, and/or the price conditions, and/or the requirements relating to transportation and importation. All of these factors have the effect of increasing the value of the strategic asset of the relevant importation channel – consolidating the conditions of high asset specificity necessary for successful exploitation of it, to the exclusion of others who do not have access to it.

Control over strategic assets that allow dominance over distribution channels has been the key driver sustaining the influence of 'Ndrangheta in European drug markets and the Mexican cartels in North America. It is also of direct relevance to the Escalade SOCGs prominence in Scotland and the UK. In a different theatre of SOC, the same factors were identified by Campana (2015b) as explaining hierarchical influence in otherwise very disparate African human trafficking networks. Although the dominant modes of organisation were best characterised as loose networks, hierarchical influence could still be detected, derived from control of bottlenecks in the transportation process. These were the channels over which hierarchical authority could be imposed through the charging of quasi-rents.

The interaction of hierarchy and networks

As indicated, the trope of opposing hierarchies to networks does not help much in terms of understanding the Scottish SOC theatre: the evidence from SOCM indicates that hierarchical SOCGs are also active participants in network arrangements. The relevant theory relating to networks can, however, provide signposts as to what conditions are likely to be more suited to network forms of association.

Where the conditions amenable to the extraction of quasi rents do *not* exist, it follows that the influence of hierarchy in criminal markets is likely to be lessened. In these conditions, loose network type arrangements are more likely to be prominent, *e.g.*, in the conduct of cross border low denomination drug transactions. The profile of the Class A drug supply chain in Scotland, characterised by the interaction of hierarchies and network, sets the challenge of devising analyses which will help explain how hierarchical SOCGs interact and manage these interactions – in particular those areas of activity where transacting participants do not enjoy strategic asset advantages, where the most common form of criminal business organisation are network formations.

Walter Powell identified networks as a means of satisfying the requirements of economic transaction making which was separate from the binary choice between top-down direction and discrete market exchange (Powell, 1990). His analysis considered the conditions under which networks were most likely to emerge – essentially fields in which knowledge and/or skills did not lend themselves to either monopoly control or expropriation by the wealthiest bidder. According to Powell, when partners were involved in ongoing complementary activities, the relationship between them was more likely to lend itself to mutually supportive information sharing. The basis of exchange was identified as essentially an exchange of distinctive competencies: "*Networks of individuals engaged in reciprocal, preferential, mutually supportive actions. Networks can be complex: they involve neither the explicit criteria of the market, nor the familiar paternalism of the hierarchy*" (Powell, 1990: 303). The exchange of distinctive competencies in terms of knowledge or skills was therefore considered more likely to occur in networks. By contrast, where competition occurred on the basis of price or manufacturing intensity, networks were less likely to be in evidence.

There is nothing, however, to prevent exchanges occurring simultaneously between entities relying on distinctive competencies for their competitiveness and other entities which rely on strategic assets to assert market dominance. The functioning of illegal markets actually requires such exchanges. The nature of Scottish drug supply chains requires a degree of co-operation between SOCGs of varying degrees of complexity and structure to enable the market to function.

This still leaves the question of how the various modes of organisation occurring within SOC gel together to provide coherent functioning markets. The answer lies in understanding the parameters relevant to the transactions that are necessary to make such markets and supply lines work; something that builds on the work of Coase and Williamson to accommodate all aspects of why one party transacts with another, and accommodates all types of structure that is relevant to the workings of SOC markets.

John Kay and the foundations of corporate success

John Kay's analysis of the factors necessary for corporate success was founded on Williamson's work on transaction cost economics (Kay, 1993). According to Kay, contract structure, and therefore organisational form, adapts to the characteristics of the type of transactions to be handled. The value of any structure therefore lies in relational contracts, and this determines the mode of business organisation. The firm (including all varieties of SOCG) is defined by its contracts (or patterns of repeat transactional behaviour in SOCG environments) and relationships. Success, or 'added value' in a commercial context, is created by putting these contracts and relationships together. Differentiating factors between firms therefore lies in the quality and distinctiveness of its contracts, with their distinctiveness being at least as important as their quality. In most efficient markets, and probably all criminal markets, there are limited opportunities to make good contracts. The question at the heart of every firm's strategy, therefore, is 'why will we be better at doing this than anyone else?'

Success is obtained by developing a set of relationships which others are unable to make. The foundation to 'adding value' (which translates to being profitable and successful), is some kind of 'competitive advantage' – some feature of its relationships which other firms lack, and cannot readily produce. Powell's exchange of competencies alluded in his analysis of network arrangements is similarly founded on complementary distinctive capabilities. But Kay's analysis can extend to all types of transacting party, whether in the context of network structures or not. The only type of circumstance where this is not the case is where a firm relies solely, not on any such distinctive capability, but on its ability to exploit a strategic asset. This may be possible in the case of certain SOCGs, where it has engineered control over a supply route, a trading channel, or a key strategic technical asset. Even in these circumstances, however, the creation of the strategic asset is usually a function of a combination of competitive advantages being applied which have been founded on different distinctive capabilities. So what are these distinctive capabilities? Kay defines them as follows:

- *Architecture* – Architecture is the network of relational contracts within, or around, the firm. Firms might establish these relationships internally (through vertical integration), externally (with partners engaged in the same activities in other theatres), or among a group of firms engaged in related activities (networks based on complementarity);

- *Reputation* – Reputation is the most mechanism for conveying information to customers – or in SOCG terms, to partners and potential competitors (perhaps backed by a necessary degree of threat, or, alternatively, through financial muscle);
- *Innovation* – Innovation can deliver competitive advantage in itself, arising from being able to do something before anyone else can. Usually, however, according to Kay, it is more often associated with generating returns as a result of combining the innovation opportunity with other distinctive capabilities.

According to this analysis, the most powerful firms combine the leverage arising from all the distinctive capabilities they have access to and use them to re-inforce each other. This in turn can amount to the creation of the kind of strategic asset that enables collection of quasi-rents. The deployment of distinctive capabilities and/or strategic assets in relevant markets confers competitive advantage, and it follows that all successful SOCGs, however they are structured, and wherever they appear in criminal supply chains, fall to be analysed in these terms. This then offers a basis for constructing a means of identifying the key elements that enable SOCGs to function and be successful.

Application of the Kay analysis to Escalade

How can this theoretical foundation be applied in such a way as to provide workable insights relevant to SOC in practice? The Escalade example lends itself to analysis using the following matrix, which is based on the business model generation matrix of Osterwalder and Pigneur (2010).

Figure 2

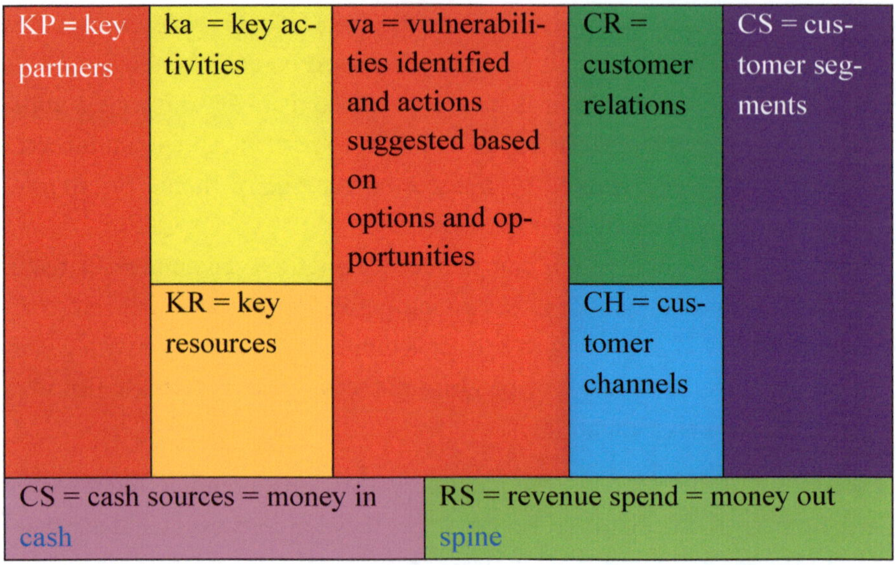

The relevant intelligence and/or information captured in relation to an SOCG can be classified according to the boxes of the matrix in order to determine its business profile. The left hand side relates to the Kay classifications of distinctive capabilities of architecture and innovation, and the right hand side relates to the distinctive capability of reputation as well as any strategic assets which can be exploited, such as control over drug distribution in a particular area or control of a key transit channel. In general terms, the K boxes taken collectively in this analysis relate to what an organisation does, and the 'C' boxes taken collectively relate to the markets it serves. In the context of an SOCG, however, the 'C' boxes usually translate to what it *controls*, since the way in which SOCGs relate to the markets they serve is usually in terms of what they control.

Applying this analysis to Escalade, in particular in respect of identifying how it acquired a dominant position in Scottish SOC, the relevant explanatory factors can be broken down into the following distinctive capabilities:

- The *key contact relationships* that allowed the Escalade group to assert itself as a major importer were those it had been able to establish with main producers and cartels in South America and Mexico. This enabled it to have control over a greater portion of the supply stages, in particular those parts offering the highest rewards, *i.e.* the phases transporting the commodity across the Atlantic to Europe and West Africa, and then from continental Europe into the UK. The Escalade group did not, therefore, rely on supplies already imported to Europe from other parties. In financial terms, this enabled the group to earn gross profits of £2 million a week from Scottish drug markets alone, or £100 million a year. This revenue enabled the Escalade group to invest in further capabilities, which had the effect of consolidating and enhancing its competitive position as detailed below;

- The *key resources* used by the Escalade group included: the warehouse network referred to, comprising storage assets in both Scotland and Europe; transport logistics over land and sea; rigorous internal control processes; and also an exclusive access to encrypted phone technology, which it also supplied to other SOCGs on a commercial basis;
- In addition to the source contacts it had acquired in South America and Mexico, the *key business partners* were prominent Scottish SOCGs, themselves often hierarchical organisations with strong roots to specific territories, who served as its primary customer base;
- *The key markets* in the UK could therefore be accessed through the network of SOCG customers it had established. These provided the local distribution capabilities necessary to access and exert a dominant hierarchical influence over the cocaine and heroin trade in the West of Scotland and much of its central belt. The financial success of the Escalade SOCG also required a means of collecting the cash realised from retail sales and securing it. The way in which this was done became apparent in the course of the law enforcement action described below.

The above outline profile identifies the key distinctive capabilities of the Escalade SOCG. The methods used by law enforcement to tackle it essentially made use of these distinctive capabilities, by turning them into vulnerabilities. The approach can be summarised as follows:

- Concerted surveillance and telephony over a 12-month period led to the identification of the principal SOCG customers of Escalade, which it supplied by with large quantities of Class A drugs. During the course of this first phase of the enquiry, the network of covertly obtained industrial premises and vehicles was identified. It was established all premises occupied had been rented under aliases. All rental payments were made in cash and in advance, limiting contact with landlords in an attempt to leave no evidential trail. Similarly, all of the vehicles identified were registered and insured to false names and addresses. Group members were observed conducting anti-surveillance prior to attending at these locations for fear of compromise.

- A further protracted period of surveillance, and other enquiries revolving around the identified warehouses, was undertaken. This had the objective of identifying as many of the covertly obtained premises and vehicles as possible. During this period, the tradecraft and hierarchy of the SOCG was identified and search warrants were obtained for all of the covertly obtained premises.
- On a Police Scotland day of 'executive action', raids were made on all the warehouse premises. This resulted in discovery of: (i) the largest weapons cache ever discovered in Scotland; (ii) an extensive collection of state-of-the-art anti-surveillance equipment and encrypted phone technology; (iii) £1,6 million in cash stored in seismic spring units for ease of secretion in lorries and other vehicles.
- DNA evidence from the weapons identified nine senior members of the Escalade SOCG. This enabled them to be evidentially linked to the torture of the debtor who had failed to pay a £30.000 drug debt.

The factors entrenching SOC hierarchical influence in Scotland's central belt

If the principal strategic asset accounting for the Escalade dominance was its contact base and supply infrastructure, what accounts for hierarchical influence attributable to its principal SOCG customers? In some cases, it relates to established dominance over a distinct geographical area; with others it relates to its broad network of contacts that enable it access to high level drug transaction negotiations. In respect of each of these SOCGs, it is the practical measures they take to secure their revenues that most obviously defines their identity as a group, and the hierarchical relationships within that are a principal feature of that group.

One of the key benefits of these arrangements is the ability to access legitimate markets. Legitimate activities are sometimes undertaken for the legal profits to be obtained from them, but in many cases, they serve, either directly or indirectly, criminal objectives – money laundering in particular.

It follows that assessment of SOCG business models must incorporate legitimate as well as illegitimate activities. The competitive position of a prominent SOCG is a function of how it manages and exploits interfaces between the two.

The most significant way in which Scottish SOCGs have done this has been to pool resources through centralised criminal money management facilities. Access to these facilities is itself a key distinctive capability which enables SOCGs to consolidate their position and accumulate wealth behind legitimate facades. The SOCGs with access to these facilities are those that feature in the top echelons of the SOCM rankings, which underline the impression that the top half of the profile of Class A drug supply in Scotland is indeed hierarchical. The extent of hierarchical influence extends down to the mid-level; aspiring SOCG players emerge from social drug networks to assume mid management roles. These roles require particular skill sets encompassing the ability to exercise discipline through threat and the management ability to secure the cash revenues that require to be secreted through money laundering portals (McLean et al., 2018). These individuals are prominent in SOCG intelligence disseminations, being the individuals most engaged at the front line, the open face of the hierarchical interests to whom they are answerable.

All of these SOCG groups, and indeed key enablers who flit between these groups, rely on established reputation to function. This often manifests as control exercised by a level of threat that is commonly perceived to be associated with that reputation; the distinctive capability which underpins how they are able to exert influence over the looser networks at the retail end of the supply chain. In essence, the expression of hierarchical influence is most obvious in the way in which relationships with looser, subordinate networks are conducted. In many senses Scottish SOC can be considered a network of these hierarchical influences, with the significant distinctive and differentiating capability common to each of them being the extent to which they are able to access and enjoy that influence in respect of these relationships.

The validity of this analysis is borne out by recent SOC developments in areas of Scotland which are beyond the usual areas of territorial control of the central belt based SOCGs (The Sunday Post, 2019). In contrast to the central belt, the northern cities of Aberdeen and Inverness do not have a tradition of dominant indigenous SOCGs. Accordingly, these markets have always been more open for infiltration by SOCGs from other areas, including England and foreign SOCGs. The strategic asset of local market dominance is not present, allowing these territories to become open to 'County Lines' drug gangs from England and beyond.

Conclusion

Understanding transactional dynamics is the key to understanding relationships within SOC, in particular hierarchical influence. It is by identifying such influence that law enforcement stands the best chance of maximising its effectiveness against SOCGs. This falls to be done by targeting not just the SOC players and groups with the most influence, but also the capabilities and strategic advantages that sustain their hierarchical position. In Scotland, the need to import illegal commodities across a sea border and persistent territorial influences have underpinned the continuing influence of hierarchical forces, which have successfully adapted to contemporary market forces and economic conditions. A key manifestation of that adaptation process is the extent to which hierarchical influence is maintained through network structures.

Given these characteristics, in order to be effective, law enforcement responses to the developing challenges of SOC in Scotland requires adoption of analytical tools that will enable understanding of SOC transactional capabilities. These capabilities are changing all the time: the networked hierarchies of SOC are particularly well suited in terms of their sets of competitive advantages to dominate and exploit many emerging dynamic criminal markets. If unchecked, they will confer increasing governance power and SOC influence over legitimate as well as illegitimate markets, which is a developing feature of SOC hierarchical influence in Scotland. Access to professional assistance at a level capable of sustaining credible presence and influence in legitimate markets, not always in sectors with which SOC has been traditionally associated, provides a further raft of distinctive capabilities which serve to confer and sustain hierarchical influence.

Failure to control the corruptive capability of such influence – which is a function of increasing accumulations of criminal profits being deployed in legitimate markets – is likely to result in increasing SOC governance across a broader range of legitimate markets and activities. The nature of the risk to developed economies is that hierarchical influences within SOC will accordingly be protected behind a screen of legitimate companies whose success in legitimate markets is underwritten by criminal revenue streams. This is the modern theatre of SOC influence and activity in Scotland, and presents law enforcement with its most potent challenge.

References

Bylund, P., *The Coasean and Williamson transaction cost theories of organisation: a critical analysis from a specialisation perspective*. University of Missouri, 2011, available at http://ageconsearch.umn.edu/bitstream/103616/2/Poster%20submit%20Bylund.pdf

Campana, P., The structure of human trafficking: lifting the bonnet on a Nigerian transnational network. *British Journal of Criminology*, 2016a, 56(1), 68-86.

Campana, P., Explaining criminal networks: strategies and potential pitfalls. *Methodological Innovations*, 2016b, 9(1), 1-10.

Coase, R.H., The nature of the firm. *Economica*, 1937, 4(16), 386-405.

Coase, R.H., The problem of social cost. *Journal of Law and Economics*, 1960, 3, 1-44.

Daily Record, 11 December 2017a, available at https://www.dailyrecord.co.uk/news/crime/torture-gang-broke-victims-leg-11677300.

Daily Record, 17 December 2017b, available at: https://www.dailyrecord.co.uk/news/crime/cocaine-gangster-faced-rap-over-11707538.

Finckenauer, J.O., Problems of definition: what is organized crime?, *Trends in Organized Crime*, 2005, 8(3), 63-82.

Financial Times, *Alarm bells ring as 'dirty cash' floods UK property market*, Cynthia O'Murchu, 16 September 2015.

The Herald, *Police still hunting for ringleaders of international cocaine smuggling operation*. 11 July 2016.

Gash, T., *Criminal – the truth about why people do bad things.* London: Allen Lane, 2016.

Hobbs, D., *Lush Life – Constructing organised crime in the UK.* Clarendon Studies in Criminology, Oxford: Oxford University Press, 2013.

Kay, J., *Foundations of corporate success.* Oxford: Oxford University Press, 1993.

McLean, R., J.A. Densley and R. Deuchar, Situating gangs within Scotland's illegal drugs markets. *Trends in Organised Crime*, 2018, 21(2), 147-171.

Morselli, C., Structuring Mr Nice: entrepreneurial opportunities and brokerage positioning in the cannabis trade. manuscript (http://citeseerx.ist.psu.edu/viewdoc/download?doi=10.1.1.464.3579), 1999.

Morselli, C., Assessing vulnerable and strategic positions in a criminal network. *Journal of Contemporary Criminal Justice*, 2010, 26(4), 382-392.

Osterwalder, A. and Y. Pigneur, *Business model generation*. Hoboken, NJ: John Wiley & Sons, 2010.

Powell, W.W., Neither market nor hierarchy – network forms of organisation. *Research in Organisational Behaviour*, 1990, 12, 295-336.

Reuter, P., *The organisation of illegal markets: an economic analysis*. Honolulu, HI: University Press of Pacific, 2004.

Scottish Government, *Serious Organised Crime (SOC) in Scotland: A Summary of the Evidence.* Edinburgh: Scottish Government, 2017.

Sunday Mail, 10 February 2019, available at www.dailyrecord.co.uk/news/scottish-news/scotlands-narcos/

Sunday Post, 10 February 2019, available at www.sundaypost.com/fp/threats-violence-and-death-as-county-lines-drugs-gangs-seize-homes-in-towns-and-villages-across-rural-scotland/

von Lampe, K., *Organized Crime: Analyzing illegal activities, criminal structures, and extra-legal governance*. Thousand Oaks, CA: Sage, 2016a.

von Lampe, K., The ties that bind: a taxonomy of associational criminal structures. In G.A. Antonopoulos (ed.), *Illegal Entrepreneurship, Organised Crime and Social Control.* Cham: Springer, 2016b.

Williamson, O.E., Transaction-cost economics: the governance of contractual relations. *Journal of Law and Economics*, 1979, 22(2), 233-261.

Williamson, O.E., Transaction cost economics. In R. Schmalensee and R.D. Willig (eds.), *Handbook of industrial organisation* (Volume 1, pp 135-182), Amsterdam: North-Holland, 1989.
Williamson, O.E., Markets and hierarchies: some elementary considerations, *American Economic Review*, 1973, 63(2), 316-325.

Changing face of organised crime
or
old and new usual suspects

Miroslav Scheinost[1]

What is the face of organised crime? Could it be represented by the faces of well-known 'organised criminals'? Let us remind ourselves of the faces of American mobsters from the golden age of prohibition – dignified men in black suits and soft hats but with a revolver in the pocket and sometimes with machine-guns in the car. We may also recall the icon of those times, Al Capone, who was sentenced not for gangster crimes but for tax evasion, or Frank Costello, the so-called "Prime Minister of the Underworld", who, for several decades, ruled one of the country's major criminal gangs. He was brought several times to court but spent only 11 months in prison, becoming a well-known figure due to the Kefauver committee hearings in 1951, but passed away tranquilly as a respectable citizen aged 91 (Kenney and Finckenauer, 1995).

Or could the face of Colombian narco-baron, Pablo Escobar, be more representative? The man who was at a certain time considered to be the richest person on earth, a man responsible for hundreds if not thousands of murders, yet mourned by thousands of common Colombians after he was killed on the run in 1993. (Thoumi, 2012)

Or is it the face of "white collar" such as Roberto Calvi, the Italian banker dubbed "God's Banker", suspected of financial machinations and money laundering whose death in 1982 has never been fully clarified?

Or is it the face of someone more up-to-date like the Russian "thief-in-law" Vyacheslav Ivankov called Yaponchik, a man whose criminal activities encompassed not only post-Soviet territory but also the U.S., and who was assassinated on a street in Moscow in 2009?

---

1 The author is director of the ICSP (Institute of Criminology and Social Prevention) Prague, Czech Republic

The faces of these men are known and distinct but the underlying face of organised crime is indistinct and more hidden. That is why the effort to delineate this multi-faceted phenomenon by some unambiguous and clear definition has failed so often (von Lampe, 2016). The strict critic may say that if the exact and generally accepted definition of the phenomenon itself is missing the analysis of its developmental changes stands on weak ground. How can we describe the intended phenomenon, its initial state and its subsequent development without having an exact definition at hand?

But while the exact contours of organised crime are contested, there is at least some agreement that by observing certain phenomena, such as systematic and planned criminal activity or hierarchically structured groups of criminals (see Musil, 2014), something can be learned about the situation and development of organised crime.

The face of organised crime in the socialist period

If we look back at the development of organised crime in the Czech Republic we may state that it is closely linked to political, social and economic developments during the period of transformation and the subsequent phase of stabilisation. It has been related not only to the phenomenon itself but also to its perception.

For the preceding period of socialist Czechoslovakia it was characteristic that the phrase 'organised crime' was not used with regard to any kind of criminal activity. Under the dominant ideology it was simply unthinkable to admit to the existence of anything like 'organised crime' within socialist society. If anything, this category was considered as something transmitted by the literature and movies, something that belonged to the alien and specific traditions of other countries.

This state of affairs was reflected also by the respective law. The Czechoslovak penal code at that time did not know the term 'organised crime' and did not take into account the potential occurrence of such forms of criminality. The penal code knew only the term "organised group" used to designate the cases when several offenders joined in order to commit some separate, concrete crime.

This does not mean that from the present perception some forms of crime in the socialist Czechoslovakia were not organised. In fact, there were some forms of 'organised' criminal groups and activities, typically in such areas as the illegal exchange of foreign currency and organised prostitution. While not labelled 'organised crime' in legal parlance or in the common language, these manifestations bore the features of organised crime, with the exception of the transnational element because the borders were hermetically closed and all contacts with foreign countries carefully supervised (Scheinost, 2001: 34).

Offenders of this 'socialist organised crime' were usually individuals who thanks to their profession had wide-ranging contacts. Take, for example, prostitution. The procurers were mostly taxi-drivers and receptionists at hotels. In contrast, those engaged in the illegal exchange of currency (called commonly "veksláci" from German "wechseln") tended to be younger people who most often pretended to be employed, for example as night watchman of some object (because it was necessary to prove a legal source of living to avoid prosecution for so-called social parasitism). The public was familiar with both these activities and especially the illegal exchange of currency that took place openly, sometimes literally before the eyes of the people (and the police). Beyond any doubt these illegal activities enjoyed some tacit approval by the general public and also the police which balanced their willingness to look the other way with the ability to garner support from criminal elements, for example by recruiting prostitutes as informants.

Another facet of the 'grey zone' of the economy was connected to illegal or semi-legal businesses involved in the illicit distribution of scarce goods. However, the Czechoslovakian shadow economy never reached the scale and level of organisation endemic, for example, in the Soviet Union. Citizens coped with the shortage of consumer goods and services through the informal exchange networks of which every citizen was a part.

Those who obtained illegal profits from these activities, either as 'organised' or simply 'economic' perpetrators, were depicted in Czech literature and movies as petty law breakers, greedy individuals not satisfied with money earned from honest work who represented the last remnants of the 'petty bourgeois' class. The '*veksláci*', on the other hand, were presented as drifting young men without firm moral principles, longing for an 'easy life'. Both these types were of course in stark contrast to the propagated model of 'socialist man' (Šinkovec, 2019).

Time of transformation

So, in the eyes of the Czechoslovak public and from the point of view of the socialist state authorities, there was no organised crime. And where some organised forms of criminality did exist, these were not understood as such. This means that the term 'organised crime' did not enter the public conscience in the CR until the social transformations of the so-called transition period began to take hold after 1989. It is important to note that under the new conditions the existence of organised crime was not tied to any of the facets of the Soviet-Era shadow economy. After all, many of the old schemes, such as the black-market exchange of currency, had lost their meaning under the new economic and financial system. Rather, the focus shifted to new forms of crime that emerged in the process of transformation against the background of a general increase in crime.

Jan van Dijk and Patricia Mayhew in their study "Criminal victimisation in the industrialised world" have argued that a high crime rate is the price paid for living in a rich, urbanised and democratic society (van Dijk and Mayhew, 1993). The post-socialist countries undoubtedly aspired to transform themselves into such a society. However, the increase in crime, including new forms of serious crime, should not be viewed as a sign that the desired goal of transformation had been realised. Rather than marking the advent of a flourishing economy, the crime trends of the 1990s were an unwanted and unanticipated consequence of the efforts to reach that goal as quickly as possible.

All post-socialist countries experienced a radical transformation both economically and politically. The common denominators of the economic transformation were far-reaching changes through the rapid privatisation of state property, the redistribution and new accumulation of capital, and the hurried – even rushed – formation of a market economy. Although the opening of borders was essential for democratic and market changes, it also opened the door to criminal activities from the outside. New institutions and processes of governance and economics were introduced in states where the natural development of social progress had been halted for decades. The state institutions, which bore the historical burden of public distrust, were left weakened by radical changes both in the constitutional framework and in the composition of staff.

The police and judiciary were among the authorities most deeply affected and undermined by these changes; and at the same time were confronted with dramatically increased workloads in the face of rising crime. As a rule, such profound social change shakes the established norms of social behaviour and social regulation and leads to the emergence of a situation of 'anomie', as predicted by Emile Durkheim (Cejp and Scheinost, 2012). And anomie increases the inclination of individuals to commit crimes especially when the new conditions create environments and fertile soil for crime in other ways as well. The emergence and growth of diverse forms of organised crime in particular where promoted in the post-socialist milieu.

When exploring the rise of organised crime in this period we may take into account a second theory apart from Durkheim's Anomie Theory: the theory of rational choice which posits that crimes are committed when potential perpetrators come to the conclusion that the benefits from crime outweigh the associated costs. Applied to the situation in transition countries it means that crime is an adaptation strategy chosen with the aim to exploit new favourable conditions quickly and effectively and with hardly any substantive risk due to the circumstance that laws and their enforcement are also in motion and, therefore, less effective in their functioning (Lubelcová, 1998: 131–134).

This form of adaptation strategy is a reaction to changes in social conscience. Under the former egalitarian model, when most of the people lived at roughly equal levels of socio-economic status, it was not useful to crop out too much. Rather, it was appropriate to remain at a plain level and avoid any unwanted attention. Individuals striving for wealth had no place in this model. In contrast, what was appreciated (at least formally) was the 'righteous work' for the common welfare of the collective. People striving for individual wealth were officially considered to be 'bourgeois types' inherited as 'survivals' from the period of class-divided society. This egalitarian model, which had prevailed for decades under the socialist regime was suddenly cast aside. It was replaced by an individualistic model which has since shaped the social climate, colouring the process of transformation and furthering a different notion of desirable social behaviour based on the principle of individual liberty, entrepreneurial success, and the display of personal wealth. The principle of competition and success has since prevailed.

Some people and social groups have been characterised by high aspirations and by their effort to accomplish a rapid vertical mobility fully taking advantage of new opportunities. Nevertheless this effort was often accompanied by impatience and by a relatively strong consumer orientation. Not all have been capable of fulfilling their ambitions in keeping with the law. Some, who with a novel vision of personal success have jumped on the opportunities provided by a free market economy, did so with weak moral standards, which is not really surprising given that under the previous regime nothing had prepared them for the new situation.

What was especially weakened was the respect for property. Because nearly all property under the socialist regime was state property, it was a "property of all people" which meant in fact that it was anonymous and effectively belonged to no one. In addition, the vision of free market economy was for most people a rather obscure notion, and something like ethical principles of enterprising or decent behaviour in the market place were remote ideas. Others found themselves marginalised due to the social changes and reacted with frustration to the loss of status and the inability to achieve prosperity (Scheinost, 1999).

We may add that the social atmosphere after 1989 was characterised by a high level of optimism. Based on research carried out in 1991, 45% of the people expected a rapid improvement of the social and economic situation in the near future, 40% counted on at least a moderate improvement (Svítková, 1992). In 1994, it was found that 33% of the population expected an improvement of their standard of living within one year, and 64% within five years (Mladá fronta Dnes, 1994).

When such high expectations come into conflict with reality, which, in fact, has been the case for many people, one can expect increasing pressure to take the risk of unlawful forms of problem solving. A rational evaluation of possible gains related to potential risks, together with a high desire for social wealth and respect, can lead to the decision to break the law. This theory seems to be adequate in order to explain at least in part the general rise of profit-motivated crimes in the period of transformation. It is possible to recall also Agnew's general strain theory – strains as the inability to achieve positively valued goals (Agnew, 2001).

If we try to explain the expansion of organised crime as a specific phenomenon against the background of this general growth of crime, the so-called 'enterprise theory' (Smith, 1980) may also prove useful. This theory describes the activities of criminal organisations in terms of market mechanisms of supply and demand. The legal market does not only fail to satisfy potential buyers of illegal goods and services, which is obvious, it even may fail to satisfy those interested in legal products and service. High demand for illegal goods (such as drugs) or services (*e.g.* the organisation of illegal migration) or scarce legal goods (art items, cars), combined with relatively low risk and high profit, provide strong incentives for illegal groups to enter the market and organize the supply in accordance with demand (Kenney and Finckenauer, 1994: 41).

This model of organised crime can be observed in various post-socialist countries. The rapidly emerging demand for drugs and cars (some of the countries in question acted as the source of the 'product' and others as its destination), the development of the sex industry, the huge numbers of refugees willing to pay for assistance in illegal migration especially during the Balkan wars, the expansion of the stolen arts trade, to name but a few 'areas of growing demand', all created profitable opportunities from which criminal groups and organisations benefited. Those who were willing to break the law in order to take advantage of these new opportunities on the one side, and people forming a demand for certain commodities that were not offered legally, on the other, met on this field of criminal enterprising.

Apart from the two groups that interacted as suppliers and customers of illegal goods and services, there was a third group of people that did not offer or buy anything. They exploited opportunities for predatory enrichment that came into being in the frame of the process of privatisation, involving such schemes as frauds, corruption, and so-called tunneling (see Baloun *et al*., 2005).

This raises the question how the face of organised crime changed in times of transition. It is possible to distinguish three elements shaping the appearance of organised crime at the time (of course as an 'ideal model'):

1. Enterprising Czechs taking advantage of new opportunities that presented themselves in a process of transition marked by such factors as

a state of anomie, a new model of social success, weakened state institutions and law enforcement authorities, and a rushed process of privatisation.
2. The Czech society with its role in creating opportunities for crime through the demand for certain goods (*e.g.*, drugs, cheap cars), unsettled social norms and changing values leading to the higher level of tolerance to socially aggressive form of behaviour, trust in quick progress etc.
3. The international influences in the form of a penetration by criminal entrepreneurs from abroad as well as a demand for illegal goods and services from abroad.

From the beginning, the attention of the public, the media and law enforcement authorities focused on this third element.

Such a penetration from abroad of course existed and cannot be denied. Many factors were favourable for organised criminal activities coming from abroad and developed on the Czech territory: an advantageous geographical position of the CR, anticipating and preparing to join the EU, instability and unpreparedness of legal norms, insufficient institutions and personnel and lack of experience of law enforcement authorities. The CR quickly became the link on the traces of transnational illegal trafficking in diverse commodities. The Czech territory served at first as transit country but gradually also as target country for some commodities such as *e.g.* drugs and trafficked women.

Organised criminal groups coming from abroad were in the first phase involved in drug trafficking, illegal migration, prostitution, racketeering *etc.* as mentioned above. They were not primarily engaged in activities carried out in economy sectors. The term 'organised crime' essentially referred to the setting and content from abroad. With regard to the Czech perpetrators organised crime was interpreted as some kind of incentive that recruits only step-by-step, domestic co-offenders, suppliers and customers.

Thus, organised crime within this initial period was interpreted especially in media as an imported phenomenon focused on its 'classical' manifestations. In this conception, organised crime was commonly represented by the activities of more or less extensive organisations and groups often interconnected in transnational networks trading illegal goods and services or illegal trafficking in legal goods and services. These 'usual' forms of organised crime probed in the new geographic areas for an attractive milieu that also encompassed newly established groups of customers, victims but also collaborators and co-offenders. They filled the field prepared by new kinds of demand or stimulated demand and offer,

The offender picture at this time corresponded to this usual interpretation: it was rather a foreigner coming from abroad as organiser of trafficking in drugs, cars, women, transport of migrants. At the second place it was his Czech collaborator: the small drug dealer, car thief, burglar of castles, museums and churches, smuggler, driver, person providing transport and accommodation of migrants *etc*. In short, mostly people at the low level of organised criminal businesses as executive members and helpers. At best the Czech co-offenders could be people acting as contacts and counsellors of foreign crime-entrepreneurs who needed their experience and orientation.

The proportion of Czechs and foreigners has been considered for years by the Police to be relatively equal but as results from expertise mentioned below the decisive role was attributed to foreigners. Especially during 1990s it was characteristic that organised crime was not understood as the product of the criminogenic potential of domestic conditions; rather it was presented as the misuse by organised groups penetrating from abroad.

Also the first governmental concept of the fight against organised crime (Concept, 1996) focused mostly on provisions how to hinder the penetration of organised crime from abroad.

Thus, this 'branch' of organised crime during the initial period of transformation may be labelled as 'traditional' or 'classic' organised crime. We may also designate it, in spite of high profits, as a 'lower' form of organised crime because it was connected to lower social strata at least at the executive level.

But if we want to understand organised forms of crime we cannot neglect changes in the legal economy, it means that it is necessary to have a look to new opportunities opened for new perpetrators in the process of transition. It is obvious that the period of transformation provided fertile grounds for the rise of criminal activities in the corporate and financial fields, in particular with regard to the process of privatisation of state property, the development of private enterprising, and the transfer of capital, all within an environment characterised by a lack of market regulation with new laws being developed and adopted only gradually and sometimes belatedly (Baloun *et al.*, 2005). Under such favourable conditions, several forms of organised illegal or semi-legal activities began to grow. Initially they were not called and presented as organised crime. In fact, for a relatively long time they did not attract any special attention, and they were not visibly connected with existing criminal organisations. Those cases that came to light concerned large privatisation investment funds such as V. Kozeny's Harvard Investment Funds, the Trend fund, or CS Funds which took advantage of coupon privatisation to amass huge quantities of investors' assets and, through a range of different financial operations, to misappropriate these assets.

Offenders coming from abroad also took part in these activities by investment of illegal profits, mostly into real estate or restaurants, but the substantial part of this kind of crime should be attributed to Czech offenders. In contrast with the above mentioned first 'branch', these forms of financial and economic crime were from the outset closely tied with the Czech environment. They arose from 'inside' and were committed mostly by Czech offenders, though in many cases there were some international ramifications especially with respect to financial transactions. For a long time these activities were not presented as organised crime, even in cases where features of organised crime were apparent, including the use of violence. For example, the so-called light fuel oil cases. The base of these cases consisted of tax fraud taking advantage of loopholes in tax law and the incoherent regulation of the designation of oil products (Baloun and Scheinost, 2002). This activity produced enormous profit for perpetrators: it was based on the co-operation of suppliers, transporters, dealers and violence was used if needed especially inside the network against unreliable members, debtors *etc*.

Development of organised crime

a. Expertise

In order to trace the development of organised crime in the CR, especially with respect to criminal activities in the economic sphere, we can draw on regular expert surveys carried out annually since 1993. The panel of experts, ranging in size between 20 and 40, has been composed mostly of police officers from specialised police units and within the last few years also included respondents from special tax service units. The survey has been part of research on organised crime carried out by the Institute of Criminology and Social Prevention. Of course, the results represent ‘soft data’, opinions of experts/practitioners, but at the same time it gives a picture of perceived trends in organised crime, as well as in the conceptualisation of this phenomenon. For comparison we may use data from 1993, 2009 and 2017 (Cejp, 2000; 2018).

One issue addressed in the surveys was the proportion of foreigners among offenders involved in organised crime. It may be surprising that throughout the entire period covered by the surveys, police experts estimated the shares of foreigners and Czech offenders to be about equal, with a slight prevalence of foreigners. However, Czech offenders were considered to be positioned more at the executing level.

In 2009 experts estimated that foreign participants comprised 55% and Czechs 45% of organised crime groups (percentage is given by the average of respondents estimation). In addition, they estimated that approximately half the groups are mixed, with almost one third composed entirely of foreigners, and only about a quarter with exclusively Czech membership. Among mixed groups, groups headed by foreigners and Czechs performing auxiliary roles were deemed to be in the majority by a small margin.

With regard to nationalities, according to the 2009 survey, Ukrainians and Russians were believed to be the two groups of foreigners most frequently involved in organised crime in the Czech Republic on a long-term basis. After 2000, Vietnamese and Albanian nationals entered this segment, and their share has steadily increased. Since 1998, the relative representation of Chinese in this first group has declined somewhat. In the 1990s, this group of strongly represented nationalities also included citizens of the former Yugoslavia. With the final disintegration of Yugoslavia into several smaller states, the share of Yugoslavs decreased significantly.

In 2017, experts estimated the share of foreigners to drop to 49% in comparison with 2009, the Czech forming 51% of the total number. With regard to the composition of criminal groups, estimates shifted even more clearly towards a prevalence of Czechs. Only 28% of groups were believed to be composed purely of foreigners, 21% mixed with a prevalence of foreigners, 21% mixed with a prevalence of Czechs, and 30% of the organised groups composed exclusively of Czechs.

With regard to nationalities we again find in 2017 Vietnamese, Ukrainians, Russians and Albanians among the nationalities most frequently mentioned, followed by Slovaks, Bulgarians and Romanians. Of lesser importance are Poles, Serbs and Nigerians as well as Chinese whose estimated numbers continue to decline.

Overall, these results suggest that the proportion of Czech and foreigners speaking of the offenders has been rather stable, but experts point out that in their opinion the share of pure or predominantly Czech groups is growing. After 2000 the most numerous nationalities (except the Czech) among offenders of organised crime have been consistently Vietnamese, Ukrainians, Russians and Albanians. The long-run tendency shows a rise of the share of Slovaks and Romanians, and within last years also Serbs. In contrast, the number of Bulgarians, Poles, Chinese and Nigerians has been decreasing (Cejp, 2018).

Apart from the national background of organised criminals the surveys sought to ascertain the opinion of experts on the most widespread forms of organised crime in the Czech Republic. The following table enables to compare at least roughly the development of typical and most widespread activities of organised crime in the CR according to the opinion of the experts. Table 1 presents the results of inquiries made in 1993, 2009 and 2017. The column under the year 1993 shows the ranking of the activity in question speaking of prevalence in this year and then the shift in its ranking in 2009 and 2017 and, of course, the ranking of newly named activities in these years.

If we compare the expert opinions expressed from 1993 to 2009, it is obvious that the most widespread activity had consistently been car theft. The organisation of prostitution decreased; theft and trafficking in stolen art items decreased very rapidly. On the other side, the production, smuggling and distribution of drugs sharply increased (since 1994).

Table 1
Surveys expert opinions

Activities	1993 N=12	2009 N=26	2017 N=41
	rank	**rank**	**rank**
Car theft	1-2	1-3	17-18
Theft of art items	1-2	18-19	24-26
Organising prostitution	3	12-16	17-18
Tax, insurance, credit frauds	4-5	4-5	3-5
Burglary	4-5	12-16	15-16
Organising illegal migration	6	7-11	12
Corruption	7-9	1-3	3-5
Handling stolen goods	7-9	20-22	21
Gambling	7-9	18-19	24-26
Money laundering	10-12	1-3	2
Extortion, racketeering	10-12	23-24	29-30
Trafficking in drugs	10-12	4-5	1
Banking frauds	-	6	19
Establishing fraudulent & fictitious companies	-	7-11	3-5
Credit card fraud	-	7-11	13-14
Document counterfeiting	-	7-11	9
Abuse of computers for criminal activities	-	7-11	7
Misuse of EU funds	-	-	6
Custom frauds	-	-	8
Illegal producing and trafficking in alcohol and cigarettes	-	-	10-11
Infringement of trade mark	-	-	10-11

N = number of experts questioned in the respective year

Even in 2009 we may see the increase of financial and economic crime in the form of tax, insurance, credit frauds and money laundering. The increase of corruption is also visible. In 2009, missing from the 'top ten' are the organisation of prostitution, handling of stolen goods, gambling and racketeering. In their place we find abuse of computers, document counterfeiting, establishing fraudulent companies, *i.e.* rather more qualified financial or economic forms of crime.

In 2017, the first place is firmly held by trafficking in drugs, followed by money laundering. Next comes corruption together with various forms of fraud at 3rd-5th place and partly of document counterfeiting in 9th place. It is important to notice that misuse of EU funds has, since 2013, ranked among the frequently mentioned activities. This year experts named some new activities such as illegal trade in pharmaceuticals and fictitious marriages contracted in order to legalise the stay in the country. All these forms of law breaking are not at top positions but still worthy of mentioning. Experts also called attention to the activities connected with the illegal trade in protected plants and animals.

These changes could indicate how organised criminal groups replace certain operations as these become less lucrative in light of new, more attractive opportunities. For example, thefts of works of art stood alongside car theft as one of the most common activities of organised crime in the first half of the 1990s. The more effective sophisticated registration of items of art and the cooperation of other European states probably led to the gradual decline of these crimes in the second half of the 1990s, and since 2000 they have fallen to a negligible level. Similarly, illegal migration declined. Violent crime against the public or even between criminal groups in connection with organised crime stepwise receded. Organised crime groups evidently make high profits in the easiest possible way through contacts, corruption and negotiation instead of violence. This is probably also one of the determinants of the shift of activities towards the economic and financial sphere (Cejp, 2018).

b. Governmental reports

The report on the security situation and public order in the CR is a document drawn up each year by the Czech police and submitted to the government and to the Parliament. Over the course of the last few years it has noted both a stabilisation of 'traditional' organised crime in the CR, accompanied by a slow decline of violent crime (murders, extortion, assault and injury), and a shift towards non-violent crime mostly of an economic character (tax fraud and evasion, credit fraud, computer crime, affecting of government and public contracts and subsidies, *etc.*). Domestic organised crime groups are in this report presented as those leading in the area of crime connected with public subsidies and public procurement. This stated general trend resonates with the notion of a close relationship of organised crime and the development of society and economy.

If we reflect on the report from 2009, we see that it stated that among typical activities of organised crime in the CR are the production, distribution and trafficking in drugs, tax frauds, organising prostitution and illegal migration, money counterfeiting, infringement of trade marks, money laundering, corruption *etc*. It was mentioned that the Czech Security and Information Service paid attention to the attempts of representatives of criminal structures to influence the decisions of state administration and to establish connections to government officials at local, regional and central levels, and to engage in money laundering and investment of criminal assets (Report on the security situation and public order 2009).

In 2013, this report speaks of a continuing trend of infiltration of organised crime into the area of legitimate business and public administration through establishing firms and companies built in order to cover financial machinations or installing own people to the key position in economic and state institutions. The decline of violent activities and growth of criminal economic activities was stated (Report on security situation and public order, 2013).

The 2016 report states that Czech organised crime groups are effectively embedded in the economic environment and dispose by high corruptive potential. These groups try to entangle into their activities people at stable positions in economy and business. The report mentions a leading role of domestic groups especially in the crime connected with public procurement and subsidies. Attempts to corrupt central as well as local public administration are characteristic, both for domestic and foreign groups (Report on security situation and public order, 2016).

The reports indicate the enormous profits generated from these kinds of economic crime in an organised and qualified way facilitated by entrepreneurial experience and accountancy qualification of perpetrators that allows them to balance on the edge of the law and avoid the intervention from law enforcement authorities. Corruption is noted especially in connection with contacts between entrepreneurs and officials especially with regard to the management of public property and public budgets (Report on the security situation and public order, 2017).

Changes in the character of organised crime

Expertise and governmental reports allow for the monitoring of developments of the qualitative characteristics of organised crime. That enables the identification of some trends. There are roughly three basic categories that are discernible based on these trends.

1. The first category pertains to changes in the overall nature and internal structures of organised crime;
2. The second concerns the way organised crime has stabilised, expanded and become institutionalised;
3. The third category points out to infiltration of organised crime into social structure and public administration.

It was observed with regard to the first category that the social and economic level of the organisations has increased. It is more sophisticated and efficient and encompasses more economic sectors. In addition to being better organised than it once was, organised crime now has a better technology at its disposal and makes use of the Internet. There has been a significant increase in the wealth of the various groups involved. Individual groups have divided up the market in illegal goods and services between themselves. Organised crime is more dangerous than in the 1990s because those who control it are now more cloaked in anonymity and control crime indirectly. Criminals are using increasingly sophisticated means to escape detection.

The second category consists of changes in the way crimes are committed. In this respect, the activities of organised criminal groups make less obvious use of violence, concentrating instead on more economic crime and fraud, and more on corruption. The range of activity is expanding to embrace more economic areas. For example, illegal production and smuggling of alcohol and cigarettes, counterfeiting, and cyber-crime are growing. There is a risk of an increase in the illegal import and export of hazardous waste, human trafficking for forced labour, abuse of EU funds and several other activities.

The third category involves changes related to the expansion of organised crime into *social structures*. It is reaching further into the public administration and undertakes larger-scale activities in the economic sphere. It tries to establish contacts within the police and other security forces.

Profits from illegal activities are laundered in legal business operations. In this respect, organised crime is causing more damage and has a damaging effect on the economy. The fact that the perpetrators already occupy high positions in the business community, and have connections in politics, local and regional administration, the media, *etc*., makes it difficult to detect their activities. The social level of activities also means that organised criminals can exploit their contacts in order to publicly discredit the authorities involved in detecting and convicting them (Cejp and Scheinost,2012).

In relation to this development it is worth mentioning the term 'godfather' as it arose around the year 2010. A content analysis of newspapers produced by the Institute of Criminology and Social Prevention in 2011 found a noteworthy shift in terminology and focus regarding the 'face of suspect'. As indicated before, the term 'organised crime' itself has been used only rarely, and for the most part it was not used with regard to events involving Czech offenders. The term 'mafia' was likewise used only rarely in relation to specific cases. More typically it was applied to different lobbies and their attempts to influence the public administration. The term 'godfather', however, was used frequently. Of course, it is a rather journalistic term, similar to 'tunnelling' the banks, companies and plants. (Baloun and Scheinost, 2002). It has not been used to designate a 'supreme boss of a criminal organisation' but as the denomination of a rich and powerful man capable of manipulating politics, at least at the local level. He has commonly been characterised as a 'controversial entrepreneur' – a businessman operating at the margins of the law and willing to go beyond if needed. It means in fact that the link of such an entrepreneur with criminal activities has not been established but is strongly presumed. Simply put, 'godfather' indicates a strong man behind the political scene with a web of contacts to dubious and shady characters (Luptáková, 2011).

Over the past few years, this term has again dropped back in media usage and in the political jargon. But its frequency around 2010 referred to the growing attention paid to the risk of the public administration being influenced by well-connected 'controversial entrepreneurs'. This direction of attention prevailed the attention paid to the peril of 'classical' organised crime. The comparison of expertise and statements incorporated in the reports on the security situation in the CR points to three basic conclusions:

1. organised crime has been stabilised on the criminal scene;

2. its traditional forms did not disappear, only have been adapted to conditions and opportunities for profit;
3. a distinct shift of organised crime activities towards the licit economy and business has been observed.

With regard to the second and third conclusion: it seems that perpetrators of organised economic criminal activities stem probably not only from high qualified strata of typical 'white collars' but also from ordinary and originally not suspicious entrepreneurs that decided to use (rather misuse) the chances in the market.

It is possible to illustrate this intersection between economic and organised crime and the involvement of such a category of offenders by the example of the so-called 'alcohol affair'. This was analysed in the frame of research carried out by Tomáš Diviák at the Institute of Criminology and Social Prevention using the method of social network analysis (see *e.g.* Borgatti *et al.*, 2013; Robins 2015; for an introduction to criminal networks see Diviák, 2018). Network is defined as: *a set of nodes and ties among them when nodes represent members/participants and ties represents the relations and interactions among them.*

The alcohol affair counted for one of the most serious criminal activities in the history of the CR. In the second half of 2012 it strongly affected the whole country: about 140 persons suffered serious health damage and more than 50 died as a consequence of consumption of alcohol contaminated by methanol. For the first time in history, the Czech government declared a temporary prohibition and control of all alcoholic beverages with an alcohol content by volume of over 20°. The prohibition was in effect during the time necessary to inspect all alcohol on the market (in shops, restaurants, bars, booths *etc.*). This also included a ban on all exports of these beverages abroad.

A broad network of perpetrators was discovered. About 70 persons were investigated. It was found that the active core of this network encompassed 32 persons.

There were two basic branches of the network. The first one was created by a long-term active criminal group that illegally produced and distributed untaxed alcohol. This illegal enterprise was covered by a legal firm; the members had their specific tasks. Leaders of this group did not hesitate to use intimidation or even physical assault in order to gain illegal profit from untaxed alcohol. Nevertheless, their product was non-toxic.

The perpetrators joined in the second branch were connected to the first one. They purchased and used their illegal product but added to it methanol. The leaders and their helpers prepared this deadly mixture and subsequently supplied it to small shopkeepers or directly to customers. These small distributors often did not know what they were in fact buying and selling – they 'only' accepted that they broke the tax regulations and traded or bought the cheaper products (tax fraud). Maybe the producers made a mistake; maybe they were not able to determine the amount of methanol, at least not in its lethal or seriously damaging quantity.

Figure 1:
Network representation

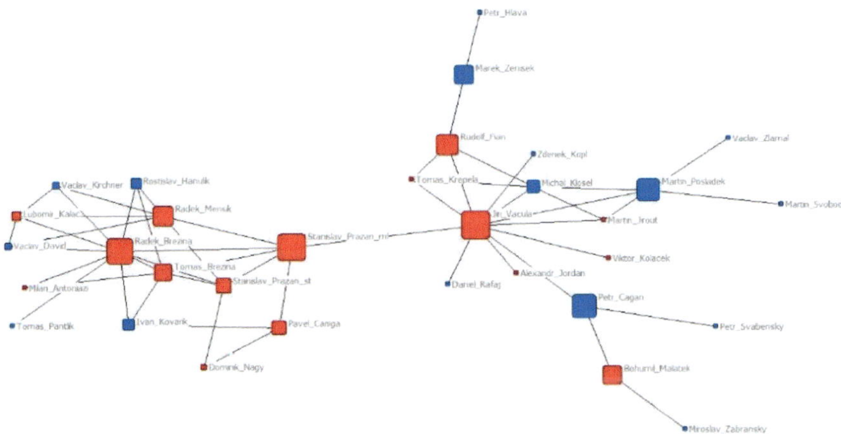

Source: Diviák (2018)

The sociogram above shows the scheme and picture of this network. Both branches are clearly visible; the perpetrators with entrepreneurial experience are coloured red; the size of the nodes indicates the relative importance of their position in the structure. As crucial aspect for the functioning and collaboration of both branches seems to be the exclusive link between two main actors – other members of both branches did not keep any contact with individuals from the respective other branch. Furthermore, Diviák and colleagues (2019) found that this network didn't fully realise its distributive potential and thus the damages done by the perpetrators could have been even more severe (Diviák, 2019).

The case was qualified as 'organised crime' and was as such prosecuted and brought to trial. The punishments were adequate: the two main leaders from the second branch were sentenced to life imprisonment. The leader of the first branch was sentenced to 13 years imprisonment.

Conclusions

The concept of organised crime in the CR has undergone significant developments. Organised crime 'old style' with the 'usual suspects' is no longer the top problem and major source of concern, at least in comparison with the public opinion during the 1990s. The threat of organised crime, instead, is found in its economic and political influence. In this regard we may remind the reader of the concept of the 'godfather' who due to his economic position and power is able to avoid law enforcement and manipulate democratic mechanisms, thereby affecting policy making by public authorities. The official reports on the security situation do not use the term 'godfather' but the threat of the influence of organised crime operating in economic sectors is distinctly articulated.

Compared to the face of the stereotypical 'organised criminal' in the 1990s – who was mostly a foreigner involved in trafficking in illegal goods, racketeering *etc.* with the tendency to violence – the imagery has definitely become less clear. There are offenders of 'classical' organised crime as they were before, there are also 'new organised criminals' acting as 'normal' entrepreneurs and 'respectable citizens'. But their picture cannot be identified with the picture of American gangster bosses from the 1920s and 1930s. It is a matter of perspective what type of criminal is to be preferred: the drug trafficker acting in the shadows on the one side, or the influential entrepreneur and businessman acting publicly on the other side. Maybe this second type resembles the Russian or Ukrainian oligarchs, but the Czech situation is still not the comparable, considering their influence.

The public as it is mentioned above has not shown much eagerness to be informed about organised crime, which is remarkable: 'organised crime' is always good for the headlines. But the evolution of 'organised crime' toward its higher involvement in economic and financial sectors evokes a growing mistrust in the honesty of the entrepreneurial class and subsequently this 'dim face' of suspects undermines the trust in policy making and many official tasks carried out in the public sphere by office holders as such.

References

Agnew, R, Building on the foundation of general strain theory: specifying the types of strain most likely to lead to crime and delinquency. *Journal of Research in Crime and Delinquency* Volume:38 Issue:4 ,2001, 319-361.

Baloun, V. and M. Scheinost, Economy and crime in the society in transition: The Czech Republic case. In: P.C. van Duyne, K. von Lampe, N. Passas, (eds.), *Upperworld and underworld in cross-border crime*, 43-60. Wolf Legal Publishers, Nijmegen, 2002, 48-51.

Baloun, V., D. Kaderabkova and M. Scheinost, Adventure capitalism and economic crime in the countries of transition: the case of the Czech Republic. In: P.C. van Duyne, K. von Lampe, M. van Dijck, J.L. Newell (eds.), *The Organised Crime Economy. Managing Crime Markets in Europe*. Wolf Legal Publishers, Nijmegen, 2005, 143-162.

Borgatti, S.P., M.G. Everett and J.C. Johnson, *Analyzing social networks*. SAGE publication, 2013.

Cejp, M., Charakteristiky organizovaného zločinu v ČR v roce 1999 [Character of organised crime in the CR in 1999]. In : Marešová,A. *et al., Kriminalita v roce 1999*. IKSP, Prague, 2000, 22-34.

Cejp, M. and M. Scheinost, A common problem – organised and economic crime. In: A. Šelih, A. Završnik, (eds.), *Crime and transition in central and eastern Europe*. Springer, 2012, 157-178.

Cejp, M., Základní charakteristiky organizovaného zločinu v ČR v roce 2017 [Basic characteristcs of organised crime in the CR 2017]. In: S.Diblíková, et al., *Analýza trendů kriminality v České republice v roce 2017*. IKSP, Prague, 2018, 71-86.

van Dijk, J.J.M. and P. Mayhew, *Kriminální viktimizace v industrializovaném světě [Criminal victimisation in the industrialised world]*.

IKSP, Prague, 1993.

Diviák,T., Síťová analýza metanolové aféry. [Network analysis of methanol affair]. In: M.Scheinost et al., *Trendy vývoje organizovaného zločinu a jeho vybraných forem.* IKSP, Prague, 2018, 111-128.

Diviák, T., Sinister connections: How to analyse organised crime with socil network analysis? *AUC philosophica nad historica* 2018(2), 115-135.

Diviák, T., J.K. Dijkstra, and T.A.B. Snijders, Poisonous connections: A case study on Czech counterfeit alcohol distribution network. *Global Crime* (forthcoming, 2019).

Kenney, D.J. and J.O. Finckenauer, *Organised crime in America.* Wadsworth, Belmont, California, 1995.

Lubelcová, G., Kriminalita v kontexte sociálnej transformácie na Slovensku [Crime in the context of social transformation in Slovakia]. In: I.Radicova (ed.), *Vieme čo odmietame a vieme čo chceme? [Do we know what we depreciate and what we want?].* SPACE, Bratislava, 1998, 131-134.

Luptáková, M., Názory české veřejnosti na problematiku organizovaného zločinu a vliv denního tisku na utváření těchto názorů [Views of the Czech public on the organised crime problem and impact of media on it]. In: *Trestněprávní revue* 2/2012, 37-42.

Mladá fronta Dnes (journal), 23.2.1994, results of surveys on public opinion.

Musil, J., Organizovaná kriminalita [Organised crime]. In: T.Gřivna,, M.Scheinost,, *I.*Zoubková,, *Kriminologie.* Wolters Kluwer, Prague, 2014, 396.

Robins, G., *Doing social network research.* London: SAGE publications, 2015.

Scheinost, M., Transnational organised crime and cross-border trafficking in human beings in the Czech Republic. In: P.C. van Duyne, V. Ruggiero, M. Scheinost and W. Valkenburg, (eds.), *Cross-border Crime in a Changing Europe.* Tilburg University, IKSP, Praha, 2000, 37-55.

Smith, D., Paragons, pariahs and pirates: A spectrum-based theory of enterprise. *Crime and Delinquency,* 1980, 26(3), 358-386.

Svítková, T., Vzpomínky na budoucnost [Memories on the future]. In*: Sociologické aktuality* 5/1992.

Šinkovec, P., Spořádaný občan také rozkrádá [A good citizen also pilfers]. Paper on the VII.th Criminological Days, Ústí nad Labem, January 21.-22. 2019.

Thoumi, F., Colombian organised crime: From drug trafficking to parastatal bands and widespread corruption. In: D. Siegel, H. van de Bunt (eds.), *Traditional organised crime in the modern world. responses to socioeconomic change*. Springer 2012, 131-148

Vold, G.K. and T.J. Bernard, *Theoretical criminology*. Oxford University Press, Oxford, 1986

von Lampe, K., *Organised Crime: Analyzing illegal activities, criminal structures, and extra-legal governance*, Thousand Oaks, CA: Sage 2016

Zpráva o situaci v oblasti vnitřní bezpečnosti a veřejného pořádku na území České republiky v roce 2009, 2013, 2016 [Report on the security situation and public order in the CR 2009, 2013, 2016], MV CR, www.mvcr.cz \

Cerca Trova: the Italian mafia on Dutch territory

Toine Spapens[1]

Introduction

An important perceived threat of transnational organised crime is that well-organised networks spread their wings across the globe (*e.g.* Williams, 1994; Castells, 2000; Shelley *et al.*, 2003; UNODC, 2010). In the Netherlands, these concerns focus particularly on the Italian mafia – here defined as the Cosa Nostra, 'Ndrangheta, Camorra and Sacra Corona Unita (SCU). Concerns were prompted by several indications. The Netherlands – together with Spain and Belgium – emerges from threat assessments as a European hub for shipments of cocaine coming in from South America and destined for Italy and the Dutch police also apprehend a relatively large number of mafia fugitives (Europol, 2017; Sarno, 2014). In 2011, the Dutch police studied the 'Ndrangheta's activities on Dutch territory and concluded that it represented a threat to the Netherlands (KLPD, 2011). Apart from that, the Italian mafia excites the imagination of many people and also piqued the interest of several Dutch enforcement officers. They were personally convinced that the Netherlands were attractive for these 'top dogs' of organised crime to open subdivisions, and lobbied their superiors intensively for the chance to delve deeper into the issue.

In 2012, the Minister of Justice and Safety commissioned a project aimed at establishing the level of subversive activities of the Italian mafia in the Netherlands.[2] The project was named *Cerca Trova*, which translates

1 The author is Professor of criminology at Tilburg University, The Netherlands

2 In the Netherlands, serious and organised crime is now referred to as '*ondermijnende criminaliteit*', which would translate into English as 'undermining', 'subversive' or 'disruptive' crime, though none of these terms is exact. Generally, it points to illegal activities that disrupt the integrity of economic life and of financial and governing institutions, but it may also refer to degradation of

from Italian as 'seek and you will find', and ran from August 2012 to December 2015. This chapter will present an overview of the main outcomes of the Cerca Trova project in which the author participated as an external advisor. I will take the opportunity to discuss these results in the broader context of the debate on globalisation of organised crime. The next section starts with a brief overview of this discussion. Then, I will describe the methodology applied by the Cerca Trova project, as well as its general and specific outcomes. The latter refers to drug trafficking; violent crime; property crime; investment in and misuse of legitimate activities; and the topic of mafia fugitives in the Netherlands, although it must be noted that hiding to escape prison is technically not a crime. I will also address the Italian mafia's activities in the former Netherlands Antilles, although the Cerca Trova project itself was limited to the mainland Netherlands.

Globalisation of organised crime: the debate

Globalisation and the fear of transnational organised crime

Globalisation is a process that can be defined as the intensification of economic, political, social and cultural relations across borders (Holm and Sorensen, 1995). Since the early 1970s, globalisation has been considered a driver of prosperity, particularly in developing countries, but also a challenge, for instance for regulators, or even a threat, for example in the shape of uncontrolled migration from the global south to the global north (IMF, 2008; Braithwaite and Drahos, 2000). Particularly since the early 1990s, globalisation has accelerated because of market liberalisation and the lowering of trade barriers, but also because of increased mobility and cheap travel, as well as rapid developments in information and communication technology, including the emergence of the Internet.

Although globalisation has been approached predominantly from a perspective of global markets, others have focused on the role of transnational

---

the environment and societal values. Although the term is most commonly used in the context of serious and organised crime, it also applies to corporate crime.

corporations. Scholars have also studied globalisation by looking at international networks of both large and small companies (Castells, 1996). From an international business perspective, multinational enterprises are considered a main agent of global integration, playing a pivotal role in linking rich and poor economies, and in transmitting capital, knowledge, ideas and value systems across borders (Meyer, 2004). However, others emphasise that multinational enterprises are also responsible for annihilating local firms; privatising resources such as drinking water; skimming off public funds through tax avoidance; and speeding up the degradation of the environment, which effects are particularly visible in the global south (Barber, 1996; Carrington et al., 2018).

Since the 1960s, organised crime researchers have often approached the provision of illegal goods and services from an economic perspective, both in terms of markets and logistics (*e.g.* Schelling 1965; Becker, 1968; Sieber and Bögel, 1993). Such approaches often result in transposing developments in legitimate economies to the criminal underworld and, not surprisingly, this also happened with the concept of globalisation. At the end of the 1980s, fear of an increase in transnational crime was also fuelled by the fall of the Iron Curtain and the subsequent implosion of the Soviet Union (Van Duyne, 1996; Hignett, 2004). Furthermore, developments in information and communication technology were expected to create new criminal opportunities and lead to the modernisation of existing illegal markets.

Next, investigative journalists and former members of the enforcement community started to compare transnational criminal organisations with multinational enterprises in books with appealing titles such as 'Octopus' (Sterling, 1990), 'McMafia' (Glenny, 2009), and 'Mafia Export' (Forgione, 2010). These books painted a picture of syndicates such as the Italian mafia, the Russian 'Mafiya', Chinese Triads and the Albanian mafia mimicking the behaviour of transnational corporations and setting up shops all over the world. From this perspective, mafias were compared to 'invasive exotics', because their level of organisational effectiveness, their methods of violence and corruption, as well as their expertise at hiding illegal activities could not be matched by indigenous criminal groups, or countered by local enforcement authorities. From an academic perspective, 'global crime' is more commonly approached in terms of networks and it is assumed that transnational organised crime groups, and particularly mafias, have increasingly forged worldwide alliances (Raine and Cilluffo,

1994; Castells, 2000). These criminal networks are assumed to be highly flexible and able to move easily to other geographical areas and set up activities wherever it is convenient (Williams, 2001; Shelley, 2005).

Fear of transnational organised crime has sparked a range of responses, of which at the global level, the United Nations Convention against Transnational Organised Crime and the protocols thereto, which opened for signature in 2000, is a notable example. However, organised crime researchers have also been critical of the picture of organised crime spreading across the world (*e.g.* Van Duyne, 1996; Van Duyne and Nelemans, 2011; Campana, 2011; Varese, 2011; Van Dijk and Spapens, 2014). I will address these views below.

A critical view on transnational organised crime from a market perspective

Critiques of warnings that crime markets are internationalising can be summarised as 'what is new'? It can indeed be argued that, for instance, trafficking of illegal substances, weapons, humans and non-human animals, as well as piracy and terrorism, have been going on for decades or even centuries (Reichel and Albanese, 2014). The same applies to transnational property crime and fraud, which were topics for Interpol already in the 1920s and 1930s (Bresler, 1992). In his memoirs, Dutch police commissioner Kallenborn, for example, describes a case of jewellery thieves in the 1920s who travelled across Europe to commit heists (Kallenborn, 1953). The notorious 'Pink Panther' gang, which originated from Serbia and robbed jewellery stores in Europe, Dubai and Japan between the mid-1990s and 2010, does not differ essentially from bands of international thieves operating as far back as the 17th and 18th centuries (Tremlett, 2010; Egmond, 2004). The only major difference in terms of crossing borders is means of transport and speed of travel. In addition, it is almost impossible to identify modern transnational crimes that did not already exist in some form in the past (Reichel and Albanese, 2014). Even cybercrimes can mostly be considered updated methods for committing theft, fraud or extortion. Hacking someone's online game to steal a valuable virtual sword may perhaps not have been possible without the Internet and computers, but in the end it is simply a theft, which probably causes similar harm to a victim as stealing his watch.

What has changed, however, is the scale and diversity of transnational illegal markets (Dandurand *et al.*, 1998; Reichel and Albanese, 2014). For example, thresholds for entering an illegal activity have been lowered. A person who is interested in producing some type of synthetic drug may nowadays order quantities of chemicals online, either on the open web or on the 'dark' web, and receive these by postal package. 'Silk road' was an example of a hidden website where users could order all sorts of narcotic drugs (Shelley and Hirst, 2017). Illegal online gambling is now estimated to be one of the most lucrative black markets (Havocscope, 2018). In the 1970s, it would probably have been a local drug addict who stole your car radio, but nowadays the perpetrator may have come from anywhere in the world. Recently in the Netherlands, the police even apprehended a group of criminals who had flown in from Chile for the sole purpose of committing burglaries (Voskuil, 2018). Increased economic prosperity in, for example, Asia also led to growing demand for protected wildlife products, such as ivory (as a status symbol), and plants and animal products (for use in traditional medicine), with disastrous effects on populations of endangered species not only in Asia itself, but also in Africa and South America (Van Uhm, 2016).

Concerns about the consequences of the fall of the Iron Curtain proved to be generally correct, although these effects were sometimes temporary and certainly not as apocalyptic as some expected. In fact, the whole of Eastern Europe certainly did not develop into a hotbed of organised crime. But nevertheless, types of crime and victims, hardly occurring before, emerged at various spots: some temporarily others more permanent. Hungarian, Romanian and Bulgarian women do represent a substantial percentage of victims of exploitation as prostitutes in Western European countries (Nationaal Rapporteur, 2014; UNODC, 2016). In the 1990s, substantial quantities of small arms and light weapons leaked from stockpiles in former Soviet and Yugoslavian states. Arms traffickers such as Viktor Bout shipped large numbers of military weapons to conflict zones, mainly in Africa (Farah and Braun, 2006). Handguns, but also automatic weapons and explosives stemming from the Balkans and other Eastern European countries, ended up in the hands of criminals and terrorists in Western Europe (Duquet and Goris, 2018). It is also clear that itinerant gangs from

Eastern and South-Eastern Europe seized the opportunity to commit property crimes in the West, and such groups are still active today (Spapens, 2008; Van Gestel, 2014).

A critical view on transnational crime from the perspective of criminal organisations

Criminologists have generally been far more critical of the idea that globalisation would enable criminal organisations to develop into multinational enterprises. Firstly, organised crime trading may be highly international, but it is also firmly embedded locally (Hobbs, 1998; Varese, 2011; Von Lampe, 2016). This is even more the case for mafia-type organisations than for trafficking networks (Gambetta, 1993; Chu, 2000). A criminal group that wants to establish a subdivision abroad must therefore be able to deal with circumstances that may be very different from those at home.

Secondly, practitioners and academics disagree about the level of organisation of mafias, especially on the question whether single groups or clans are governed by some overarching body and thus operate as a coordinated entity that would resemble a national or transnational corporation. When we look at the Italian mafia, for example, investigative journalists and current and former law enforcement officials mostly assume that such ruling bodies exist: the Cosa Nostra's two *Cupola* and the 'Ndrangheta's *Crimine* or *Provincia*. However, academics do not agree that these represent some form of higher management (e.g. Paoli, 2014). For example, the Camorra and SCU do not have comparable Commissions; the *Cupola* were established only in the 1950s and the *Crimine* not even before the 1990s (Dickie, 2013; Sciarrone, 2014). The Cosa Nostra's *Cupola* were established upon American advice mainly because the heroin trade required financial investments which were beyond the reach of a single clan (Dickie, 2013). Later, their main function was to prevent or solve violent conflicts between the clans, which sometimes caused hundreds of deaths. Indeed, such internal wars do not as such support the image of a well-managed syndicate.

Of course, examples of mafia groups establishing themselves on foreign territory did and still do exist, but without exception these concern single clans and individual members, and proof that a 'top management' is steering global expansion is missing (*e.g.* Campana, 2011). Furthermore, Varese (2011) concludes that criminals move to another country not because of choice but because of necessity, for instance because they were forced to leave their country of origin which because of police attention or fellow criminals had become a too hot place. In practice, when foreign crime groups develop illegal activities on foreign territory voluntarily, we can observe two basic mechanisms. The first is through immigrant communities; the second is through affiliation with indigenous criminal groups. In practice, these mechanisms are often entwined to some extent.

Germany, Canada and Australia, for example, have substantial immigrant communities stemming from Calabria and indications exist that this allowed 'Ndrangheta clans to establish cells (*'ndrine*) there (Forgione, 2010; Gratteri and Nicasso, 2007). Mafia members extort the locals and may force them to support other illegal activities, for instance by making available housing and transport, often under threat of retribution against family members who reside in the country of origin. Comparable methods can be observed, for example, within Albanian and Chinese immigrant communities in Belgium and the Netherlands, respectively (Farcy 2002; Spapens 2008). However, 'outsiders' are usually not targeted for extortion because they cannot be intimidated in similar ways.

Thirdly, instead of battling indigenous crime groups for territories or markets, it will usually be more lucrative for foreign groups to seek cooperation. Alliances may be ad-hoc, for instance to organise a shipment of illicit goods, but may develop further over time. An example is synthetic drugs production in the Dutch-Belgian border area. Here, Dutch criminal groups started to set up laboratories from the beginning of the 1990s onwards (Van Duyne, 1995). These activities were established in cooperation with Belgians, although in most cases they were led by Dutch criminals, but gradually an integrated criminal network emerged (Spapens, 2006; 2008; Colman et al., 2018).

The idea of foreign criminal groups as 'invasive exotics' can also be challenged. The main assumptions seem to be that newcomers are more violent and better at hiding their activities, which gives them the advantage over indigenous criminals and law enforcement. However, applying violence is not the smartest thing to do and there seems to be little reason why local criminals should not quickly be able to match foreign groups in this respect (Van Dijk and Spapens, 2014). Secondly, newcomers may instead be even less effective in screening off their activities in a new environment, for instance when they are unfamiliar with local law enforcement tactics. In the 1990s, for example, American buyers who were sent to the Netherlands to acquire large quantities of ecstasy pills were not accustomed to the Dutch police's extensive wiretapping and, despite ample warnings from their Dutch suppliers, they persisted in talking too much over the phone (Spapens, 2006).

If foreign criminal groups establish themselves in countries where law enforcement is weak, the situation may, however, be different. An example is the *Mara Salvatrucha* or MS-13 gang, which was originally formed by El Salvadorian youths in Los Angeles in the 1980s. Large numbers of its members were expelled to El Salvador – for the moment I will leave aside that because of this they were technically not foreigners – and continued with criminal activities there, to which the government, weakened by civil war, was unable to respond effectively (Malone and Malone-Rowe, 2014). Furthermore, MS-13 also established itself in other Central American countries, such as Honduras and Guatemala, whilst retaining a strong presence in the United States.

Outlaw motorcycle gangs might be brought up as another example of syndicates that succeed in setting up chapters in different parts of the world. However, these chapters are mostly composed of local members who are not under foreign leadership. It is unclear to what extent such chapters are directly 'managed' from abroad or remain instead relatively independent in choosing their criminal and other activities. The latter option seems to be more realistic (UNODC, 2002). Furthermore, OMCG chapters may be heavily involved in crime, but they are also highly visible. All in all, these gangs do not seem to qualify very well as invasive exotics who may someday succeed in replacing local criminals.

In conclusion, globalisation has obviously increased opportunities for transnational organised crime on the one hand, but on the other, we must not forget that especially mafia-type illegal activities, such as protection/extortion and collusion with authorities to acquire public funds, are deeply embedded in local settings. In the remainder of this paper, I will look at activities of Italian organised crime in the Netherlands and then reflect on these findings from the perspectives described above. The next section first discusses data collection.

Cerca Trova: data collection and analysis

Cerca Trova operated as a joint team composed of staff of the Dutch police, the tax authorities, the Fiscal Intelligence and Investigation Service (FIOD), and the Public Prosecution Service. It consisted of practitioners, *i.e.* experienced detectives, intelligence analysts of different agencies, students at the police academy who did research for the team in the context of their bachelor thesis, and a public prosecutor. Several members of the team were fluent in Italian, and some already held extensive knowledge about the Italian mafia out of personal interest. The present author was attached to the project to provide advice and safeguard scientific quality and edited the final report (Cerca Trova, 2017).

The aim of the project was first to produce a reliable intelligence picture, which was to be made available to the Dutch Parliament in an anonymised and public format. Second, the team was to support regular investigative work related to Italian organised crime. In practice, this meant that team members acted as intermediaries between Italian and Dutch enforcement agencies in ongoing cross-border cases, and provided information to regular Dutch police investigation teams for further consideration.

The team relied for the most part on information available from the Dutch police and the judiciary, the Tax Administration and administrative agencies, as well as on information coming from Italy in letters rogatory. Team members also collected open source information and conducted interviews with practitioners in the Netherlands, Belgium, Germany and Italy, as well as with five academic researchers of Italian organised crime. Cerca Trova's preliminary findings were presented to, and discussed with, Italian law enforcement officials during visits to Rome and Reggio Calabria in January 2015.

Data collection resulted in a database of 276 mafia-related crime cases which were investigated from 1989 to 2014. Most cases were initially retrieved from a database of requests for mutual legal assistance kept by the Dutch police liaison post in Rome, to which information was added from case files and intelligence sources; interviews with detectives who were involved (if necessary); and open sources.

a. The past and present of Italian mafia activities in the Netherlands

The presence of the Italian mafia in the Netherlands has been documented since the 1970s. At that time, the Camorra, for example, acquired illegal cigarettes in Rotterdam, which were smuggled to, and sold in, Italy (Arlacchi, 1993, p. 123). In 1992, the Dutch police analysed 30 investigation cases related to Italy which mainly concerned cocaine trafficking, but also money laundering, murder and small-scale arms trafficking (CRI, 1992). Mafia-affiliated individuals had started Italian restaurants as early as in the 1980s and these establishments became meeting places for members of the Italian criminal underworld who visited the Netherlands, whilst some owners were themselves actively involved in the drug trade. The police observed links with several clans of the Camorra, such as the Annunziata, the La Torre and the Stolder clans, whereas other restaurant owners could also be linked to the Cosa Nostra (CRI, 1992).

In 1995, a research group drew a picture of organised crime in the Netherlands in the context of a parliamentary enquiry (Tweede Kamer, 1995). Information on the Italian mafia, however, was scarce, because only one substantial investigation had been completed since 1992. This operation, codenamed Campina (Camorra-Pizzeria-Naples), had confirmed earlier findings that the Camorra was involved in trafficking cocaine from the Netherlands to Italy. Camorra representatives bought the drugs on behalf of different clans, and sometimes for other mafia groups as well. Small and medium-sized shipments were transported by road with couriers, sometimes hidden between flowers, whereas larger shipments were allegedly sent to Southern Italy by ship. Mafia members met in Italian restaurants with Colombian, Turkish, Surinamese and Netherlands-Antillean drug suppliers (Tweede Kamer, 1995). However, the research group found no indications that Italian organised crime had managed to set up a permanent bridgehead in the Netherlands. In 2001, the police updated its 1992 analysis, but this brought no additional insights. Almost 10 years later, the police published a new report which focused specifically on the 'Ndrangheta (KLPD, 2011). This report was again based on police information, but also on a substantial number of interviews with Italian and other enforcement representatives. As mentioned above, the Cerca Trova project was the most recent effort to draw a picture of the Italian mafia's activities on Dutch territory.

The Cerca Trova team compiled a database spanning a period of 25 years, and Table 1 presents an overview of the type of activities mentioned in these files for mutual legal assistance. In total, 461 different illegal activities were mentioned. Almost 60% of mafia-related activities concerned different types of narcotic drugs, mostly cocaine. Remarkably, only 2% of the cases involved synthetic drugs, although the Netherlands are viewed as a main producer of ecstasy and amphetamine (Tops *et al.*, 2018). Other activities mentioned relatively often are money laundering and the hiding of mafia members from the Italian authorities in the Netherlands.

Table 1
Illegal activities mentioned in requests for mutual legal assistance (1989–2014)

Illegal activity	**Number**	**%**
Cocaine	131	28
Cannabis and hashish	34	7
Heroin	3	1
Synthetic drugs	10	2
Narcotic drugs unspecified	113	25
Money laundering	40	9
Mafia fugitives	37	8
Violent crimes/murder/firearms	14	3
Fraud	12	3
Extortion	9	2
Other	27	6
Unknown	31	7
Total	**461**	**100**

Although the cases are mafia-related, only 68% of the subjects mentioned held either Italian or Dutch nationality (both 34%). Italian-Dutch criminal cooperation which involves mafia members is more international than that. German, Spanish, Belgian and Colombian nationals account for another 14%. In total, 61 different nationalities were mentioned in the case files, showing the interconnectedness of transnational criminal networks. The next sections address the main types of illegal activities.

b. Drug trafficking

The database shows that Camorra and 'Ndrangheta are prominent in the context of drug trafficking. They account for 90% of the cases in which a specific mafia was mentioned. By comparison, the roles of Cosa Nostra (4%) and Sacra Corona Unita (6%) are modest. In half and a third of the cases, respectively, Cosa Nostra and SCU cooperated with the Camorra. Cooperation between Camorra and 'Ndrangheta is less common, and was observed in only 6 cases. Earlier research showed that different clans invest together in drug shipments and Cerca Trova again confirmed this (Tweede Kamer, 1995; KLPD, 2011). Available information shows that the Netherlands is not the territory of specific clans.

The Netherlands and Spain are the main European ports of entry for cocaine (Europol, 2013). The case files did not reveal why Italian mafias use the Netherlands (and Spain) for this purpose and do not ship cocaine directly from South America to Italy. According to Italian law enforcement officers, this could be explained by the fact that ports in Italy are under much stronger surveillance than the Dutch and Spanish harbours. This explanation is not very convincing, however, because the long Italian coastline presents ample opportunity to circumvent ports altogether and pick up and deliver shipments with small motorboats, for example. Occasionally, cocaine shipments are indeed intercepted in Italy, for instance in 2010 when police seized 1.000 kilos in a Calabrian port. Strangely, the press reported that the shipment was destined for the Netherlands and the United Kingdom instead of Italy (De Gelderlander, 2010). However, in almost all cases the cocaine shipped through the Netherlands was destined for Italy.

Mafia-affiliated Italian immigrants and fugitives who hide in the Netherlands play an important role in maintaining contacts with Dutch criminal groups. It is unknown whether Dutch criminals were solely hired to take care of shipments, or invested in cocaine together with the mafia and other groups. Dutch criminals know their way around the ports and possibly also maintain contacts with corrupt Customs officials. Several cases of corruption in the port of Rotterdam have come to light in recent years (Rovers, 2018).

Police observations of meetings suggest that the mafia also does business directly with Colombian suppliers. These meetings may concern incoming shipments, but it is also possible that business relations have evolved to the extent that orders can be placed directly with representatives of cocaine producers who reside in the Netherlands and no longer require to visit to Colombia. In the few cases in which the mafia seemed to operate independently from Dutch criminals, Albanians and Romanians removed the drugs from containers that had arrived in the port of Rotterdam, whilst mafia members monitored the operation from a distance. Entering container terminals illegally by simply climbing over a fence and removing packets of drugs from containers before they go through customs is a rather crude method. The risk of getting caught is substantial, because entry to these terminals is guarded with fences, cameras and other detection equipment, which seems to suggest that cooperation with Dutch criminals who do not need to apply such cowboy methods is indeed a safer bet.

Drugs that have entered the Netherlands are usually forwarded to Italy by road, either by couriers in private vehicles or hidden between truckloads of regular goods such as flowers and fruit. Because of the abolition of fixed border controls in the Schengen area – most of the European mainland – traffickers do not need to take extensive measures to conceal illicit goods, because the risk of being stopped and searched is almost zero if one drives carefully and avoids weekend nights (Spapens, 2008). Individual shipments tend to be relatively small, often just a few up to several tens of kilos, and can easily be hidden in empty spaces in private cars, for example in the doors.

Couriers, usually young males who reside in Italy but hold all sorts of nationalities, receive an airline ticket to the Netherlands and some pocket money to enjoy a few days of leisure, and are then tasked with driving a car back in which drugs are hidden. Smuggling drugs between flowers is also an effective method because flowers are distributed to even the smallest villages. The police are aware of this method, but they will only stop and search a transport when they are certain that the cargo contains drugs, because flowers are both valuable and vulnerable and if nothing illegal is found, the authorities will face substantial claims for damages.

c. Violent crime on Dutch territory

Italian organised crime is reputed for its violence. Cerca Trova, therefore, expected that mafia presence on Dutch territory would be visible in underworld killings. Between 1988 and 2014, 13 persons were the victim of mafia-initiated murders, including one case in which the Dutch police intervened and prevented the killing.[3] In addition, Cerca Trova identified four possible murders, three of which were mentioned by crown witnesses in statements but could not be confirmed because no bodies were ever found. The fourth case concerned the suicide of a Camorra fugitive in which there were indications that he was in fact murdered. Except in two cases, all actual or possible murders were committed before 2002, especially by the SCU (six, possibly eight) and the Camorra (five, all before 1992). Most killings were drug-related, or appeared to be, for instance because subsequent investigation pointed to business conflicts related to drugs or theft ('ripping') of drugs.

Acts of punishment could rarely be identified, because in a relatively large number of cases, the police were unable to collect sufficient evidence to allow a conviction, and in some cases, perpetrators managed to escape long prison terms by becoming a *collaboratore di giustizia*, the most notable example being Filippo Cerfeda, a SCU member who killed four people in the Netherlands. Giorgio Basile, another *pentito*, also confessed to an unknown murder (Ulrich, 2005).

All in all, the level of mafia violence on Dutch territory is rather limited and almost no killings have taken place in the past 16 years, which seems to underline that its members prefer to stay under the radar and avoid attracting attention to the drug trade. The fact that the SCU was held responsible for most killings is also an indication of unplanned violence because its members have a reputation for lack of discipline (Massari, 2014).

Some members of the Cerca Trova team assumed that the mafia has simply become better in hiding its murders, for instance by disguising them as suicides or by employing non-Italian killers. However, looking into several potentially suspicious killings which involved suspects or victims of Italian nationality or descent did not produce any connections with mafia clans. On the one hand, this still does not rule out that the mafia ordered murders of non-Italians and hired non-Italians to commit them. On the

[3] In 2017, after Cerca Trova was finished, one more mafia murder was committed, which could be attributed to a conflict in Italy. The victim had unsuccessfully sought refuge in the Netherlands.

other hand, underworld killings are often also meant as a message and it will be at least partly ineffective if no one knows who sent it.

d. Property crimes

In Italy, the mafia is well-known for committing property crimes. Extortion of legitimate businesses is generally seen as a classic mafia-style crime, but its members are also involved in other types of property crimes. The Cerca Trova database contained 28 examples of property crimes, with fraud (12) and extortion (9) being the largest categories.

At first glance, extortion seems to be a relatively large category, but in fact none of these cases took place on Dutch territory. All but one concerned investigations of extortion committed in Italy by mafia members who had fled to or took up residence in the Netherlands. The remaining case involved a restaurant owner who was also a drug dealer and the police established that extortion had in fact been a financial conflict with a SCU member because of a failed transaction.

In the 1990s, there had been indications that the mafia extorted Italian restaurants in the Netherlands, but these had been too vague to lead to further investigation. Cerca Trova did not find or receive more recent signals of mafia-related extortion. It must be noted that this type of crime is difficult to detect because the victims are often reluctant to report it to the police. The team therefore looked at cases in which Italian restaurants or businesses owned by Italian nationals became the victim of inexplicable violence or arson, which might indicate an unwillingness to pay protection money or refusal to buy specific ingredients from 'designated' companies in Italy. The *Bundeskriminalamt* had observed the latter in investigations in Germany. However, this rendered only one case in which a recently opened restaurant was severely damaged for no apparent reason, but mafia involvement could not be established. In 2017, the Dutch police issued a press release about another case in which two restaurants were attacked, after which an Italian national was arrested in Spain, but again no mafia affiliation was mentioned (Nationale politie, 2017).

In 2016, a major criminal investigation in the Netherlands made clear that the brothers Vincenzo and Giuseppe Crupi, who the Italian police saw as members of the 'Ndrangheta's Commisso clan, controlled a Dutch flower export company. The Dutch police assumed that this company was originally established for trafficking drugs, but that the owners had now also expanded to a range of property crimes (Anesi et al, 2017; De Jong and Voskuil, 2017). The most important of these was long firm fraud: the company ordered large quantities of flowers from Dutch suppliers but failed to pay the bills. Several suppliers went bankrupt as a result, and representatives who called for payment received serious verbal threats, although this did not scare them from reporting to the police. In addition, the investigation also linked suspects to bankruptcy fraud and VAT fraud, as well as to the fencing of expensive Swiss chocolate. The case also led to a large-scale investigation in Calabria and the Italian authorities seized assets to the value of €30 million. In Italy, the clan had invested money in 13 flower companies, 21 stores, 22 apartments and two hotels (De Jong and Voskuil 2017). The 'Ndrangheta is allegedly still active in the Dutch flower trade: another person originating from Calabria started a new business and employs most of the former staff of the mafia-controlled company (De Jong and Voskuil, 2017). However, new instances of fraud involving this company have so far not been reported, although flower traders must remain highly alert for Italian buyers who never pay their bills.

e. Investments in and misuse of legitimate businesses

The flower trade is one trade sector in which Italian organised crime invested in the Netherlands. Another sector that appeared to be vulnerable is the Italian catering sector. Analyses indicated that 22 Italian restaurants might be associated with the mafia (out of 1.205 venues). The project team was unable to determine whether the venues were specifically set up by the Italian mafia to facilitate criminal activities in the Netherlands or instead to launder money. In three cases, existing or former restaurant owners were convicted of mafia membership in Italy; in eight cases, police information showed that mafia members used the venue as a meeting place; and in a further eight cases, officers observed contacts between the owner and known mafia members. The remaining restaurant owners were suspected of involvement in serious or organised crime and the venues were frequented by criminals active in the drug trade, but no direct mafia links could be established.

Analysis also showed no indications of large-scale mafia-initiated investments or fraud schemes in other economic sectors in the Netherlands.

However, there were at the time several cases under investigation in which the Italian mafia was suspected of having used Dutch companies and financial service providers as intermediaries to move capital to and from Italy. The Netherlands has many Trust Offices (legal entities, partnerships or natural persons that provide one or more trust services on a commercial basis), which are vulnerable to being misused for this purpose. In one case under investigation, capital originating from different countries was invested in companies that wanted to buy real estate the Italian authorities had earlier seized from the mafia. Dutch legal persons represented by a Trust Office in Amsterdam participated in these companies to the value of €2 billion. This and a few other, similar, cases are still under investigation in the Netherlands and Italy, but at the time of writing, enforcement agencies had not been able to produce concrete evidence of mafia-related money laundering.

In Italy, the mafia is known to be involved in procuring government contracts, particularly for construction work in which mafia-controlled companies can acquire contracts via corrupt local or other officials. To curb this problem, the Italian authorities have implemented anti-mafia legislation that includes thorough screening of any private company that wants to work for the government or apply for a subsidy. Setting up a company in another EU Member State may make it possible to circumvent these background checks. Within the current legal framework, it is difficult to exchange police intelligence, on which effective screening often depends, for purposes other than criminal investigation; but this case concerned administrative screening (Spapens *et al.*, 2015). In one concrete example, the Italian authorities requested background information on a Dutch company that was hired to do installation work at the Milan Expo, but this was refused by the Dutch public prosecution service because of a lack of clarity regarding the legal provisions for mutual assistance in criminal matters (Spapens *et al.*, 2015). Although this situation presents a loophole to criminals, Cerca Trova did not find examples of Dutch companies that might have been set up to avoid anti-mafia background checks in Italy.

f. The Netherlands as a hiding place for mafia fugitives

Finally, the Cerca Trova project looked at mafia fugitives who use the Netherlands as a hiding place. Over the years, a relatively large number of wanted mafia members have been apprehended in the Netherlands. Between 1992 and 2014, the Dutch authorities arrested 55 mafia members who had been living there for shorter or longer periods. The Italian authorities provided information on a further 38 individuals who could not be traced in time. Most fugitives were members of the 'Ndrangheta and Camorra. Cosa Nostra members are relatively rare. According to Italian enforcement officers we interviewed, they usually choose to hide in Sicily. Fugitives do not belong to specific clans, although a relatively large number were members of the Calabrian Strangio-Nirta clan.

The media usually refer to apprehended mafia members as kingpins but in fact they are mostly lower to middle-ranking within their clans. The leaders prefer to stick close to their territory in Italy. Although the relative number of *latitanti* is higher than in all other European countries except for Spain, the Cerca Trova project was unable to establish with certainty why the Netherlands is attractive to mafia fugitives. Apprehended suspects logically provide no information on this. From interviews with enforcement officers, two potential explanations arise.

The first is that fugitives usually choose countries where they feel at home to some extent. *Latitanti* who went to the Netherlands had probably visited the country before and established contacts with persons who were willing to help them organise their stay, for instance by discreetly providing housing and a job. Apart from using a false identity, many took no specific precautions to avoid being found and worked, for instance in an Italian restaurant, or had their own business. Others received social benefits, one person even in his own name. Apparently, most fugitives felt completely safe, except for those who were hunted by rival clans. Although the Dutch weather is usually less attractive than that of Spain, for example, and cultural and language barriers may be greater, the country's international orientation, its excellent infrastructure and airline connections with Italy, as well as the fact that almost all Dutch think positively of Italian culture and lifestyle, were also thought to be reasons why mafia members favour the Netherlands (KLPD, 2011).

However, Italian police officers we interviewed largely dismissed those factors and stated that all North-Western European countries are similar in these respects. Instead, they pointed to a second explanation: the fact that in the Netherlands – as in Spain – fugitives can continue to play a useful role in drug trafficking operations. Several indications support this explanation. It was observed, for instance, that some mafia fugitives maintained contacts with South-American cocaine suppliers. *Latitanti* also supported mafia members who visited the Netherlands to negotiate drug deals, and assisted drug and money couriers who came to the country. In several cases, large sums of cash were found when the police apprehended a fugitive, much more than was necessary for covering the costs of living, and possibly intended for buying drugs.

g. Mafia infiltration in the former Netherlands Antilles

The Cerca Trova project was limited to the Netherlands itself, but the media have reported on several cases of mafia infiltration in what were then the Netherlands Antilles. These refer to the islands of Sint Maarten and Curaçao, which have held an independent status within the Kingdom of the Netherlands since 2010, although the judiciary and the police, for example, remain the responsibility of the Dutch authorities. It must be noted that Dutch legislation does not include provisions for convicting a person of mafia membership, and that all persons mentioned below have always denied being part of – or even affiliated with – the mafia.

On Sint Maarten, reports of mafia infiltration date from as early as the 1970s (De Jong and Voskuil, 2017). This started when Sicilian businessman Rosario Spadaro bought a hotel which he developed into a casino. Spadaro was linked to the Italian-American Cellini family, which participated in the illegal gambling operations of Meyer Lansky. Originally, one of the Cellinis co-owned the casino, but the Dutch authorities had refused him an operating licence. From unknown sources, Spadaro then raised money to buy out Cellini and gradually acquired a substantial number of properties and businesses on the island. Inevitably, warm contacts developed between Spadaro and local top politicians, culminating at the end of the 1980s in a joint venture for expanding the island's airport and harbour. Italian companies were hired to do the construction work, whilst Italian banks provided funding. Companies set up by Spadaro and his political friends inflated the costs of the projects by €18,8 million and in 1995, Spadaro was sentenced to 12 months' imprisonment for this fraud (De Jong and Voskuil, 2017).

At the end of the 1970s, another Sicilian native named Gaetano Corallo also appeared on Sint Maarten to open a gaming house. He already owned several casinos in Italy and sought to expand his business to the Netherlands Antilles. In 1983, however, he was suspected of working for the Cosa Nostra's Santapaola clan and fled to Florida, where he was arrested and extradited to Italy in 1989. By that time, he had already entrusted his son Francesco with the Sint Maarten casino (De Jong and Voskuil, 2017). Over the following years, the younger Corallo acquired casinos in several countries, and he also became one of the largest operators of electronic gaming machines in Italy. He too developed close relations with politicians in the Netherlands Antilles, most noticeably Gerrit Schotte, who in 2010 became the first prime minister of (semi) independent Curaçao. Almost immediately after taking office, Schotte faced increasingly severe allegations of corruption. These also implicated Corallo, who was suspected of having financed Schotte in return for an important public position (GHJ, 2017).

The Dutch public prosecution service started an investigation and the Italian authorities provided information in which Corallo, although he had never been convicted, was identified as a mafia member and accused of being involved in drug trafficking and money laundering (De Jong and Voskuil, 2017). In August 2012, Corallo was put on Interpol's red notice list. In 2016, the court sentenced Schotte to three years' imprisonment for accepting bribes from Corallo, and the sentence was confirmed on appeal in July 2017 (GHJ, 2017). In December 2016, Dutch authorities arrested Corallo and, after having spent eight months in pre-trial detention, he was extradited to Italy on charges of large-scale tax evasion, money laundering and bribery, related to his gambling machines. However, the Italian judiciary apparently failed to build a credible case against him, because in Italy, Corallo's pre-trial detention was discontinued immediately upon his arrival. When his passport was also returned to him in July 2018, he returned to Sint Maarten, prompting quite a few raised eyebrows (Zwart, 2018; Antilliaans Dagblad, 2018). Dutch authorities had expected that Corallo would receive a long prison term in Italy, but must now decide whether to prosecute him for bribing Schotte.

Discussion and conclusion

Based on the information available, Cerca Trova confirmed that the Italian mafia is indeed active on Dutch territory, particularly the 'Ndrangheta and Camorra. Almost all activities are related to the drug trade, for which several clans have maintained a stable presence in the Netherlands since the 1980s. Its members regularly visit the country to negotiate with drug suppliers and to organise shipments, or perform similar tasks while hiding from the Italian police or rival clans. The mafia has access to, or has established, a supporting infrastructure, for instance in the shape of restaurants where meetings can be organised safely, and companies in economic sectors that are useful for trafficking drugs, such as the flower trade. Individuals, Italian as well as Dutch nationals, provide assistance such as housing and transport.

However, there is always a risk that criminals who are present in a country for one reason seek to expand their business for their own reasons. The fact that 'Ndrangheta members thought it a good idea to start ordering flowers without paying for them illustrates this. Given the risks involved, it is hard to imagine that a sensible and well-organised crime syndicate managing things from Italy would have allowed them to do so, given the risk of detection.

Occurrences in the former Netherlands Antilles demonstrate the disruptive effect mafia infiltration may have when economies are weak and authorities lack integrity. Of course, any person who invests substantial sums in a local economy will rapidly build influence with politicians. If the latter are prone to corruption, the relationship may be misused to acquire government contracts or positions. Although this opens the way to classic mafia-type crimes, it does not necessarily require a mafia organisation; any white-collar criminal might do the same. Once again, we cannot assess whether, for instance, Francesco Corallo was under the direct control of Sicilian 'masters' or was operating independently.

In the Netherlands, the Italian mafia is not an 'invasive exotic'. It did not attempt to take over existing illegal markets or to open new ones. Instead, in the drug trade we mostly see close cooperation with Dutch and other criminals. Involvement in the flower trade and possibly the Italian catering branch did not spark conflict with the indigenous criminal underworld.

A protective factor for the Netherlands seems to be the lack of a substantial Italian community originating from the southern part of Italy. Most Italian immigrants who came to the Netherlands after the First World War and have since acquired Dutch citizenship, come from the north of Italy. The number of Italian nationals is about 50.000 and thus rather small, and it is partly made up of students and others who reside in the Netherlands temporarily. There are no concentrations of Italians in specific neighbourhoods. This makes it much harder for the mafia to parasitize on their fellow countrymen than, for instance, in Germany, Canada and Australia – countries with relatively large and concentrated communities originating from southern Italy.

In the Netherlands, the Italian mafia has not introduced more effective or more violent methods of organised crime. Since 2002, the mafia has virtually refrained from openly committing murders on Dutch territory and indications of extortion-related violence and threats are almost non-existent. When it comes to applying methods to avoid detection and prevent enforcement agencies from acquiring evidence, the picture is rather mixed. The police did notice mafia members who were very apprehensive of being wiretapped and followed, and they also used false identities. However, Dutch criminals apply the same methods. Remarkably, other mafia members hardly took any precautions to avoid being identified, and some fugitives even used their real names. Furthermore, it only took a phone call to Italy to tie businessmen such as the Corallos and the Crupis to the mafia. Although they were running a legal business on paper, this does not seem to match the image of a highly professional criminal organisation trying to set up shop abroad and remain undetected.

It is important to discuss whether the available information indeed paints a reliable picture of the mafia's activities on Dutch territory. Within the Cerca Trova team, this question was from time to time fiercely debated. To begin with, a general weakness of information collected by law enforcement is that it mostly represents investigative priorities and does not necessarily provide insight into the full range of activities of the criminal underworld (Hobbs and Antonopoulos, 2014). Apart from that, police information may be flawed by practical issues. As mentioned above, most cases included in the Cerca Trova database had Italian letters rogatory as a starting point and these usually emphasise illegal activities which are known priorities in the requested country, to ensure maximum assistance. Therefore, property crimes and trafficking of marijuana, which hardly spur the Dutch public prosecutors into action, may have been mentioned less than, for instance, cocaine. In addition, crimes without a direct international link, such as extortion of local businesses, may not be visible at all in international assistance requests. Also, peculiarities of the Dutch Police Information Act (*Wet Politiegegevens*) made it difficult to obtain information older than five years, and if questions arose, it was sometimes problematic to find additional material regarding old cases. However, a more fundamental issue in organised crime research – or any study of an 'invisible' illegal activity – will always be to what extent missing information implies that no substantial problems exist, or instead that we are dealing with extremely smart criminals.

Some Cerca Trova team members held the latter opinion, which they underpinned, among other things, by pointing to statements delivered by *collaboratore di giustizia* such as Cerfeda and Basile about hitherto unknown crimes they had committed in the Netherlands. In addition, Italian police officers explained that in some cases, only far-reaching long-term investigations had supplied the necessary evidence, and that this had required, for instance, wiretapping of hundreds of subjects. According to them, it was particularly difficult to prove crimes of collusion, with Rome's *mafia capitale* case as an example. Of course, such efforts had been impossible in the context of Cerca Trova, and this deeply frustrated several team members who felt they had had no proper chance to uncover what was potentially hidden.

Others, including the author, took a more pragmatic approach. Although organised crime groups are sometimes compared to secret societies, it is very unlikely that they can keep their activities completely hidden, whilst at the same time exerting highly disruptive effects on society. It may be necessary to go to great lengths to acquire evidence to prove your case in court, but here we were only looking for indications of mafia activity. If the mafia had indeed infiltrated deeply into the Dutch economy, or had for decades systematically applied methods such as extortion, chances are slim that enforcement agencies would not have received any signal at all. In fact, intelligence on mafia activities in the Netherlands had been consistent since the 1990s. Infiltration of legitimate businesses and politics did indeed succeed in the former Netherlands Antilles, but this merely proves the point that politicians who are susceptible to corruption are vulnerable to any type of villain, mafia affiliated or otherwise. So far, we have no indications that in the Netherlands itself it is equally easy to find influential politicians who would not mind colluding with the mafia.

Regardless of how one views the question of whether Cerca Trova did or did not provide the full picture, the project made it clear that the Italian mafia's activities in the Netherlands should be monitored and disrupted where possible. As a follow-up, a small police team was established for this purpose.

In the context of the debate on globalisation of organised crime, we may conclude, however, that developments in the past three or four decades have not structurally changed the market for the Italian mafia in the Netherlands, and that the mafia has not managed to alter the indigenous Dutch criminal underworld or (even partly) replace it.

References

Anesi, C., G. Rubino and K. Voskuil, Maffia nog steeds actief op bloemenveiling. *AD*, 27 March 2017.

Antilliaans dagblad, 'Corallo wordt vrijgesproken', 5 August 2018.

Arlacchi, P., *Leven in de mafia; Het verhaal van Antonino Calderone*. Amsterdam, Nijgh en Van Ditmar, 1993.

Barber, B. *Jihad vs McWorld.* New York, Times Books, 1995.

Becker, G., Crime and punishment: An economic approach, *Journal of Political Economy*, Vol. 76, 1968, 169-217.

Braithwaite, D. and P. Drahos, *Global business regulation*. Cambridge, Cambridge University Press, 2000.

Bresler, F., *Interpol.* London, Sinclair-Stevenson Ltd, 1992.

Campana, P., Eavesdropping on the Mob: the functional diversification of Mafia activities across territories. *European Journal of Criminology*, 8 (3), 2011, 213-228.

Carrington, K., R. Hogg, J. Scott and M. Sozzo, (eds.), *The Palgrave handbook of criminology and the Global South*. Cham, Palgrave McMillan, 2018.

Castells, M., *The rise of the network society*. Cambridge and Oxford, Blackwell, 1996.

Castells, M., The perverse connection: The global criminal economy. In: M. Castells, *End of millennium, the information age: Economy, society and culture vol. III*. Oxford, Blackwell Publishers, 2000.

Cerca Trova, *Cerca Trova. Een analyse van de Italiaanse maffia in Nederland*. The Hague, Ministerie van Justitie en Veiligheid, 2017.

Chu Y.K., *The Triads as Business*. London and New York, Routledge, 2000.

Colman, C., F. De Middeleer, T. Spapens, S. van Nimwegen, R. Ceulen, S Gerbrands, L. Paoli, E. Roevens, E., *De grens voorbij?* The Hague, Boom Criminologie, 2018.

CRI, *Italiaanse Misdaadorganisaties in relatie tot Nederland*. Zoetermeer, 1992.

Dandurand, Y. B. Tkachuk and A. Castle, Recent international efforts to address transnational crime. Paper presented at the *International Conference on Crime and Criminal Justice in a Borderless Era*, Kyoto, 2 November 1998.

De Gelderlander, *Enorme drugsvangst in Italië*, 15 November 2010.

Dickie, J., *Mafia Republic*. London, Hodder and Stoughton, 2013.

Duquet, N. and K. Goris, *Firearms acquisition by terrorists in Europe. Research findings and policy recommendations of Project SAFTE*. Brussels, Flemish Peace Institute, 2018.

Duyne, P.C. van, The phantom and threat of organised crime. *Crime, Law and Social Change*, 24, 1996, 341-377.

Duyne, P.C. van and M. Nelemans, Transnational organised crime: Thinking in and out of Plato's cave. In: F. Allum and S. Gilmour, *Handbook of transnational crime*. London: Routledge.

Dijk, J. van and T. Spapens, Transnational organized crime networks across the world. In: J. Albanese and P. Reichel, *Transnational organized crime: An overview from six continents.* Thousand Oaks, Sage, 2014.

Egmond, F., Multiple underworlds in the Dutch Republic of the Seventeenth and Eighteenth Centuries. In: C. Fijnaut and L. Paoli, *Organised crime in Europe*. Dordrecht, Springer, 2004, 77-107.

Europol, *SOCTA 2013. Europol serious and organized crime threat assessment*. The Hague, 2013.

Europol, *Serious and organised crime threat assessment 2017*, The Hague, 2017.

Farah, D. and S. Braun, *Merchant of death*. New Jersey, Wiley, 2006.

Farcy, F., *How is the Albanian Mafia setting up; locally, nationally and in Europe*. Paris, Institut de criminologie. Département de recherche sur les menaces criminelles contemporaines, December 2002.

Forgione, F. *Mafia export. Come 'Ndrangheta, Cosa Nostra e Camorra hanno colonizzato il mondo.* Milan, Baldini Castoldi Dalai, 2010.

Gambetta, D., *The Sicilian Mafia*. Cambridge MA, Harvard University Press, 1993.

GHJ (Gemeenschappelijk Hof van Justitie van Aruba, Curaçao, Sint Maarten en van Bonaire, Sint Eustatius en Saba), *Zaaknummer: H-38/16, strafvonnis*. 21 July 2017.

Gestel, van, B., *Facilitering van mobiele bendes*. The Hague, WODC, 2014.

Glenny, M. *McMafia: A Journey Through the Global Criminal Underworld*. New York, Vintage books, 2009.

Gratteri, N. and A. Nicaso, *Fratelli di sangue: storie, boss e affari della 'Ndrangheta, la mafia più potente del mondo*. Milan, Oscar Mondadori, 2010.

Havocscope, *Global black-market information*. Available at: havocscope.com. Accessed 18 October 2018.

Hignett, K. Organized crime in East Central Europe: the Czech Republic, Hungary and Poland. *Global Crime*, Vol. 6, Nr. 1, 2004, 70-83.

Hobbs, D., Going down the glocal. *The Howard Journal of Criminal Justice*, volume 37(4), 1998, 1-19.

Hobbs, D. and G.A. Antonopoulos, How to research organized crime. In: L. Paoli, *The Oxford handbook of organized crime*. Oxford, Oxford University Press, 2014.

Holm, H. and G. Sorensen, Introduction: what has changed? In: H. Holm and G. Sorensen, *Whose world order: uneven globalisation and the end of the Cold War*. Westview Press, Boulder Colorado, 1995.

IMF, Globalization: a brief overview. *Issues Brief*, May 2008.

Jong, de S. and K. Voskuil, *Maffia paradijs*. Amsterdam, Meulenhoff, 2017.

Kallenborn, H., *Strijd tegen internationale misdadigers*. Amsterdam, Keesing, 1953.

KLPD, *De 'Ndrangheta in Nederland. Aard, criminele activiteiten en werkwijze op Nederlandse bodem*. Driebergen, Dienst Nationale Recherche, 2011.

Lampe, von, K., *Organized crime. Analyzing illegal activities, criminal structures and extra-legal governance*. Thousand Oaks CA, Sage, 2016.

Malone, M. and C. Malone-Rowe, Organized crime in Latin America. In: P. Reichel and J. Albanese, *Handbook of Transnational Crime and Justice, 2nd edition*. Thousand Oaks, Sage, 2014, 471-482.

Massari, M., The Sacra Corona Unita: Origins, Characteristics, and Strategies. In: N. Serenata, *The 'Ndrangheta and Sacra Corona Unita. The history, organization and operations of two unknown Mafia groups*. Cham, Springer, 2014, 101-116.

Meyer, K. Perspectives on Multinational Enterprises in Emerging Economies. *Journal of International Business Studies*, Vol. 35, No. 4, 2004, 259-276.

Nationale politie, Verdachte van brandstichting Italiaans restaurant Nieuwstraat aangehouden. *Press release*, 16 September 2017.

Nationaal Rapporteur Mensenhandel en Seksueel Geweld tegen Kinderen, *Mensenhandel in en uit beeld II. Cijfermatige rapportage 2008-2012*. The Hague, Nationaal Rapporteur, 2014.

Paoli, L. The Italian Mafia. In: L. Paoli (ed.), *The Oxford Handbook of Organized Crime*. Oxford, Oxford University Press, 2014, 121-141.

Raine, L. and F. Cilluffo, (eds.), *Global organized crime: the new empire of evil*. Washington, DC, Center for Strategic and International Studies, 1994.

Reichel, P. and J. Albanese, Historical overview of transnational crime. In: P. Reichel and J. Albanese, *Handbook of Transnational Crime and Justice, 2nd Edition*. Thousand Oaks, CA, Sage, 2014, 1-22.

Rovers, B. Corruption in the Rotterdam Sea Port: Iceberg or Fish Story? Paper presented at the *18th Annual conference of the European Society of Criminology*, Sarajevo, 29 August – 1 September 2018.

Sarno, F., Italian mafias in Europe: between perception and reality. A comparison of press articles in Spain, Germany and the Netherlands, *Trends in Organized Crime*, 17, 2014, 313–341.

Schelling, T., Economics and Criminal Enterprise, *Public Interest*, 7, 1965, 61-78.

Sciarrone R., Ndrangheta: A rectular organization. In: N. Serenata, *The 'Ndrangheta and Sacra Corona Unita. The history, organization and operations of two unknown Mafia groups*. Cham, Springer, 2014, 81-99.

Shelley, L., J. Picarelli and C. Corpora, Global Crime Inc. In: M. Cusimano, *Beyond sovereignty: Issues for a global agenda.* Florence KY, Thomson/Wadsworth, 2003.

Shelley, L., The globalization of crime. In: M. Natarajan, *Introduction to International Criminal Justice*. Boston, McGraw Hill, 2005, 3-10.

Shelley, L. and N. Hirst, *Transnational threats: current and future trends*. Paper presented at the Annual Security Review Conference, Vienna, 27-29 June 2017.

Sieber, U. and M. Bögel, *Logistik der organisierten Kriminalität*, Wiesbaden, Bundeskriminalamt, 1993.

Spapens, T., *Interactie tussen criminaliteit en opsporing*. Antwerp and Oxford, Intersentia, 2006.

Spapens, T., *Georganiseerde misdaad en strafrechtelijke samenwerking in de Nederlandse grensgebieden*. Antwerp and Oxford, Intersentia, 2008.

Spapens, T., M. Peters and D. van Daele, D., *Administrative measures to prevent and tackle crime*. The Hague, Eleven International Publishing, 2015.

Sterling. C., *Octopus. The long reach of the international Sicilian mafia*. New York, Simon and Schuster, 1990.

Tops, P., J. van Valkenhoef, E. van der Torre and L. van Spijk, L., *The Netherlands and synthetic drugs: an inconvenient truth*. The Hague, Eleven International Publishing, 2018.

Tremlett, G., The hunt for the Pink Panther gang, *The Guardian*, 23 August 2010.

Tweede Kamer, *Kamerstukken II*, Vergaderjaar 1995/96, 24 072, nr. 17, 1995.

Uhm, van, D., *Uncovering the illegal wildlife trade*, Utrecht, Phd thesis, 2016.

Ulrich, A., *Das Engelsgesicht. Die Geschichte eines Mafia-Killers aus Deutschland*. München and Hamburg, DVA and Spiegel Buchverlag, 2005.

UNODC, *Results of a pilot survey of forty selected organized criminal groups in sixteen countries*. Vienna, 2002.

UNODC, *The globalization of crime: a transnational organized crime threat assessment*. Vienna, 2010.

UNODC, *Global report on trafficking in persons 2016*, Vienna, 2016.

Voskuil, K., Zuid-Amerikaanse bende pleegt golf van inbraken in ons land. *AD*, 25 May 2018.

Williams, P. Transnational Criminal Organisations and International Security, *Survival*, Vol. 36, No. 1, 1994, 96–113.

Williams, P., Transnational criminal networks. In: J. Arquilla and D. Ronfeldt (eds.), *Networks and netwars: The future of terror, crime, and militancy.* Washington DC, Rand Corporation, 2001.

Zwart, R., Comeback van een maffiabaas. *Koninkrijksrelaties.nu*, 27 July 2018.

Do firearms link organised crime and terrorism in the Netherlands? A Social Network Analysis exploration

Niels van Wanrooij and *Saraï Sapulete*[1]

Introduction and research question

a. Introduction

Attacks by (jihadi) terrorists have become more frequent over the past decade. As the neighbouring countries experienced more frequent and more deadly terrorist attacks (see Figure 1), the Dutch authorities grew increasingly concerned about the possibility of similar attacks happening in the Netherlands. In particular, the threat of Dutch (jihadi) terrorists acquiring heavy firearms to conduct Bataclan-like attacks loomed in the back of policymakers' minds. Preventing such heavy firearms from falling into the wrong hands became a top policy priority. In 2016, this led the Dutch Ministry of Justice and Security to commission a study on how firearms are acquired by terrorists, specifically

1 The authors are research consultants at Ecorys Netherlands, an international research and consultancy organisation. This chapter is based on a study for the Scientific Research and Documentation Centre (WODC) of the Dutch Ministry of Justice and Security, which was completed by a project team consisting of Dr. Brigitte Slot, Dr. Saraï Sapulete, Niels van Wanrooij MSc (Ecorys) and Ms. Monique Bruinsma (Bureau Bruinsma) in 2016-2017. We are very grateful for the assistance by the WODC and by the generous collaboration offered by the National Police, especially by one of their analysts– who aided our data collection immensely – as well as the National Team Firearms Expertise and the National Team Counter-Terrorism and Radicalism.

looking at interactions between firearms dealers, organised crime, and terrorists (suspects).

Figure 1.
Selected terrorist attacks in Europe, 2004 - 2017

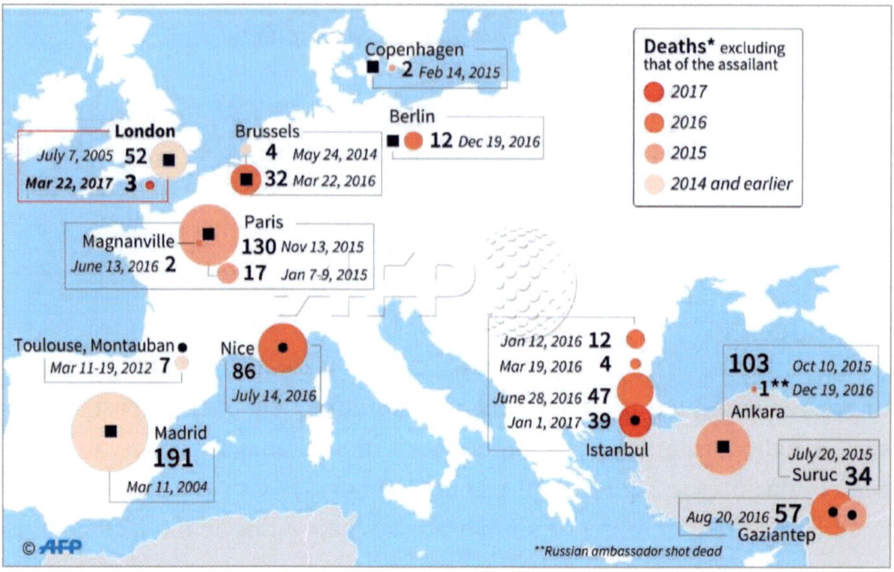

Source: AFP

An extensive literature exists on the presumed connection between organised crime and terrorism, in academia (for example, Laqueur, 2000; Makarenko, 2004; Basra, Neumann and Brunner, 2016) and, in line with the development of the phenomenon in Europe, in European policy papers (for example Makarenko and Mesquitaa, 2014; West Sands Advisory LLP, 2012; Renard, 2016; Adviesraad Internationale Vraagstukken, 2013). In addition, much has been written specifically about how the firearms trade operates in Europe (Centre for Strategy and Evaluation Services, 2014; Flemish Peace Institute, 2018) and on the firearms used in mass shootings (Duquet, 2016).

At the same time, while media report about the routes travelled by jihadis and their firearms proliferated (see Figure 2; Der Spiegel, 24 March 2016; NRC, 15 July 2016;) very little empirical research is conducted on the relationship between terrorism and organised crime (Hübschle, 2011). Although presumably intelligence services and law enforcement agencies have access to the relevant data – and one expects they exploit this data to counteract potential threats – such information is not shared with the public. While this is understandable from the point of view of law enforcement, it does not help address questions about the (development of the) nature of the phenomenon, hampering a better understanding and a public debate on the issues.

Figure 2.
Delivery route of firearms used in terrorist attacks in Europe

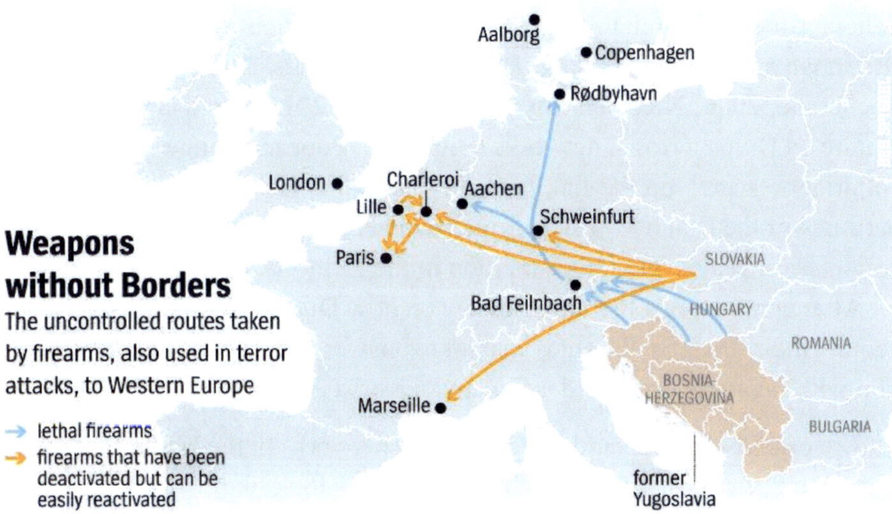

Source: Der Spiegel (24 March 2016)

b. Research question

Two main assertions follow from the literature on the organised crime-terror nexus. On the one hand, terrorist groups are posited to increasingly act like organised crime groups in order to obtain their money. On the other hand, profit-maximising criminal groups will not ask too many questions when they are able to sell their products to whomever, jihadis included.

Research regarding the profiles of Dutch jihadi terrorists has shown that in many cases, they have a criminal history (Poot and Sonnenschein, 2009; Bie, 2016). Research by Veldhuis (2016) implicates prisons as pivotal locations where criminals and terrorists meet, and in some cases petty criminals can be recruited as terrorists. It seems the attacks in Paris (2015) and Denmark (2015) were committed by petty criminals thus recruited (NCTV, 2015). The terrorists were able to rely on their old criminal networks to obtain their firearms, and the suppliers of the firearms seem not in all cases to be aware that their old buddy has become a terrorist.

The situation described above holds for the case of the Netherlands as well: although there is a reliable literature on the operation of the firearms trade (Boerman and Bruinsma, 2012; Bruinsma and Moors, 2005; Dienst Nationale Recherche, 2006; NRC, 13 July 2016a; 13 July 2016b), and an emerging literature on Dutch terrorist networks (Bie, 2016; Poot and Sonnenschein, 2009), empirical research on the link between the two is lacking. The scientific department of the Dutch Ministry of Justice and Security recognised this gap and commissioned a study on the situation in the Netherlands.

After conducting a literature review on how Dutch (jihadi) terrorist groups acquire their firearms, the study sought to answer the following research question with regard to organised crime and terrorists:

> Are organised crime and jihadi terrorist networks in the Netherlands interwoven? If so, what does this interwovenness look like?

The concept 'interwoven networks' is defined as follows: the lack of a clear boundary between two networks, characterised by a (partial, but structural) overlap of networks. As applied and operationalised in our Social Network Analysis (SNA) methodology, overlapping networks would be characterised by members of a network being part of both an organised crime network and a jihadi terrorist network.

This question has been explored by way of a SNA (Social Network Analysis on a specific case, namely that of the Slovakian firearms dealer AFG (see below). The identification of the starting group was crucial to the potential of the study itself. An extensive consultation was organised to identify the most relevant, and potentially fruitful 'case', and inputs were gathered from experts at the National Police, the Public Prosecutor's Office, the counter-terrorism coordinator (NCTV), and the intelligence service (AIVD).

The SNA was thus applied to a major case involving organised crime, firearms dealers and – as became apparent – terrorist suspects. The study can best be understood as an explorative case study (Gerring, 2007) where a tentative link is explored and opportunities for further research are developed.

Research design

a. Social network analysis

The main body of the study consisted of a Social Network Analysis. Such an analysis provides a method to study social structures. The focus is not on individual actors (or nodes), but on the relationships between them. Actors can be individuals, but also organisations, countries, *etc*. The relationship can be defined by several types of links, *e.g*. kinship, friendship, financial transactions, *etc*. Social network analysis thus gives us a "formal, conceptual means for thinking about the social world" (Wasserman and Faust, 1994). The social network analysis method gives an in-depth insight into the dynamics and links between actors. Moreover, it allows for identifying main actors and their function (*e.g*. connectors, influencers) within the network.

Social network analysis provides added-value by showing not only how actors are interlinked but also who are the essential actors within a particular network. Moreover, a social network analysis allows for an easy comparability with other networks by analysing the network characteristics (fragmented or fully connected structures) and the ease of interaction (ability to form connections) between actors.

b. The case: the AFG firearms dealer

Since 2014, European law enforcement investigators have been observing the Slovakian (web)shop AFG, located in the small town of Partizánske. This shop sells deactivated firearms throughout Europe on their premises and via their website (see Figure 3). The German *Bundeskriminalamt* (Federal Police) estimated in 2016 that some 14.000 of these firearms were in circulation in the EU. These firearms were deactivated in a way that made reactivation into 'live' firearms relatively easy. Because of a loophole in European legislation this method of deactivation was legal at the time, even if reactivating them was not.

This presented an opportunity and an easy supply of firepower to satisfy the demands of actors with malicious intent, both criminals and terrorists. And indeed, reactivated firearms from this 'AFG line' have made their way to French terrorists, UK gangsters, and German neo-Nazis (Der Spiegel, 24 March 2016).

Figure 3.
Deactivated submachine gun (CZ vz 58) on AFG web shop

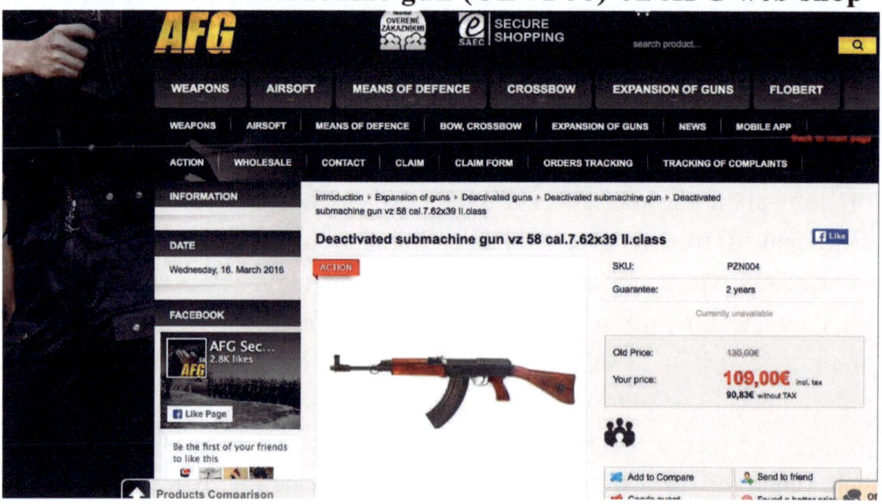

Source: AFG website

The most recent Dutch National Threat Assessment (*Nationaal Dreigingsbeeld, 2017*) indicates that such reactivated firearms make up a large proportion of the supply of firearms in the Netherlands, with almost 200 're-cycled' automatic firearms found since 2012: rifles from manufacturer CZ akin to the famous AK 47, Skorpion machine-pistols as well as various pistols. Crucially, police investigations show that the majority of these firearms can be traced back to the AFG webshop, with (illegal) reactivation taking place in Germany or the Netherlands.

While it is unclear exactly how many steps there are between reactivation of the firearms and their appearance on the market, it is clear that the final step before reaching the 'customer' was through (illegal) firearms dealers. Within the context of this study, it is this latter group of firearms dealers that represents the salient network(s) of organised crime.

Because of this case's importance for law enforcement, the National Police had started to compile an AFG-database listing details about the apprehensions and investigations where AFG firearms were found, including which persons were present when a firearm was discovered, how they were connected to the firearm(s) (such as 'in possession at time of apprehension', 'present but not in possession') and whether there had been active police investigations into these persons. In total, more than 2.000 persons were listed in this way. This provided a rich data source that was leveraged as the starting point for the SNA.

As it was known that firearms dealers were involved in this case, our research question could focus on whether, starting from this group, connections to terrorist cells could be discovered.

c. Data collection

Following the identification of the relevant case, the framework for the Social Network Analysis was developed. This was done by developing a data collection protocol (which criteria are relevant to our research questions), and a database template.

Our research adopted an open-ended approach: neither the size of the group nor the individuals within it were known beforehand. The only 'known' was the point of departure: the initial group of subjects whose social network would be mapped. Their connections, and their connections' connections, became only (fully) known during the course of the data collection.[2] Theoretically, the pool of people in the databases could have been known if all of them were researched beforehand, but the salient relations between subsections of them could not have been.[3]

The study was able to draw on 'raw' police data present in the various databases of the Dutch National Police: information on the criminal record and history of apprehensions, arrests and convictions of all Dutch citizens, as well as information about family relations. Working arrangements were made to work on-site at the National Police premises, so that queries of these databases were either performed or supervised by an authorised police analyst at all times. The extracted information has been coded, anonymised and processed into a large database, indicating the personal characteristics and relations between (code-named) subjects.

To be able to work with the case, the group of over 2.000 subjects had to be reduced. First, this was necessary as it included many subjects that were simply not relevant for our purposes: innocent bystanders; (deceased) victims; those with only a very tenuous link to firearms. Second, as SNA is a labour-intensive methodology that increases the number of subjects included exponentially with each step, the starting group needed to be as small and focused as possible to avoid the noise overpowering the signal. We limited our file analysis to persons with a *criminal record* (persons implicated as suspects and those convicted of crimes).

To focus our efforts and eliminate non-relevant persons, a number of steps were followed to filter the 700 remaining subjects into three relevant roles. First, a distinction was made between those subjects that had been found in direct possession of a firearm, and those that had not been. The former were assigned the role of *firearms possessor*.

---

2 This is in contrast to when an SNA is applied to, for example, a typical company, where all the relevant persons (the employees) are known to the researchers beforehand.

3 The only way this would have been possible is if it had been possible to engage with the detectives who handled the investigations. (This would have had the drawback of potentially steering the focus of the SNA towards particularly vivid cases for these investigators.)

Separately, the whole dataset was cross-checked in two ways:

1. With police experts on the Dutch firearms trade, to identify (known) *firearms dealers* – the second role in our SNA;
2. With police experts monitoring extremists and (known) terrorists, to identify *(suspected) terrorists* – the third role in our SNA.

Those subjects that were not assigned any of the three roles were subsequently expunged from our dataset. Following these steps, we obtained a list of 40 persons divided into three relevant roles: 5 firearms dealers; 15 terrorist suspects; 20 firearms possessors. Every person was assigned a single role. Logically, those identified as firearms dealers and terrorist suspects could also have possessed firearms, while those in the firearms possessors subgroup could not have been identified as firearms dealers or suspected terrorists as this would have meant changing their classification.

This group of 40 formed the starting point of the SNA. We then proceeded with 'snowball sampling' from our focal actors: each individual's police file had a section elaborating the individuals associated with it through past (suspected) crimes. This list of co-suspects and –convicts was added to the SNA as a first layer of contacts. Each of these newly added individuals was subsequently subjected to the same exercise, again analysing their police file for persons associated through past (suspected) crimes.

While building our database, we collected both relational and personal attributes. The relational attribute answered whether subject *a* had a relation to subject *b*, based on association in their criminal record (they had been apprehended and/or convicted together in one or more cases). We also noted recorded whether these persons were identified as firearms dealers, terrorist suspects (labelled 'CTER actors' to distinguish them from the start group) or firearms possessors. An overview of the data groups used in the study is given in Table 1.

Table 1.
Data groups used in the study

Data group	Definition
Starting group	40 persons identified from the AFG case, comprised of the 3 subgroups 'firearms dealers', 'terrorist suspects', and 'firearms possessors'.
Firearms dealers [start group]	5 persons from the AFG case identified by police experts as known firearms dealers in the Netherlands
Terrorist suspects [start group]	15 persons from the AFG case identified by police experts as terrorist suspects in the Netherlands
Firearms possessors [starting group]	20 persons from the AFG case with a conviction for a firearms-related offence
CTER actors	All persons in the SNA database, identified as terrorist suspects in the Netherlands by police experts
Firearms possessors	All persons in the SNA database, identified as having a conviction for a firearms-related offence

d. Measures

Key in social network analysis is the concept of *centrality.* A strong, central network position of an actor is not only determined by the number of contacts the actor has, but also by the position the actor holds in the network, and the connectedness of his or her contacts. The following structural network characteristics define the centrality of actors (see *e.g.*, Freeman et al. 1991, Borgatti 2005):

- *Degree centrality*. Degree centrality measures the number of relations an actor has with other actors. It is higher the more connections an actor holds with other actors. In a directed – or asymmetric – network, we distinguish in-degree and out-degree, being the number of incoming ties, and the number of outgoing ties.
- *Betweenness centrality.* Betweenness centrality measures the importance of one actor in acting as a bridge between actors who would otherwise not be connected (Burt, 1992). These connecting actors do not necessarily need to have a high degree centrality but need just to act as a bridge between

two distant communities. By taking the position between two non-connected groups, a 'structural hole' is filled (Burt, 1992). Taking such a bridge position is also known by the term 'brokerage'. Betweenness centrality is measured by the number of times an actor fulfils a bridge position on the shortest path (defined by the number of dyadic ties) between two other actors within the network.

- *Closeness centrality*. Closeness centrality measures the distance of one actor to all other actors in the network. The more direct relations exist between actors, the higher closeness centrality is. It can be regarded as a measure of how long it will take to spread information from one actor to all other actors. Closeness centrality is calculated via the sum of the length of the shortest paths between an actor and all other actors in the network.
- *Eigenvector centrality*. Eigenvector centrality takes into account the *relative importance* of the relations of actors, instead of merely the number of relations. In networks that are larger and more complex, measuring only closeness centrality does not always suffice. Eigenvector centrality provides a relative score, in which actors who have relations with more central actors, score higher than actors with the same number of relations, but with less central actors. Thus, actors with high eigenvector centrality have more relations to others who are themselves well-connected.

Findings

a. Network characteristics

The 40 key actors who were central to our analysis have led to a network of 724 actors, who have 4.340 connections with each other, defined by (suspected) co-offending ties (see Table 2). This is a low density or sparse network, indicated by the network density of 0,8%, meaning 0,8% of all possible relations between the actors has been established. Of course, the nature of the network is a logical consequence of the methodological choice to base relations solely on associations through a criminal record. It remains an open question what this says about the density of the underlying social networks.

Furthermore, we see that the network exists of 22 components, which are isolated from each other. Based on our data collection and analysis, we see no overarching network emerging. This is (also) a consequence of our method of snowball sampling starting with 40 focal actors (start group), which were not connected to each other up-front.

Table 2.
Network characteristics

Aspect	Number
Actors	724
CTER actors identified	108
CTER actors currently under investigation	37
Connections	4.340
Density	0,008
Components	22

We have identified nine of the 22 components as crucial for answering our research question, based on the following indicators:

1. The component "DEALERS" contains all *five* identified firearms dealers;
2. Seven of the components contain terrorist suspects (TERROR 1 -7);
3. One of the components (TERROR 8) identifies terrorist suspects in the network of a person in the start group.

The other network components are either too small or contain no relevant subjects from our starting group. We first describe the network characteristics of the start group, followed by a description of the components in detail.

As we do not have information on the complete network of all actors identified, the network measures are skewed for those actors in the start group: because we have more information for the start group, their centrality is higher by definition. Therefore, we report the centrality measures regarding our 40 persons from the start group. The centrality measures are based on the centrality within the component the actor is located in. We have presented the measures for the firearms dealers, terrorist suspects as well as the start group as a whole.

Table 3.
Degree centrality start group

Group	Mean	Min - max	N
Degree centrality			
Start group	18,8	3 – 73	40
Firearms dealers	11,6	3 – 19	5
Terrorist suspects (start group)	24,5	3 – 73	15
Closeness centrality			
Start group	0,01	(0,00 – 0,11)	40
Firearms dealers	0,00	(0,00 – 0,00)	5
Terrorist suspects (start group)	0,02	(0,00 – 0,11)	15
Betweenness centrality			
Start group	0,57	(0 – 5,09)	40
Firearms dealers	0,19	(0 – 0,40)	5
Terrorist suspects (start group)	0,80	(0 – 5,09)	15
Eigenvector centrality			
Start group	0,27	(0 – 0,69)	40
Firearms dealers	0,07	(0 – 0,30)	5
Terrorist suspects (start group)	0,23	(0 – 0,56)	15

For degree centrality, we see an average score of 18,8 indicating that actors in the start group are related to an average of about 19 other nodes in their respective components. The maximum of actors someone is related to is 73 in the case of a terrorist suspect, which skews the average of the terrorist suspects group (average of 24,5). The average degree centrality score for the firearms dealers is lower (11,6; N=5). Terrorist suspects (N=15) have more relations than firearms dealers. The other centrality measures also indicate that terrorist suspects are more central than firearms dealers.

b. Network of firearms dealers

After looking at the start group, we zoom in on the relevant components. All firearms dealers can be found in one component with 55 actors (component DEALERS; see Figure 4). In this sense, the SNA 'shows' that they are part of the same space in the underworld. At the same time the firearms dealers have a rather peripheral position in the overall network of 724 actors. Relatively speaking they do not have many connections and do not occupy a central position.

The firearms dealers are not all connected to each other directly, and mostly fulfil bridge positions to each other's ego-centric networks (see Figure 4). Weapon dealers 1 and 2 score high on betweenness centrality in component DEALERS: they connect other networks of actors within the component. Weapon dealer 4 scores highest on eigenvector centrality, indicating he has most relations to others who are themselves well-connected.

Figure 4.
Component DEALERS, five firearms dealers

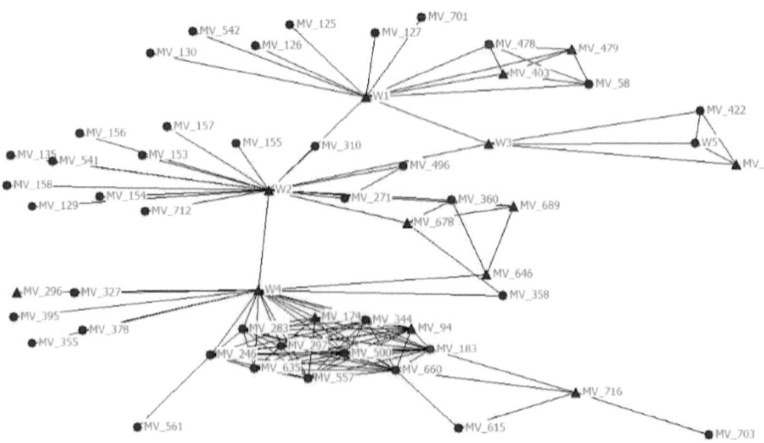

Legend:

- *W1-W5: firearms dealers*
- *Red: present on the CTER suspect list*
- *Triangle: convicted for firearms possession ('Wwm-feit' under Dutch law), proxy for possessor of firearms*

Furthermore, there are three actors in this sub-network, who are in the CTER database. Two of these have a direct connection to one of the firearms dealers. This indicates that firearms dealers are in direct contact with subjects that are flagged as persons of interest regarding potential terrorist motives. These actors are highly likely to be able to obtain firearms from their connections.

c. Networks of terrorist suspects

We identified seven components around terrorist suspects in our start group (see Figure 5). Within these components, there are almost invariably subjects that have been found to be in possession of firearms. In other words, in most cases firearms are in circulation within the networks of terrorist suspects. One can surmise these would be relatively easy to acquire by these subjects.

Figure 5 shows the seven components. This visualisation reveals that the size of these sub-networks varies substantially, ranging from 4 to 204 actors per component. As a consequence of our data collection method, the terrorist suspects have most connections. Several clusters within the components in which they are prominently represented, are connected by bridging actors. In other networks, the terrorist suspects fulfil bridge positions themselves.

In component TERROR 1 there are 38 actors. One of the terrorist suspects (rcd triangle) is most central, and also convicted for firearms possession. Component TERROR 2 is the largest component with 204 actors. Again, one of the terrorist suspects is most central in this component. Furthermore, a number of actors who are not included in the start group have been identified as central. Component TERROR 3 is the smallest component, with 4 actors, 2 of which are terrorist suspects. Both of them are connected to all others in the component, while no direct link exists between the two non-terrorist suspects.

Component TERROR 4 contains 81 actors, who are connected by two central bridge positions, fulfilled by terrorist suspects, who have been also convicted for firearms possession. Component TERROR 5 consist of 21 actors, built around a terrorist suspect. Four other actors – outside of the start group, but known in the terrorist database – are identified as being highly central in the component. Those four actors are all directly connected to the terrorist suspect in the most central position.

Component 6 consists of 112 actors. In this network, two terrorist suspects and three non-start group actors are highly central. The terrorist suspects score high on eigenvector centrality, while the non-start group actors mostly have high scores regarding betweenness centrality. Finally, component 7 contains 22 actors, revolving around one central terrorist suspect.

The information from these components reveals that the terrorist suspects are (indirectly) connected to each other within the components, but also to a large network of persons with a criminal background, especially visible in subnetworks 2 and 6. Also, weapons are within arm's reach for many actors within these components. This may indicate that terrorist suspects can obtain a firearm relatively easily.

Figure 5.
Components containing terrorist suspects

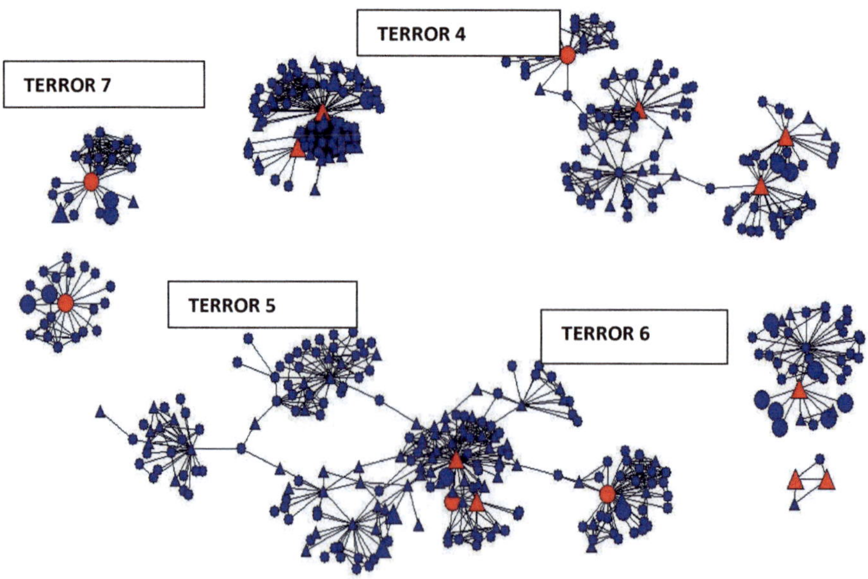

Legend:

- *Red: terrorist suspects part of start group*
- *Size: bigger symbol indicates subject now or in the past under active investigation on counter-terrorism concerns*
- *Triangle: convicted for firearms possession ('Wwm-feit' under Dutch law), proxy for possessor of firearms*

d. Network with identified terrorist suspects

Apart from the component including the five arms dealers, and the seven components comprising terrorist suspects, there is a ninth component (TERROR 8; see Figure 6) relevant for our analysis, which revolves around an actor identified in the start group who is neither an arms dealer nor a suspected terrorist. This individual (SG_13) was identified in the start group due to a direct link to an AFG-weapon (for which he had not been convicted during the timespan of our study). In drawing up the connections of this individual (SG_13), four actors were identified who are known in the terrorist database, and of which one was known in a terrorist investigation at the time of our study.

Component TERROR 8 consists of 27 actors, of which SG_13 as well as three other individuals occupy the most central positions. One of the latter three individuals (MV_560) is known in the terrorist database. The connection between SG_13 and MV_560 may indicate a relation between AFG and terrorism given SG_13's direct link to an AFG sourced weapon.

Figure 6.
Component TERROR 8, network with terrorist suspects

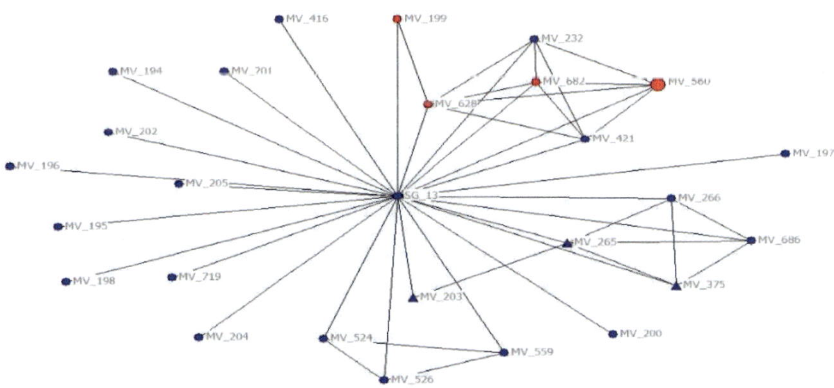

Legend:
- *Red: terrorist suspects part of start group*
- *Size: bigger symbol indicates subject now or in the past under active investigation on counter-terrorism concerns*
- *Triangle: convicted for firearms possession ('Wwm-feit' under Dutch law), proxy for possessor of firearms.*

Conclusion

a. On acquisition of firearms

In this section we reflect on how the findings relate to the research question and draw a number of (tentative) conclusions.

At an early stage of the case study, it became clear that the terrorist suspects had access to firearms from the AFG supply line. Crucially, within the 'firearms dealers network' (component 10) we have identified several terrorist suspects who have either a direct (one step) or indirect (two steps) link to these dealers. Further research (or police investigation) at subject-level into how exactly they acquired those firearms would be fruitful. However, the characteristics of the network(s) arising from our SNA indicates it is highly likely these were directly or indirectly acquired via Dutch firearms dealers, seems to lend support to what we would expect based on the alleged crime-terror link discussed in the (academic) literature.

b. On the interwovenness of organised crime and terrorism

At the same time, some of our findings are noteworthy. Most importantly, our case study does not show evidence that there is an interwovenness between organised crime and terrorism. This conclusion can be broken down into a number of distinct elements.

The results of our case study seem to imply that the firearms trade in the Netherlands can rightly be considered as 'organised' crime: all five firearms dealers identified within the case are linked through their presence in one network and it is not farfetched to assume they know each other.

Structurally speaking, the case study does not reveal a coherent terrorist network in the Netherlands. Rather, we find many smaller sub-networks that contain a few terrorist suspects and many criminals who interact with each other. One conclusion is therefore that at the *individual level*, there is an interwovenness or interconnectedness between criminals and terrorists (who often are or have been criminals themselves). In some cases, terrorist suspects perform a central role in a network, or act as a 'bridge' between otherwise unconnected networks. However, this cannot be qualified as an organised crime nexus: that would require a more comprehensive, structural interface between the two types of networks.

At the same time, as we have not seen a coherent terrorist organisation emerge from our data, it logically follows that based on our study it cannot be concluded that there is an interwovenness of organised crime and terrorism at the *group* or *structural level.*

In relation to this point, it is important to explicitly note that the absence of interwovenness also (logically) cannot be confirmed: we have not seen these networks in our case, but this absence could be caused either by their non-existence or be a result of the scope of the study. Perhaps these would have emerged if the network were mapped to one additional degree of relations. The arrests of a number of terrorist suspects last year (2 in June, 7 in September and 5 in December 2018; see Trouw, 29 December 2018), who have all been charged with membership of a terrorist network and with conspiring to plan a terrorist attack, indicates that looser terrorist networks or cells are present in the Netherlands. It is important to monitor the progress of these court cases, to identify the nature of these looser networks and, in case these suspects had already acquired weapons, to trace how these have been obtained.

Discussion and the way forward

a. Avenues for further research

Our study has been able to draw on primary sources from the police in order to build our SNA database. Coding has been based on police files, validated and complemented by inputs from specialised police teams. It has not been possible to include 'richer' information on the context of specific cases and subjects, which would be present with the detectives responsible for working the cases. As a result, our research has been able to lay bare the 'bone structure' of the networks.

A fruitful next step would be to 'put some flesh on the bones' by involving those detectives and enriching the analysis with a contextual understanding. Subject *a* is related to subject *b,* but are they casual acquaintances, close friends, or partners turned enemies? Did they actually know each other?[4] Firearms dealer *x* knows terrorist subject *y,* but what is the meaning of this relationship – are they childhood friends, or 'accidentally' connected by a common acquaintance? Considering how labour-intense this unravelling could be, our suggestion would be to focus on the 15 persons that our SNA has highlighted as being of particular relevance, due to (the combination of) their personal characteristics and their position in their respective networks.

Based on the experience gained during the study, SNA is a very fruitful approach for further (applied) criminological research. The method is scalable, so that any characteristic or type of relationship that is deemed relevant can be included in a specific model.

The method is also adaptive: it can relatively easily be applied to other areas of interest, such as outlaw motor gangs and the drugs trade. The only limiting precondition is that sufficient data needs to be available. Through combining primary data from police databases with expert knowledge from specialist police teams (further complemented by outside experts), this is a hurdle that can be overcome.

Although coding of the subjects and the creation of the database can be time-consuming, on the whole the method could prove to be a time saver for police analysts and investigators, for whom the need to prioritise is immense. Using network positions and personal characteristics, it is possible to identify a select number of key subjects, on whom an investigation could usefully focus.

In addition, mapping the structure of a network allows previously unseen (because indirect) links between phenomena to be recognised, and potential blind spots to be discovered more easily. Police work would stand to gain from more structurally implementing these approaches.

4 In the worst case, they could have been incidentally lumped together in the system by careless registration.

In our case, some 15 subjects already known to the police have been flagged as of interest for further investigation, and two new subjects have been flagged as of interest from a counter-terrorism and radicalism perspective.

b. Reflections on the applicability for police work

Although SNA is not an alien methodology for many police analysts, it seems that mapping of a social network often only occurs on a subject basis (who is this suspect in contact with?) and not on a phenomenon or more strategic level (what, if any, are the links between different criminal groups?).

The applied method of systematically combining information from different fields of expertise (in our case: intelligence on firearms and on terrorism) leads to new insights. The added value can be seen on two levels:

- By mapping the social network of suspects, relationships are uncovered that may be instructive when assessing threats and whom to prioritise. A systematic approach allows for clear-cut choices in this prioritisation, which can lead to more efficient use of resources (personnel, time and money).
- Regular cross-checks of actors from different fields (firearms dealers, extremists, firearms users), their connections, density of their networks can lead to the identification of overlap between phenomena that had not been recognised before. This furthers our (theoretical) understanding of the subjects of this study

A further deepening of this theme is recommended as a result of this exploration. In the context of this research, a number of concrete possibilities have been described for how to apply SNA within the police agencies to this theme and related issues. SNA can support the process of gathering further information regarding the nexus of organised crime and terrorist jihadi groups, and can assist in the decision-making concerning how to prioritise follow-up investigatory work.

c. Limitations and opportunities for further research

A fundamental question is to what extent social structures can meaningfully be captured with the network model. This discussion is beyond the scope of this article, although we note that the often transactional nature of criminal relations would seem *a priori* to be suitable for a network model.

In addition, this study has some more specific limitations that need to be recognised – which hint at opportunities for further fruitful research. These fall into three categories:

- Data: the information (made) available to us was limited to primary data from the police databases, supplemented by specialist expertise. Further research would benefit from involving detectives involved in specific cases. Concretely, one should consult the investigators who have 'human intelligence' on those identified as key actors within a social network.
- Reliability: it is known that primary police databases suffer from a certain level of data pollution as a result of incorrect or incomplete registrations. Researchers should recognise this, and adopt the strategy outlined in the previous point: consult the relevant detectives.
- Robustness: our findings are liable to change if further layers of connections are added to the network. It could be that such an expansion of the network in will reveals for example, a network of loosely federated terrorist cells. Future studies need to keep in mind that there should be a balance between on the one hand 'completeness' of the networks, and on the other the strength of the connections thus discovered (to what extent are third-degree connections indicative of a robust organisation?), compounded by practical concerns about the trade-off with the time spent on gathering and interpreting the data.

References

Adviesraad Internationale Vraagstukken, Criminaliteit, Corruptie en Instabiliteit: een Verkennend Advies'. *Advies*. The Hague: AIV, 2013.

Basra R., P. Neumann and C. Brunner C., *Criminal pasts, terrorist futures: European jihadists and the new crime-terror nexus*. London: ICSR, 2016.

Bie, J.L. de, *How jihadist networks operate. A grounded understanding of changing organizational structures, activities, and involvement mechanisms of jihadist networks in the Netherlands*. Leiden: Universiteit Leiden, 2016.

Boerman, F. and M. Bruinsma, *De illegale handel in vuurwapens en explosieven*. Zoetermeer: Dienst Nationale Recherche Informatie, 2012.

Borgatti, S.P., Centrality and network flow. *Social Networks,* 2005, 27(1), 55-71.

Bruinsma, M. and H. Moors, *Illegale vuurwapens. Gebruik, bezit en handel in Nederland, 2001 – 2003*. Tilburg: IVA, 2005.

Burt, R.S., *Structural holes: The social structure of competition*. Cambridge, Mass.: Harvard University Press, 1992.

Centre for Strategy and Evaluation Services, *Study to Support an Impact Assessment on Options for Combatting Illicit Firearms Trafficking in the European Union*. European Commission: DG Migration and Home Affairs, 2014.

Der Spiegel / European Investigative Collaboration (24 March 2016), 'How EU Failures Helped Terrorists Obtain Weapons'.

Dienst Nationale Recherche, 'Illegale wapenhandel'. In *Justitiële Verkenningen,* 2006, 4(8).

Duquet N., *Armed to kill: An exploratory analysis of the guns used in recent public mass shooting in Europe*. Brussels: Flemish Peace Institute, 2016.

Duquet N. (2016), 'Firearms acquisition and the terrorism-criminality nexus'. In Renard T. (ed.), *Counterterrorism in Belgium: key challenges and policy options*. Egmont Institute: Egmont Paper 89, 2016.

Dutch National Police, *Nationaal Dreigingsbeeld 2017*, 2017.

Europol, *European Union Terrorism Situation and Trend Report 2015*. The Hague: Europol, 2015.

Flemish Peace Institute, *Project SAFTE*. Brussels: European Commission Directorate-General for Migration and Home Affairs, 2018.

Freeman L.C. and S.P. Borgatti, Centrality in valued graphs. *Social Networks,* 1991, 13(2), 141-154.

Gerring J., *Case study research. principles and practices*. Cambridge: Cambridge University Press, 2007.

Hanneman, R.A. and M. Riddle, *Introduction to social network methods*. Riverside, CA: University of California, Riverside, 2005.

Hübschle A., 'From Theory to Practice: Exploring the organized crime-terror nexus in Sub-Saharan Africa'. *Perspectives on Terrorism,* 2011, 5(3-4).

Laqueur, W., *The new terrorism*. Oxford: Oxford University Press, 2000.

Makarenko, T., *The terror-crime continuum: tracing the interplay between transnational organised crime and terrorism*, 2004

Makarenko, T, and M. Mesquitaa, 'Categorising the crime–terror nexus in the European Union', *Global Crime,* 2014, 15(3-4), 259-274.

NCTV, *Beleidsimplicaties dreigingsbeeld terrorisme Nederland 38*. The Hague: NCTV, 7 April 2015.

NRC, 'Hoe het vuurwapengeweld in Nederland explodeerde', 13 July 2016a.

NRC, 'Onderzoek naar Slowaakse wapens in Nederland', 13 July 2016b.

NRC, 'De Slowakijeroute en het terrorisme', 15 July 2016.

Poot, C.J. de and A. Sonnenschein, 'Jihadistisch terrorisme in Nederland. Een beschrijving op basis van afgesloten opsporingsonderzoeken'. *In Onderzoek en beleid no281.* The Hague: WODC, 2009.

Trouw, 'Politie Rotterdam arresteert verdachten in terrorisme-onderzoek', 29 December 2018

Veldhuis T., *Prisoner radicalization and terrorism detention policy: Institutionalized fear or evidence-based policy making?* London: Routledge, 2016.

Wasserman, S. and K. Faust, *Social Network Analysis. Methods and Applications.* New York: Cambridge University Press, 1994.

West Sands Advisory LLP, *Europe's crime-terror nexus: links between terrorist and organized crime groups in the European Union*. Brussels: European Parliament, Directorate-General for Internal Policies, Policy Department Citizens' Rights and Constitutional Affairs, 2012.

The perception of corruption in the daily life of Ukraine

Anna Markovska, Alexey Serdyuk, Petrus C. van Duyne and Konstantin Bugaychuk[1]

Introduction

In the course of the last quarter of the 20th century corruption became not only a social, but also a political issue both on the international and domestic levels. Politically this has entailed international organisations addressing the subject to ensure that conventions or international treaties can be ratified. Domestically, it has entailed that even endemically corrupt countries have found it difficult to stay out of campaigns against corruption. This situation applies to Ukraine.

Since independence in 1991, Ukraine has always scored highly on a scale of corruption of Transparency International Corruption Perception Index. At the international political level, fighting corruption has often entailed the signing of relevant protocols. Thus, Ukraine has developed a complex legal framework providing for the application of anti-corruption measures. For example, when Ukraine ratified the UN Convention Against Corruption (UNCAC) and adopted its measures on the 31st October 2003, it accepted the following obligations: to support the introduction and development of initiatives designed to target corruption; to support international collaboration intended to challenge

1 Anna Markovska is a Principal Lecturer in Criminology at the School of Humanities and Social Sciences, Anglia Ruskin University, Cambridge, UK. Alexey Serdyuk is Deputy Head of Research Lab on Crime Enforcement of Kharkiv National University of Internal Affairs, Ukraine. Petrus C. van Duyne is professor (em.) of empirical penal law at Utrecht University, The Netherlands. Konstantin Bugaychuk is Head of Research Lab on Crime Enforcement of Kharkiv National University of Internal Affairs, Ukraine.

corruption (including technical facilitation, collaboration and assistance in anti-money laundering procedures); and to facilitate honesty, responsibility and transparency in managing its state, budget and assets.

These procedures may be considered as a breakthrough; providing an array of resources to tackle corruption. However, the efficient execution of these measures by the state remains unmonitored, making them in effect little more than diplomatic signposts indicating compliance without detailing any successful outcomes. Indeed, the implementation of anti-corruption directives has proved to be largely ineffective, and not only in Ukraine.

UNCAC is considered to be a first global legally binding anticorruption instrument. Mungiu-Pippidi (2015) notes that the most challenging aspect to the implementation of this convention is the lack of "an effective follow-up monitoring mechanism" (p.189). Once countries such as Ukraine adopt the provisions of the UNCAC as national law, it has proved extremely difficult to put them into effect (*ibid.*). Despite the fact that there is presently no evidence that such countries that have adopted the UNCAC have deployed their anti-corruption measures efficiently, the importance of their diplomatic significance should not be underestimated. Their very recognition is an acknowledgement of the importance of anti-corruption reform movements: a point of departure.

In 2014, fighting domestic corruption was highlighted as being a major priority for Ukraine. In fact, the demonstration of effective anti-corruption initiatives has now become a prerequisite to obtaining political and especially financial support from western donors whose perception of the situation in Ukraine is crucial. For example, a Dutch referendum on the EU-associate agreement failed because of the Dutch perception of Ukraine being a corrupt country.

Though there is a degree of international unity concerning the importance of fighting domestic corruption, the definition of what qualifies as such is vague. "Integrity" (or the lack of it) is often seen as being a vital element of the definition but it is badly demarcated. For the purpose of our research this is not necessarily a problem as we are not dealing here with demarcations of basic concepts but with the *perceptions* of citizens.

It is important to understand corruption and the perception of corruption as being cultural phenomena because these are related to the ways societies understand its rules and compliance with those rules (Melgar *et al.*, 2010). People's perception of corruption depends on their "values and moral views" (*ibid.*). Some may never have paid a bribe in their lifetime, but are aware nevertheless, that others are engaged in corruption, a situation that has the potential to make them regard their entire society as being corrupt.

Why then is it important to study corruption perception? A short answer would be that it directly affects the issue of trust. Melgar *et al.*, (2010) point out that "high levels of corruption perception could have more devastating effects than corruption itself; it generates a 'culture of distrust' towards some institutions and may create a cultural tradition of gift giving and hence, raising corruption". Mungiu-Pippidi (2015) develops this notion further in discussing the importance of the cultural context in implementing anti-corruption measures.

'Perception' is not necessarily a vague concept here. There are a number of internationally recognised indicators of corruption which attempt to capture statistically the experience of people (households and business communities). Some well-known surveys are: Global Corruption Barometer, the Global Competitiveness Report, the International Country Risk Guide and the World Bank Worldwide Governance Indicator for the Control of Corruption. These analyse representative population samples and also the perception of businessmen and experts on corruption: their findings are used widely in developing policy initiatives, hence, even if subjective, perception matters.

The analysis of cultural settings is often considered essential to provide an estimate of the scale of corruption in a country. Investigating the endemic nature of corruption among the elite in Ukraine is one way to begin to understand such cultural settings. The 'elite' of Ukraine includes political, military, and public service representatives. Illegal profits gained from corrupt exchanges often depends on hierarchical positions within the state, proximity to state budget control and/or legislative power.

It is difficult to find any sphere of life in Ukraine that is not affected by corruption. Schools, hospitals, ministries, and both state and privately owned factories have all been implicated in corruption scandals. Below we have selected some recent examples investigated post 2014.

Various cases have provoked different degrees of concern. In 2017 the case of the State Enterprise (SE) Lviv Armor Vehicle Factory, that after a tender won the supply of new B-46-6 engines to the Armored Command Center (ACC) of the Armed Forces of Ukraine, was a particularly striking example arising from the military conflict in the east of the country (NABU, 2017). According to retrieved documents "LAVF bought engines from Limited liability company (LLC) Bullet Line and supplied them to the ACC of the Armed Forces of Ukraine for 28.560.000 UAH[2]". Detectives of the National Anti-Corruption Bureau (NABU) investigated the deal and found that "the engines were supplied by a third party without any documents. The contracts with LLC were in fact fictitious". The investigation also revealed that "the supplied engines had been sold to enterprises in the domestic market as surplus assets of the Ministry of Defense". Such effective stealing from the armed forces was considered by the Ukrainian media at the time as being a new low for the Ukrainian 'elite'.

The illegal extraction of amber in Western Ukraine, facilitated by Members of Parliament, is an example of a different cultural context of corruption: that of natural resources (NABU, 2017). The illegal extraction of amber in Western Ukraine has been reported by the Ukrainian media over a long period (Fakty, 2016; Lebed, 2015). Lebed (2015) reports that depending on the nation's presidency, the official policy against illegal extraction differed significantly. For example, in the time of President Kuchma the illegal extraction of amber was in effect a state enterprise, but during the Yushchenko regime it became directly exploited by criminals. Lebed (2015) also states that following a moratorium on illegal amber extraction the documentation concerning the activity and possible state involvement in it was intentionally chaotic, making any investigation virtually impossible. In a similar way Ukrainian officials were implicated in the "organisation of a criminal scheme of purchase of ilmenite, routine, zirconium and salmonite concentrates extracted at low prices" (NABU, 2017).

---

2 As of 13 February 2019, 28.560.000 UAH is approximately 935.000 Euro.

The first two decades of Ukrainian independence created a fruitful ground for the elite to abuse their power without being subject to sanctions, the consequent loss of public trust is therefore hardly surprising, and had serious consequences. Johnson (2014) studied the nature of political trust following democratic reforms in Poland and Ukraine, and found that in Ukraine there exists a negative association between support for democracy and trust in political institutions. People believe in democracy but they do not trust the political elite.

This chapter presents the results of a five year corruption perception survey undertaken in the city of Kharkiv in order to critically address the structural factors and models with which to assess the level of corruption in Ukraine. We aim to facilitate ongoing discussion regarding effective anti-corruption reforms.

Ukraine and the fight against domestic corruption

The Maidan Revolt engendered a real hope that endemic corruption in Ukrainian politics and society would be tackled seriously. Such a hope was, however, soon disappointed. Freedom House (2017) reported that since the revolution of 2014, anti-corruption reforms had not progressed according to the expectation of local reformers and the international community. "Corruption still permeates the state, and it is clear that the political will at the top of the government has not been sufficient to dismantle the old system" (Ibid.). The Ukrainian public still rated corruption as the nation's most serious problem. 44% of people interviewed by the Fund for Democratic Initiatives (2017) considered corruption as its most serious problem, while 90% believed that corruption was widespread. In the same study the most corrupt institutions were identified as being the courts, the Verkhovna Rada (the Parliament of Ukraine), the Prosecutor's Office, and the Government. Only the church and NGOs received higher ratings in terms of trust (*ibid.*). For many ordinary Ukrainians, it is precisely the political will to address and tackle corruption that is lacking. A factor that makes the fight against corruption ever more difficult is the continuing armed conflict in the east of the country and the consequent increasing number of cases of corruption related to that conflict (Markovska and Serdyuk, 2018).

Among significant changes identified by the Freedom House in 2017 was the initiative of Ukrainian civil society groups, backed by international organisations or governments (The United States, the European Union, and the International Monetary Fund), in effecting structural changes to accommodate new organisations to control corruption. For example, in 2015 the Ukrainian government established the National Anti-Corruption Bureau (NABU), an independent law enforcement organisation with significant powers to investigate high level corruption. This body works in conjunction with the Specialised Anti-Corruption Prosecution Office (SAPO) which has powers to prosecute upper level criminality. However, as Markovska and Van Duyne (2019) note "the data available (or lack of it) thus far does not show that their integrated approach is efficient and effective". Nevertheless, the budget of NABU has been increased from 486,6 mln Hrv in 2016 to 857 mln Hrv in 2018, and as of 31st March 2018 it has secured 19 convictions. For some this is considered to be a success, but others raise the issue of undue political influence to explain the relatively small number of successful prosecutions. This may point to the activity of a clandestine opposition against an intensive anti-corruption policy at a higher level. Indeed, the immediate future will be crucial for the ability of NABU to establish its credibility and independent investigative authority.

Over the past four years the Ukrainian parliament has "passed wide-ranging judicial reforms, including important constitutional changes to establish a comprehensive anti-corruption framework modelled on EU best practices" (Freedom House, 2017). The conclusion drawn by Freedom House (2017) was that as "long as Ukraine's international partners remain clear about the fundamental principles that will lead to success, and continue to back change with both short-term and long-term incentives, the country will have no choice but to press ahead with major reforms". The question remains as to how realistic is it to suggest that the progress against Ukrainian domestic corruption will in fact continue even when the international partners withdraw from Ukraine?

For an answer to this question we refer to the study conducted by Mungiu-Pippidi (2015) who analysed different understandings of the causal mechanisms of corruption, and the policy initiatives employed in their suppression. Mungiu-Pippidi (2015) argues that there are at least three distinct models used to explain the rationale behind corruption control initiatives:

1. structural factors that are facilitated by the external events (for example financial crises or war);
2. institutional legal instruments and the establishment of a legal framework to fight corruption;
3. corruption control as one element in a wide spectrum of economic reforms.

In order to understand the 'what works agenda', we need to go beyond attempts at control and look at the social, political and geographical setting of a particular country that facilitates corruption (Ibid.), consequently, Mungiu-Pippidi (2015) elaborates on structural factors such as size of population, ethnic diversity, the existence of a principle of ethic universalism (equality before the law) and regional variation in living conditions and rates of modernisation (including political modernisation). Her purpose is to determine whether developing countries can impose "a superstructure of rational and legal administration" (p.97) in order to create an environment conducive to good governance and the application of the measures demanded by anti-corruption reform. Mungiu-Pippidi (2015) identifies a problem in the process of modernisation enforced from above that has the potential to create significant discord between official norms, and how society operates (*ibid.*). By ratifying the UNCAC, Ukraine has accepted the role assigned to it by the international community and continued to co-operate in the development of comprehensive institutional legal instruments (one of the three rationales behind corruption control mentioned above). However, this does not necessarily mean that "government and society are in some state of transition to modernity" implying therefore different cultural norms (*ibid.*:97). In this chapter we understand the 'transition to modernity' as being a move to principles of good governance, accountability and transparency. Many countries in the world have been 'modernised' but only a selected few have managed to implement accountability and transparency in standards of governance.

What then can be said of the impact of international anti-corruption initiatives? In response, Mungiu-Pippidi (2015) investigated institutional interventions to control corruption arguing that "the bivariate regressions show that neither of the tested anti-corruption interventions has a positive significant effect on control of corruption. The presence of an anti-corruption agency is even associated with a deterioration in the control of corruption" (p. 106). The researcher concedes that in order to study any individual country, country-specific information must be tested to understand the actual effectiveness of its relevant measures. That is why an understanding of the national context of Ukraine is very important in assessing the success of its anti-corruption measures.

In this chapter we discuss the results of a 5-year survey beginning in 2013 and concurrent with an anti-corruption movement that led to political unrest against the background of military conflict in the east of the country. In an attempt to understand the sentiment of the citizens of Kharkiv prior to, during and in the aftermath of a series of anti-corruption measures that were supported by both local enthusiasts and international donors.

Methodology

Since December 2013, five annual surveys have been conducted in Kharkiv in eastern Ukraine. The first survey was conducted in December 2013, the second in October 2014, and repeated annually in October 2015, 2016 and 2017. Each survey was conducted over a three-day period. In the 2017 survey, 662 respondents aged 16 and above were interviewed. The survey was conducted as part of the "Program for ensuring public safety and order in the territory of the Kharkiv Region for 2016-2017" implemented by the Kharkiv National University of Internal Affairs. To gather data, selected members of the general public were interviewed face-to-face for 10-15 minutes by 36 interviewers from the University of Internal Affairs using a structured paper questionnaire.

A quota sampling method was used to select respondents by demographics (sex, age) and geographical characteristics (district of residence in the city).

The selected cohort was selected to be representative of the general population of Kharkiv (population 1.451.377 as of 01-10-2017) according to age, sex and place of residence. The measurement errors at a 95% confidence limit were calculated as being: for indicators approaching 50% ± 3,94%; for indicators approaching 25% ± 3,4%; for indicators approaching 10% ± 2,36%; for indicators approaching 5% ± 1,71%.

The questionnaire includes 19 items measured by Likert scale and three sets of questions:

1. Perception of corruption (seriousness of the problem of corruption, level of corruption, assessment of the effect of corruption, readiness of respondents themselves to participate in corrupt practices, the 'image' of corruption that respondents create for themselves, personal "policy" towards bribery, ways to eliminate corruption);
2. Experience of corruption (% of Kharkiv residents who have personally experienced corruption during the contacts with 19 types of the official institutions, "bribes on demand", voluntary offer of bribes, use of personal connections, official complaint against corruption);
3. Social and demographic characteristics of participants (sex, age, education, income, district of residence).

SPSS (v 22.0) was used in statistical analysis.

Findings

In this chapter we discuss selected questions that deal with the public perception of corruption; in particular, just how do people perceive corruption, and why does this matter?

In order to understand the participants' perception of the seriousness of corruption, they were asked to answer the following question, "In your opinion, how serious is the problem of corruption in Ukraine?". Table 1 below shows their responses to this question starting 2013 onwards. In 2017, 65% of respondents believed that corruption was a serious problem in Ukraine. Interestingly, in comparison with 2013, by 2017 the number of people who held corruption to be a very serious problem was lower. Is it the case that the anti-corruption reforms in post-Maidan Ukraine started to work, or is it because the other social and political issues become more prominent?

Table 1:
How serious is the problem of corruption in Ukraine?

	2013 %	2014 %	2015 %	2016 %	2017 %	Mean
Very serious	45	53	35	39	25	39
Serious	35	30	34	32	40	34
Difficult to answer	17	13	20	17	24	18
Not serious	3	2	6	8	8	5
Absolutely not serious	0	2	4	4	2	2
100% = N	492	581	533	1016	622	-
Index*	**0,6**	**0,65**	**0,45**	**0,46**	**0,38**	-

*Index calculated by recoding responses into digital values: Very serious = +1; Serious = +0,5; Difficult to answer = 0; Not serious = -0,5; Absolutely not serious = -1. Index varies from +1 to - 1. Please note that 'difficult to answer' is important because it can change our mean (and index) by increasing the general number of respondents (our denominator). So this category must be included in the table, "difficult to answer" was therefore coded as "missing value" and excluded from further analysis.

A more visual means of understanding the trend over the last five years is by analysing the index calculated according to the responses: here +1 means the problem is "very serious" and -1 means that the problem is "not serious at all". We identify two discernible groups: one representing those who believe in the seriousness of corruption as a social issue and a smaller group who does not think there is a serious problem. It is interesting to observe that over the five years of the study there was a fluctuation in the number of respondents choosing not to give a definitive answer. It is this group of respondents that is of major interest to us. There are several ways to interpret the 'difficult to answer' entry. Some researchers argue that often the 'difficult to answer' option represents a lazy way of responding to a questionnaire (Krosnick and Presser, 2010). By contrast, we suggest that this is in fact an important indicator of public difficulty make a definitive choice. According to us, the increasing number of respondents choosing the 'difficult to answer' option might point to the emergence of new concerns in Ukrainian society where the perception of the seriousness of corruption is overshadowed by concerns about the military conflict on the one hand, and the worsening economic situation of ordinary citizens on the other. In a survey of the general public undertaken in 2018, the Fund of the Democratic Initiatives (FDI, 2018) reported that 36% of respondents assessed life in Ukraine as being difficult, and 46% as being unbearable.

Graph 1 below represents responses to the question "How would you rate the level of corruption in Ukraine and in the city of Kharkiv?" Results have been recoded into the index from 0 to 1, where 0 is "very low level of corruption" and 1 is "very high level of corruption". Index calculated by recoding answers to digital values: Very high = 1; Higher than average = 0,75; Average = 0,5; Lower than average = 0,25; Very low = 0.

Graph 1.
"How would you rate the level of corruption in Ukraine and Kharkiv?"*

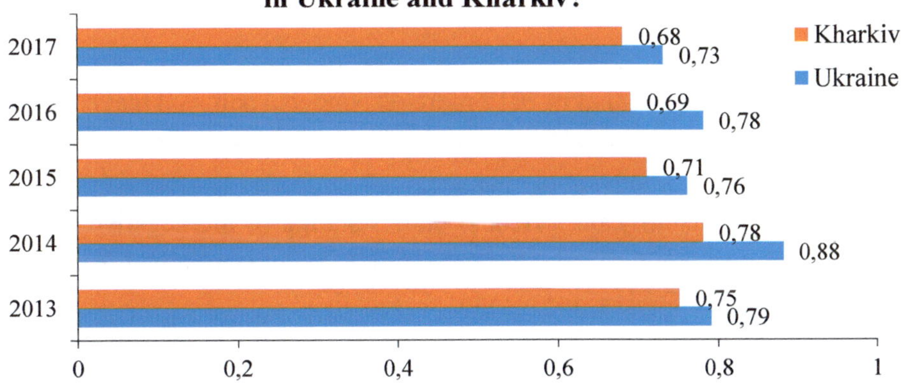

*The index estimate varies from 0 – very low level to 1 – very high level

We observe that normally the respondents from Kharkiv rated the issue of corruption as being worse for Ukraine than for their home city of Kharkiv; emphasising the corrupting influence if the outsiders rather than that of their fellow Kharkiv citizens.

Question 3 was designed to measure changes in perception of the level of corruption over the last 12 months by asking: "In your opinion, has the level of corruption changed in the last 12 months?"

Table 2.
Has the level of corruption changed in the last 12 months (%)

	2013	**2014**	**2015**	**2016**	**2017**
Increased a lot	17	17	11	9	12
Increased a little	27	19	17	19	19
Has not changed	46	46	49	43	48
Decreased a little	4	10	12	16	13
Decreased a lot	1	1	3	4	2
Difficult to answer	5	7	8	10	6
100% = N	492	581	533	1016	622
Index*	**0,29**	**0,22**	**0,11**	**0,07**	**0,13**

*Index calculated by recoding answers to digital values: Increased a lot = +1; Increased a little = +0,5; Has not changed = 0; Decreased a little = -0,5; Decreased a lot = -1; Difficult to answer = missing value. Index varies from +1 to -1.

It is interesting to note that in 2017 more respondents believed that corruption had increased (31% in total) whereas about 48% of respondents believe that the level of corruption had not changed.

In order to quantify the personal understanding of the negative effect of corruption, question 5 asked, “In your opinion, is corruption bad for the state and citizens in general or bad for you personally?”

Table 3.
Is corruption bad for citizens and state or bad for you personally?

	2013		2014		2015		2016		2017	
	Citizen %	**Person %**	**Citizen %**	**Person %**	**Citizen %**	**Person %**	**Citizen %**	**Person %**	**Citizen %**	**Person %**
es, negative npact	57	40	68	56	60	46	60	42	51	38
ather negative npact	37	42	24	19	24	26	25	26	34	37
ather no negave impact	4	10	3	13	8	15	5	12	8	14
o impact	1	5	2	9	4	9	4	11	3	7
ifficult to anwer	2	4	4	4	4	4	5	9	3	4
00% = N	492	492	581	581	533	533	1016	1016	622	622
ndex*	**0,7**	**0,4**	**0,8**	**0,5**	**0,65**	**0,4**	**0,7**	**0,4**	**0,6**	**0,41**

*Index calculated by recoding answers to digital values: Yes, negative impact = +1; Rather negative impact = +0,5; Rather no = -0,5; No impact = -1; Difficult to answer = 0. Index varies from +1 to -1.

Table 3 shows that in general, respondents believed that corruption was bad for all citizens and the state. However, with regard to themselves, they rated the seriousness of the impact of corruption across the years as being universally lower.

In order to quantify the readiness of respondents themselves to participate in corrupt practices, question 5 asked "In your opinion, can you justify bribery, unofficial services or presents, if it is important to you in solving a certain problem?"

Our Graph 2 reveals that in 2014 only 16% of respondents categorically objected to corrupt practices, but this proportion increased to 31% by 2017. However, more than half of respondents (60%) were prepared to justify corruption depending on the situation. This we believe is due to the peculiar feature of the cultural context of Ukraine.

Graph 2.
Can corruption be justified?

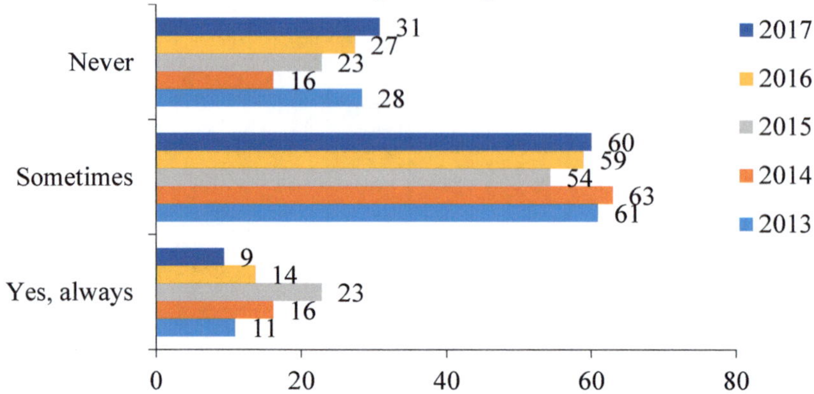

In order to understand the 'image' of corruption that respondents create for themselves we asked "In your opinion, what does corruption mean for people in society and for yourself?" Respondents were asked to select 4 answers out of a possible 8.

According to Graph 3, 40% of respondents believed in the overall negative influence of corruption and expressed an awareness that corruption has a devastating impact on society and state institutions. However, more than a third (39%) indicated that corruption was nevertheless "a quick way to solve complex problems without bureaucracy and red tape." Both opinions it seems could be held by the same respondent. This is illustrated by a fifth of respondents agreeing with the old saying "if you don't oil, you don't move" indicating that corruption is still accepted in certain situations. For example, informally settling a parking fine by negotiating and bribing the police. While evidently understanding the negative impact of corruption, the respondents revealed a surprising ambivalence to the issue.

Graph 3.
Perception of corruption
(The image of corruption that respondents create for themselves)

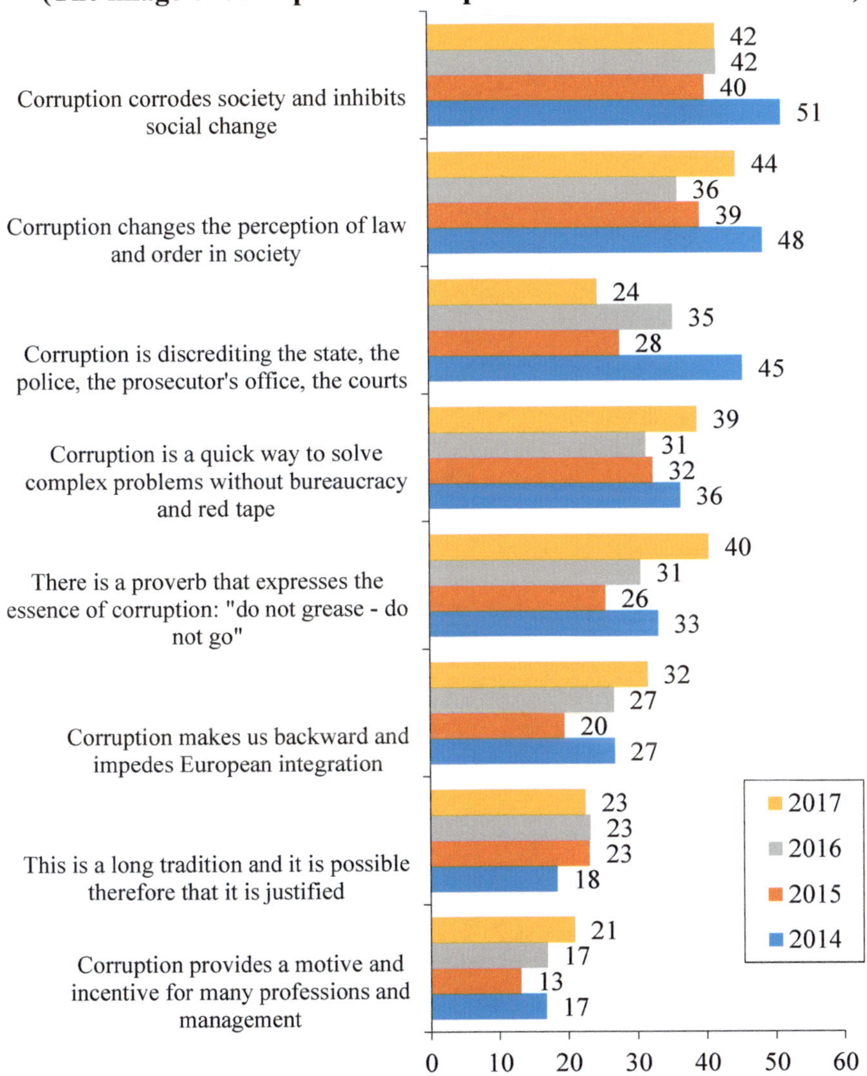

In order to understand personal conduct in relation to bribery we posed the further question: "What is your personal "policy" towards bribery?" of which the results are summarised in Graph 4.

Graph 4.
Personal "policy" towards bribery.

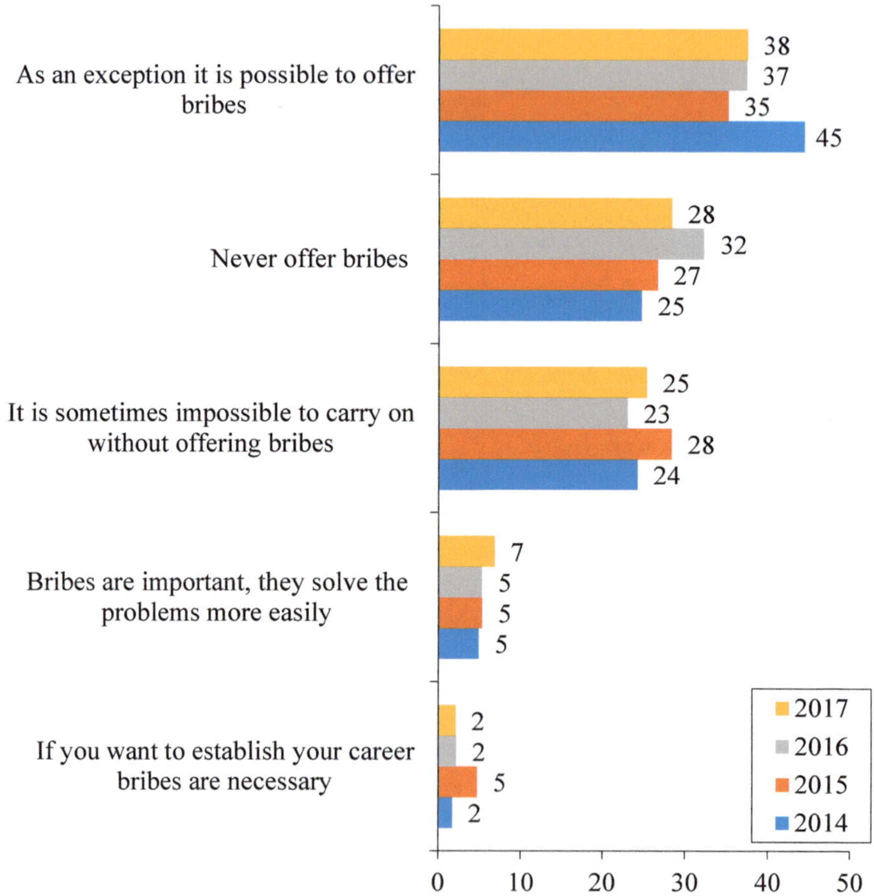

More than a third of respondents personally justified bribery, when faced with a hopeless situation (from their point of view) or where they "very much needed a result." A quarter believed that some corruption could be avoided. However, less than a third of respondents refused participation in corrupt practices and believed that bribes should never be given in any circumstances.

It is interesting to observe that around 6% of people claimed to be comfortable with corruption, and that this proportion has not changed significantly since 2016, though the percentage of those who believe that one should never offer a bribe has decreased over the same period. Overall, the respondents tend to be increasingly tolerant towards corruption.

Our next question asked "What possible steps might be undertaken to eliminate corruption"?

Graph 5.

Possible ways to eliminate corruption

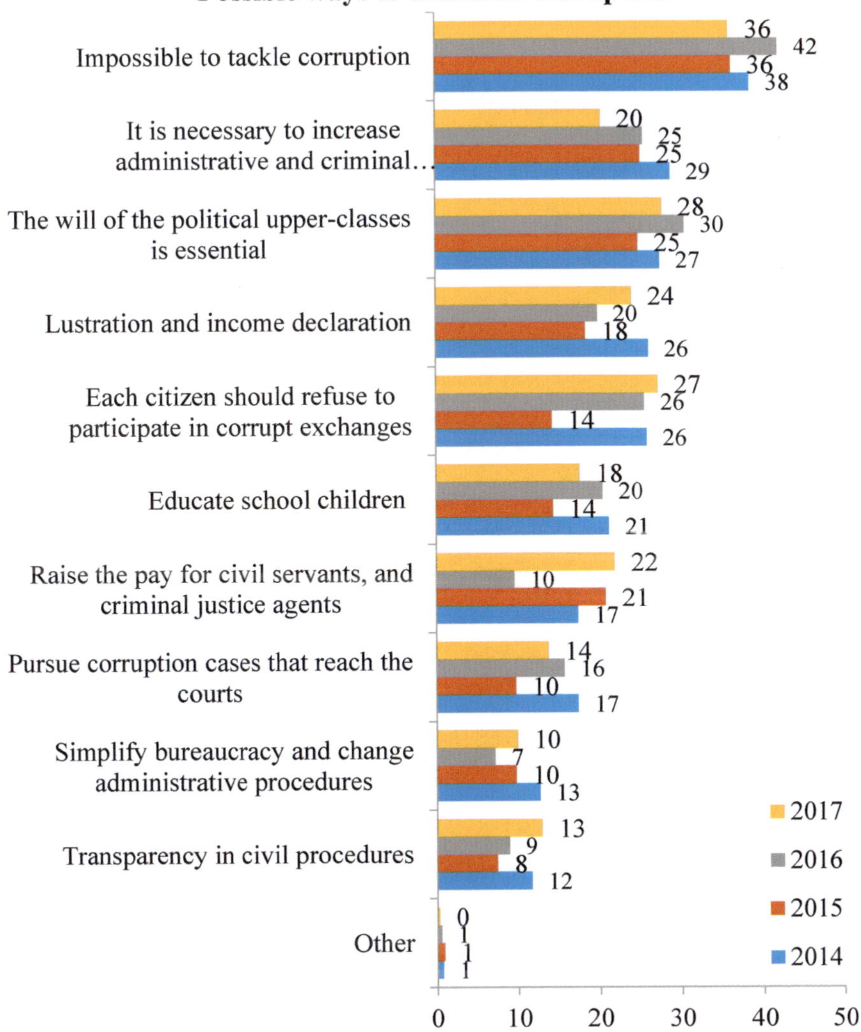

Kharkiv respondents tend to believe that corruption is practically impossible to supress (36% in 2017, 42% in 2016 and 36% in 2015) and a third of respondents believe that the authorities lack any real will to tackle corruption.

The survey also investigated respondents' personal experience of corruption. In 2017 as compared with 2016, less people reported that they had been solicited for a bribe though more reported that they had offered a bribe voluntarily. Surprisingly however, the FDU (2018) national survey reported that 60% of Ukrainians prioritised the implementation of anti-corruption reforms.

Graph 6.
Personal experience of corruption
% of Kharkiv residents who have personally experienced corruption

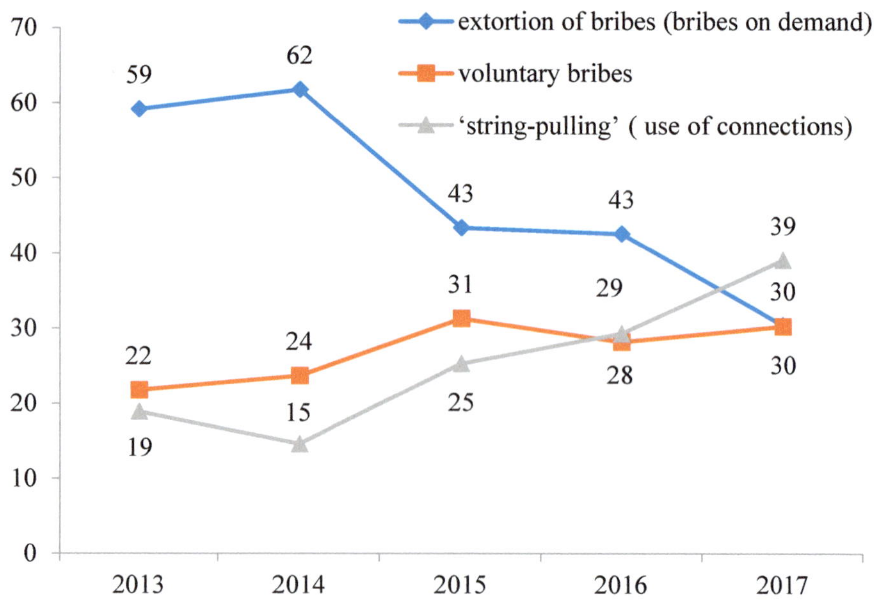

Against the background of a general reduction in the experience of "bribes on demand", there was a slight increase in the voluntary offer of bribes and a large increase in the use of personal connections. This is important, because it implies that an 'enabling network' of like-minded people of questionable integrity exists, signalling a hidden economy of corrupt exchange, which implies all previously noted forms of corruption, but one which employs them with greater caution.

The following graph shows the percentage of respondents who had personally experienced corruption and made an official complaint against it.

Graph 7.
Did you make an official complain about corruption? ("Yes", %)

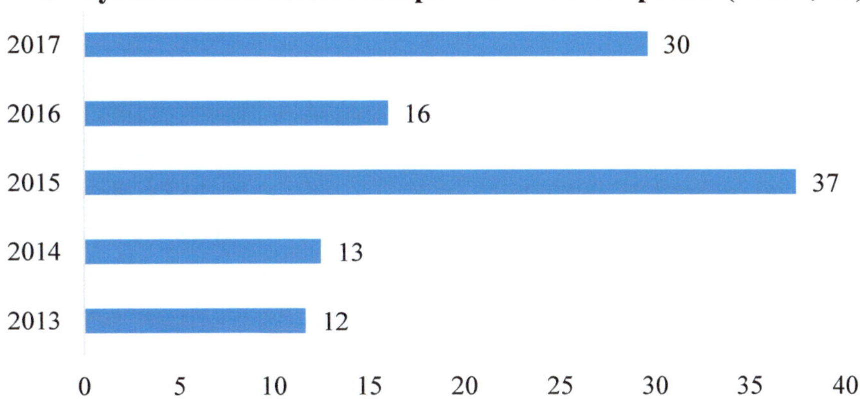

It will be noticed that the percentage of those who have complained of corruption has increased: from 16% to 30% between 2016 and 2017, showing that there are now a growing number of Ukrainians who are less tolerant to corrupt practices. Our previous two graphs provide us with some interesting material for consideration. While 39% of our respondents had themselves offered bribes on a voluntary basis, 30% of respondents had complained officially about corruption! While intolerance of corruption is growing, the same can be said of a pragmatic personal tolerance of it.

Discussion and conclusions

The 2017 Kharkiv survey highlighted significant ambiguity in public attitudes towards corruption. As stated above we have observed a growing intolerance of corrupt conduct while also accepting it as part of daily life. Mungiu-Pippidi

(2015) notes that in the context of developing countries, as in our case, this ambivalent attitude towards corruption, challenges the assumption of Western anti-corruption donors that corruption is a deviation from the rule of law and seeks to impose 'zero-tolerance' of it. We can perhaps conclude that 'pathologising' corruption has not yet been effective in Ukraine, and may not necessarily be the most expedient way to cure this malaise.

A second significant observation is that of a lack of political will in tackling corrupt practices. This issue is evidently connected with the ambiguity towards corruption noted above and the seeming acceptance of it by a third of our respondents. In 2017, 36% of Kharkiv respondents believed that it is impossible to tackle corruption. This is in agreement with a 2017 national survey that revealed 90% of Ukrainians as believing corruption to be widespread (FDI, 2017). The problem of corruption in transitional societies is often associated with political power. Unfortunately, up to the present donors have attempted to counter corruption through the encouragement of technical expertise and training (Mungiu-Pippidi, 2015). The danger with this approach in Ukraine is that the task of controlling the implementation of an anti-corruption policy is often in the charge of a political elite which is corrupt and controls access to the state resources. Since 2014 Ukraine has made substantial progress in founding and developing independent institutions to investigate corruption cases and prosecute guilty parties even if often actively opposed by. But even then it was an uphill struggle achieved because donors threatened to withdraw funding.

The third topic that deserves further study is that of the growth in *voluntary bribes* being offered by members of the general public in exchange for favourable official decisions and the use of informal links and social connections to influence that decision making. This phenomenon accords with the '*blat* system' as described by Ledeneva (2018) where corrupt practices are "associated with sociability, *i.e.* the use of personal networks, but also serve an instrumental purpose in gaining influence or accessing limited resources" (Ledeneva, 2018). In Soviet times the term was used to describe mutual assistance in gaining goods or services that were in short supply (and where financial payment was often not required). Voluntarily offered bribes in Ukraine are similarly likely to occur concerning obtaining a favourable decision from service providers. For example, extractors of amber from the fields of the western Ukraine used to offer bribes to the local police to keep their illegal extraction from the notice of the authorities (Lebed, 2015). Our 2017 Kharkiv study suggests that in a time of political instability and conflict, the employment of social connections and informal links could be seen as beneficial and less blameworthy. It is also less likely to be investigated by the new anti-corruption organisations if any exchange is classified as ‘security cleared and pre-arranged’, no matter how that exchange was achieved.

Regarding the effectiveness of anti-corruption initiatives Kaufmann (1997) argues that they must relate to available information, decisive leadership and collective action. Mungiu-Pippidi (2015) notes that while many Western donors understand the importance of civil society and the media in creating the social climate necessary to tackle corruption, not many understand the importance of collective action. Successful anti-corruption projects must be multi-dimensional and involve a broad range of actors (*ibid.*).

In 2017 Kharkiv residents no longer described corruption as the most challenging issue faced by country. There are many factors that may have influenced this change. Among them are: the worsening economic situation for ordinary Ukrainians and the continuing military conflict in the east of the country. The priority for most ordinary people is simply to survive financially in this worsening economic and political situation. Many ordinary people view the effectiveness of anti-corruption measures with more than a pinch of scepticism. On a local level respondents believe that the level of corruption in the city of Kharkiv is stable. One in five believes that corruption does not impact on their daily lives (see Table 3). A prevalent sentiment is that although corruption is bad it can be good for you personally. Consequently, in comparison with the 2016 survey by 2017 more respondents were willing to justify corrupt actions. At the same time, however, respondents increasingly argue categorically against corruption in all its aspects. We believe therefore that it is possible to argue that we are observing a degree of ‘inner polarisation’ indicated by the evident internal ambiguity in these views. On the one hand, a rejection of corruption in principle while on the other hand, tolerating it in personal practice. Those who complain about corruption often view themselves as the 'prisoners' of the phenomenon having very little ability to challenge the system in which they are forced to function.

Anti-corruption initiatives in Ukraine have in the past targeted specific individuals, and have consequently failed to challenge the institutional framework or the systems of governance within which those individuals operate. In addition, those in power have failed to present a good example of transparent governance and personal probity. In 2016 in an attempt to tackle corruption and placate western donors, specifically the International Monetary Fund, the government of Ukraine "launched the wealth database for legislators and civil servants" (Prentice, 2018). About one million civil servants had to complete an on-line e-declaration. As a result of the information being made public ordinary citizens have learned of the luxurious life style of many politicians and senior civil servants. Nevertheless, it is telling that the National Agency on Corruption Prevention that is supposed to check the e-declaration data, has never really been fully operational (*ibid.*). This half-baked implementation explains the remaining and substantial degree of scepticism on the part of the general public. It seems that although information on corrupt officials is increasingly available, systemic concrete actions to end corruption have not yet started.

In such a context one can see why voluntary bribe offering becomes a norm: the administrative structure remains the same and most newly appointed officials tend to operate under the same norm. To simply survive it becomes necessary to 'play the system'; to offer a bribe when necessary.

References

Facty, Reseller of amber: "Militiamen underestimate the weight of the seized solar stone. Do they steal it?" https://fakty.ua/217239-perekupcshik-yantarya-pravoohraniteli-zanizhayut-ves-izyatogo-solnechnogo-kamnya-eto-takaya-taktika-ili-oni-ego-prosto-voruyut, 2016.

FDI, Monitoring 2018. [On-line]. Available at: https://dif.org.ua/article/monitoring2018-osnovni-tendentsii-zmin-gromadskoi-dumki, 2018.

Freedom House, Nations in transit 2017: The false promise of populism. [On-line]. Available at: https://freedomhouse.org/report/nations-transit/nations-transit-2017, 2017.

Johnson, I., Political trust in societies under transformation: a comparative analysis of Poland and Ukraine. *International Journal of Sociology*, 2014, Volume 35, Issue 2.

Kaufmann, D., Corruption: The facts. *Foreign Policy*, 1997, No. 107, [On-line]. Available at: http://web.worldbank.org/archive/website00818/WEB/PDF/FP_SUMME.PDF, 1997.

Krosnick, J.A. and S. Presser, Questions and questionnaire design. In *Handbook of Survey Research*. London: Emerald Ltd, 2010.

Lebed, R., Камень преткновения: что делать с украинским янтарем? https://www.bbc.com/ukrainian/ukraine_in_russian/2015/11/151109_ru_s_amber_story, 2015.

Ledeneva, E., Global informality project. [On-line]. Available at: http://www.in-formality.com/wiki/index.php?title=Global_Informality_Project, 2018.

Markovska, A. and A. Serdyuk, The normalisation of arms trafficking in times of conflict: the Ukrainian experience. Van Duyne et al., *The Janus-faces of cross-border crime in Europe*. The Hague: Eleven International Publishing, 2018.

Markovska, A. and P.C. van Duyne, Power and trust networks in the organisation of crime in Ukraine. In Hufnagel, S., Moiseienko, A. (ed.). *Criminal networks and law enforcement: global perspectives on illegal enterprise*. London: Routledge, 2019.

Melgar., N., M. Rossi and T. Smith, The perception of corruption. *International Journal of Public Opinion.* 2010, Vol. 22, No.1.

Mungiu-Pippidi, A., *The quest for good governance: how societies develop control of corruption*. Cambridge: CUP, 2015.

NABU, Court dismissed from his position the suspected Director of the Lviv Armor Vehicle Factory.
https://nabu.gov.ua/en/novyny/court-dismissed-his-position-suspected-director-lviv-armor-vehicle-factory, 2017.
Prentice, A., Ukrainian asset declarations reform seen letting corrupt officials off hook. [On-line]. Available at: https://www.reuters.com/article/us-ukraine-corruption-nabu/ukrainian-asset-declarations-reform-seen-letting-corrupt-officials-off-hook/.

Police reform in Ukraine.
A reconnaissance of perceptions

Igor Sviatokum, Alexey Serdyuk and *Petrus C. van Duyne*[1]

Introduction: the need for police reform in Ukraine

After proclaiming independence in 1991, Ukraine inherited the old Soviet police system without introducing significant changes. Basically, the structure remained in place, and the first national law "*On militsiya*", adopted in 1990, while, technically, Ukraine was still a Soviet Republic, did not change anything in the ways the old and then new law enforcement body worked. The *militsiya* continued to function as a clearly militarised, heavily centralised system under the Ministry of Internal Affairs. The latter and the former were not organisationally separated, meaning that the ministry concurrently served as a central managing body of the *militsiya*, with the minister being *de facto* head of the *militsiya* (*de jure,* the relevant position did not even exist). The Soviet legacy also manifested itself in the way the performance of the *militsiya* was measured. Performance assessment was based primarily on the criminal statistics, measuring such indicators as number of registered crimes, clearance rate, conviction rate *etc.* (Markovska and Serdyuk, 2013). Indicators of the current period were compared to the relevant numbers from the previous period, making it necessary to either keep the indicators on the same level or to constantly "improve" them, but within a plausible range. This system created strong incentives for the officers to manipulate numbers in order to achieve required goals and, thus, was geared towards presenting the public with biased

---

1 The first two authors are, respectively, researcher at and deputy head of the Research Lab on Crime Enforcement of Kharkiv National University of Internal Affairs, Ukraine. Petrus C. van Duyne is Professor of criminal law (em) and visiting professor at Utrecht University, The Netherlands. The authors want to express their gratitude to Stefano Donati, Presidential Award Fellow at Northern Arizona University, whose grant made this research possible.

figures from a manipulated assessment process (Markovska and Serdyuk, 2013).

The first major document expressing serious intentions of the Ukrainian government to reform the *militsiya* is the *Resolution of the Cabinet of Ministers of Ukraine on the framework of development of the system of Ministry of Internal Affairs* in 1996. The document did not address aforementioned issues, but focusing instead on the development of the *militsiya* within the existing framework. Later, the issue of reforming the Ministry of Internal Affairs and the *militsiya* had been periodically raised (in 1996-1998, in 2003, in 2005, in 2010 *etc.*) and dropped again. While in certain cases some changes have indeed been implemented, the *militsiya* still largely retained its centralised nature, plan-based performance assessment and other features inherited from the Soviet period.

We will not attempt to analyse each of these instances in detail; instead, in this chapter we focus our attention on the two more publicised cases of reforms, namely, the attempt to abolish the traffic police (*DAI*) in 2005 and the reform of the criminal procedural law in 2012.

Two cases of the previous reform attempts

The decision to abolish the *DAI* was taken in the wake of large-scale mass protests in the autumn and winter of 2004, dubbed the Orange Revolution, and subsequent government change. As the law-enforcement agencies were widely associated with an 'old regime'[2], there existed a significant public pressure to reform them. The choice of the DAI was, in many respects, dictated by the fact that, being a branch of the public service, it had a regular contact with the citizens and was therefore important for image building. At the time, that image was bad: it was considered to be one of the more corrupt services. This

2 One of the points of discontent during the Orange revolution was the Gongadze case. In 2000, Ukrainian journalist Georgiy Gongadze was kidnapped and murdered. In the same year recordings implicating the then incumbent President Kuchma and minister of internal affairs Kravchenko in his disappearance were published, leading to the so-called *Cassette Scandal*. Four former officials of the Ministry of Internal Affairs were subsequently charged with his murder and sentenced to various terms of imprisonment. Former minister Kravchenko committed suicide not long after the Orange revolution. The case on the Gongadze murder is still open as of September of 2018.

image primarily originated from the wide-spread practice of accepting and/or soliciting bribes from the drivers in exchange for overlooking traffic violations. Still, it is worth pointing out that the contemporary studies, while confirming a significantly high level of corruption in the DAI, hardly singled out this branch of service as uniquely problematic. For example, Martynenko (2004), surveyed criminal records of the charges filed against the *militsiya* officers, and showed that while the DAI indeed contributed significantly to the number of criminal cases opened against its officers (58 of 528 in 2002) and the number of officers that were convicted (11 of 78 in 2002), it was hardly the most or the only problematic branch of the police service. For instance, the criminal investigation branch of the *militsiya* at the same period had 99 cases opened against its officers and 22 officers convicted (Martynenko, 2004: 79).

The reform policy followed on this pressure does not look very consistent. It went as follows. On July 19, 2005, the President issued a decree, ordering the liquidation of the DAI and split it into two separate services: the patrol service and the road *militsiya*. While the patrol service was indeed established, the DAI itself had *never* been liquidated, and continued to exist (although in a truncated form). No official explanation had been provided, but already in May 2006, the Minister of Internal Affairs stated that the reform of the DAI had been finished. Despite that, in September of the same year he argued, that the President meant the reform of the DAI, not its liquidation. Thus, the much announced liquidation of the DAI did not happen at that time: it continued to exist, although, with some organisational changes and in a significantly reduced size.

While no reasons were given, the most plausible explanation for not abolishing the DAI, is that due to that lack of planning, sudden changes in the traffic police service would have made driving significantly less safe, increasing the number of traffic accidents. This was emphasized by Zozulia (2008) in his article on this reform. He points out, that according to official data of the Ministry of Internal Affairs, the adopted changes "significantly decreased the efficiency of the DAI" (Zozulia, 2008: 168).

The second intended reform, that of the Criminal Procedural Law in 2012, while not reforming the *militsiya* directly, affected policing significantly, especially the criminal investigative branch of *militsiya.* This reform was aimed at replacing the old Criminal Procedural Code, inherited from the Soviet times. In this case, the reform showed a much better planning, in both formulating its aims and drafting of relevant bills. Its primary goal was to make the criminal procedure more transparent and fair. It addressed, for example, the issue of the officers refusing to open criminal cases, mentioned as a quite widespread irregularity in the study by Martynenko we quoted earlier (Martynenko, 2004: 79). By making rules of crime registration significantly more stringent such that refused cases surface easier and quicker thereby preventing unaccountable discretion.

It is noteworthy that the second stage of the reform envisioned the adoption of a new classification of criminal offences: there are crimes *per se* being more serious, and criminal misdemeanours representing petty offences. Consequently, the Criminal Procedural Code provides for much simpler procedures for the investigation of criminal misdemeanours and stipulates the establishment of a separate service to deal with them. However, the provisions of this second stage were adopted only in November of 2018 and will become effective in 2020. Until then, both petty and serious crimes have to be processed by the same criminal procedure, increasing the workload per officer dramatically. Therefore, while the necessity and the conditions of this reform were stated much clearer than for the first one, its implementation stopped halfway, leading to ambivalent results at best. In various branches it increased the workload.

The history of these two policies illustrate a disturbing tendency of the police reforms to either evaporate because of bad planning, unrealistic goals and problems of implementation (as it happened with the DAI), or somewhere in the middle of the process they grind to a halt due to changes in political priorities (as it happened with the reform of criminal proceedings). In addition, to make things worse, virtually every change of the Ministry of Internal Affairs itself went hand in hand with staff reduction, the current police reform not excepted. While, admittedly, some units seemed to have been overstaffed, this correlation between reforms and dismissals did anything but improving the motivation of the officers for further reforms.

Therefore, frequent 'reforms' that brought few improvements to the police, have given rise to an attitude of suspicion to further changes: a mixture of scepticism ("it's just changing a nameplate"), fear for their position and irritation with the meddling from 'above' *etc*., or, in general, a 'reorganisation fatigue'.

The Maidan and the current police reform

The push to the current reform came under tragic circumstances. While there existed a public pressure for comprehensive reforms in 2005, the events of the winter of 2014 made it much more vocal and strong. The events on Maidan led to a critical point, where trust in the law enforcement agencies plummeted, making at least some reaction from the post-revolutionary government necessary.[3] We should mention, though, that while driving policy-makers to implement police reform, this public pressure also created its own challenges. The necessity to react does not equal to understanding of what kind of a reform is needed. Indeed, the first measures of the new government look like *ad hoc* decisions; symbolically, one of the first measures taken, in fact, was re-abolition of the DAI (this time, for good).

The objections against the old *militsiya* system were summarised in the policy document of the current reform, *Strategy of the Development of the Agencies of Internal Affairs*, adopted by the Cabinet of Ministers of Ukraine on 22 October, 2014. After reflecting upon the role of law enforcement agencies in the tragic events of the winter of 2013-2014, the document stated that "the post-Soviet militarised model of the Ministry of Internal Affairs continued to cultivate an image of an 'exclusive crime fighter', whose success, in general, did not depend on the public support, and whose efficiency was measured by an antiquated system of quantitative indicators of the crime fighting". The document also highlighted such problems as "systematic underfunding", "extensive system of internal corruption", substandard labour conditions and lack of transparency and accountability in the *militsiya* and Ministry of Internal Affairs in general.

These considerations led to essential differences of the current reform compared to the previous attempts. The first of them is its scope. Where previously reforms were implemented piecemeal, being regulated primarily by the secondary legislation (governmental resolutions, presidential decrees *etc.*), the current reform envisions a more comprehensive overhaul of the policing

3 The Maidan Revolution is called after the square in the centre of Kyiv, where people came together to protest against President Yanukovc' refusal to sign the Association Agreement with the EU: the Euromaidan movement. In February 2014 this led to serious violence with the riot police followed by the ousting of Yanukovyc.

praxis, the main points of which have already been enshrined in the new Law on the National Police.

The second difference is that the new law establishes the police as a separate body, under oversight of, but separate from, the Ministry of Internal Affairs. The law stipulates that the main tasks of the police is to provide police services, representing a dramatic shift towards a citizen-oriented policing rather than acting as an agent of state repression. To this end, a new branch of the police has been established: the Patrol Police. This new branch is intended to both bring 'fresh blood' into the force and to open a window to a closer police-citizen cooperation. The establishment of this branch included a well-publicised recruiting campaign, aimed at inviting young people to serve in the police and promoting reform to the general public.

Public confidence and the new look of the Patrol Police

On closer examination, though, the reform suffers from the same slow and often reluctant implementation, as the previous reforms. The most relevant example for us is the intended introduction of the new system of police *performance assessment* based on *public confidence* in the police, which is another important dimension of the shift towards a citizen-oriented policing. The law on National Police adopted in 2015 (art. 11 par. 3) stipulates that the level of public confidence in the police is the main criterion of the police performance assessment. The law also stipulates that the level of public confidence is measured by independent sociological services in the manner determined by the Cabinet of Ministers of Ukraine. However, the regulation by the

Ukrainian government that established procedure for such measurement has only been adopted in the winter of 2018. Therefore, for nearly three years the new system of performance assessment required by the law existed only on paper. In the meantime, the police had either to use the old evaluation system or come up with *ad hoc* solutions. This ambivalence is at odds with the idea of using the judgments of public opinion as a proper evaluation tool for police performance.

In itself, the direct formulation of this system in the Law on the National Police represents a large step forward. This idea, of course is hardly new in the 'West'; neither is it new for the Ukrainian academia. Publications presenting public opinion as an important source for police performance evaluation existed as early as in 2005 (*e.g.*, Maltsev, 2005).

Despite this lacuna, a series of surveys in the Kharkiv Region spanning 2013-2018 should be mentioned (Serdyuk, 2018: 45). In 2013, the percentage of those who trusted or "somewhat trusted" their local *pre*-reform *militsiya* division in the region was 24 and 39% opposed to 10 and 13% of those who distrusted or 'somewhat' distrusted it.

By 2018 only 15% trusted the police with additional 40% "somewhat" trusting it. On the other hand, the percentage of those who distrusted or "somewhat" distrusted it decreased slightly to 6 and 11%. Asked specifically about the trust to their local Patrol Police (*ibid.*: 50), 11% stated they trusted it, 45% "somewhat" trusted the new division; 3 and 11% distrusted or "somewhat" distrusted it. While we must caution, that this survey represents only one region of Ukraine, it shows that the reform still has a long way to go before it reaches its goals in building public trust in the police.

On the whole, the current reform is not doomed to failure by itself. Nevertheless, its implementation shares much of the same characteristics, which led to the less than spectacular results. One of them, arguably, is lack of regard by the policy makers of the effects that reforms have on the day-to-day tasks and working conditions of the police officers. How do they experience these changes? As they have to carry out the reform, it is important to learn their perceptions. Another important reason to gauge the perception of the reform by the police officers is, of course, the fact that the aforementioned shift towards more citizen-oriented policing depends largely on the rank-and-file making efforts to implement these changes in their day-to-day work. This led to the research question of how the goals and changes due to this reform are perceived by the police officers.

Methodology

Questionnaire and data collection

From spring to autumn 2017 a survey was conducted which included the use of two data collection methods:

1. Web-based survey on the Qualtrics online survey platform in spring 2017 resulting in 194 responses;
2. Face-to-face interviews during the autumn 2017, with a structured paper questionnaire filled by 385 respondents personally and anonymously. The participation was voluntary.

The composition of the paper questionnaire consisted of 41 closed questions (indicators) with 75 items (generally Likert type ordinal or interval scales). The web-based questionnaire included additional open-ended questions, the Herzberg motivational scale and personality questionnaire Big Five Inventory (BFI-10). The outcomes of these additional subjects are not discussed in this paper.

In this paper we focus on respondents' answers concerning the following clusters of content:

1. The respondents' perception of the police reform with an emphasis on the interaction with the public;
2. The respondents' perception of the police organisation as a 'fair employer', particularly where it concerns the protection of social and labour rights;
3. Working conditions as a background, comprising salary as well as the availability of office facilities and tools.[4]

For the processing and analysis of data the statistical software package SPSS Statistics v.25 and Microsoft Office Excel were used.

This survey built on preceding investigations carried out between 2013 and 2017 as mentioned above. In these surveys, respondents from the police had been asked to express their opinion about the importance of public trust for the police. Now police officers were asked to formulate their perception of their interactions with the public as well as their view on the police reform and their police organisation.

---

4 An analysis of the full range of questions will be provided by the final report of this project.

The sample

The intended sample size was 500, but in the end, a sample size of 552 was achieved. The determination of the intended sample size was based on the data about number of police officers per branch and a previously conducted research project in 2007 devoted to the same topic: the police reform and social guarantees for the police. The approximate number of police officers in 2017 was 8000 and for the end of 2018 it was reduced to 7.892.[5] The number of patrol police officers by staffing schedule in 2017 is 1.478, but the actual number in 2018 was 1.359.[6] Our total sampling population is approximately 9.300. The number of selected respondents per branch is based on the estimate of the general number of positions per specific branch. An estimate is necessary here, because the police service in the Kharkiv region does not provide public information about the number of actually employed officers by specific branch. The approximate sampling characteristics were kept similar to those of the 2007 research project in order to enable the comparison between the 'old' militia and the 'new' police force (Bielousov, Kobzin, Sviezhentseva, Serdyuk *et al*, 2008). The adoption of the face-to-face paper-based method of data collection in the second stage of research was made necessary because of the low response rate achieved in the web-based survey.

The sampling method implemented in this study is a Quota sampling per branch of police service. We use only one inclusion criterion for the subsets of participants: the branch of the police service. There is no exclusion criteria or any restrictions based on demographic or socio-economic characteristics (*e.g*., age, sex, ethnicity, socioeconomic status).

The sample from the Ukraine National Police of the Kharkiv region consists of the following branches which participated in the survey.

---

5 From official website https://hk.npu.gov.ua/about/struktura/shtat-ta-chiselnist.html

6 From the response for official letter: https://ukr.lb.ua/news/2019/01/16/417300_nedokomplekt_patrulnoi_politsii.html?fbclid=IwAR1uQHR-GfCfeEr75Cq2dLfU3Itj_pxgA65jbEXaj0dq0MYzxqjvWlkciTlg

Table 1
Respondents by branch of service according to the 2017 questionnaire

Type police service	Frequency	Valid %
Criminal police	114	21,3
Pre-trial investigation	47	9,5
Department for prevention	46	9,3
Regional Police Directorate	42	8,5
SWAT*	23	4,7
Battalion Kharkiv*	25	5,1
East Oriental Corps*	25	5,1
Other division Pol	27	5,5
Patrol Police	144	29,2
Total	493	100,0

Missing values: 59

**In the later analysis the Battalions and the SWAT have been dropped after an initial test: they have more defence tasks and little interaction with the public.*

From the reform perspective (more citizen orientation of the police), the most important division is between the Patrol Police and the other service branches: the Patrol Police is intended to have more direct interaction with the people. This branch has its own chain of command and is not a part of the Regional Directorates that act as territorial branches of the police at the oblast level. This does not imply that the other branches were not touched by the police reform. Changes in education and health care are mentioned as well as the bringing together of the functions of operations officers and criminal investigators. How deep that reform penetrated into the branches other than the Patrol Police is difficult to determine. Some experiments, such as crime mapping, have been carried out in these branches, but systematic surveys or evaluation of these changes are lacking. Although in the police reform the Patrol Police has a special place, we will compare their perceptions and background variables of its officers with those of the staff of the other branches.

Findings

a. Perception of the police reform by officers

1. Understanding and the 'right direction'

The first question concerns the general level of understanding of the reform: its tasks and objectives as far as the respondents themselves declared to understand the reform, whether fully, partly or not at all. As this implies some scale of understanding, we designed the following levels of understanding scale:

- Completely understand the reform
- Understand the reform somewhat
- Somewhat don't understand it
-
- Don't understand the reform at all

Naturally, the two middle categories are fluid, but they still represents the opinion of the respondent of what he or she thinks to understand. We did not examine his or her *real* knowledge of the reform, only their *perception* of their understanding.

Table 2

Self-assessed understanding within the police branches.

Police branch / *Level of understanding*	Crime. police %	Pre-trial invest. %	Prevention %	Reg. pol. direct. %	Patrol Police %	Other division %	Total N	%
Completely	33	33	30	36	54	37	168	*40*
Somewhat yes	12	16	35	26	24	41	93	*22*
Diff to answer	26	36	22	19	13	11	85	*20*
Somewhat no	20	11	11	12	8	11	53	*13*
Not at all	9	4	2	7	1	0	18	*4*
Total = 100%	114	45	46	42	143	27	417	*100*
Missing 62								
Index*	**1.92**	**2.21**	**2.19**	**2.12**	**2.49**	**2.29**	**2.27**	

*For the illustrative purposes, we converted percentages into indices on the scale from 0 to 3 (don't understand = 0, rather don't understand = 1, somewhat understand = 2, understand completely = 3, in order to prevent dilution of the index, the option 'difficult to answer' was treated as a missing value).

It is essential that the police officers across all branches of service have at least some knowledge of the reform and its goals as they are the ones who will, ultimately, implement its principles in their daily work. In the case of the Patrol Police, a high level of understanding follows logically from the fact that this branch was established in the course of the reform; additionally, the training of the recruits for the Patrol Police included explanation of the goals of the police reform. Table 2 provides an overview of the police branches and the self- assessment of understanding. As the Table indicates most respondents think they have a fair (22%) to a full understanding (40%) of the reform process. This score is somewhat veiled because 20% of the respondents found it difficult to answer this question. This option was inserted for the respondents who do not feel that they can express their opinion or knowledge of the reform coherently.

Apart from that, most Patrol Police officers rated the assessment of their knowledge complete (54%) or more or less sufficient (24%). The next highly self-assessing categories are the division of pre-trial investigation (33% full understanding and 16% rather well understanding) and department of prevention (30% full understanding and 35% rather well understanding). Both have a significant score of "difficult to answer", however.

This self-assessment of understanding gains meaning if connected to a number of functional 'features' of the respondents: age, length of service or kind of police division or education. Is there a relation between length of service or age of the respondents? There was indeed a small but significant 'age' or 'years of service' effect on the understanding levels: the group that expressed complete understanding has a mean age of 30,3 years compared to 33 years in the category of "not understand at all": an inverse significant correlation between age and expressed level of understanding (r = -0,117; sign. 0,001, two sided). The same observation is made concerning the *length of service*, which as a time variable is not independent from the basic age variable. Indeed, there is again an inverse relation between service time and understanding: respondents reporting a "complete understanding" have an average service length of 8,6 years, compared to 11,5 years for the 'not-understanding' group and 12,9 service years for the 'not fully understand' group. So there is a length-of-service effect in the understanding of the reform, but again the correlations are small, though statistically significant (Spearman rho = -0,197; 0,001 two sided).

The following question of interest concerns the perceived change: reform without awareness of change does not look very satisfying. However, the general 'change perception' may conceal the more specific effects on various aspects of the police tasks and organisation.

Table 3.
What changes did the reform bring to your work?

	Sign. impr. %	Some impr. %	No change %	Little worse %	Sign. worse %	Hard to answer %	Ind.*	Total N= 100%
Organisation of work	21	28	30	7	8	7	*0.25*	473
Legal frame	10	23	37	9	15	5	*0.02*	466
Coop. police	12	24	37	8	16	3	*0.05*	465
Coop. publ. agencies	10	20	47	8	10	5	*0.07*	473
Coop. citiz.	9	18	48	8	10	7	*0.05*	470
Salary	14	23	41	8	10	4	*0.12*	464
Supplies	15	36	21	8	13	6	*0.17*	469
Social guarantees	5	8	44	10	26	7	*-0.25*	466
Legal safeguard	5	6	42	10	30	7	*-0.29*	469
Average	11	21	39	8	15	6		

*For illustrative purposes, we converted percentages into indices on the scale from -1 to 1 (significant worsening = -1, some worsening = -0.5, no change = 0, some improvement = +0.5, significant improvement = +1, in order to prevent dilution of the index, the option 'hard to answer' was treated as a missing value).

The first interesting finding is that on average 39% of the respondents thought they experienced no change in their organisation or their working environment. There is one exception: the provision of *supplies*. Supplies, in this case, mean all the equipment and facilities necessary for the police officers to perform their duties (See Table 10). For 51% of the respondents this implied an improvement: for 15% a significant one and for 36% only a minor improvement. Still, 21% noticed a worsening.

Most approval was expressed concerning the *organisation* of their work: 21% observed a significant and 20 some improvement; the Patrol Police being most satisfied (65%) and the Department of Prevention least (33%).

The outcomes of the *cooperation* variables, one of the targets of the reform project (cooperation with other police forces, public agencies and the citizens) do not seem to meet expectations. On average 44% saw no change: least with the citizens' cooperation (48%) and best regarding the cooperation with *other police forces*, though most respondents rated this change rather modestly (24% 'somewhat'; 12% 'significantly').

It should be noted that most respondents did not express much satisfaction about *personal guarantees*, whether social or legal. Around 44% saw no change and on average 26% mentioned even a significant worsening.

Using the index values to gauge perception of the changes by the different branches of service, yielded the following picture. Officers from the Patrol Police were the most satisfied about changes to the organisation of work (0,42), legal framework (0,15), cooperation with other police divisions (0,28), cooperation with other public agencies (0,17), cooperation with the citizens (0,16), salary (0.24) and supplies (0,22). When it comes to the spheres where the majority of the respondents claimed deterioration (social and legal guarantees), the least dissatisfied were respondents of the Pre-trial Investigation (-0,15) and department of prevention (-0,19) respectively. In general, it seems that the Patrol Police tend to regard the changes better than their colleagues. This also corresponds with the breakdown of the index values by the length of service. Officers with the shorter term of service (especially those serving less than 3 years) tend to view changes more positively than the officers who served longer. This can be contributed to the Patrol Police officers' average years of service: 5 years compared to 10 years of the whole sample. The notable exception is the situation with the supplies, where, in fact, the officers who served more than 20 years showed the largest value of the index.

These findings raise the question whether the respondents consider this project going into the right direction. Taken all the respondents together, one third thought the reform went fully or partly into the right direction. Another third thought the opposite, while 32% thought it difficult to answer this question. To what extent this affected the motivation is not easy to determine. Staying or leaving the police force may be an indicator of motivation. One would expect that those who thought the project went into the wrong direction would more frequently say that they would leave the service. In fact, there was such a tendency: respondents who questioned the right direction also indicated a bigger willingness to leave the police in the coming 1-3 years. However, the correlation (Spearman rho) between these variables is low (0,108) but just significant (0,025). Indeed, the opinion about the direction seems to yield little more than this trend.

As the participating police branches may have different interests, we inspected the outcomes of the 'branch of service' variable. In total, only 8% of the respondents thought the project was going into the right direction, with little variation between the police units (range: 6% Patrol Police and 9% pre-trial investigation). 24% thought the project went 'rather or somewhat' into the right direction, a modest judgement. A large part of the Patrol Police (38%) expressed this meagre valuation, followed by the pre-trial investigation (24%). There is a confusing 'knowledge effect' already presented in Table 2: of the 75 respondents who said they did not (fully) understand the project, 59 (79%) of them still thought it did not go into the right direction. This, however, could be explained by the fact that, while these officers do not understand the reform, they still feel its consequences in their day-to-day jobs, which they do not like or, otherwise, do not see any changes they would expect from the reform.

It should be noted that around a third of the respondents did not know how to answer these questions. This is in contrast to the relatively low percentage of the officers who did not know how to answer the questions about the *specific* changes to their work, ranging only from 3 to 7 % (see Table 4). One possible interpretation of this phenomenon could be that instead of the big picture, envisioned by the authors of the reform, police officers themselves are more focused on the more mundane aspects of their job.

2. Perception of police tasks and citizens

Having surveyed the officers' understanding of the reform project and the evaluation of its direction, the question should be raised how this relates to one of the key objectives: increasing public confidence in the police. By the nature of this survey – police perceptions – this relationship cannot be assessed directly as the research project does not contain a parallel citizen opinion survey. Instead, the respondents were asked whether they were of the opinion that public trust in the police is an adequate criterion to assess the officers' work. This question relates closely to the understanding of the reform by police officers, as reorienting policing towards a more service-based model is one of the basic principles of the reform.The respondents answered to this question relatively positive: 17% thought that this was "completely" the case and 31% "to a certain extent". However, 20% thought that the public trust is rather not an indicator of the efficiency of policing, and 6% strongly disagreed with the notion that their work can be adequately assessed by measuring the public trust.

This is a positive finding, which should also be reflected in the related '*co-operation with citizen*' variable as presented in Table 4. However, only 9% of the respondents answered positive to this related question about '*citizen cooperation*': 9% thought it "significantly improved" and 18% "somewhat". That is moderate compared to the finding that 48% of the respondents reported *no change* while 18% saw the cooperation worsening (7% could not answer this question). For this reason, we combined the two variables and calculated their correlation. The cross-tabulation is presented in Table 4. It reveals a tendency to rate the importance of the public confidence higher when there is also a significant improvement in cooperation as indicated. However, there were many respondents who felt on the one hand, that public trust adequately assesses the quality of their work, while on the other hand, that the cooperation with the citizens had become worse. Indeed, the Spearman's rho correlation is weak, though statistically significant (0,149; 2 tailed significant 0,002). Some of the branches differed widely on this variable: for example, 18% of the Criminal Police mentioned a significant worsening of the cooperation but 31% of the Patrol Police noted some improvement and 11% a significant improvement.

Table 4

Cooperation police-citizen by reflected confidence

Coop. Cit.	Sign.	Insign.	No	Little	Much	Diff.	Total	
Confidence	impr. %	impr. %	change %	worse %	worse %	to an-swer %	N	%
Sign. impr.	34	19	15	6	7	0	72	*16*
Insign. impr.	31	45	32	15	24	14	143	*32*
Diff. to an-swer	21	18	27	45	27	50	118	*26*
Little worse	9	12	24	27	30	29	92	*20*
Much worse	4	7	4	6	11	7	25	*6*
Total = 100%	56	108	169	33	70	14	450	*100*
%	*12*	*24*	*38*	*7*	*16*	*3*	*100*	

Missing values: 29

We may conclude that the respondents were moderately satisfied with the improvement of cooperation and that there are reasons to deduce that this influences their acceptance of the importance of the public trust in their work. However, the relation is not that strong that it justifies the assumption of a stronger causality.

The questionnaire also asked for other facets of the police citizen interaction, as far as perceived by the respondents. Two questions addressed two almost opposing motivations or responses related to the public-police interaction: (1) *avoiding* complaints from the citizens and (2) *gaining* approval by the citizens.

In the first case, we can assume that the importance of gaining trust from citizens translates into the professional and proper conduct that avoids evoking complaints. Indeed, 130 respondents (28%) indicated that in their work they "keep this constantly in mind". 114 respondents (24%) said to have this principle "often in mind". Both subsets were also sensitive to what we call the 'confidence effect', as presented in Table 5.

Table 5

Avoiding complaints broken down by citizens' confidence

Avoid complaint / **Confidence**	Constantly %	Often %	Rarely %	Never %	Diff. to answer %	Total N	%
Completely	25	12	14	18	6	75	*16*
Somewhat	31	38	35	16	25	143	*31*
Diff. to answer	21	28	28	19	47	121	*26*
Rather not	21	17	18	32	17	93	*20*
Not at all	3	5	4	14	6	6	6
Total	130	114	116	62	36	458	100
%	*28*	*24*	*25*	*14*	*8*	100	

Missing values: 21

More than half of the 130 respondents who said to avoid complaints from citizens were aware of the importance of the public confidence (25% "completely" and 31% "somewhat"). However, 14% of the respondents who rarely paid attention to avoiding complaints still reported they "completely" thought the public confidence is an important yardstick of their work, with another 35% of this subset stating it is a "somewhat" important yardstick. Indeed, the correlation of the complaint variable with the public confidence variable is low: Spearman rho, 0,153, though 0,001 statistically significant. A similar low correlation is found with the *cooperation* variable of citizens with the police: Spearman rho, 0,117, significant at 0,013.

Relating the avoidance variable to the particular branches of service, it was observed that the Criminal Police was most keen to avoid complaints: 56%; the Department of Prevention the least: 31%. This may be a function of the kind of tasks these branches perform, however. The Criminal Police, acting under the stringent rules of criminal procedure, face much more significant risks because of citizens' complaints, than the Prevention Department, whose officers more often deal with administrative cases.

A stronger correlation was found between the perception of public confidence and the need to obtain positive feedback from citizens: Spearmen rho 0,272; significance 0,000. Those who were most sensitive to public confidence (59% 'completely') were constantly aware of the need of positive feedback. However, 33% who said they rather did not think of public confidence still were constantly aware of the need of positive feedback. Between the need of feedback and kind of service there was no significant correlation.

Table 6

Citizens' confidence broken down by need of positive feedback

Citizens' confidence / **Need feed-back**	Completely %	Somewhat %	Diff. to answer %	Rather not %	Not at all %	Total N	%
Constantly	59	28	25	33	15	148	*33*
Often	25	49	29	22	23	149	*33*
Rarely	13	18	29	23	35	100	*22*
Never	0	4	6	16	19	32	*7*
Diff. to answer	3	2	11	7	8	26	*6*
Total	75	144	118	92	26	455	*100*
%	*16*	*32*	*26*	*20*	*6*	*100*	

Missing values 24

In general, the respondents displayed an awareness of the public confidence as a reflection of the quality of their professional conduct, the importance to avoid complaints and the importance of feedback. However, we have no yardstick to determine whether this is a result of the police reform itself. The highest score of "completely reflects police conduct" with 16% of the respondents (see Table 6, first column) is certainly modest. The other variables have a higher score, but the correlations between the variables is modest. Though there is a tendency, there is certainly no clear pattern, let alone a causality.

3. Some material and organisational background facets

While the targets of the police reform are to a large extent of a social, organisational and institutional (cooperation with other police forces and civil institutions) nature, attention should also be devoted to the perception of the facets of the tangible working environment. Though officers may rationally recognise the need for reform and express their appreciation of many positive aspects, their perception of the working environment may have more influence on their motivation than politically correct statements about reform themes. Moreover, as observed earlier, police officers tend to have opinions that are more related to the day-to-day job conditions than to the more general aspects of the reform.

This is a broad angle, which for the purpose of this chapter must be narrowed to what we assume is motivationally relevant. Two aspects stand out:

a. Material and legal labour conditions;
b. Protection of health and position.

The distinction is a matter of convenience: protection can be interpreted as a labour condition and the other way round.

a. The perception of material and legal working conditions

Obviously, the general perception of working conditions are important: it is the 'mental frame', within which other perceptions are ordered. In this research, the mental frame consists of the answers to the question about *fair labour conditions*. The majority of the answers to this question pointed clearly into one direction: of the 443 respondents 170 said they experience "no" and 95 "rather no" fair labour conditions (38% and 21%). Only 38 (9%) rated their labour conditions as fully fair. Asked for more precision 71% stated that they think their social and labour rights are violated.

A fairly strong correlation was found between the perception of the fairness of the working conditions and the perception of the violations of labour and social rights: Spearmen rho -0,468; significance 0,000. 82% of those who consider their working conditions unfair responded also that their labour and social rights are violated; of those who consider their working conditions fair only 26% reported no labour and social rights violations (with an additional 18% responding "somewhat no").

Table 7
Fairness of labour conditions against labour and social rights violations

Fair conditions	Yes	Somewhat	Somewhat no	Not at all	Total	
Rights violated	%	%	%	%	N	%
Yes	21	16	34	82	148	*38*
Somewhat	34	38	42	13	149	*34*
Somewhat no	18	43	22	1	100	*24*
No	26	4	2	4	32	*5*
Total	38	140	170	95	446	*100*
%	*9*	*32*	*38*	*21*	*100*	

Missing values: 33

a1. Getting paid

We assume that one type of violations of rights impacting directly on the officers' perception concerns the payment of salaries: do they get their full legal pay? This question was answered negatively by 29% of the respondents while 45% said they did not know, both remarkably high numbers for this important labour condition. Still it may even be flattering, given the finding that 96% respectively 94% does not get full compensation for overtime or night-time work even if it is compensated by extra days off. But what if these days off accumulate endlessly?

Income, as a component of the material working conditions is important in another way: many officers reported difficulties of making ends meet, as presented in Table 8.

Table 8
Salary improvement by 'sufficient salary to maintain family'

Improvement / Sufficient salary	Sign. impr. %	Insign. Impr. %	No change %	A bit worse %	Sign. worse %	Diff. to answer %	Total N	%
Yes	15	7	1	0	7	6	21	*5*
Rather yes	12	12	9	9	13	6	43	*10*
Rather no	30	33	35	46	22	25	138	*33*
No	44	48	55	46	58	63	219	*52*
Total N=100%	61	87	177	35	45	16	421	
In %	*14*	*21*	*42*	*8*	*11*	*4*		

Missing values: 58

As can be deduced from Table 8, the salaries tend to be generally perceived as insufficient income to maintain a family, even though 44% of the surveyed officers report a significant improvement in the salary. On the whole, 85% thought the pay was insufficient to maintain a family, whether an improvement was mentioned or not. The Patrol Police seems to have gained most: 51% of them mentioned an improvement in salary against only 20% of the Criminal Police.

Not surprisingly, respondents generally declared modest living expenses in their households. 58% stated that they spend all their money on basic, inexpensive goods, 29% – that while their households' income was generally sufficient, it was still difficult to purchase some goods, such as furniture, TV, refrigerator *etc*. 9% claimed that they don't have enough money even for the most essential goods.

a2. Feeling protected

Another matter concerns the feeling of being *protected*. This issue has many facets, which are part of the general perception of the protection of human rights and freedoms in Ukraine. Within this broader framework, we project the perceptions of protection derived from specific regulations such as the regulatory framework of the use of force, and weapons training. Protection of police officers also concerns their rights and freedoms in relation to citizens as well as their protection in court: do police officers enjoy the same protection as citizens?

Going from the broadest protection circle and narrowing our focus, we find that the respondents' perception of human rights protection in Ukraine does not reflect much trust: 43% thought the protection in general not sufficient and 9% completely absent. Does this have any influence on the perception of the reform? In focus groups it was mentioned that protection of rights is an important issue for police officers. These frequently mentioned concerns were converted into specific survey questions relating to officer-citizen legal interactions, for example, who "enjoys better protection: the police officer or a common citizen?" Obviously, there should be equality of justice, but perception may be different as presented in Table 9.

Table 9
Perception of equality of legal protection of citizens and police officers: In general and at trial

Equality in protection?	General protection %	At trial %
Police more than citizen	1	2
Equally	22	28
Citizen more than police	77	71
N = 100%	479	479

The answers to these specific questions point clearly into one direction: officers feel that in legal proceedings with citizens there is a preferential treatment of the citizens. This perception is expressed in all services, independent of the perceived level of social protection and the kind of service.

One may hypothesise that trust in a fair employer may act as a counterbalance to this bias such that officers may generally feel socially protected. In the perception of the respondents that appeared not to be the case. 60% of the respondents do not consider the police organisation a fair employer (41% a bit unfair and 20% not fair at all) and 83% feel to be "rather not" or 'not at all protected'.

Table 10
Police organisation as employer and sense of social protection

Fairness employer / *Socially protected*	Fair %	Somewhat fair %	Somewhat unfair %	Not fair %	N	%
Yes	27	2	1	1	16	*4*
Somewhat yes	21	22	9	1	53	*12*
Somewhat not	32	53	52	20	189	*44*
No	21	23	39	78	169	*40*
N = 100%	44	126	176	81	427	
%	*10*	*30*	*41*	*20*		

Missing values: 52

As can be observed, the perception of not being protected is predominant. Even among the respondents who think the police organisation a fair employer, more than half (53%: that is 32% "somewhat" plus 21% "not at all") have (severe) doubts about their social protection. However, this is only a small subset of the population: the vast majority doubts the fairness of the employer as well as the prospect of proper protection.

Many facets of the police work entail the risk of getting harmed, physically or mentally, against which the police organisation is required to provide protection. As protecting health and safety may in actual work situations be complex we also asked the respondents whether they got sufficient training on this point. This proved to be the case: 72% thought they had either "fully sufficient" (18%) or "generally sufficient" (54%) training to protect their health. However, when it came to actual sickness, only 4% said that the necessary treatment was provided, while 84% said that this did not happen: "fully" 53% or "not fully" 31%.

a3. Being supplied

Against the background of the perception of the fairness of the police organisation it is of importance to take stock of the provisions, facilities and tools needed for the execution of police tasks, as is becoming of a good and fair employer in the implementation of an important reform. Formulated simply: what is the point of reform if in the end you still sit on wooden boxes in an unheated office with no gas for the car to do patrols? This question is not new: in the 2007 survey (Bielousov, 2008) there was also a question about material provisions of officers in their stations. We provide the findings of 2007 together with those of 2017, obviously with warnings of methodological caveats.[7] The comparison is only partial because some of the implied services no longer exist. Despite these differences, the figures give an indication of changes over time.

Table 11

Equipment and provisions of police stations: 2007 and 2017

	Year	Sufficiently provided	Partially provided	Not provided
Workplaces	2017	42	41	17
	2007	*48*	*43*	*10*
Stationery	2017	16	38	47
	2007	*11*	*27*	*63*
Means of communication	2017	18	46	36
	2007	*32*	*47*	*21*
Computers	2017	15	49	36
	2007	*13*	*49*	*38*
Internet access	2017	26	37	37
	2007	*9*	*21*	*70*
Access to the police databases	2017	40	40	20
	2007	*15*	*30*	*55*
Furniture	2017	22	53	25
	2007	*18*	*51*	*31*
Transport/cars	2017	15	39	46
	2007	*14*	*39*	*47*
Fuel	2017	15	48	37
	2007	*12*	*29*	*59*

Answers to the questions of the present survey on how the officers are provided with different kinds of tools and facilities shows a number of problems. Only with respect to the workplaces, the most common response was "fully provided" (42%); the option "partially provided" was the most common for other supplies such as means of communication; computers; Internet access;

[7] The 2007 survey covered the whole country and had a sample of 3000 officers. Ukraine, for the purposes of the study, was divided into 7 regions, Kharkiv Oblast being chosen as a typical for the northern region (Kharkiv, Sumy and Chernihiv Oblasts) and was represented by 355 officers (according to the percentage of the officers from the region in the *militsiya*).

furniture; fuel for cars; access to the police databases. For the latter, however, the difference between the options "sufficiently provided" and "partially provided" was negligible. It should be noted that despite the usual "partly provided," on average 36% said to have no means of communication, computer or internet access. For the transport and stationery, the most common response was that they are 'not provided'. It could also happen that there were cars, but no fuel or fuel without cars (9 respondents).

Compared to the results of the 2007 study, there seems to be general improvement, however very modest. Two notable exceptions are, on one hand, the worsening of the perception of the supplies of workplaces and means of communication, and, on the other hand, significant improvement of the availability of Internet access and access to the police databases, which can be attributed more to the general technological development.

b. The police viewed as an organisation

In table 10 we present what the respondents thought of their organisation as a 'fair employer', a proposition which the majority of 60% denied. However, their assessments of other aspects of the police as an organization tend to be more positive.

Two questions addressed the assessment of the police efficiency by the officers themselves, concerning police as a whole and the particular branch of the police, to which they belong. Answering the first question, the majority of the respondents thought that the police is in general efficient or "rather efficient" (13 and 40%). However, respondents tend to assess their own branch of service as more effective than the police in general (30 and 47%). The respondents of the Parole Police displayed the most enthusiasm for the police in general (11% efficient and 56% "rather efficient") as well as their own branch (26 and 58%).

Two questions concerned the assessment of the police on the scales of "order-chaos" and "reason-absurdity". While, in both cases, the majority of the respondents characterised the police as "orderly" or "more orderly than not" (15 and 52%) and as reasonable or "more reasonable than not" (19 and 52%), 26% of the respondents thought there was "more chaos than order" in the police work and 24% that there was more absurdity than reason. Of the respondents who thought their service to be inefficient, 45% thought "more chaos than order" is an adequate description of the police system. Unsurprisingly, those who found more chaos in the police system (110) also perceived more absurdity in their work (62%).

Of the services the pre-trial investigation respondents were most critical on the 'order-chaos' variable (45% more chaos) as well as on the 'reason-absurdity' variable (40% more absurd), with more than 10% above the average for both variables (32% and 28%).

The other aspect of the police organisation addressed in the questionnaire was the perceived influence of the respondents' service on their personal self-fulfilment. The majority of the respondents stated that their job was either fully or somewhat beneficial to their self-fulfilment (12% and 60%).

Another facet of the relations between the police officers and the organization is their readiness to quit the police completely or to change their branch of service. While respondents mentioned significant problems with their jobs, only a small percentage of them expressed a readiness to transfer to another police division or to quit the police entirely. 40% stated they are not going to leave the police, another 41% indicated that they do not have any specific plans to leave. Only 5% stated they are going to leave in a period of a year, 9% plan to leave in 2-3 years, 4% – no earlier than in 4 years. It should be noted, however, that it was the patrol police that showed the biggest readiness to leave the police: 9% stated readiness to leave in 1 year, 10% in 2-3 years.

Conclusion and discussion

In the introduction we discussed two of the reforms and changes the police in Ukraine had to undergo in the past decades. It appeared that the design and implementation of these measures proved to be little consistent.

The first reform was aimed at abolishing the DAI, the then traffic police, widely perceived as a corrupt division. However, it continued to exist: policymakers backtracked on their plans, declaring that the goals they set had been accomplished – that was a counterfactual statement. The second reform changed the rules of the criminal procedure under which a large section of the police officers operate. While it was implemented more or less consistently, the crucial legislation necessary to support it had not been enacted yet. As we mentioned, these were the two most obvious examples of the numerous changes and reforms that affected Ukrainian police since the country declared independence in 1991. Thus, the current reform that has been initiated in the wake of Maidan Revolt might be seen as 'just another one' in a series of half-baked policies: achieving little but burdening police officers in their day-to-day task fulfilment.

Despite this (justified) expectation, the current reform actually differed from the previous ones, most importantly in its scope. It established the National Police in place of the old *militsiya* and formulated progressive principles of policing. Most importantly, it placed much more emphasis on service- and citizen-oriented policing and the related importance of the public trust. This led to a new system of police *performance assessment* based on this *public trust*. Unfortunately, the implementation of this new assessment was delayed keeping it in the state of 'paper reform'. Currently this new assessment system is still under production and may be ready by 2020. In addition, there was the establishment of the Patrol Police, largely staffed with newly recruited police officers.

The reverse side of the perception by the public of the police reform is that of the police officers: The present study sought to elucidate how police officers view the reform and the conditions under which they perform their duties. Obviously, a lot depends on the level of understanding of the reform, which 64% of the respondents self-assessed as complete or as partial. However, irrespective of this self-assessed knowledge almost 40% of the respondents observed no change in their work despite the reform. Singling out the two target variables of 'cooperation with the public' and 'cooperation with public agencies', we see that on these variables on average 48,5% of the respondents see no change either. When we look at the Patrol Police respondents, they perceive a positive change more often, including perceived improvements with regard to cooperation with other police forces. Unsurprisingly, Patrol Officers, more than the other respondents, thought the reform went in the right direction (44% against 31% of the whole sample), given that the very existence of their agency was a core part of the reform.

Closely related to the perception of the reform were questions designed to estimate the officers' sensitivity for their interaction with the public. These questions concerned acceptance of the public trust as an indicator of the police efficiency, avoiding citizens' complaints and the need for a positive feedback. Additionally, this set of questions was closely related to the perception by the police officers of the improvement in cooperation with the public (48% of the respondents saw no changes).

Does this also apply to work conditions, from salary to legal and social protection as perceived by the respondents? A common point of these conditions is the perceived *fairness* of the police organisation as a responsible employer taking care of its personnel.

In general, the respondents were rather critical of the degree of fairness of their employer: the general fairness rating of the police organisation appeared to be low. Only 40% considered the police organisation fair ("completely fair" 10% and "a bit fair" 30%) to its personnel. This is reflected in the perceptions of the salaries, protection of social and legal rights as well as the care for officers' families and proper care in cases of illness. This concerns particularly the protection in cases of legal procedures with citizens and protection against the own police organisation concerning labour and social aspects. Whether in general or in a court of law, more than 70% of the respondents felt that the common citizens are better protected than the police officers. This is a feeling of uncertainty that may affect the professional risk taking in conflict situations. The feeling of rights violation by the employer causes even more uncertainty. More than 70% thought that such was the case. Unsurprisingly, the majority of them also consider their employer to be unfair. This negative perception of rights infringements was underscored by 60% of the respondents who did not think the police organisation to be a fair employer. This points at a deep-seated lack of trust in the employer, *i.e.* the state in general and the police as a whole in particular, which was shared by all branches, but with the highest percentage (77%) among respondents from the ranks of the Patrol Police, the flagship of the police reform. The situation is aggravated by the perceived insufficiency of the supplies the officers needed in order to perform their duties. This is a problem the reform still has to address.

This contrasts, however, with the apparent commitment the officers seem to feel towards their job. 72% of the police officers expressed the opinion that their job fully or somewhat contributes to their self-fulfilment. 53% of the officers assessed the work of the police *as a whole* efficient or "rather efficient". Assessing their own department, they were even more generous: 77% thought it was efficient or rather efficient. Moreover, despite being dissatisfied with the conditions of their work, the respondents did not show much inclination to leave the police. Only 18% of the respondents expressed a willingness to quit their jobs. It should be noted, however, that it was the officers from the Patrol Police who were the most eager to quit. This corresponds with the greater willingness of the young officers (duration of service less than 3 years and 3 to 5 years) to quit.

To what should we attribute this attitude? There is no unambiguous answer: younger staff may more optimistically perceive job opportunities even in a halting labour market, while older staff may be more pessimistic and prefer a 'fixed job'. In addition, there may be a loyalty to their service where they worked for many years.

These observations lead to two conclusions. In the first place, a significant part of respondents claim to understand the importance of the public opinion for their work. Still, a large part of the officers show ambivalence towards the reform, stating that it is difficult for them to assess their understanding of the reform, to determine whether it moves into the right direction or whether the public trust is an adequate reflection of their work.

A nation-wide survey is required in order to gain a fuller picture across the country; however, it seems that there remains a lot to do in order to instil in the officers a willingness to actively implement provisions of the reform in their day-to-day job.

This relates to our second conclusion. To maintain this positive momentum the police organisation should invest more effort in its relationship with its employees: the driver must instil trust in his horses that pull the reform cart. It is naïve to expect the police officers to accept the police reform enthusiastically if it does not also improve their working and living conditions. The other, more general aspect of this is the trust of the police officers in their organisation they are working for, *i.e.* the police and the state more generally, to ensure their legal and social protection. If it is the aim that the public trust is the reflection of the quality of the police work, the trust of the police officers must be a reflection of the quality of the National Police as a fair employer.

References

Maltsev, V. V., *Hromadska dumka u systemi otsinky diialnosti orhaniv vnutrishnikh sprav Ukrainy [Public Opinion in the System of Performance Evaluation of the Bodies of Internal Affairs of Ukraine]* (Candidate of Sciences Dissertation), 2005.

Markovska, A. and A. Serduyk, Dysfunctional social institutions as an obstacle to tackle crime: exploring the dilemma of a good Ukrainian policeman. In: P.C. van Duyne, J. Harvey, G.A. Antonopoulos, K. von Lampe, A. Maljevic, Jon Spencer (eds.). *Human dimensions in organised crime, money laundering and corruption.* Nijmegen: Wolf Legal Publishers, 2013.

Martynenko, O.A., Kryminolohichna kharakterystyka pravopo rushen, shcho vchyniuiutsia pratsivnykamy OVS Ukrainy [Criminological Characteristics of the Offences Perpetrated by the Employees of the Bodies of Interior]. *Pravo i bezpeka* [*Law and Security*] 2004, 3(2), 78-82.

Serdyuk O. O., *Publichna bezpeka ta dovira do pravookhoronnykh orhaniv. Za rezul'tatamy doslidzhen' 2013-2018 rokiv, provedenykh v Kharkivs'kii oblasti [Public security and confidence in the law enforcement agencies. Based on the results of the studies of 2013-2018, conducted in Kharkiv Oblast] : naukovyi zvit* [report]. Kharkiv, 2018.

Stan zakhyshchenosti prav, osnovnykh svobod i sotsial'nykh harantii pratsivnykiv OVS Ukrainy [State of protection of the rights, basic liberties and social guarantees in the agencies of interior of Ukraine] : monograph / Yu.L. Bielousov, D.O. Kobzin, Yu.O. Sviezhentseva *et al.*; ed. by K.B. Levchenko. Kyiv, 2008.

Zozulia I.V., Derzhavna avtoinspektsiia yak obiekt reformuvannia v systemi MVS Ukrainy [State Automobile Inspection as an Object of Reform in the System of MIA of Ukraine]. *Forum prava* [*Forum of Law*], 1, 164-186.

Moldova: Small country – big problem! Corruption and a mono-garchy

Petrus C. Van Duyne and *Brendan Quirke*[1]

Introduction

What is corruption? One of the many answers to this question is: "It is a misuse of public office for private gain" (Svensson, 2005: 19). Though this short definition is widely used, it is imprecise. It intends to cover a too wide range of law breaking, from bribery to embezzlement to fraud, clientelism and secret dealings. We prefer to bring all these modes of conduct under the umbrella of *breach of integrity*. However, the concept of integrity needs further precision. The online Oxford Dictionary brings us one step further with the following definition of integrity: "The quality of being honest and having strong moral principles." That leaves us to define the constituting elements of honesty and moral principles. We suggest that these concern truthfulness and behaving according to yardsticks. According to Van Duyne (2001), what is central in the concept is the decision making according to yardsticks: corruption erodes the *integrity of decision making* and leads to bending or evading its standards which an honest decision maker should refuse. Van Duyne (2001) formulates it as follows:

> "Corruption is an improbity or decay in the decision-making process in which a decision-maker (in a private corporation or in a public service) consents or demands to deviate from the criterion, which should rule his decision making, in exchange for a reward, the promise or expectation of it".

We will use the concepts of corruption and integrity breaches interchangeably, but always within the framework of the integrity of decision making.

---

1 The authors are based, respectively, at Utrecht University, The Netherlands, and at Manchester University, UK.

As we will see, it is the deep and pervasive erosion of the integrity of the decision making in the public administration and private sector, which affects the welfare of the peoples. In our study this awkward predicament concerns Moldova, which does not stand alone in this regard. In fact, the whole western Black Sea and Balkan region is characterised by a high level of corruption (Emerson *et al.*, 2017; McDevit, 2015; Kononczuk *et al.*, 2017). On the Corruption Perceptions Index 2017 of Transparency International, of which the scale ranges from 10 (highly corrupt) and 100 (very clean) and with a global average of 43, Moldova scores 31; Ukraine 30; Bosnia and Herzegovina 38; Albania 38; Macedonia 35; Serbia 41; Bulgaria 43; Montenegro 43 and Romania 48 (Transparency International, 2018). It is clear that Moldova together with Ukraine, is at the bottom of this apparently deeply corrupt region.

Corruption is a global concern and Moldova underwrites this: it is (or will become) a signatory of a number of international conventions against corruption.[2] However, this legal compliance did not make the country less corrupt though we still lack a systematic knowledge of the backgrounds and facets of corruption in Moldova. This chapter aims to make a reconnaissance by bringing together what is known about corruption in this country. The sources for this study are not rich: corruption in Moldova seems to be under-researched. The consulted sources consist mainly of open English language sources, mainly from Moldovan institutions and local authors whose publications were uploaded on various websites.

We will first look at the common denominator underlying the corruption in this region: the Soviet heritage.

---

2 The *United Nations Convention against Corruption of the United Nations*, in force since 14 December 2005; the *Inter-American Convention against Corruption of the Organization of American States*, in force since 6 March 1997; the *Civil Law Convention on Corruption of the Council of Europe*, adopted 4 November 1999; the *Criminal Law Convention on Corruption of the Council of Europe*, adopted 27 January 1999; the *EU Convention against Corruption involving officials of the European Union*, adopted on 25 June 1997; the *African Union Convention on Preventing and Combating Corruption*, adopted in 2003; the *OECD Anti-Bribery Convention*.

The Soviet corruption heritage

Moldova is a small, relatively underdeveloped country sandwiched between Romania and Ukraine. The principality of Moldova was founded in the 1350s. It was controlled by the Ottoman Empire for almost 500 years until 1812, when the north-eastern part of the principality – Bessarabia – was annexed by the Russian Empire. In 1918, Bessarabia became part of Romania but in 1940 was annexed again by the Soviet Union.

Whether in Tsarist or Soviet times, corruption has been endemic. As Markovska (2007) comments, in Pre- and Post-Revolutionary Russia, officials were often expected to 'live off the job' by extracting every penny they could from those who depended on their services (Markovska, 2007: 227). For Moldova it can be interpreted as a continuation of the Turkish style of governing the outlying provinces: officials (often Greek aristocrats) had to rent their position and reclaimed the expenses by living off their districts (the Phanariote era; Kurat and Bromley, 1976). Civil service positions became a commodity that could be sold or inherited (Chalidze (1977) quoted by Markovska and Isaeva (2007: 228). This was continued under the Bolshevik rule.

Jowitt (1983) observed that in the Soviet Union bribes "are being offered and taken for everything, ranging from certificates of place of residence, to apartments, to ministerial posts in the republics" which in his opinion were practices that sustained the privileged political cadre. Jowitt (1983) comments that the purchase and sale of positions for large sums of money signifies the profound institutionalisation of a structure of bribery and graft, from the bottom to the top of the pyramid of power.

Stefes (2003) quotes Konstantin Simis, a Jewish lawyer who was forced to leave the Soviet Union, who aptly observed: "it can be stated without fear of exaggeration that the average Soviet citizen was accompanied by bribery from womb to tomb". It exerted control over the distribution of the most basic scarce resources and services, causing a frantic search (Stefes, 2003; Clark and Wildavsky, 1990: 217). There were no control mechanisms in the one party state. Corrupt conduct was expected from most leading cadre: declining participation was unofficially sanctioned (Simis, 1982: 218). Finally, the rules that structured corrupt activities were refined and commonly known (Vaksberg, 1991: 6).

Stefes (2003) poses the question: how did the myriad of opportunities to take bribes turn into a *system* of corruption? He believes that this was enabled by a system of *clientelism* within the state-party apparatus. He believes clientelism was built initially around the career ambitions of Soviet officials who realised that without the patronage there were no career prospects as socialist orthodoxy prevented a meritocratic promotion system to develop. So promotion became based on patronage.

This system created a profitable leverage towards citizens in need of permits and licenses (Simis, 1977: 38). Given the civil servants' power to stall, the citizens were accomplices as well as extorted victims (Stefes, 2003; Simis, 1982: 230). All ex-Soviet states shared this system.

Towards capturing the Moldova state

Apparently the Moldovan people accepted this heritage of 'corrupt business as usual': paying bribes as an expected expense in getting served by underpaid officials who considered these as regular fringe benefits.

Apart from this heritage, 'liberated' Moldova was the only Soviet successor state, which did not welcome its birth: the majority of the population speaks Romanian and wanted to join Romania. This was not to the liking of the Russian speaking minority (9%) living east of the Dniester. With Russian armed support the Russian minority revolted in March 1992 and declared its own state: Transnistria, recognised by no other state but Russia. Meanwhile the Romanian state, just having cast off the oppression of its socialist leader Ceaucescu, showed little enthusiasm to embrace 'little sister' Modova (Całus, 2016: 16). "Where to belong to?" remained an unanswered question: should Moldova move to the west and the EU or towards Putin's Russia? In populist versions this easy to understand divide remained dominant in all rhetoric. This went at the expense of proper democratic policy building from a social and economic ideas and conceptions.

As a corollary Moldova had to start its life without popular identification, feelings of belonging to a shared tradition, history, or a national pride. Who loves Moldova? Its own citizens in the last place, a sentiment reinforced by the dislike of its corrupt elite (Całus, 2016; Ch. 1 and p. 34). This is a socio-political undertone explaining the fragile state building.

Given this Soviet pre-history, corruption was not a new problem, as Markovska (2007) observed. New was Moldova's road to an authoritarian regime. Unlike in its neighbour state Ukraine (Konończuk *et al.*, 2017), Moldova developed in the first decade of its existence a genuine multi-party system and at every election the voters removed the then ruling party or coalition from office. The pluralism was also reflected in the many-sided media. However, as indicated above, this pluralism had no internal content derived from social-economic ideas. Actually, the Moldovan people experienced all this pluralism not as a democracy but as chaos and inefficiency. In an opinion survey in 2001, 57% of the interviewees expressed their preference for an old-fashioned one-party system, which was also considered to be less corrupt (Całus, 2016a: 24). Apparently the people had not learned much from history.

At the election of 2001, the people got what it wanted, but at the expense of more corruption and a captured state. The Party of Communists obtained a majority in Parliament of 71 out of 101 seats. Its leader, Vladimir Voronin, became the President. Though formally the President has little power, Voronin controlled his party fully and through that Parliament. Nominating his cabinet allowed him to rule as if constitutional restrictions on the presidency did not exist (Całus, 2016a). Not only did he pack the cabinet with loyal followers, he also succeeded in subordinating the system of justice to his will by appointing loyal judges and prosecutors (Prosecutor General Office and Supreme Court). Next he extended his party's influence to the public media. An important extension of power consisted of weakening the local administrative units which numbers were enlarged from 12 to 32 by splitting them up (2002). This shrinking of size made them financially more dependent on the central government that now could better influence local elections. After capturing the state apparatus, the real 'big grab' was done by Voronin's son Oleg using his father's influence and connections to extend his businesses. Apart from intimidations, he claimed that firms owed him money and used false court orders from a bribed judge to reclaim these fake 'debts' (Całus, 2016a: 24).

Voronin completed the constitutional two terms as president till 2009, after which elections were held. After a lot of bickering for the election of a President[3], Parliament was dissolved and snap elections were held, in which the Communists were defeated by what has been called the *Alliance for European Integration* (AEI), consisting of four opposition parties. The two oligarch party leaders of the two biggest parties were Vlad Filat (Liberal Democrats) and Vlad Plahotniuc (Democratic Party Moldova). Did this herald a change from the grabbing and greed of Voronin and son?

Perfecting state capture

Other than the name of the new coalition suggests – working towards Europe and its standards – the leaders of the parties in power showed hardly genuine interest in working towards the EU unless their interests were not threatened (BTI, Country report Moldova, 2018: §14). In fact, there is no other real programme but to enjoy the benefits of a EU rapprochement, in particular the coveted visa free travelling and EU development funds. There is a lot of lip service to keep EU delegates and international partners happy.

The two leaders who mattered are Vladimir Plahotniuc and Vladimir Filat. Plahotniuc is chairman of the Democratic Party (PDM). He is considered to be the wealthiest businessman in the country, with his net worth estimated at hundreds of million to over a billion dollars. Filat was a former Prime Minister and the President of Moldova's center-right Liberal Democratic Party (PLDM). His critics accuse him of having profited from corrupt privatisation practices.

In October 2009, less than a month after the AEI was sworn in, it made Parliament to adopt a law on public functions and the statute of the civil servants. This allowed the government to appoint or dismiss staff of the judiciary, law enforcement and regulatory bodies. For example: chairpersons and vice-chairpersons, the Prosecutor General and deputies, judges of the Constitutional Court (CC), the Supreme Council of Magistracy (SCM), and director and deputies of National Bank, the National Anti-corruption

[3] According to Wikileak cables Voronin offered Marian Lupu who had recently crossed-over from the Communist to the Democratic Party, $ 10 million for power sharing: he would become Speaker and Lupu president. But Lupu declined. www.theguardian.com/world/2010/dec/02/wikileaks-cables-moldova-voronin-bribe Accessed 7-10-2018.

Centre and Chairperson and members of the Central Election Commission.[4] In a ruling of 29 December 2010, concerning the dismissal of the Chairperson of the Supreme Court the Constitutional Court mitigated this arrogation of power by differentiating between the institutions of high *political* and high *public* interest, such as the courts which should be protected against political interference. However, the government mostly flouted this mandatory ruling. In fact, the coalition followed the lines of its secret agreement of August 2008 on the division of the positions between the three member parties. The Liberal Democrats under Filat 'got' the Central Election Commission (Transparency International *et al.,* 2017: 8). The Democratic Party of Moldova (DPM) of Plahotniuc 'got' a strong foothold in the justice system which proved later to be of a most strategic value: the General Prosecutor's Office, that he did not hesitate to use for his own purposes. In addition, he got a preponderant influence over the Supreme Court, the Supreme Council of Magistracy and indirectly the courts of justice. With a touch of wry irony, Plahotniuc also got the anti-corruption bodies in his grip.

These two oligarchs, Filat of the Liberals Democratic Party of Moldova (DLPM) and Plahotniuc of the Democratic Party of Moldova shared the centre of political power. They proved also to be serious rivals, which is a formula for political instability. However, during the first coalition years they kept up appearances of stability to the EU in view of the coveted Association Agreement with the EU and the liberalisation of the EU visa regime in 2014. Also, as their majority was slim, it was in their interest to avoid new elections, though tensions were mounting. Prime Minister Filat, expressed after a few years his misgivings about the appointment policy and warned on July 2011 against what he qualified as the *mafiotisation* of the Republic (TI *et al*., 2017: 6). He also admitted that his party got control of the Central Election Commission, a perfect position for election manipulation. These outpourings lowered his trust with the population of whom two third considers elections unfair (Transparency International and CMI, 2017).

Filat's influence declined after an attempt to reclaim control over the General Prosecutor's Office in 2013 and lost subsequently his position as

4 For a full list see Transparency International *et al*., 2017, p. 5

Prime Minister. Meanwhile, Plahotniuc' influence was increasing by bribery and intimidation (Całus, 2016a). The final battle between the two oligarchs two years later is of interest because it revealed how subserviently the Prosecutor General Office, Mr Harunjen, and the courts operated.

The opportunity to settle accounts came when the One Billion Banking Theft came to the open and Filat was accused by the main suspect Ilan Shor of passive corruption. As Plahotniuc 'owns' the General Prosecution Office he made the deputy Prosecutor come into rapid action against his rival. On October 2015, Parliament was informed of the alleged Filat's wrongdoing and while violating its own procedural rules, hastily stripped him of his immunity, whereupon the Prosecutor General had him arrested immediately (TI, 2017). After a trial *behind closed doors* he was convicted to nine years prison. Now Plahotniuc was the only main oligarch left. He could be satisfied: he was now a 'mono-garch'. Having no other public position, he could dominate the 'ship of state' without any accountability.

The functioning of the 'ship of state'

The 'ship of state' is a metaphor for describing the government as standing on the command bridge; as the legislative determining the course; the mechanisms of the rule of law system to maintain order, and the executive to follow orders to keep the ship afloat. How is the Moldovan ship of state sailing?

1. Parliament and political parties

When there is systematic and grand corruption, there is most often a direct political link because at this level political decision making processes are affected. This does not only concern the direct benefits, but also the system of mutual protection: corrupt actors must have the clout to thwart anti-corruption measures and policies. That is often denoted with the abstract euphemism: "there is no political will to fight corruption". That is too free-floating: one must look at the perpetrators and all who abet their corrupt conduct. In our narrative this concerns corrupt politicians and their parties in the Moldovan Parliament of which the most important are:

- The Liberal Democratic Party (PLDM)
- Party of Socialists of Republic of Moldova (PSRM)
- Party of Communists of Republic Moldova (PCRM)
- The Democratic Party of Moldova (DPM)
- The Liberal Party (LP)

We have noted earlier that in Moldovan politics the content of party programmes are irrelevant. Relevant are the leading persons, or as the chairman of the Constitutional Court observed: "*Moldovan political parties are authoritarian entities, dominated by 'Leader's cult', without internal democracy and political visions*".[5] Hence we focus on politically leading actors: not a full picture gallery of 'who is who', but only those of whom enough is known in relation to systematic corruption.

In the previous sections we have already met Vladimir Voronin of the communist party PCRM who ruled two terms from 2001-2009. As mentioned, he is important because he set out to subordinate the administration of justice by skilfully appointing colourless and pliant figures on key positions (Całus, 2016). As we have seen, next came the regional administration, made financially dependent on the central government: non-communist districts got less money (Całus, 2016a: 24). His son Oleg benefitted from public contracts and preferences. With the support of corrupt judges he raided allegedly indebted corporations.

The scene changed in 2009, when this 'one-party grabbing' was replaced by a series of coalition governments of parties who were also not averse of sharing the grabbing spree.

Apart from that, the coalition worked uneasily together under their umbrella of the Alliance for European Integration. Nominally pro-Europe, their main energy was devoted to dividing the spoils including the 'rights' to nominate the top ranks of the law enforcement and supervisory institutions such as prosecutor general, chief of the fiscal service, governor of the National Bank of Moldova or the chief of the Central Electoral Commission (included in a confidential protocol August 2009). Tensions between the liberals under Filat and Democrats under Plahotniuc soured their relation. It came to a culmination with the arrest of the Filat (October, 2015)

5 https://www.europalibera.org/a/27209223.html.

because of suspicions of passive corruption involvement and his hasty trial as described in the previous section (see p. 384).

With the main rival neutralised the power relation in Parliament had changed. Still, Plahotniuc' DPM was too small: it got only 12-16% of the votes at the elections. To get more seats the businessman came to the fore: Bribery was one of the convincing methods to lure MPs from another parties ('floor crossing'). A communist MP recalled: "An MP from DPM proposed me a very consistent remuneration and functions for relatives to leave the faction" (Transparency International *et al.*, 2017: 14). The result was a 'floor crossing' to the DPM: 14 communist MPs, two liberal and one socialist MP and 17 of the liberal democrats changed sides to the DPM.[6] With this outcome one can say that the mono-garch, Plahotniuc, succeeded in capturing the Moldovan legislature, while he has no official position in any of the branches of public administration or Parliament.

Floor crossing was the leverage to get controversial bills accepted. For example, against all advice and protests from western partners (US, EU) and international institutions (IMF, OECD), Parliament adopted in July 2018 the Fiscal Reform Package, together with Capital Amnesty implying that illegal or non-reported funds or assets can be legalised at a 3% payment of the declared value, while the normal income tax rate is 7-18%. The withheld assets declarations can be submitted 1 December 2018 till 28 February 2019. In fact this is money laundering by law.

2. The functioning of the juridical system

It is difficult to determine to what extent the law enforcement system operates adequately and impartially: what are the yardsticks for a 'fair trial'? This is a matter of interpretation. In some cases, there is little room for interpretation. For example, the useless display of police power in the trial against Filat compared to the soft treatment of the main criminal operator, Ilan Shor. Therefore, we restrict our search to explicit critical mentions in the studies and reports on the administration of justice.

There are different aims for abusing the judicial system. In the first place, one can exert pressure to get a favourable verdict or ruling from the

6 Unsurprisingly, three attempts to introduce a bill against this practice of floor crossing were halted.

court; in the second place, the law enforcement system can be used to intimidate opponents or, in the third place, to punish officials for 'wrong decisions': against the interest of the ruling party or to deter others. Examples will be given below.

One of the early critical mentions came from one of the main actors: Filat himself, criticising that the DPM (rather, Plahotniuc himself) has a decisive influence on appointments for the top functions: in the judiciary, General Prosecution Office and National Anti-Corruption Centre (Transparency International *el al.*, 2017) and other supervisory and regulatory bodies. This is what Filat called the *mafiotization* of top appointments (see, TI, 2017: 5): staffing essential institutions with compliant personnel. However, this is a strong statement from someone being directly 'in the know' while regretting that his influence was on the wane. Are there more sources which may shed light on this delicate matter of lack of judicial integrity?

Though systematic research is lacking, the cases described in the literature and sometimes also the public upheaval caused by a suspicious verdict provide good illustrations of how the legal apparatus can be abused. Should that all be attributed to the DPM and behind that Vlad Plahotniuc? There is consensus about this among authors (Całus, 2016a; Gribincea, 2017; Hriptievski, 2017; Prohnitchi, 2018), however, consensus is no proof. Allegations that the Supreme Court of Justice is under influence of Plahotniuc through his power of appointment is of course refuted by the president of this Court, but questions remain. The same applies to the Prosecutor General, Harunjen, under whose management the Anti-Corruption Prosecution Service hardly functioned, who showed very little zeal in handling the One Billion Bank Theft, and who lives in a dwelling which cannot be paid from his salary. All this was no hindrance to an expeditious appointment on 8 December 2016, behind closed doors (Transparency International, 2017; Gribincea, 2017). In the next section we provide a selection of examples of (ab)using the system of justice.

a. Favouritism, intimidation or punishment

Sorin Pleşca

The case against Sorin Pleşca may illustrate the political influence on the outcome of a prosecution. In March 2016 Sorin Pleşca shot his brother "by accident". He ran away and stayed two weeks in hiding after which he was found. He was charged with "murder from imprudence" ("death by criminal negligence"), but after two and a half month the case was closed as "the parties reached an agreement". How could the prosecutor reach such a decision in a man-slaughter case? At the end of the year Sorin got a job at the embassy of Moldova in Turkey and his father, Nae-Simion Pleşca, sitting in Parliament for the LDPM defected to the DPM of Plahotniuc. Together with five other turncoats he helped to install the new Filip government of the same DPM. (TI *et al.*, 2017: 27).

Valeriu Guma

This MP for the DPM (Plahotniuc) was convicted in April 2013, in Romania for corrupting the General Director of the State Assets Recovery to four years imprisonment. However, Guma absconded to Moldova. Thereupon, the Court in Bucharest requested the Moldovan authorities to recognise the verdict and execute the punishment (transfer of execution of verdicts). But Guma as MP still enjoyed the privilege of immunity, which the Parliament did not want to withdraw. When his immunity expired, the Moldavian Court ignored the Romanian request and converted the punishment into a suspended imprisonment of four years.

Mayor Filipov of the town Taraclia

Mayor Filipov was accused of cutting 31 trees in the courtyard of the town hall, though this was the responsibility of specialised services in the municipality. He was nevertheless prosecuted for causing damage, but was in first instance acquitted. However, the Cahul Court of Appeal convicted him to a fine and compensation of the damage. More important, in addition, he was also deprived of the right to hold public office for two years, which effectively crippled him politically. The SCJ annulled this sentence and referred the case for retrial. The mayor stated that this was a revenge for his refusal to join the DPM in the local elections in 2015 (Gribincea, 2017).[7]

---

7 To many this did not appear a loose accusation. The Congress of Local Authorities from Moldova demanded reinstalling him as mayor. Even the EU ambassador and the US embassy expressed their concern, a very exceptionally step.

The case of Basarabeasca's mayor

In March 2017 the mayor of Basarabeasca, Valentin Cumpoies, was arrested and put into preventive custody for 30 days. The charge was negligence in preventing a citizen to abuse his 13 year old daughter to provide sexual services. Whether this misconduct or the mayor's liability was proven is not known: the case is pending, but the damage to the mayor is done. Cumpoies is member of Our Party, an extra-parliamentary party highly critical of Plahotniuc and his DPM. The Congress of Local Authorities of Moldova protested strongly against this "unprecedented and unjustified arrest" (TI *et al.*, 2017: 30).

The three stealing ministers

In the Moldovan media these examples were discussed as examples of 'selective justice' with three ministers who were accused of abuse of office: illegally selling state property in February 2013. One minister was of the democratic party (Plahotniuc), the others liberal democrats. The latter accused saw their case quickly sent to court. The democrat minister's case was halted, despite documented accusations by the accountant (May 2013). This got public, but still no prosecution followed (Gribincea, 2017: 5).

The case of judge Manole

The case of Domnica Manole, judge at the Chisinau Court of Appeals, is illustrative for the whole judicial system in Moldova. The case concerns an attempt of a group of citizens to organise a referendum on the constitution. This is only possible with 200.000 signatures including 20.000 from at least half the administrative units as counted in 2000. The referendum group met these conditions, but Central Election Commission (CEC) refused to organise a referendum. In appeal the Court annulled the ruling of the CEC, which went in appeal against at the Supreme Court of Justice (SCJ). April 2016, the appeal verdict was annulled and the decision of the CEC upheld. The reason was that after the referendum law of 2000, under the communist leadership of Voronin a new regional division of the country was determined in 2002 with many more but smaller units. This implied that meeting the referendum conditions became impossible: some units did not even have enough voters. However, the referendum law was never adapted to this new regional division. So, judge Manole interpreted the law such that this referendum can work with the old regional division of 2000, while the SCJ ruled that only the 2002 division was valid. That was not the end of the matter. The SCJ took seriously offence at judge Manole daring to interpret the law: that is the privilege of the Constitutional Court. Subsequently, on 23rd May 2016, the CEC submitted a criminal complaint of abuse of office against the judge to the General Prosecution Office. The next day, with unusual speed, the Interim Prosecutor requested the Superior Council of Magistrates permission to initiate criminal procedures. In a *closed session* the Council gave permission, against which Manole appealed at the SCJ, but now the procedure began to stall: after a year the case still has not been reviewed and judge Manole remains suspended.

The case of Manole was considered important for the independence of the judiciary and caused much upheaval. Judges from the Chisinau Court of appeal expressed their support for the judge and also the EU and the US embassies expressed again their concern.

The struggle of judge Manola with the hierarchy of the justice system is important for three reasons. In the first place, the referendum on the constitution was the last thing the ruling elite wanted: it was prepared to do anything to forestall it. In the second place, though the danger of a referendum was in the end averted by the SCJ, the DPM – through their proxies in the CEC and General Prosecutor – may have aimed to make their point: "don't dare to interpret the constitution by yourself or else we initiate a criminal investigation", even if interpreting laws is the main metier of judges. In the third place, by making this point the ruling elite clearly set a limit to the judicial independence, as was also observed by one of the protesting SCJ judges: to "initiate criminal investigation in this case sets a dangerous precedent for the independence of judiciary".

Transparency International *et al.*, (2018) is more direct in their conclusion: there are strong reasons to doubt the independence of the judiciary. The appointment power of the DPM regarding the top echelons of the judiciary, stemming from the informal interparty agreement 2009/2010, and a personnel policy (see below) enables a powerful influence on the work of the courts. We will therefore discuss these personnel management tools next.

b. Appointment and promotion

Appointment and promotion can be considered very effective bribes: it is a once in a lifetime corruption, after which one remains entangled in a patron-client relationship. And it is cheap: no money changes hands.

Concerning the important function of the President of the Supreme Court of Justice, there is no documented evidence supporting Filat's claim that the Liberal Party had the 'right' to nominate the President or other staff. With the demise of Filat, Plahotniuc would have taken over. Naturally the President, Poalelungi, denies emphatically that he would be a 'Plahotniuc man'. Nevertheless, there are no examples of SCJ decisions which were opposed to the interests of DPM or the business network of Plahotniuc. See Manola's fate above, who issued a verdict that could harm the elite's interests.

The legal procedure of appointment and promotion looks solidly based on merits. The selection of candidate judges or the promotion of judges proceeds in a two-step way (Transparency International *et al.*, 2017; Hriptievschi, 2017). There are: (1) the graduation examination at the National Institute of Justice (for candidate judges) or performance evaluation (for judges) and (2) the evaluation by the *Career and Selection Board.* This Career Board inspects the points in the selection and promotion reports and gives a reasoned judgment. This is subsequently presented to the Superior Council of Magistracy (SCM), the supervisory body partly politically appointed. The SCM must propose the candidates or judges with the highest marks to the President of Moldova for an appointment or promotion. What do we know about this procedure based on merits only?

It appears that the SCM hardly takes notice of the marking by the Career Board. Transparency International *et al.* (2017: 17) Hriptievschi (2017) and (Gribinscea, 2017) observed that candidates or judges with lower points are systematically preferred to candidates with higher points: the authors mention eleven cases (six for the Courts of Appeal and five for the Supreme Court) while no reasons were given for ignoring the rating of the Career Board.

There are also many cases with 'integrity issues', in which proposed candidates or judges' promotions were refused by the President: about 80 in the period 2002-2015. The President's reasons were: discrediting justice; lack of objectivity; possession of unjustified wealth or other 'integrity issues'. The SCM has a considerable power to ignore the refusal of the President, because he can refuse only *once*: by again proposing the rejected candidate with a two-third majority the SCM proposal must be accepted, whether reasons are given or not (mostly). So, despite the serious reasons of the President for not accepting candidates or promotions, the SCM maintained 55 questionable proposals: again no reasons provided (Transparency International, *et al*., 2017: 18).

The way the top position of deputy President of the Supreme Court was filled, is telling. First, on April 2015, a vacancy was created by accusing the then deputy President of manipulating a new Integrated Case Management System. She felt pressured to resign which may have been the intention: nothing was heard of this serious allegation, while the vacancy remained open. The candidate judge for this position, an outspoken personality, was passed, again no reasons given. At the end (December 2016) an inconspicuous judge with a history of controversial decisions was proposed instead (Hriptievschi, 2017).

It is also striking that not having declared one's income and assets fully, remained unheeded, also with appointments at the SCJ which should be a role model. One judge was low in the ranking, had little experience and failed asset declaration: she stated that her Porsch was bought for only € 500. Still, she was hastily proposed for appointment – even before the investigation of her asset declaration. In a Public Appeal on 8 February 2016, Civil Society Organisations expressed their concern about the nomination policy of the SCM, repeatedly ignoring the Presidents references at 'integrity issues' of candidates.[8]

There are also indications that in 2012, the SCM was warned by the Security and Intelligence Service of the involvement of judges in the Russian Laundromat. However, the SCM did not interfere till 2016. Then a number of judges involved got a positive evaluation and were promoted to administrative positions or the Court of Appeal (TI *et al*., 2017: 32).

It is almost a euphemism to say that the functioning of the Superior Council of Magistracy in matters of appointment and promotion is worrying. It is selective and non-transparent, giving the impression of punishing judges with a frank mind and furthering judges with an integrity risk. By

---

8 http://crjm.org/wp-content/uploads/2016/02/2016-02-08-Apel-CarieraJudecatori-ENG.pdf

not giving reasons for its decisions the SCM shirks public accountability (Hriptievschi (2017).

c. Tools against integrity breaches in the judiciary

Within the structure of the justice system there are tools to prevent or sanction breaches of integrity principles. How do these function? TI *et al.* (2017: 20) and Hriptievschi (2017) inspected a number of cases to determine how the internal correction system responded to signs of breaches of integrity. As far as the signs came from civil society, for example from investigative journalists, the correction system is hardly functioning, reinforcing the lack of trust of 89,6% expressed by respondents in the Public Opinion Barometer.[9]

As we have already observed in the sections above, the asset declaration by judges is repeatedly ignored. If that is brought to the attention of the superiors, no action follows with one exception: one judge was fined with € 750 for defects in her asset declaration.

A tool to prevent corruption is to randomise the distribution of cases over the judges in the courts. However, this system is also vulnerable to manipulation or suitable to accuse someone of having done so. We mentioned the example of the deputy President of the SCJ who was in 2015 accused of such a manipulation, allegedly just to get rid of the judge, an often observed ploy to harass someone out of the organisation.

The procedure for establishing disciplinary responsibility is a complicated tool: it exists of five levels. On each level a disciplinary case can be halted, while serious doubts about the integrity of the judge remain. The first level is the *Judicial Inspection,* which examines the complaint which it can reject. There were suspicions that the Judicial Inspection do not investigate sufficiently, particularly in cases in which chairpersons or judges from higher courts were involved (Hriptievschi, 2017). In one case the Judge-Inspector was himself in conflict of interest.[10] Evidence can also be ignored, such as the audio-recording of the President of the Rîşcani Court, shouting and fulminating against a defence attorney and threatening his

9 Institute for Public Policies, Public Opinion Barometer, October 2016: http://www.bop.ipp.md/result?type=bar.

10 The President of the Court he investigated was the judge who examined a case in which the Inspector's wife was involved (Transparency International, *et al.*, 2017:21).

client. The Disciplinary Board stopped the procedure for lack of evidence. In various cases in which judges from the SCJ were involved the SCM annulled the disciplinary sanctions (Transparency International *et al.*, 2017: 21-22).

To conclude, there are serious indications that the disciplinary procedures are used selectively and ineffectively. They cannot be considered to have a preventive or 'self-cleaning' function to further integrity.

Altogether there are ample indications that the system of justice is ill-equipped to keep its own part of the 'ship of state' clean. There are severe doubts of its independence: it is often selective and non-transparent. How that looks like is illustrated by the ill-famous Billion Bank Theft.

d. The Billion Bank Theft

The great Moldovan Bank Robbery sounds like the title of a caper movie – it isn't! Over a period of two years, approximately 1 billion dollars were embezzled from three Moldovan banks causing them to collapse in November 2014. The banks concerned were: *Unibank* (UB); *Banka Sociala* (BS) and *Banca de Economii Moldova* (BEM). According to a report in February 2017 by the London based auditing firm, Kroll, the three banks were subject to a large co-ordinated fraud from 2012 to 2014. The fraud was committed by issuing of hundreds of loans to linked companies. The majority of the loans with no or fake collateral were processed or laundered through two Latvian banks. Part of the loan funds were then channelled back to Moldova to repay existing loans and to allow the continuation of more dubious lending. At least $600 million was distributed to other destinations: shell firms in the UK and offshore corporations (Kroll, 2017).

A large number of Moldovan companies were judged to be working together on this fraud. The companies were linked to a Mr Ilan Shor, high manager of the BEM and of the Shor Group. According to Kroll (2017), at least 77 companies with accounts at the three Moldovan banks concerned made up this group of companies. Individuals and companies linked to the Shor group increased their ownership interest by buying shares in the three Moldovan banks allowing them control of management. Companies linked to the Shor group also provided the required corporate and bank structures enabling this fraud.

The aftermath: trials, convictions and asset recovery

Though this heist was enormous and well organised, what is important in our narrative is the way it was handled. In the first place, according to the Centre for Combating Economic Crime and Corruption (no date), the response of the government was slow, secretive and selective, mainly targeting political rivals in the ruling coalition: most important the earlier mentioned Vlad Filat.[11] In the second place, there was also not much transparency in the handling of this case: the extent of the fraud came only piecemeal to the open. The Kroll investigative report was not intended for publication but was leaked anyhow. The investigative team of journalists, working in an association Zeppelin Investigations (2018), judged the report shallow and incomplete. The follow-up report is not yet available. The secret attempt to bail out three affected banks was revealed nevertheless and led to steep inflation, the fall of the government and broad public protests.

Naturally, the protest of the public was directed against the political and economic elite suspected of having a stake in the scam, in the first place the oligarch Plachotniuc. However, there was no evidence of his direct involvement: no "smoking gun". It remained unclear who benefitted of this robbery: the number of beneficiaries should be far larger than the handful prosecuted defendants. Fourteen acting or former judges and three bailiffs have been arrested for their alleged involvement Reuters (2017) mentions that 40 people have either benefitted from the scam or facilitated it.

The three defendants getting the main law enforcement and media attention were: Vlad Filat, the ex-Prime Minister and now opponent to Plahotniuc; the young rich businessman and politician, Ilat Shor, the previous chairman of Banca di Economii and mayor of the small town Orhei in the centre of Moldova. The third defendant was Veaceslav Platon, businessman and parliamentarian.

As mentioned, Shor was leading the so-called Shor Group and was the main operator of the scheme. He was arrested and placed under house arrest in May 2015 but nevertheless allowed to run for mayor of the small town Orhei, which he surprisingly won with 62% of the votes. In June 2016, he was arrested again and charged, but after two months custody released after denouncing all accomplices involved, in particular disclosing the bribes ($250 million and expensive cars) he gave to ex-Prime Minister Filat. However, for this active bribery he was not prosecuted. That

11 http://www.cccec.md/the-moldovan-banking-scandal/

omission did not save him: in June 2017, he was convicted for fraud and money laundering and sentenced to seven years and six months imprisonment. He called it all a conspiracy of the government and NGOs against him. He appealed against this sentence and pending this appeal was released to return to the mayor's office (Transparency International *et al.*, 2017).

His investigation and trial took more than two years with the appeal procedure still on-going. At the time of writing he succeeded in drawing out the trial procedures (or was allowed to).

Filat got a rougher and also much quicker treatment: six months till the verdict in first instance, and eight month for the appeal procedure (Transparency International *et al.*, 2017: 12). As mentioned in the previous section, after being accused by Shor to have received money and cars, the Prosecutor General had him arrested in Parliament with a lot of police showing. In Juni 2016, Filat was sentenced for passive corruption and convicted to nine years imprisonment. In addition, he was banned from holding public offices for the term of five years. The trial was behind closed doors and the verdict was not publicised. Only PublikaTV of Vlad Plahotniuc was allowed to be present. Throughout the trial he was surrounded by an excessive number of Special Forces officers.[12] Filat appealed to the Supreme Court of Justice and the European Court for Human Rights of which the procedure is still pending.

This was still mild compared to the sentence meted out to the third perpetrator in this scheme: Veaceslav Platon, with Shor also heavily involved in the $ 20 billion Russian laundromat which ran through Moldovan banks (Zeppelin investigations, 2018). He was charged with stealing $40 million from the Banca de Economii. Platon was barred from his trial because of 'bad behaviour'. Also to the public, the trial proceeded behind closed doors. Only the verdict was read in public (April 2017), with the defendant present. He used to occasion to shout to his judges: "Judges, look into my eye! Aren't you ashamed? This is not a sentence, this is a politically rigged inquisition orchestrated by your master, Vlad Plahotniuc, who should be

12 https://en.crimemoldova.com/news/social/vlad-filat-sues-moldova-to-the-european-court-of-human-rights-for-violating-his-rights-in-the-trial/
http://www.intellinews.com/former-pm-filat-sues-moldova-through-european-court-of-human-rights-127058/

put in prison himself! This is not a trial, this is Plahotniuc's menagerie." Platon was convicted to 18 years imprisonment.[13]

The aftermath of the mega fraud in terms of *asset recovery* remains unmentioned as nothing has been recovered thus far. The same applies to the beneficiaries of these huge sums of money. There are persistent indications that the National Bank, some MPs and the Supreme Council of Magistracy were informed at an early stage of the scam. Also the Prosecutor General showed no sense of urgency to come into action (Gribincea, 2018). Despite lofty intentions about funds recovery, there is no orderly asset recovery report available. Also the EU foreign affairs Commissioner Morgherini called in May 2018 for more recovery action, but in vain.

To summarise: the prosecution and trials displayed a high degree of selectivity, bias in terms of treatment and severity of sentence and lack of transparency. The main criminal operator, Shor, was allowed to draw out all procedures, remaining at large as mayor of Orhei, while the other defendants were immediately put in custody. There was no legal transparency: the trials were behind closed doors and verdicts were not publicised.

3. The executive and corruption

Extending the metaphor of the ship of state to the executive of Moldova, would depict a boat's 'bridge' with the Prime Minister 'at the helm' supported by his responsible ministers and deputy ministers with the President as a ceremonial captain. However, this picture is far removed from the present state of affairs. Since 2009 there have been six governments. The changes were not a consequence of a battle of ideas derived from party programmes but of a of the disagreement of the division of the spoils between the democrats (DPM-Plahotniuc), the Liberal Democratic Party (LDPM-Filat) and the Liberal under Ghimpiu. This bickering went on and off, thinly concealed from the wester sponsors of the poor country. The big 1-Billion bank robbery caused additional instability and street protests. The government resigned.

---

13 https://en.interfax.com.ua/news/general/416902.html
Apart from these leading suspects, two other accomplices were mentioned as convicted for this scam to four and five year imprisonment.

The new government (Democrats and Liberals), was headed by the weak and pliant Plahotniuc-man: Paval Filip. He was installed in January 2016 during an undisclosed, late-night ceremony which was only later confirmed by a press release from the president's office (Transparency International *et al.*, 2017: 36).[14]

This was a grubby beginning but it reflected the real Plahotniuc' success: as the NGO Freedomhouse and Transparency International (2017) observed, the premier and the speaker of parliament were now also in his hands, "an unusual concentration of power" of a party whose ranking at the 2014 election was only fourth. As mentioned, the DPM was further strengthened by 22 MPs 'crossing floor' from the Liberals and Communists.[15] In May 2017 the coalition broke up and the PLDM was replaced by the socialists (PSRM). Again, the majority of the ministers were appointed by the DPM, that is: Plahotniuc.

It bodes ill for the anti-corruption reforms in particular when it concerns the implementation of the reform laws that have been enacted since 2009.

In the first place, there is the reform of the *Prosecution Office*, August 2016. First there is the questionable appointment of the Prosecutor General Office: Mr. Harunjen having an income and property mismatch and otherwise a low performance in his previous job in the Anti-corruption Prosecution Service. To this comes the appointment of the deputy chief anti-corruption prosecutor with also a low skills score and a comparable asset declaration problem (Gribincea, 2017: 4). These officials manage the Anti-corruption Prosecution Office (APO) consisting of 50 prosecutors' positions: nine filled thus far. While it is the intention that they will handle high-level corruption cases, 75% of the cases are still petty corruption cases (Gribincea, 2017; Prohnitchi, 2018; Stefan *et al.*, 2018). Meanwhile APO's budget lacks special funds to be used for special investigation activities. APO is further burdened by a too broad mandate under which it must also deal with cases that have nothing to do with corruption, such as fraud in the private sector or terrorist finances (Stefan *et al.*, 2018: 14. APO's statistics look good, but its workload does not reflect a real prioritisation corrupt state capture.

---

14 https://freedomhouse.org/report/nations-transit/2017/moldova

15 By joining the Alliance for European Integration the communist defectors showed no qualms to forsake their pledge to the voters to steer Moldova towards Putin's Eurasia.

Thus far, the attention for high-level corruption cases looks very biased: prosecution and conviction of members of the ruling parties and their associates are hard to find (one example, deputy minister of Economy, Triboi, March 2017 (TI *et al.*, 2017,). This reinforces the impression that the anti-corruption system is mainly used against opponents.

The "guardian institutions"

The Moldovan legal system is not without 'guardian institutions' whose functions are enshrined in law. But the question is not whether there are sufficient regulations, but how they are implemented. The following sections provide an outline of their functioning. For a proper evaluation more data are not available.

a. The National Anti-Corruption Centre

The NAC resulted from a reorganisation of the Center for Combating Economic Crimes and Corruption in 2012 and became an independent central public organisation, directly under the responsibility of the parliament. It is tasked to prevent, investigate and combat corruption and related offences. It has a personnel of 350 officers: among them 40 staff for prevention and ten analysts.

The political responsibility for the NAC is the (DPM dominated) parliament. According to Gribincea (2017) this is reflected in the investigation pattern: no corrupt DPM members or officials have been arrested with the exception of the Minister of Economy, Valeriu Triboi and Minister of Agriculture, Eduard Grama.[16]

---

[16] Triboi bought a building for a low price from a state enterprise and had it renovated by other state enterprises. That was known for years. But now another development may have plaid a role in bringing this to the open: a gas deal with Ukraine or Transnistria. The minister favoured the Ukraine agreement, but was arrested just before concluding it, preventing the deal. A few months later the gas agreement was made with Transnistria after all (TI, *et al.*, 2017; p. 27-28). Grama was arrested in relation to a contested land deal, and was detained for 72 hours. http://www.moldova.org/en/minister-agriculture-eduard-grama-arrested-72-hours-corruption-charges/

NAC issued a Progress Report 2014-2015, which has also a chapter with a series of quantitative findings. Unfortunately the statistics are rather crude and elementary and must be used cautiously. Obviously they concern only concern *detected* cases. One can assume here a high 'dark number': most types of corruptions are consensual. Moreover, who will report a satisfactory criminal transaction to the authorities that are generally distrusted anyhow.

In the two reporting years the NAC detected 1.031 cases of corruption or corruption related crimes of which 66% were rated as "severe and extremely severe"; 24% as "less severe" and 10% as "minor". However, these qualifications are not operationalised, neither in terms of damage or in terms of affected morality.

Unfortunately the report does not provide a breakdown of these three severity categories over other variables, such as the suspected persons or the type of public services in which detected cases of corruption happened.

The data of the report indicate that more than 50% of the input consists of cases against police officers, doctors and 'individuals'. The text of the NAC report does not allow further differentiation, devaluating this statistical effort.

On a few subjects the NAC report provides us some interesting glimpses on sanctioning, also in relation of the size of the bribes. Of the 585 cases reviewed by the courts the judges pronounced in 83% a guilty verdict. If a prison sentence was imposed this was in 31% suspended.

The amount of money involved in the bribery seems modest: on average € 1.161 in 2014 and € 2.751 in 2015. However, without a frequency distribution, a breakdown by other variables and the values of the medians, these figures rather raise the question why such an analysis has not been carried out. The same applies to the strange finding of the NAC that there is an inverse relationship between the value of the bribe and the fine imposed. With a bribe sum of less than € 2.500 the relation between bribe and fine is 1:4; with a bribe between € 2.500 and € 5.000 the relation is 1:1; but with a bribe exceeding € 5.000 the relationship changed to 4:1. The higher the bribe, the lower the fine. This finding goes at the heart of the principle of equality of justice.

b. The Anticorruption Prosecution Office

The prosecution of corruption offences is naturally in the hands of the Prosecution Office, which was reinforced by the new Law on Prosecution Service of 2016, a (slow) follow-up of the 2011 Justice Sector Reform Strategy. The law strengthened the independence of the prosecutors. To lower the 'temptation' the salary of was doubled. An anticorruption Prosecution Office was established, intended for cases of high-level corruption cases.

Unfortunately this is an illustration of a successful reform on paper but failing in the implementation. The earlier mentioned appointment of the Prosecutor General Harunjen (see pp. 384, 387 and 399) head of the previous Anti-corruption Prosecution Centre raised suspicions. Summarised: little zeal; undeclared wealth and after a hasty procedure he was sworn in behind closed doors (Gribincea, 2017: 3). The selection of the deputy, also with a wealth-declaration issue and moderate ranking (a third place) cannot be considered as inspiring. It may be too early for a judgement, but Gribincea's (2017) observation that 75% of the workload of these specialised prosecutors still consists of small case strengthens the impression of another half-baked reform.

c. The National Integrity Authority

While the NAC is a law enforcement criminal law institution, the new broad integrity organisation will be the National Integrity Authority. This body, established by law in 2016, should result from the reorganisation of the National Integrity Commission to be accomplished by the Integrity Council. However, this did not appear to work. For unexplained reasons various deadlines for carrying out tasks were extended. It also proved difficult to fill the position of (deputy) president leading to substantial delays. In its annual survey of the governance of Moldova 2018, Freedom House concludes to a failure for 2017 and a "lack of political will" (which is rather a Plahotniuc issue) to see through the NIA reform and fight corruption.

According to Transparency International (2018: 2):

"*more than one year after the adoption of the laws from the Integrity Package, their implementation did not go further than organizing the competition to fill the positions of Chair and Vice-Chair of the NIA, the procedures not yet being finalized. Obviously, delaying the reorganization of this institution jeopardizes the process of control of wealth and personal interests.*"

Perhaps the latter point is this issue at stake: processing the almost 65.000 declarations of assets and interests. Asset declaration can be an important tool for furthering integrity – if heeded at all. However, the landscape has changed and not in favour of this integrity tool. In an earlier section (p. xx) we pointed at the Capital Amnesty Law (August 2018) allowing a post hoc declaration of hidden (criminal) assets which will then be taxed by only 3% of its declared value. Though not mentioned explicitly, this seems at odds with the assets and interests declaration. Why report assets when all the fruits of corruption and other profitable crimes can be legalised by filling a form? The opposition and (western) foreign partners have expressed their concern that this act may turn Moldova into a laundering hub for the region and beyond. Given the experience with the Russian Laundromat no an exaggerated worry.

Meanwhile the National Integrity Authority is struggling to get born by an apparently disinterested political midwife. Against the background of this Capital Amnesty Law, the question arises whether the *National Strategy of Integrity and Anticorruption* (SNIA) for 2017–2020 (and within it the NIA) should be taken seriously in the first place (Prohnitchi, 2018).

d. Independent media: shedding and shunning light

The relation between corruption and the media is not a direct one. In our formal definition the concept of 'media' has no place unless the chief editor of a newspaper or TV station is bribed in their capacity of decision makers. However, that is a too formal approach. One of the functions of the media is shedding light on political or societal importance. The opposite, shunning light, is the built-in consequence of integrity breaches. Hence, for the corrupt elite capturing the media is an important requirement to keep the light out. It is therefore no accident that we so often find the mention of 'behind closed doors', behind which there is no room for a free press. Apart from closing doors there are smarter ways to neutralise the free media. How does that look like in this mono-garchy?

The simplest and legal approach is to establish a news firm oneself; then to take over an ailing company; or to increase influence on supervisory bodies and to get a grip on the revenue side of the media: the *advertisement* market. If that does not work sufficiently, old-fashioned Soviet means can be used: physical and psychological intimidation of journalists, such as assaulting, having journalists a few days detained by a willing police unit, stalking, spying and death threats, also against relatives (Freedom House, 2017: 8; 2018: 8).

Freedom House observes in their 2017 and 2018 reports a continuation of a near monopoly of Plahotniuc' news corporations, whether printed, radio or through television. He owns or controls through his proxies (his favoured mode of operation) four out of five nation TV stations, cable television channels, and three radio stations and controls a number of newspapers. His share of the media market is estimated between 60-70%. In addition he has a firm grip (about 70%) on the advertisement market, enabling him to put pressure on displeasing new stations as well as the state media regulator. In individual cases he can also make cable operators cut disagreeable broadcasts: putting the 'television on black' (Całus, 2017: 40-41).[17] Of course, there is a law against media concentration, which is, however, circumvented by nominating straw men.

As a result, a 'light shunning' media system has developed to protect the interests of a small elite or to hide their deeds. The media actors themselves do not need to be directly bribed. A manipulation of advertising revenues, a captured police and judiciary and occasionally beating up a journalist, does not require bribing.

Final state: the mono-garchy

Given the available documentation about the legislative, the judiciary and the executive, as well as business conglomerate, Moldova differs clearly from the oligarchic power network of the neighbouring Ukraine

[17] This happened on 20 January 2016, when Moldtelecom controlled by Plahotniuc blocked the signal of TV stations covering protests against the new government of Filip, Plahotniuc's nominee as Prime Minister. Another kind of interference occurred 27 August 2016: Moldova 1, cut covering independence day as soon as protesters showed up (Całus, 2017: 40).

(Konończuk *et al.*, 2017; Całus, 2016a). In this country a plurality of oligarchs persevered in maintaining a precarious balance of power, though the clan around Yanukovich lost its influence. In contrast, in Moldova the struggle for political dominance has (thus far) resulted in one surviving oligarch, Plahotniuc. So instead of an oligarchy one can speak of a monogarchy. This does not mean a return to a one party system which would formalise his power. Surveying the way Plahotniuc has operated since he reanimated the small Democratic Party after the Voronin era, one can observe that he uses to work via proxies. He is no office holder but a businessman who is just also acts as the chairman of the DPM. But otherwise he is rarely at the front line. While protecting his business interests by political means he remains unaccountable, but still in control.

What are the consequences of this state of the country? The positive side is that compared to the instability during the power sharing with co-oligarch Filat, a certain stability has returned. However, this is a stability with stagnation, to protect business interests of one clan

Conclusions

Moldova a small country with a big problem: it had to make a difficult transition into the post-Soviet world. It has been hampered by a poorly performing economy, outdated laws, the dominance of oligarchs and the lack of 'political will' of the political elite to tackle endemic corruption. More precise, the oligarchy stands in the way of any reform that may harm their interests. However, in this country, one rather uses the plural term – oligarchs. There is only one oligarch of any importance and influence left: Mr Vlad Plahotniuc. His rival oligarchs are either disgraced or in jail or both. He is the puppet master for the entire country – nothing is decided or done without he says so (Całus, 2016b; Rahman, 2017: 6).

There is institutional weakness everywhere in Moldova. In particular the judiciary is weak and corrupt. The judiciary can act corruptively and engage in embezzlement and money laundering and again there are few convictions. Judges with low rankings can still be promoted to senior positions just because they are acceptable to Plahotniuc. Outspoken personalities in the judiciary are at risk of being harassed by allegations of wrong doing and the initiation of criminal investigations. After having caused professional and personal damage, these investigations usually come to an unexplained halt.

The banking sector is weak and prone to be victimized or undermined by internal corruption. The Laundromat case is a telling example. A billion dollars can disappear from the banks and hardly anyone is held accountable. Serious asset recovery has thus far not been undertaken. Who cares?

There are institutional 'guardians' against corruption. But the NAC and the Anti-corruption Prosecution office handled thus far mainly 'small fry'. The National Integrity Authority still demonstrates embarrassing delays. These institutions appear to be weak and less than transparent. It is very difficult to find any reports about their activities and any sort of accountability. Critics from civil society are of the opinion that the 'guardian' institutions are kept deliberately weak by appointing mediocracies in the leading ranks, especially in the system of justice and law enforcement.

The EU had made the transfer of final tranches of its aid funds dependent on real progress in judicial reform. Apart from such pressure, the EU should do more concerning training and expertise on the ground in Moldova to assist civil society involved in the fight against corruption.

Meanwhile, the reality on the ground is that nothing will happen against the interests of Plahotniuc and his clan, despite his unpopularity: in opinion polls 95% of interviewees say they distrust him (Całus, 2016b). If there is any chance of removing this obstacle, it will come from civil society that has to be strengthened.

References

BTI Moldova Report, *BTI 2018 Country Report – Moldova.*, Gutersloh: Bertelsmann & Stiftung, 2018.

Butkovic, H. and V. Samardzija, The fight against corruption in Moldova: What can be learned from Croatian Experiences, *The Development of Democracy Conference,* Zagreb 28-29 April, 2015.

Całus, K., *The unfinished state. 25 years of independent Moldova.* OSV Studies, 2016a.

Całus, K., *Moldova: from oligarchic pluralism to Plahotniuc's hegemony*. Centre for Eastern Studies. No 208, 2016b.

Carasciuc, L., Corruption and Quality of Governance. 2001. Available on http://www.transparencyinternational.md. Accessed on September 10th, 2017.

Chalidze, V., *Criminal Russia*, P.S. Falla, 1977.

Centre for Combating Economic Crime and Corruption. No date. Available at http://www.cccec.md/the-moldovan-banking-scandal/.

Clark, J. and A. Wildavsky, Why Communism Collapses: The moral and material failures of command economies are intertwined, *Journal of Public Policy*, 1990, Vol. 10 (4), 361-390.

Council of Europe, *Report on the Corruption Risk Assessment within the Public Prosecution Service of Moldova*, 2016. Available on *http;//coe.int*. Accessed 12 May 2018.

Cozonac, C., L. Stefan, S. Parvu and M. Podumlijak, *Conflicts of Interest and Incompatibilities in Eastern Europe, Romania, Croatia, Moldova*. 2012. http://expertforum.ro/wp-content/uploads/2013/03/Conflicts-of-Interest and incompatibilities in Eastern Europe (Accessed 1 March 2018).

DKP Consulting, *Moldova Anti-Corruption Assessment Final Report*, USAID, 2006.

Duyne, P.C. van, Will Caligula go transparent? Corruption in Acts & Attitude, *Forum on Crime & Society*, 2001, Vol.1(2), 73-98.

European Commission, Report on Implementation by the Republic of Moldova of the Action Plan on Visa Liberalisation, 2012, available on http://ec.europa.eu/dgs/home-affairs/ Accessed on 15 March 2018.

Emerson M., N. Hriptievschi, O. Kalitenko,T. Kovziridze, E. Pochnitchi, *Anti-corruption policies in Georgia, Moldova and Ukraine*. 2017. www.3dcftas.eu/.

Feldbrugge, F.J.M., Government and Shadow Economy in the Soviet Union, *Soviet Studies*, 1984, 36(4), 528-543.

Freedom House, *Moldova: A country in transit*, Freedom House, 2018.

Gamurair, L. and C. Ghinea, It has only just begun: EU and anti-corruption institutions in Moldova, EPC Policy Brief 1 August 2014. Available on *http://www.epc.eu/documents/uploads/pub 4683*, Accessed on April 20th, 2018.

Gribincea, V., *Moldova: Investigating high level corruption – progress or illusion?,* Soros Foundation: Moldova, 2017.

Gribincea, V., *Analysis of the strategy for the recovery of funds defrauded from the banking system of the Republic of Moldova*, Discussion Paper, 2018.

Hriptievschi, N., *Independence & accountability of Moldova's judiciary under threat*. Legal Resource Center, Moldova, 2017.

Institute for Public Policies, *Public Opinion Barometer*, October, 2016

Jowitt, K., Soviet neo-traditionalism: The political Corruption of a Leninist Regime, *Soviet Studies*, 1983, 35(3), 275-297.

Kaufman, D., Corruption: The Facts, *Foreign Policy*, 1997 (107), 114-131.

Konończuk, W., D. Cenușa and K. Kakachia,. *Oligarchs in Ukraine, Moldova and Georgia as key obstacles to reforms*. 2017. www.3dcftas.eu/.

Kurat, A.N. and J.S. Bromley, The retreat of the Turks, 1683-1730. In M.A. Cook (ed.), *A history of the Ottoman empire to 1730*. Cambridge University Press, 1976.

Los Angeles Times, Soviets Uncover massive Corruption: Billions Lost in Uzbekistan Case Involving Brezhnev Kin, 1988. Available on: http://articles.latimes.com/1988-01-24/news/mn-38144_1_soviet-union. Accessed on June 3rd, 2018.

Markovska, A and A. Isaeva, Public Sector Corruption: Lessons to be learned from the Ukranian Experience, *Crime Prevention & Community Safety*, 2007, Vol.9 (2), 118-129

McDevit, J., *The state of corruption in Armenia, Azerbaijan, Moldova and Ukraine.* 2015, EU.

NAC, *Progress Report of the National Anti-Corruption Centre 2014-2015.* 2016.

Novak, R., Corruption and Transition Economies, Paper presented to the *9th OSCE Economic Forum*, Bucharest, 27-28 March, 2001.

Prohnitchi, E., *A fight against corruption in Moldova: what's wrong and what can be done?,* Soros Foundation, Moldova, 2018.

Reuters,https://www.reuters.com/article/moldova-banking-platon/moldovan-businessman-jailed-for-role-in-1-billion-bank-fraud-idUSL8N1HS3T0.

Simis, K., The machinery of corruption in the Soviet Union. *Survey*, 1977, Vol.23(4), 35-55.

Sobjak, A., *Anti-corruption in Moldova & Ukraine*. The Polish Institute of International Affairs, 2015. Available on http://www.pism.pl. Accessed on April 20th, 2018.

Soloviev, V., *Moldova: the failing champion of European integration*. Legatum Institute, 2014.

Stefan, L., N. Hriptievschi and V. Gribincea, *Position paper: the anti-corruption prosecution office should investigate only high-level corruption*. Legal Resources Centre from Moldova (LRCM) and Expert Forum from Romania (EFOR), 2018.

Stefes, C., *New faces in post-soviet politics: does it really matter?* Paper presented at Central Eurasian Studies Annual Conference, Cambridge, Massachusetts, 2003.

Svensson, J., Eight Questions about Corruption, *Journal of Economic Perspectives,* 2005, 19(3), 19-42.

Transparency International, Adept, LRCM, Legal Resources Centre from Moldova and DIS, *State capture: the case of Moldova*, Chisinau, 2017

Transparency International, CMI, *Moldova: an overview of corruption and anti-corruption with a focus on the health care and procurement sectors*. Anti-corruption Resource Centre, www.U4. no.

Transparency International, *Exporting Corruption, Progress Report 2018: assessing enforcement of the OECD Anti-Bribery Convention*, Transparency International, 2018.

UNDP, United Nations Development Programme Moldova. *Strengthening Prevention and Analysis Functions of the National Anti-Corruption Centre (NAC),* 2018. Available on www.undpmoldova.md Accessed on 20 April 2018.

UNDP, *Assessment Report of corruption risks in public procurement in the Republic of Moldova*, 2016. Available on http;//www.undpmoldova.md Accessed on 20 March 2018.

Vaksberg, A., *Soviet Mafia*, St. Martin's Press,1991.

www.europalibera.org/a/27209223.html Accessed on 8 June 2018.

www.reuters.com/moldova-banking?moldovan businessmanjailed for role in £1 billion bank fraud, Accessed on 26 August 2018.

Zeppelin Investigations, *Moldova: LAUNDROMAT*, June, 2018.

Assessing the outcomes of anti-money laundering policies. Ambitions and reality

Brigitte Slot and *Linette de Swart*[1]

Introduction

Combatting money-laundering ranks highly on the political agenda, both internationally and in the Netherlands. Much effort has been put into the prevention of money laundering, as well as detecting and prosecuting criminals who actually have spent their ill-gotten money in the legal economy. Not only has the legal framework been strengthened, *e.g.* the implementation of the fourth anti-money laundering directive and fine-tuning of the Dutch Penal Code, several financial programs have been introduced in order to strengthen the position of both the police and special investigators as well as the public prosecution. In addition, cooperation between the public and private sector is encouraged and several informal and formal networks combatting money laundering have been established.

Anti-money laundering policies are part of the political agenda and many resources have been made available – both in terms of public money and human capacity. However, it is unknown what the impacts of these actions are on money laundering in particular and on crime in general. The Financial Action Task Force (FATF) has recently set-up a framework for assessing the effectiveness of anti-money laundering policies. In their fourth round of mutual evaluations, this new framework is applied for the first time. The mutual evaluation of the Netherlands is planned for 2020. In preparation of the coming mutual evaluation, the Dutch Ministry of Justice commissioned a study to investigate the extent to which the activities

1 Both authors are researchers at Ecorys Netherlands.

and the actual outcomes of the anti-money laundering policies in the Netherlands comply with the objectives of the anti-money laundering policies as formulated by the FATF.[2] This chapter highlights the main outcomes of this exercise.

Anti-money laundering in perspective

The Financial Action Task Force (FATF) was created in 1989 by the G-7[3] with the goal of combatting money laundering as a strategy in the fight against drugs. After the attacks on the World Trade Centre in 2001, terrorism financing was added to the FATF mandate. In 2008, the FATF scope was further extended to the financing of proliferation of weapons of mass destruction.

Central to the FATF architecture are the 40 Recommendations, which provide international standards on how countries should organise their fight against money laundering and terrorist financing, as well as the financing of proliferation. Countries shall implement and adapt these standards to their specific legal and institutional circumstances and characteristics of their financial sector.[4]

The FATF Recommendations refer, amongst others, to establishing well-functioning financial intelligence unit, pursuing risk-based policies and having an operational sanctioning system. The extent to which a country has implemented the Recommendations is evaluated via a system of regular mutual evaluations, in which, per Recommendation, the evaluators

---

2 This study is a follow-up of an earlier study that also aimed to assess the state of play of the Dutch anti-money laundering system. That study, prepared by Decide in 2015, provides information for the period 2010 – 2013 and is seen as a snapshot of anti-money laundering policies in that period.

3 Canada, France, Germany, Italy, Japan, the United Kingdom and the United States of America.

4 Implementation of the FATF recommendations in the European Union is regulated via the EU Anti-Money Laundering Directives of which the first was adopted in 1990. The current fourth iteration of the EU Anti-Money Laundering Directive was published on 5 June 2015. The fifth will come into force on the 10th January 2020.

indicate whether the country is either largely compliant, partially compliant or not compliant at all. To pass the evaluation successfully, countries are urged to remedy any biases and strategic deficiencies.

The 40 FATF Recommendations primarily focus on the 'technical' aspects of their anti-money laundering and terrorist financing architecture. It concentrates primarily on the question whether countries have the required legal and institutional frameworks in place and whether their competent authorities have sufficient powers to prevent and fight money laundering, terrorism financing and proliferation in an internationally harmonised manner.

This system of technical compliance only indicates whether certain measures, laws and institutions are in place. The system does not provide any insights into the effectiveness of the deployed systems. Alternatively, the system does not indicate whether less money was laundered, terrorism and proliferation were prevented or more criminals were caught as a result of the measures.

This implies that establishing the right FATF-approved system does not automatically imply that money laundering and terrorist financing are addressed successfully. In a paper on the merits and downsides of the FATF-approach Halliday *et al.*, (2014) conclude that the FATF has been very successful in establishing global standards in anti-money laundering and terrorist financing regimes. However, at the same time the FATF is remarkably vague and generic in its objectives and how to get there. The FATF Recommendations are based on a 'belief' that money laundering and the financing of terrorism are more likely to be reduced if countries comply with the FATF requirements (Halliday *et al.*, 2014).

This chapter focuses on the FATF-approach towards money laundering. The core question is: to what extent does the FATF provide sufficient guidance on assessing the results of their own anti-money laundering regime.

New ambitions

Building upon a successful worldwide implementation of the FATF regime, the FATF realises that the extent to which its overall objectives are being achieved is still an open question. In order to address this omission, and to thereby reach a 'next level' of country assessments, the FATF revised its evaluation system in 2012 (FATF, 2012). Next to the 40 technical Recommendations, which were reviewed simultaneously, the FATF adopted a new system to measure the effectiveness of national anti-money laundering.

First a 'high-level objective' was formulated, which echoes the 'raison d'être' of the FATF by stating that: "Financial systems and the broader economy shall be protected from the threats of money laundering and the financing of terrorism and proliferation, thereby strengthening financial sector integrity and contributing to safety and security."

This high-level objective still raises many unresolved conceptual questions, such as the meaning of the term 'money laundering', which is not unproblematic as legal definitions differ from the colloquial use of the term money laundering, and countries also vary in their criminal code definitions of the phenomenon. Secondly, one may still question what is meant by the supposed 'threat of money laundering to the financial system.' For example, Van Duyne and Soudijn, 2013 argue that money of a criminal will function no differently in the bank than an account with legally acquired money.[5]

In order to specify the generic high level objective, three 'intermediate outcomes' and eleven 'immediate outcomes' have been formulated. The first eight immediate outcomes directly relate to fighting money laundering, while immediate outcomes nine to eleven focus on combatting terrorism and proliferation financing (see Figure 1).

[5] As put differently by the authors: the excavated Viking silver hoards in Britain were less threatening than the Vikings themselves (Van Duyne and Soudijn, 2013).

Figure 1.
FATF Framework for evaluating effectiveness

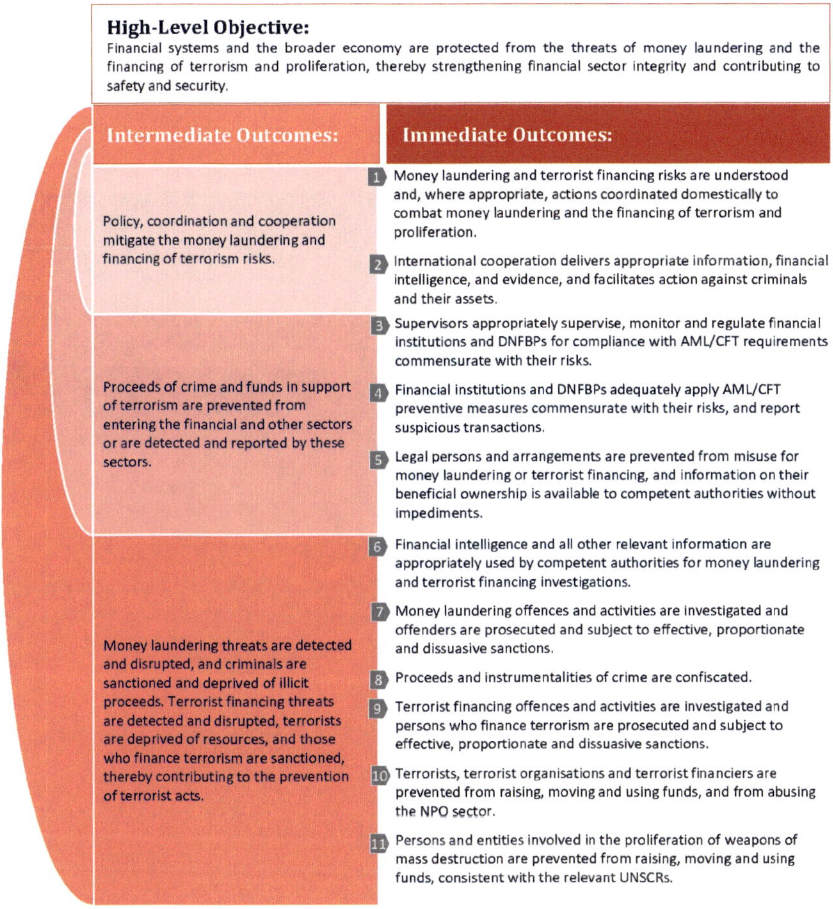

Source: FATF Methodology (2013)

The new FATF effectiveness-assessment methodology was adopted in 2013 (FATF, 2013). In order to operationalise how effectiveness shall be achieved, for each of the immediate outcomes multiple 'core issues' were formulated. And to strengthen the system even further, the FATF issued a guidance document on data requirements in which, per core issue, several data suggestions are provided (FATF, 2015).

As described above, the FATF developed an extensive Framework for evaluating the effectiveness of national anti-money laundering systems. By linking the different FATF publications, a concise evaluation framework becomes apparent. Below is an example of one core issue combined with the data suggestions and linked to the relevant immediate outcome is presented.

Figure 2.
Combining the FATF documents into one evaluation framework

Immediate Outcome 7

Money laundering offences and activities are investigated and offenders are prosecuted and subject to effective, proportionate and dissuasive sanctions

Core issue 7.3

To what extent are different types of ML cases prosecuted (e.g., foreign predicate offence, third-party laundering, stand-alone offences etc.) and offenders convicted?

Data suggestions

* Number of ML convictions (broken down to show the underlying predicate offence)

* Number of ML convictions relating to:
- Third-party laundering
- A stand-alone ML offence
- Self-laundering
- Foreign predicate offences

Source: FATF (2012, 2013, 2015)

With this new methodology, the FATF's focus is changing from a predominantly technical evaluation of laws and systems to a more mixed evaluation in which outcomes of anti-money laundering investigations and prosecutions are systematically being assessed. This new approach is applied in the fourth round of mutual evaluations that started in 2013. More concretely, each mutual evaluation shall also analyse the actual results ('outcomes') of time and money invested in fighting money laundering. The question is whether, and to what extent, the new FATF methodology provides sufficient guidance to do so.

Anti-money laundering in the Netherlands

Anti-money laundering policies in the Netherlands have two interrelated goals: (i) the prevention and fight against crime, and (ii) the protection of the integrity of the financial sector. The Netherlands does not have an overall national anti-money laundering policy framework, for example, as it is embedded in its national anti-organised crime policies on the one hand, and policies aimed at stimulating financial integrity on the other hand. The two responsible ministries are the Ministry of Justice (organised crime section) and the Ministry of Finance (financial sector integrity).

Strictly speaking, this complicates the assessment of the effectiveness of the anti-money laundering measures. The successes of anti-money laundering policies strongly depend on how successful a country (the Netherlands) is in preventing and fighting crime in general. Similarly, stimulating financial integrity is the result of a complex set of rules of conduct and of financial surveillance measures, which is much wider than the fight against money laundering alone. Anti-money laundering policies cannot, in other words, be assessed on their own merits alone.

The fourth FATF-evaluation of the Netherlands is scheduled from October to November 2020. In order to start timely preparations of this evaluation, and with the objective to gauge its own anti-money laundering policies on a regular basis, the Ministry of Justice commissioned the development of an 'Anti-money laundering policy monitor' (Ecorys, 2018). One of the specific objectives of this monitor was to explore the application of the new FATF-effectiveness assessment to the situation in the Netherlands. The monitor covers the years 2014 – 2016.

Methodology of the monitor

The research conducted in the context of this monitor consisted of a comprehensive literature review of (Dutch and international) academic literature and policy documents, the collection and analysis of publicly available quantitative data, and interviews with a large number of relevant stakeholders from Dutch policymaking and anti-money laundering circles.

The monitor's core unit of measurement is derived from an analysis of actors within the anti-money laundering enforcement network in the Netherlands, including: various supervisory agencies, the Financial Intelligence Unit (FIU-Nederland), the National Police, the Dutch Fiscal Information and Investigation Service (FIOD), the Anti Money Laundering Centre (AMLC), the Prosecutors Office and Judiciary, the Central Judicial Debt Collection Agency (CJIB), national customs agencies, and the Ministries of Justice and Finance.

For each actor, a comprehensive overview was prepared, describing their role in the anti-money laundering system, their goals, the available resources (both in terms of FTE and in terms of financial means), their main activities and the results thereof. Where possible, a comparison between the period 2010 – 2013 and the period 2014 – 2016 was made.

Based on these individual analyses, an assessment of the overall Dutch anti-money laundering system was made. In this analysis, the FATF framework was tested and for each data suggestion and core issue an indication is provided as to whether it is possible to provide the requested information.

Main findings

a. from a practical research perspective

Collecting the information required by the FATF is a challenging task, especially for independent researchers. Over a period of almost two years with multiple interviews per actor, phone calls and emails, the amount of information collected remained limited. Traditional data, such as the number of suspicious transaction reports (STRs), the number of convictions, and the amount of confiscations can be retrieved rather easily. Nevertheless, when more details are required, such as the type of money laundering offence,[6] the sanction imposed and the number of police investigations, it already becomes more difficult.

---

[6] For instance, self-laundering or third party laundering.

On the one hand, actors are reluctant to share information. Some indicated that sharing requested information would be contradictory to the confidentiality of the data (*e.g.* on administrative sanctions imposed by the supervisory agencies), while others did not wish to collaborate with independent researchers. On the other hand, much of the data requested by the FATF is simply not available within the organisations. For each of the data suggestions (FATF, 2015), an assessment was made about which actor should have the required information. Several of the actors indicated that they do not collect the information requested and in some cases they also pointed out that they do not see the relevance of collecting such information. It should be noted that the Netherlands is, compared to many other countries, well above average in the presentation and analysis of judicial data (Levi *et al.,* 2017).

Overall, collecting quantitative data to assess the effectiveness is a time consuming and difficult task. Much of the requested information is not available or actors are not willing to share this. From this practical point of view, assessing the effectiveness of the Dutch anti-money laundering system turned out to be impossible. Some indications of the results obtained could be given, but assessing whether or not the efforts made are effective, is still an open-ended question.

b. from a more theoretical perspective

Difficulties with the effectiveness assessment did not only derive from a lack of data, as described above. Even when it would have been possible to collect all the required data, an analysis of the effectiveness of the anti-money laundering system would have remained a methodological obstacle. Several, more essential problems, will remain and need to be addressed, namely:

- There is no credible methodology for measuring the total amounts of money laundered;
- The FATF overlooks the need for constructing a proper baseline or zero measurement;
- Data, as suggested by the FATF, allow different and even contradictory conclusions;
- Prevention is not sufficiently delineated by the new FATF-methodology, which renders it unmeasurable;

- The FATF implicitly assumes a predominantly criminal law approach to money laundering.

In the following paragraphs, examples are presented to illustrate the above stated points. This is based on the earlier mentioned study for the Dutch Ministry of Justice (Ecorys, 2018).

First, quantification of the outcomes (effectiveness) is problematic as long as it remains unknown how much money is actually being laundered. Despite several attempts to assess the size of the money laundering, no unequivocal methodology for measuring money laundering has been provided thus far. Attempts to quantify the total amount of money laundered – see for example Tanzi (1996), Schneider (2004, 2015) Unger (2006, 2018), Soudijn (2012) – are based on numerous assumptions and econometric modelling, which create much discussion, both within academia and among policymakers. These estimates are too uncertain for assessing the effectiveness of anti-money laundering policies over the years.

None of the methods is based on the extrapolation of prosecution data and for good reasons. First prosecution data are not useful in assessing the amounts of money laundered. One of the problems with prosecution data is that the prosecutor can by default impose money laundering for any crime-for-profit. Public prosecutors do not always follow this route, because (i) the extra burden of proof needed for a money laundering charge has no added value in terms of sentencing; (ii) charging money-laundering offences might unnecessarily reasons slow down the trail efficiency and (iii) the proceeds of crime may be reclaimed with demanding a court recovery order or sentence.

Second, to assess the effectiveness of anti-money laundering measures a baseline is required. Such a baseline is not part of the current FATF methodology, while a baseline is a critical reference point for assessing the changes due to anti-money laundering activities and for understanding the effectiveness of an anti-money laundering regime. The current fourth round of mutual evaluations should explicitly have aimed to provide a baseline for future effectiveness assessments. Strictly speaking, without a baseline no proper judgements on the effectiveness can be made. The FATF seems to have overlooked this.

Third, the FATF presents numerous data suggestions to substantiate the immediate outcomes (FATF, 2015). In its guidance, the FATF indicates that an assessment of the effectiveness should be beyond a purely statistical exercise. Assessors should use data and statistics, as well as other qualitative information, when reaching an informed judgement about how well an outcome is being achieved. Data should be 'interpreted critically' and placed in the context of a country's circumstances. This is another core problem of the new methodology. The suggested approach appears to be based on 'hard data', but in the end, the interpretation is fully qualitative and subjective. This is in line with a general contemporary critique in social sciences on the tendency to overvalue statistics and to undervalue the validity thereof (Levi *et al.,* 2017).

In addition, country reports of the fourth round of mutual FATF evaluations conducted thus far, reveal a remarkable lack of data. Also a variation between countries in types of data presented, and in the levels of detail thereof, became apparent. A short analysis of a selection country reports[7] shows that:

- None of the countries presented data in the context of Immediate Outcome (IO) 1 (anti-money laundering policy framework).
- The narratives of IO 6, 7 and 8 (detection, prosecution and sanctioning respectively) are most data rich.
- Data are being used multiple times to explain more than one IO.
- Assessments of IO 3 (supervisors) highly depend on the internal data made available by specific supervisors, while there is wide variation across countries on how supervision is organised, which complicates cross-country comparisons.
- The level of detail between the presented data differs substantially across countries and across types of data. Nevertheless, more detailed data do not automatically lead to a higher evaluation result.[8]
- There is no proper validity test of the presented data, which makes them questionable for evaluation purposes.

The availability of data as suggested by the FATF-methodology is also

---

7 In the context of the study for the Ministry of Justice, the following country reports were analysed: Austria, Australia, Belgium, Canada, Hungary, Italy, Norway, Spain, Sweden, Switzerland and USA.

8 During a mutual FATF evaluation, all immediate outcomes are assessed. Based on the assessment, the country receives per immediate outcome an effectiveness mark, *e.g.* low, moderate or substantial level of effectiveness'. The assessment is based on both quantitative and mainly qualitative information. How these are combined remains undeterminated.

a problem in the Netherlands. Two years before the fourth mutual evaluation of the Netherlands, much of the data, as suggested in the FATF-assessment methodology, were not (yet) available.

A more pressing pitfall is that the data may tell different and even opposing stories. For instance, what does a high number of money laundering cases prosecuted (core issue 7,3) mean? Is this an indication that money laundering is actively and successfully detected, investigated and prosecuted? Or is the underlying problem so large, that in practice the efforts made are only a drop in the ocean? Reversing this argument, does a low number of money laundering cases mean that crime is not actively detected and prosecuted? Or is the problem simply of a limited dimension? Or is there an successful level of prevention?

Another example concerns the implicit message in many of the FATF evaluations is that a high number of STRs or an increase in the number of STRs is considered as a sign of a good or better functioning anti-money laundering system. However, an increase in STRs may reflect several developments. It may point at enhanced FATF-compliance, as more cases of suspected money laundering are reported to the authorities. It could also be the result of an increase in underlying money laundering activities. Changes in the numbers of STRs may also simply result from a change in anti-money laundering regulations, for instance when new reporting entities are brought under the anti-money laundering regulations. This illustrates that a good understanding of the context is crucial to draw conclusions on the real-world meaning of the data.

In addition, the number of money laundering cases detected, investigated, prosecuted or money laundering convictions does not take into account the size, nature and complexity of the cases. As an example, Figure 2 presents the number of money laundering cases prosecuted in the Netherlands in the period 2010 to 2016. The data reveal a decrease between 2012 and 2015. What does this mean? Was the Dutch public prosecution doing less well? Without any additional information, the question cannot be answered unambiguously. It is possible, that the public prosecution focused on several larger and more complicated cases. Successful prosecution of such complex cases may yield better results in terms of discouraging money laundering practices than prosecuting multiple smaller cases such as the many cases of 'self-laundering': the small fry that feeds the statistics. Nevertheless, the FATF data suggestions seem to favour a high number of cases prosecuted above the prosecution of a more limited number of large and complex cases. A deliberate focus on the latter, might in an evaluation falsely be labelled as a less effective policy.

Figure 3
Number of money laundering cases prosecuted

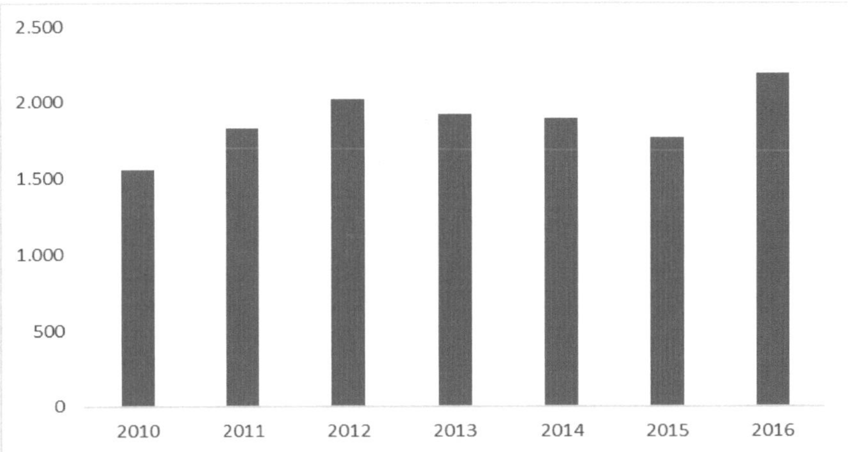

Source: Ecorys (2018)

Fourth, assessing prevention is problematic. Prevention is an important pillar under anti-money laundering policies and practices. The second intermediate outcome explicitly refers to prevention, by stating that proceeds of crime shall be prevented from entering the financial and other sectors. Prevention is explicitly referred to in immediate outcome 4 according to which financial institutions and other economic entities have to apply adequate anti-money laundering preventive measures. Immediate outcome 5 also refers to the prevention of misuse for money laundering.

As an illustration, stakeholders in the Netherlands claim that the focus in the fight against money laundering is shifting towards an increase in activities aimed at prevention. Many of the stakeholders interviewed in the context of this study indicated that more time and resources have been devoted to make the Netherlands an unattractive country for money laundering. Nevertheless, it is difficult to support these statements, as determining the impact of these efforts is difficult, especially in a quantitative way.[9]

9 Evaluating crime prevention is a developed area of research within criminology. A variety of different approaches to measures crime prevention outcomes

The FATF itself hardly provides any guidance on this issue, as the most elaborated core issues still focus on detecting and prosecuting money laundering activities, and not on preventing it. Based on the information collected in the Netherlands, it is not possible to indicate how much money laundering was prevented, which share of it directly relates to anti-money laundering policies and how much is caused by external factors measured from a determined point in time. Again, a prevention assessment without a baseline (zero-measurement) is void.

Connected to the above argument is the fact that money-laundering activities might change and thereby slip off the detection radar. For example, the methods to launder the money might change to a yet unknown area for the relevant authorities or, more importantly, money-laundering activities might move to other countries, with less stringent regimes. Increasing national efforts to combat money-laundering lead to an increased pressure on the systems of other (often neighbouring) countries. As a result, international cross-border cooperation becomes more important in the fight against crime. Although many stakeholders, including the European Commission and the FATF, recognise the importance of cross-border cooperation, reality shows that international cooperation remains a struggle.

Finally, the FATF-methodology for assessing the effectiveness of anti-money laundering policies implicitly assumes a predominant criminal law approach. Although the FATF indicates that, the data suggestions are not exhaustive and not mandatory, the new evaluation system still has a criminal law bias. There are no data suggestions on alternative repressive approaches, which in fact might be highly effective. For example, a multitude of sanctions can be taken against perpetrators of money laundering, making use of instruments available under criminal law, administrative law, fiscal law and disciplinary law. In the different areas, fines can be imposed and the values of those fines can be combined. However, in administrative law also other sanctions might be imposed, such as the revoking of licenses. These measures might be more effective in combatting money laundering than imposing fines. Nonetheless, they are easily forgotten in the effectiveness assessment, as it is easier to count convictions or euros confiscated

---

have been developed, including experimental research designs, qualitative research, participatory evaluations and theory driven approaches (see Morgan and Homel, 2013). These methods could potentially enrich the FATF approach to measure the preventive effectiveness of the anti-money laundering regime.

than assessing the impact of an individually revoked permit.

Conclusions

The FATF has been successful in establishing global standards in anti-money laundering laws, institutions and polices. Since 2012, the FATF evaluation system not only focuses on technical compliance to the FATF standards but also on the effectiveness of the deployed systems. This new approach is currently implemented in the fourth round of mutual evaluations.

Despite these valid intentions, the application of the new FATF evaluations evaluation framework to real world anti-money laundering activities raises many questions.

Assessing the impact of anti-money laundering policies is by definition a challenge as there is no methodology for measuring the size of the underlying problem (the amounts of money that are actually being laundered in a country).

Besides this core problem, two aspects of the new methodology should be addressed in order to further improve the effectiveness assessment method. One the one hand, the FATF data suggestions centre around traditional – and relatively easy-to-get – data, such as numbers of suspicious transaction reports, money laundering investigations and prosecutions. These data may be interpreted in contradictory directions. For example, an increase in STRs may be the result of both enhanced and weaker anti-money laundering policies, and of an increase of the underlying problem. The conclusion is that 'hard data' become soft, as a qualitative and sometimes subjective interpretation is needed. Moreover, anti-money laundering policies and practices are changing rapidly in some countries, such as the Netherlands, where a traditional judicial approach to money laundering is replaced by a combination of penal, fiscal and administrative instruments. This should be better addressed in the FATF evaluation framework.

On the other hand, several methodological challenges are open to be addressed in the future. First of all, as prevention is crucial in the international anti-money laundering regime a credible method for assessing the preventive impacts would be greatly enhance the effectiveness assessment framework. Also, the FATF should develop guidance on validation of the presented data. In addition, the FATF effectiveness assessment would become more credible with the explicit introduction of a baseline assessment.

In order to address the current weaknesses in the FATF evaluation methodology, the FATF should appoint a panel of independent academic experts and assign them with the task to address current data and methodological shortcomings. The current FATF system of a high-level objective, intermediate outcomes and immediate outcomes is predominantly the result of international negotiations, rather than strict analytical thinking. This is the fundamental shortcoming of the current methodology. The interpretation of the evaluation *outcomes* may be subject to politics while evaluation *methodologies* are non-negotiable by definition.

References

Ecorys, *Monitor anti-money laundering 2014 – 2016*, 2018.

Ecorys, University of Utrecht and Free University of Amsterdam, *Amount and effects of criminal expenses*, 2018.

FATF, *International standards on combating money laundering and the financing of terrorism & proliferation – The FATF recommendations*, 2012.

FATF, *Methodology for assessing technical compliance with the FATF recommendations and the effectiveness of AML/CFT systems*, 2013.

FATF, *FATF guidance - AML/CFT-related data and statistics,* 2015.

Halliday, T.C., M. Levi and P. Reuter, P., *Global surveillance of dirty money: assessing assessment of regimes to control money-laundering and combat the financing of terrorism*, 2014.

Levi, M., P. Reuter and T.C. Halliday, *Can the AML system be evaluated without better data?*, 2017

Morgan, A. and P. Homel, Evaluating crime prevention: Lessons from large-scale community Programs. *Australian Institute of Criminology, trends and issues in crime and criminal justice*, No. 458, 2013.

Schneider, F., The size of the shadow economies of 145 countries all over the world, 2014.

Schneider, J.F., Size and development of the shadow economy of 31 European and 5 other OECD countries from 2003 to 2015: different developments, 2015.

Soudijn M.R.J. & Th. Akse, *Witwassen.* Criminaliteitsbeeldanalyse - KLPD, Dienst Nationale Recherche, 2012.

Tanzi, V., Money laundering and the international financial system, IMF working paper, Number 96/55, 1996.

Unger, B., G. Rawlings, M. Busuioc, J. Ferwerda, M. Siegel, W. de Kruijf and K. Wokke, *The amounts and the effects of money laundering.* Den Haag: Ministerie van Financiën, 2006.

van Duyne, P.C. and M.R.J. Soudijn, Crime money in the financial system - What we fear and what we know, 2010.

van Duyne, P.C., J.H. Harvey and L.Y. Gelemerova, *The critical handbook of money laundering – policy, analysis and myths.* London: Palgrave, 2019.

Is corporate social responsibility anything more than a mask for multinational (oil) companies?

Matjaž Jager, Ciril Keršmanc and *Katja Šugman Stubbs*[1]

Introduction

In this chapter we address a certain problematic use of corporate social responsibility (CSR). After first stopping at various CSR definitions, we ask ourselves what kind of responsibility CSR really is? We continue by pointing out its contested rationale and ask ourselves whether CSR is legitimate and ought to be desirable? Within this debate, we discuss the proposition that CSR can be tolerated only in the case when it is employed as a veil for increasing the corporation's profits. One such use is the case when a corporation employs CSR as a tool for creating a fake façade or a mask over its unethical, illegal or criminal conduct. Bearing such cases in mind, some scholars (*cf.* Bakan, 2004; Babiak and Hare, 2007) have suggested the analogy between a (deviant) corporation and a human psychopath. We present this analogy in some detail and show various examples of using CSR as a mask by some multinational oil corporations. In conclusion, we answer the question posed in the title.

1 Matjaž Jager is a Senior researcher and Director of the Institute of Criminology at the Faculty of Law, University of Ljubljana. Dr. Ciril Keršmanc is a judge at the District court in Ljubljana. Katja Šugman Stubbs is a judge at the Constitutional court of the Republic of Slovenia, Professor of law at the Faculty of Law, University of Ljubljana and a Senior researcher at the Institute of Criminology at the Faculty of Law Ljubljana. The authors wish to acknowledge the financial support of the Slovenian Research Agency (Grant number J5-8242).

Organisational choices in relation to the law

Looked at from the binary and sometimes simplified, legalistic ("either legal or illegal") perspective, the main choices of a corporation as a subject of the law are rather simple: 1) it can either comply or 2) not comply with the law.[2] Needless to add, these two options or perhaps better – short or long terms attitudes – are in most cases not fixed once and for all; they may be shifting in time and may be partially or selectively applied. We also know that some smart corporations try to influence the substance of the law in their favour beforehand, thus avoiding being tempted by the risky second option. But for our purpose here we are principally interested in a third choice they may also make; they may voluntarily go beyond the duties of the law. This is, in fact, a kind of a proverbial additional effort of 'going an extra mile'. And, legally speaking, this is the main idea of corporate social responsibility. It starts where the legal obligation ends. For some reason, corporations decide to take additional obligations in favour of, for example, their employees, customers and/or the society at large, as in the case of environmental protection measures. Legally speaking these obligations, as a rule, cannot be legally enforced by the beneficiaries and thus fall within the so-called 'soft law'. This said, it is also clear that the formal notion of going beyond legal obligations does not tell us much about the content of this effort.

What does corporate social responsibility cover?

A clear definition always goes a long way in securing a rational debate. In this respect, it is unfortunate that the concept of CSR does not yet have a uniform definition but rather a small sea of them. Zerk for example, in her book *Multinationals and Corporate Social Responsibility* (2006) goes through different definitions put forward by the European Commission, the United Kingdom government, Canadian-based non-governmental organisation Ethics in Action, CSR Wire, The World Economic Forum and The Confederation of British Industries, before she defines CSR as:

---

2 On the (sub)option of being »legal but not right« or »lawful but awful«, see, *e.g.*, Passas and Goodwin (2004).

"the notion that each business enterprise, as a member of society, has a responsibility to operate ethically and in accordance with its legal obligations and to strive to minimise any adverse effects of its operations and activities on the environment, society, and human health" (Zerk, 2006: 32).

CSR is also called 'corporate social performance', 'corporate social responsiveness', 'corporate citizenship' and similar (*cf.* Carroll, 1999). One business dictionary defines it perhaps more adequately broadly as "[a] *company's sense of responsibility towards the community and environment in which it operates.*" Or, one can see CSR as a result of a pressure from outside, *i.e.*, as a "*requirement placed on an organisation to be accountable for its impact on all stakeholders*" (Okodudu cited in Wosu, 2013: 16). In practice CSR may range from classical philanthropy to a much more encompassing CSR paradigm of "managing for stakeholders": customers, suppliers, employees, financiers and not least communities (Freeman *et al.*, 2007). It appears that two motives that may be decisive are either a genuine concern for the issues addressed or self-interest.

In a globalised world where multinational companies (MNC) operate, different states may have different conventional and legal standards. What is considered to be illegal and unacceptable in one country, may be legal or at least tolerated in another. As a result, what is a mandatory legal requirement outside the scope of voluntary CSR in one country may be above and beyond the legal requirements and only considered to be voluntary CSR in another. One can see how this mismatch of standards might contribute to a muddled notion of what voluntary CSR might or should in fact be. A good example is the flaring of associated gas in oil extraction by MNCs, a practice which will be analysed later – alongside others – to illustrate how the CSR may be used to negate and evade the responsibility and appear more socially responsible than one in fact is.

Because of the lack of a clear and broadly accepted definition, the fragmented approach to CSR outlined above is what we have at present. Expectations simply vary, despite the initiatives to create worldwide CSR standards at least in some areas. For example, there is a growing effort to establish coordinated standards for human rights abuses by businesses; the United Nations put forward the 2011 UN Guiding Principles on Business and Human Rights, while the EU proposed its 2016 Council of Europe

Recommendations on human rights and businesses, to name only a few of the most general initiatives.

1. But is it legitimate?

Before jumping ahead, we may ask ourselves whether CSR is, in fact, to be desired and why? Surprisingly the idea is controversial, at least in theory. The Nobel Prize winner for economics Milton Friedman did not like it at all. In his book *Capitalism and Freedom*, he called CSR a "fundamentally subversive doctrine" unsuitable for a free society (Friedman, 1962: 133). In his essay "The Social Responsibility of Business is to Increase its Profits" that appeared in *The New Your Times* magazine in 1970 (Friedman, 1970: 126) he made his point clear:

> ". . . there is only one and only social responsibility of business – to use its resources and engage in activities designed to increase its profits so long as it stays within the rules of the game, which is to say, engages in open and free competition without deception or fraud."

In a nutshell: the wider social goals are not for business leaders but for the legislature to decide. In the aftermath, one of the ruling figures of the economic analysis of law, Judge Richard Posner, articulated similar concerns in his *Economic Analysis of Law* (1998: 460-463). This understanding of what the corporation is all about is based on the so-called "nexus of contracts" view of the corporation which posits the shareholders' profit maximisation as its sole legitimate goal and sees CSR as a step in the opposite direction (*cf.* Avi-Yonah, 2006: 3-5).

This position on the legitimacy of CSR did raise some academic debate. It became obvious that one's position on CSR depends on one's view of the underlying theory of the purpose of the corporation. Thus, Friedman's negative position on CSR is a logical implication of the view that the sole obligation of the management is to deliver the highest possible profits to the shareholders. Interestingly, however, the interventions of Friedman and his followers did not, in fact, influence the development in corporate CSR practice. Today there is hardly a Fortune 500 corporation that does not issue a kind of a CSR annual report on various issues from environmental protection to traditional charity (*cf.* Spence, 2011: 61).

Hence, CSR is today a widely accepted form of (international) business practice. The idea that started as voluntary internal organisational policy or strategy at the level of individual corporations is witnessing a shift towards wider, more coordinated schemes, standards and soft law recommendations at regional, national and transnational levels (the UN, the EU, *etc.*).

Interestingly, however, the only instance where Milton Friedman would reluctantly tolerate CSR is when it is not used as an "end in itself". In other words, he would tolerate it when it is used as a means to increase profits, even though that does not change the fact that it is still a "hypocritical window dressing", *i.e.* a little bit of a deception, that someone could "disdain as approaching fraud" (Friedman, 1970: 125). As Bakan summarised Friedman's point: "The executive who treats social and environmental values as a means to maximise shareholders' wealth – not as ends in themselves – commits no wrong. It is like 'putting a good-looking girl in front of an automobile to sell an automobile'". This is indeed "hypocritical window dressing" but serves the bottom line (Bakan, 2005: 34). In other words, CSR may only be used as an instrument of increasing the profitability of a business, be it short, mid or long term. In fact, in this respect, it becomes something internal and not external to the business strategy of the corporation as its integral and valuable "profit hub".

Therefore, it looks like the law-abiding corporation faces the following options regarding CSR:

a) not to use CSR at all and proceed with business-as-usual;
b) make CSR part of a business plan and by its effort try to increase profit even more than in case (a); and finally,
c) deliberately employ CSR for intrinsic reasons while taking into account that the profits could (but need not) be lower than without CSR effort.

The division between option b) and c) may not be strict at all. The corporation may believe in intrinsic reasons for CSR and still think this is the best for profit and stability in particular in the long run (a kind of intrinsic 'win-win' situation).

2. Another possible combination

So far, we have assumed that the corporation stays within the limits of (hard) law of the land. But this is not always the case. Even in the case when the corporation decides to break the law it must/may still decide among the same three options concerning the CSR that we outlined above (*i.e.* do nothing, CSR as part of a business plan, or intrinsic CSR).

We are interested in one variation of the second option; a deviant corporation with a CSR mask. This combination may not be so uncommon. For example, the corporation fails to comply with hard and/or self-imposed soft law and at the same time continues to use CSR tools as a deliberate deception or a mask to hide its (primary) deviance. It would be like pretending to go an extra mile without even finishing the required primary distance. A good example would be Enron. We may read in the literature that the notorious Enron Corporation had a special CSR task force with a substantial number of employees. It won many awards for its CSR efforts, including a Climate Protection Award, and a 'Corporate Conscience Award'. Despite the image of a high 'corporate conscience' and a good 'corporate citizenship' that they carefully produced and maintained, its main business activities turned out to have disastrous and criminal consequences on many levels, including environmental protection. One of the main protagonists, Enron's president Jeff Skilling, could not have described it better when he clarified to one of his energy department executives: "*Mike . . . we are a green energy company, but the green stands for money*" (*cit.* in Bradley, 2009: 309-310, *cf.* Bakan, 2005: 57-58).

Consequently, we can expand our classification even further. There are two types of using CSR as a 'hypocritical window dressing', *i.e.* as a mask: (1) by a law-*abiding* corporation to appear compassionate and concerned (in order to increase profits) and (2) by a law-*breaking* corporation to appear compassionate and concerned (in order to increase profits or deflect law enforcement attention). In both cases, we assume profit maximisation as the final goal.[3] The second type employs CSR mostly as a kind of a PR, cover up or a pre-emptive damage control activity.

This brings us to the analogy that we want to explore further. Using CSR as a deception in order to hide unethical, illegal or even criminal activities may signal certain corporate "character traits". Joel Bakan pointed this out in his renowned work *The Corporation* (2005). He asked himself whether a parallel between deviant modern multinational corporations and human psychopaths is possible. It appeared to him that:

> "Human psychopaths are notorious for their ability to use charm as a mask to hide their dangerously self-obsessed personalities. For corporations, social responsibility may play the same role. Through it, they can present themselves as compassionate and concerned about others when, in fact, they lack the ability to care about anyone or anything but themselves" (Bakan, 2005: 57).

He decided to present this question to one of the highest authorities on the issue of human psychopathy – Robert D. Hare – a researcher renowned in the field of criminal psychology, who in the 1970s developed a diagnostic tool called the psychopathy checklist (PCL). He asked him to apply the test to corporations in general. Hare observed numerous similarities, summarized by Bakan as follows: "The corporation is *irresponsible*, Dr. Hare said, because "*in an attempt to satisfy the corporate goal, everybody else is put at risk.*" Corporations try to "*manipulate everything, including public opinion*", and they are *grandiose*, always insisting *that we're number one, we're the best.*" A *lack of empathy* and *asocial tendencies* are also key characteristics of the corporation, says Hare – "*their behaviour indicates they don't really concern themselves with their victims*"; and corporations often "*refuse to accept responsibility for their own actions* and are *unable to feel remorse*: *if* [corporations] *get caught* [breaking the law], *they pay big fines and they . . . continue doing what they did before anyway.*" And in fact, in many cases, the fines and the penalties paid by

3 The financial profitability of CSR for the corporation has been assessed empirically. Conclusions are not unanimous; early studies reported positive, negative and neutral financial impact. A meta-study published in 2003 concluded that CSR actually pays off (Orlitzky, Schmidt, Rynes, 2003).

the organisation are trivial compared to the profits that they rake in. Finally, according to Dr. Hare, corporations relate to others *superficially* – "*their whole goal is to present themselves to the public in a way that is appealing to the public [but] in fact may not be representative of what th[e] organisation is really like*" (Bakan, 2005: 57). After going through the entire PCL checklist in this manner, the conclusion he was able to make was the following:

> ". . . it would be pretty hard for us not to look at the corporate structure itself as not being psychopathic. They would have all the characteristics. And in fact, I suppose one could argue that in many respects a corporation of that sort is of the prototypical psychopath, at the corporate level instead of the individual level" (Bakan, 2005: 56-57).[4]

In other words, Hare agreed with Bakan that the analogy could be meaningful. Superficial, grandiose, manipulative, irresponsible, impulsive, striving for short-term goals, asocial, without empathy or remorse and without the ability to accept responsibility – these are the traits that a modern corporation and a psychopath have in common. The only symptom on his PCL that Hare was not able to identify was poor behavioural control, which in fact is still greater cause for concern, as it may indicate clear rational intent.

Some examples of CSR (mis)use by multinational oil companies

Undoubtedly, some of the accidents in the oil industry are results of the nature and intrinsic danger of this activity.[5] On the other hand, oil and gas

---

4 Dr. Hare was also included in the documentary based on and named the same as Bakan's book, *The Corporation*.

5 The Exxon Valdez oil accident, in the aftermath of which 11 million gallons of crude oil spilled and polluted 1.932 kilometer of Alaska's Prince William Sound coastline in 1989, did involve reckless action, but as the US Supreme Court found in *Exxon Shipping et al. v. Grant Baker et al.* "it was without intentional or malicious conduct, and without behaviour driven primarily by desire for gain" (para.40). In this case, the US Supreme Court recognised that not all accidents can be treated equally and capped punitive damages in cases

MNCs are repeatedly mentioned in connection to intentional labour and human rights law violations, not to mention the environmental pollution. They typically function in a trans-border, multi-jurisdictional business environment, many times involving developing countries with an ineffective legal system in place. But, even if their legal obligations are muddled or not enforced effectively, they still have CSR tools at their disposal.

On a generic level, codes of conduct, principles, guidelines/standards (including management and reporting systems), benchmarks, networks and multi-partner organisations, awards, to name but a few, are all considered to be voluntary CSR tools. Multinational oil companies have at their disposal all of the CSR tools intended for general use (such as for example the United Nations Global Compact, Global Reporting Initiative (GRI), Voluntary Principles on Security and Human Rights, AA1000 Assurance Standard, etc.)[6] as well as those put in place specifically for extractive industries (such as for example Extractive Industries Transparency Initiative (EITI), Publish What You Pay (PWYP) and Global Gas Flaring Reduction (GGFR).[7]

These tools can also be used as a mask, but to get the better picture one should look at it in greater detail. At the same time we may also try to identify some of the 'psychopathic' traits mentioned by Hare. Some MNC were accused of complicity in grave human rights violations, such as forced labour, rape, and murder in the case of the Unocal gas pipeline construction in Myanmar[8] or alleged killings in Nigeria in the *Wiwa v. Royal Dutch Petroleum Co.*[9] and *Bowoto v. Chevron*[10] cases. In addition, multi-

---

of reckless action profitless for the tortfeasor to 1:1 in relation to compensatory damages, consequently reducing punitive damages from $ 2.5 billion to $ 500 million.

6 *See* http://www.unglobalcompact.org/, http://www.globalreporting.org/Home, http://www.voluntaryprinciples.org/, http://www.accountability21.net/

7 *See* http://www.publishwhatyoupay.org/, http://web.worldbank.org/WBSITE/EXTERNAL/TOPICS/EXTOGMC/EXTGGFR/

8 The *Doe v. Unocal* case was brought before a U.S. court and settled before it ended. *See* Girion (2004) and also Rosencranz and Louk (2005).

9 Wiwa v. Royal Dutch Petroleum, 226 F.3d 88 (2nd Cir. 2000)

10 Bowoto v. Chevron Texaco Corp., 312 F. Supp. 2nd 1229 (N.D. Cal. 2004)

national oil corporations have dubious records in upholding their environmental pledges, despite their going green and promising responsibility towards the environment. Because of this, NGOs frequently accuse corporations of greenwashing, that is of "*unjustified appropriation of environmental virtue by a company . . . to create a pro-environmental image, sell a product or a policy, or to try and rehabilitate their standing with the public and decision makers after being embroiled in controversy*" (Source Watch 2010: 55). Similarly the term 'blue wash' is used to characterise the abuse of goodwill towards the United Nations by those participants of the Global Compact that wrap themselves in the flag of the UN, while still violating human rights, labour and environmental standards. Many times there is a lack of any monitoring or enforcement of standards by the UN itself (Kenny and Karliner, 2000: 39). Not surprisingly, multinational oil corporations figure highly in such indictments (*e.g.* Solman, 2008; Moreci, 2008; Cheeseman, 2008).

A particular example is gas flaring in the Niger Delta, which we want to look at in greater detail. It occurs when natural gas is released as a consequence of oil production. Since it is unprofitable to collect, it is burnt on the site. The near-constant combustion this entails has severely detrimental effects on the local environment and people. (*cf.* Earth Report/BBC, 2010: 18). In the Niger Delta, in particular, gas flaring has been going on for decades with disastrous consequences for the environment and the inhabitants of the area.[11]

If one looks at the codes of conduct of Royal Dutch Shell, Chevron and Exxon/Mobil, which are among the biggest players in Nigerian oil production, all are highly committed to protecting the environment[12], yet have still to curtail or are very slow in curtailing the harmful gas flaring in the Niger

---

11 *Cf.* Wosu (2013) for the comprehensive overview of the various forms of harmful externalities of oil exploration in the Niger Delta. For a very recent overview of the situation see, e.g., Jerič (2018).

12 For example Royal Dutch Shell in its code of conduct states that it is "committed to the goal of doing no harm to people and protecting the environment" while "contributing to the communities in which we operate as good neighbours, creating lasting social benefits." (Royal Dutch Shell, Code of conduct). Chevron states: "We place the highest priority on the health and safety of our workforce and protection of our assets, communities and the environment" (Chevron, The Chevron way). Exxon Mobil conducts its business". . . in a manner that is responsive of the environment and economic needs of the communities in which we operate". (ExxonMobil, Environmental performance).

Delta oil production. The first legislative acts aimed at reducing gas flaring go back as far as 1973, yet without much success. Way back in 1999 the Nigerian government and the oil industry operators had agreed to end flaring by 2008 but no substantive improvement has been achieved so far (*cf.* Ukwuoma, 2008). This reluctance or extreme tardiness in tackling gas flaring is symptomatic for the entire oil community in Nigeria. Thus the conclusion: "*the history of commitment on this issue is that of broken promises, ground-shifting, shady deals and ignored legislation.*" (*ibid.*)

It is not difficult to see how this description of the oil companies' conduct in Nigeria accords with Hare's diagnosis of psychopathic behaviour. It would, of course, be biased not to take into account the technical and practical difficulties involved in diverting associated gas to other uses, which is the usual explanation given by the oil corporations. Yet, as the Director of the Department of Petroleum Resources (DPR), Chukwueke, pointed out:

> "The federal government and the oil companies agreed on the zero gas flaring date. In fact, it was the oil companies that chose the date. So, they do not have any reason for not meeting with the deadline [. . .] The zero gas flaring was supposed to be January 1, 2008, but some of them in the industry were arguing that it should be December 31, next year, now they are also saying we should give them till 2010 [. . .] the industry knew the context when it agreed on the 2008 date" (*ibid.*).

Even today, more than ten years after the agreed upon but many times extended "deadline", the situation has not improved substantially. It is therefore not so much a case of technical difficulties as one of short-term cost/benefit calculation for the multinational oil corporations concerned.[13] There is a price tag on multinational oil corporations' environmental concern.

---

[13] This is supported by the following: "According to *The Guardian* source, the oil companies submitted that putting a deadline on gas flare *without adequate funding arrangements* for oil and gas projects would not help the course of the government in addressing environmental and economic factors associated with gas flaring in the country" (Ukwuoma, 2008). In 2009 the Nigerian senate set a new date to end gas flaring – December 2010. With the expiry of this deadline, the flaring of gas was supposed to become a criminal offence in Nigeria; except, typically, for those who get a special permit of exception from the minister concerned (for start-ups, equipment failure, and other considerations).

The main obstacles to accountability

Multinational oil corporations adhere to double or often multiple standards. They have to follow one set of rules, usually highly regulated and enforced in their home state (or a developed host-state), while they follow "international best practices for oil production" in developing host states (Global Gas Flaring Reduction). The latter are just "best practices" and any enforcement in developing and usually corrupt host state is notoriously difficult to achieve, as the case of Niger Delta gas flaring illustrates.

Separate legal personalities of MNC's subsidiaries (or contracting partners) in each state where the multinational corporation operates create jurisdictional problems which arise as a result of that separation. This presents obstacles in establishing any kind of accountability on the side of the multinational oil corporation as a whole (Zerk, 2006: 104 *et seq.*). If there is a major incident, one grave enough to be reported internationally, the consequences for the corporation concerned usually go no further than some bad publicity, a temporary reduction in its stock prices or, at worst, the liquidation of a subsidiary. Nonetheless, human rights standards[14] and the emerging international standards of conduct regarding the environment[15] and labour[16] may be creating a level of tolerance which, if broken, can result in civil and criminal[17] liability in the corporation's home state,

---

[14] *See* the Universal Declaration of Human Rights (G.A. Res. 217A (III), U.N. Doc. A/810 at 71 (1948); International Covenant on Economic, Social and Cultural Rights, 993 U.N.T.S. 3; S. Exec. Doc. D, 95-2 (1978); 6 ILM 360 (1967); International Covenant on Civil and Political Rights, 999 U.N.T.S. 171; S. Exec. Doc. E, 95-2 (1978); 6 ILM 368 (1967).

[15] *See* the Rio Declaration on Environment and Development (31 ILM 874), which lists 27 (environmental) principles including the precautionary principle, the "polluter pays" principle, environmental impact assessment and the concept of sustainable development.

[16] *See* the ILO Declaration on Fundamental Principles and Rights at Work, 37 ILM 1233 (1998).

[17] The nationality principle, for example, permits a country to exercise criminal jurisdiction over any of its nationals accused of criminal offences in another state. In Slovenia, for example, there are special substantive criminal law provisions pertaining specifically to juridical persons, meaning that a corporation based in Slovenia can be put on trial as a corporation/juridical person and a

despite possible laxity in its host country's legislation or powers of enforcement.

Emerging solutions /remedies?

As to 'hard law' violations – the only ones that can be legally enforced – Zerk suggests that

> "it is possible that, given timc, more general or procedural obligations for multinationals could emerge, such as a prohibition on double standards, an obligation to carry out environmental impact assessments and apply a precautionary approach, and an obligation to warn affected employees, communities and consumers of health, safety, and environmental risks" (Zerk, 2006: 298).

In her book, she examines two possible solutions for regulating multinational corporations, specifically home state regulation and international regulation and generally appears to favour (future) international regulation (Zerk, 2006: 299-310). However, given the reluctance of states to surrender their sovereignty and the time it will take to establish and implement the international bodies and adopt mandatory regulation[18], home state regulation would seem to be the only choice for the time being.

---

conviction can ultimately result in its liquidation. *See Zakon o odgovornosti pravnih oseb za kazniva dejanja*, Ur. l. RS 98/2004, 65/2008 (SLO).

18 A practical example is well presented by Stephen Kabel (2004: 477-478). He describes an unsuccessful process of negotiation to bring legal persons within the jurisdiction of the International Criminal Court (ICC). The French proposal was ultimately withdrawn. The author argues, though, that the jurisdiction over legal persons, although not express, is implicitly recognised. *See* also Šugman and Jager (2009) for an EU case study on sovereignty in criminal matters (specifically regarding environmental protection).

1. Tort law

In addition, home state regulation already exists. Zerk identifies four groups of theories on parent company liability which can be utilised to establish accountability in a parent company or subsidiary, once the case is accepted by a home state court (Zerk, 2006: 215-233). The amount or lack of control exercised by the parent company seems to be the deciding factor and it is here that voluntary CSR tools can play a role. Especially initiatives to increase transparency (such as GRI) or set operational standards (such as ISO 26000 or AA 1000 AS) can make it easier to prove effective control in a court of law by leaving behind a clear paper trail and also detailing misconduct such as misrepresentation or lack of due care. Therefore, even though CSR initiatives are voluntary by nature, they can aid in establishing/proving accountability once they are in place.

2. Criminal law

As for criminal liability and home state prosecution, one needs to distinguish two categories, namely, the prosecution of individuals working for multinational companies and the prosecution of the parent company as a juridical person. The former lies outside the scope of the present chapter, while the criminal responsibility of legal persons has gradually been established in common law as well as on the continent. Selinšek notes that while in most continental European states[19] the criminal responsibility of juridical persons is seen as an accessory to that of the physical person who is acting in its name, the evolution, especially of the US law, appears to be moving towards accepting the independent and principal responsibility of corporations (Selinšek, 2005: 192).

Slovenia, for example, has adopted a Criminal Liability of Legal Entities Act[20], which in article 3/3 states that a domestic legal entity is responsible also for a felony committed abroad against a foreign state, citizen or legal entity. According to the act, there are five possible sanctions for a legal entity found guilty of such a felony, namely:

---

[19] An exception she makes note of is Belgium, where the conviction of a corporation generally excludes criminal responsibility on the part of the agent acting for it unless the agent acts intentionally. *See* also Faure (1999: 111).

[20] Zakon o odgovornosti pravnih oseb za kazniva dejanja (Criminal Liability of Legal Entities Act), Ur. l. RS 98/2004, 65/2008 (SLO).

1. a monetary fine;
2. confiscation of property;
3. liquidation (with confiscation of property);
4. ineligibility for participating in public tenders and
5. a prohibition from trading with financial instruments (art. 12).

In addition, a conviction may also result in the revocation of issued concessions/licenses and inadmissibility from entering new bids for licenses/concessions (art. 21). In the US, a corporation may, for example, be found guilty of knowing endangerment and fined under the Federal Water pollution Control Act (sec. 309).[21] The US also has the so-called charter revocation laws and, notably, the notorious multinational oil company Unocal was among the first in the modern age to be threatened with a corporate death sentence (Mokhiber, 1998).

The global nature of multinational corporations adds yet another layer of complexity to the debate. As with tort law, there are legal obstacles preventing one from treating a multinational corporation/enterprise as a single (accountable) entity. When several separate legal entities in a 'home' state are involved, the concept of aiding and abetting can sometimes be of help (Selinšek, 2005: 209-225). However, given the accessory nature[22] of this concept, it often fails when different jurisdictions and substantive standards are involved. If there is no underlying violation by a principal in a foreign state due to a different substantive criminal provision there, aiding and abetting should theoretically be excluded from further consideration. There is a simple solution to the problem, nevertheless. As with the classic textbook example of a separate criminal offence of aiding and abetting in connection to suicide, the legislative body of the home state can always transform aiding and abetting into an independent felony; it can criminalise aiding and abetting in connection to a specific crime.

As in the case of tort law, we may come to the same conclusion concerning the importance of CSR tools in relation to criminal law responsibility; CSR tools once in place can aid in establishing/proving accountability.

---

21 Federal Water Pollution Control Act, 33 USC 1251 *et seq.* (US).

22 By "accessory nature" one should understand the requirement of double criminality, because if the act of the principal (in a host-developing state) is not a criminal act, then according to accepted theory, aiding and abetting should not be criminalised either.

Conclusion

Milton Friedman argued that the only legitimate social responsibility of business is to increase its profits no matter what, "*so long as it stays within the rules of the game, which is to say, engages in open and free competition without deception or fraud*" (Friedman, 1970: 126). Even if we – for a moment – remain in this frame of mind, we see that he must have assumed a developed, relatively non-corrupt and effective legal system that in principle punishes businesses practicing 'deception or fraud'. Yet, in many if not most of the developing countries of the world, this is, unfortunately for the majority of their citizens, not the case. The government does not do its job properly, and some of these countries are wholly or partly 'failed states".

On top of that some of them may suffer the so-called 'oil curse' (*cf.* Collier, 2008), the idea that sometimes petroleum wealth creates more harm than good for the oil-rich country. In a highly globalised business of oil extraction multinational oil corporations operate in such Third World, corrupt, legally underdeveloped and partly or totally failed states. In comparison to their home – mostly First World – country, the business environment of a host country may be more muddled and less concerned about the standards of applicable laws and regulations, to say the least. In such a situation, Friedman's "*profits at all costs seeking*" MNC will delay the implementation of costly environmental improvements as the risk of being "*effectively, proportionately and dissuasively*" sanctioned will be very small. Meanwhile, it will try to maintain the green image in order to reduce the eventual reputational damage. The case of gas flaring in the Niger Delta illustrates how corporations, using CSR as PR, want to appear more socially responsible than they actually are.

To conclude – widespread CSR efforts of corporations acknowledge the fact that they do not operate in a social void. There are instances of genuine ethically driven CSR and CSR initiatives that begin to take into account all those that have a stake in activities of a business. But clearly, CSR is also much too often misused as a mask, analogous to the way a human psychopath uses his charm as a fake façade hiding his self-absorbed personality.

Nonetheless, to answer our question in the title of this essay, even in these cases, once the CSR tools with their procedures and standards are in place, they may leave behind paper trails, which can make it easier to prove illegal misconduct in the court of law either in a tort, administrative or criminal case.

References

Babiak, P., R. Hare, *Snakes in suits: when psychopaths go to work*, New York, Harper Business, reprint ed. 2007.

Bakan, J., *The Corporation: The Pathological Pursuit of Profit and Power*, London, Constable & Robinson, 2005.

Bradley, R., *Capitalism at work: business, government, and energy*. M & M Scrivers Press, 2009.

Carroll, A.B., Corporate social responsibility: evolution of a definitional construct, *Business & Society*, Vol. 38, No. 3, 1999, 268-295.

Chevron, *The Chevron Way,* http://www.chevron.com/about/chevronway/ (20-12-2018).

Earth Report/BBC, *Billion Dollar Bonfire*, date at www.tve.org/earthreport/archive/doc.cfm?aid=1842 (20-12-2018).

ExxonMobil, Environmental performance, at https://corporate.exxonmobil.com/en/environment/environmental-performance (20-12-2018).

Faure, M.G., Criminal responsibilities of legal and collective entities: developments in Belgium, In A. Eser, G. Heine, B. Huber (eds.) *Criminal responsibility of legal and collective entities*. International Colloquium, Freiburg in Breisgau 111, 1999.

Friedman, M., The social responsibility of business is to increase its profits, *NY Times* Sept. 13, 1970.

Friedman, M., *Capitalism and freedom*, Chicago, The Chicago University Press, 1962.

Girion, L., Myanmar: Unocal to settle rights claims, *Los Angeles Times*, 14 December 2004.

Global Gas Flaring Reduction: A public-private partnership. *Regulation of associated gas flaring and venting: a global overview and lessons,* at-www-wds.worldbank.org/external/default/WDSContent-Server/WDSP/IB/2004/07/16/000012009_20040716133951/Rendered/PDF/295540Regulati1aring0no10301public1.pdf (20. 12. 2018).

Hare, D.R., *Without conscience: the disturbing world of psychopaths among us*. London, Warner Books, 1994.

Jerič. A.P., V delti Nigra: kjer domačini "dihajo in pijejo Shellovo umazanijo", Ljubljana *MMC RTV SLO*, date at https://www.rtvslo.si/svet/v-delti-nigra-kjer-domacini-dihajo-in-pijejo-shellovo-umazanijo/473379 (20-12-2018)

Kabel, S., Our business is people (even if it kills them): the contribution of multinational enterprises to the conflict in the Democratic Republic of Congo, *12 Tul. J. Int'l & Comp. L.* 461-485, 2004.

Kenny, B. and J. Karliner, Tangled up in blue: corporate partnerships at the United Nations, TRAC – Transnational resource & Action Center, 2000. (at http://www.corpwatch.org/article/tangled-blue) (20-12-2018)

Mokhiber, R. The death penalty for corporations comes of age. *Business Ethics,* 1 November 1998., also available at http://www.corpwatch.org/article.php?id=1810 (20-12-2018).

Moreci, M., Beyond propaganda: oil giant BP greenwashes Alberta Tarsands. *These Times*, March 19, 2008, also available at www.inthesetimes.com/article/3568/beyond_propaganda/(2-12-2018).

Orlitzky, M., F.L. Schmidt, S.L. Rynes, Corporate social and financial performance: a meta-analysis. *Organization Studies*, Vol. 24, No. 3: 403-441, 2003.

Passas, N. and N. Goodwin (eds.) *It's legal but it ain't right: harmful social consequences of legal industries*, Ann Arbor, University of Michigan Press, 2004.

PBS Frontline, *The Spill* (documentary), at www.pbs.org/wgbh/pages/frontline/the-spill/ at min 47. (20-12-2018)

Posner, R., *Law and economics*, 5th ed., New York, Aspen Law & Business, 1998.

Rosencranz A., D. Louk, Doe v. Unocal: holding corporations liable for human rights abuses on their watch, 8 *Chapman Law Review*, 135, 2005.

Royal Dutch Shell, *Our Code of Conduct*, at https://www.shell.com/promos/code-of-conduct-enlish/_jcr_content.stream/1519787681925/7244ccb63d094acac56f9ee1b8305aaf0a728a605803121504ef4bceb12fec27/codeofconduct-english-2015.pdf 20-12-2018)

Selinšek, L., Korporacijska delinkvenca s poudar-kom na posebnem delu Kazenskega zakonika.Univerza v Mariboru, Pravna Fakulteta, 2005.
Solman, G., BP: Coloring public opinion, *Adweek*, January 14, 2008, also available at www.adweek.com/brand-marketing/bp-coloring-public-opinion-91662/ (20. 12. 2018).
Spence, D.B., Corporate social responsibility in the oil and gas industry: the importance of reputational risk, 86 *Chicago-Kent Law Review* Vol. 59/1, 2011.
Source Watch, (2010) *Greenwashing*, at http://www.sourcewatch.org/index.php?title=Greenwashing (20. 12. 2018)
Šugman-Stubbs, K., M. Jager, Judicial resolution of "the battle of pillars" and the idea of using criminal law as the "self-evidently necessary" policy tool, in S. Braum, A., Weyembergh (eds.), *Le contrôle juridictionnel dans l'espace pénal européen*, Bruxelles, Editions de l'Université de Bruxelles, 2009.
Cheeseman, G-M., Oil companies and greenwashing, *TriplePundit*, May 5, 2008, at http://www.triplepundit.com/2008/05/oil-companies-and-greenwashing/ (20-12-2018)
Ukwuoma, B., Government, oil companies in a battle of wits over gas flaring, *The Guardian (Nigeria),* 16 January 2008, also available at http://www.guardiannewsngr.com/focus_record/article01//indexn2_html?pdate=160108&ptitle=Govt, (2-12-2018)
Yonah, A., Corporate social responsibility and strategic tax behavior, *Law and Economics Working Papers Archive*, 2003-2009, Art. 65, 2006.
Wosu, E., Oil exploration and corporate social responsibility – a case of SPDC global memorandum of understanding (GMou), *Global Journal of Human Social Science, Sociology & Culture*, Vol. 13, No.2, 2013.
Zerk, A.J., *Multinationals and corporate social responsibility: limitations and opportunities in international law*. Cambridge, Cambridge University Press, 2006.

Participants at the Kharkiv Colloquium